RECLAIMING THE GAME

COLLEGE SPORTS
AND EDUCATIONAL VALUES

William G. Bowen and Sarah A. Levin

IN COLLABORATION WITH

James L. Shulman, Colin G. Campbell,
Susanne C. Pichler, and Martin A. Kurzweil

PRINCETON UNIVERSITY PRESS   PRINCETON AND OXFORD

Library of Congress Cataloging-in-Publication Data

ISBN: 0-691-11620-2
Library of Congress Control Number: 2003100409

British Library Cataloging-in-Publication Data is available

This book has been composed in Adobe New Baskerville
by Princeton Editorial Associates, Inc., Scottsdale, Arizona

Printed on acid-free paper. ∞

www.pupress.princeton.edu

Printed in the United States of America

1 3 5 7 9 10 8 6 4 2

Contents

CONTENTS

CHAPTER 1

Introduction

IN NO OTHER country in the world is athletics so embedded within the institutional structure of higher education as in the United States. This is true at all levels of play, from the highly publicized big-time programs that compete under the Division I banner of the National Collegiate Athletic Association (NCAA) to small college programs that are of interest primarily to their own campus and alumni/ae communities. But to many sports fans, "serious" college sports are thought of almost exclusively in terms of Division I competition between highly skilled teams composed of students holding athletic scholarships. It is no surprise, therefore, that the ranking of the best and worst college sports programs introduced by *U.S. News & World Report* is concerned, at least in the first instance, only with play at this level.[1]

However, as both university presidents and readers of the sports pages know well, the public exposure these programs receive is not always positive: the extensive reporting of events such as the resurgence of Notre Dame football, the bowl championship series, and basketball's "March Madness" is regularly accompanied by commentary on the "dark side" of big-time sports.[2] In 2001 the Knight Commission published a second report calling for reform of Division I sports in stronger terms than ever before,[3] and a week does not pass without one or more stories detailing some new recruiting scandal or lapse in academic standards, debating gender equity issues, commenting on rowdy behavior by athletes and other students, or speculating on the future course of the NCAA.

The academic downside of big-time sports has been recognized for a very long time—indeed, for at least a century.[4] The generally unstated—or at least untested—assumption has been that all is well at colleges and universities that provide no athletic scholarships and treat college sports as a part of campus life, not as mass entertainment. The positive contribution of athletics in these contexts is emphasized on the sports pages of student newspapers, alumni/ae magazines, and official publications, which, taken together, provide a generally healthy corrective to a societal tendency to emphasize problems.[5] The director of athletics and physical education at Bryn Mawr, Amy Campbell, surely spoke for many dedicated coaches and administrators at such schools when she wrote: "College athletics is a prized endeavor and one that enriches the experience of college students. The question should not be 'at what price athletics' but rather how to structure athletic programs that serve both the student athletic interest and the greater goals of liberal arts institutions."[6]

We identify strongly with this pro-sports mindset and cannot imagine American college life without intercollegiate teams, playing fields, and vigorous intramural as well as recreational sports programs. But we are concerned that all is not well with athletic programs at many colleges and universities outside the orbit of big-time sports. One of our principal concerns is that widely publicized excesses and more subtle issues of balance and emphasis may undermine what many of us see as the beneficial impact of athletics. "Save us from our friends" is an old adage, and it has real applicability here. Zealous efforts to "improve programs," boost won-lost records, and gain national prominence can have untoward effects that may erode the very values that athletic programs exist to promote—as well as the educational values that should be central to any college or university. From our perspective, the challenge is to strengthen, not weaken, the contribution that athletics makes to the overall educational experience of students and to the sense of "community" that is important not only to current students but also to graduates, faculty members, staff, and others who enjoy following college sports.

THIS BOOK—AND HOW IT DIFFERS FROM *THE GAME OF LIFE*

A principal thesis of this study is that there is an urgent need to recognize that the traditional values of college sports are threatened by the emergence of a growing "divide" between intercollegiate athletics and the academic missions of many institutions that are free of the special problems of "big-time" sports. Until recently, this problem was largely unrecognized. Readers (and reviewers) were very surprised by the evidence in our previous study, *The Game of Life,* that documented a persistent and widening split between academics and athletics at selective colleges and universities that offer no athletic scholarships, do not compete at the Division IA level, and presumably exemplify the "amateur" ideal.[7]

This new book is a direct response to requests by presidents of colleges and universities (and other interested parties) that we address a number of questions raised but not answered by *The Game of Life.*[8] Many observers of the educational scene (including those of us who conducted the original study) were taken aback by the degree to which athletes at Ivy League universities and highly selective liberal arts colleges have underperformed academically, by which we mean that they have done less well academically than they would have been expected to do on the basis of their incoming academic credentials. (A box with definitions of frequently used terms, including *underperformance,* is provided later in this section.) To be sure, there were suspicions that increasing specialization in athletics, more intensive recruitment, and growing pressures to compete successfully in the post-season as well as during the regular season (combined with rising academic standards in general) were taking a toll on the academic performance of these athletes relative to that of their classmates. But no one could be sure this was true because no systematic data existed. The need to "find the facts" is what motivated the first study; the need to find more of the facts, and to understand them better, is what motivated this follow-up study.[9]

In seeking to fill in gaps that *The Game of Life* left open, *Reclaiming the Game* has several distinctive features.

First, the coverage of schools is both more inclusive and more focused. This study includes all 8 of the Ivy League universities and all 11 members of the New England Small College Athletic Conference (NESCAC); it also includes more universities in the University Athletic Association (UAA), an association of leading urban universities, and more liberal arts colleges outside the East.[10] At the same time, it does not present new data for the Division IA private and public universities such as Stanford and Michigan that were part of the original study. The issues facing the big-time programs, although similar in some respects to the issues we are discussing here, are so different in other respects that it did not seem sensible to tackle both sets of questions in the same study.

Second, this book contains data for a much more recent class (the putative class of 1999, which entered college in the fall of 1995). This updating allows us to answer the important question of whether the increasing and spreading academic underperformance among athletes noted in *The Game of Life* had reached a peak at the time of the 1989 entering cohort (the most recent entering cohort included in that study) or whether this disturbing trend has continued.

Third, and perhaps most important, this new study incorporates an important methodological innovation: we are now able, as we were not in *The Game of Life,* to distinguish *recruited athletes* (those who were on coaches' lists presented to admissions deans) from all other athletes (whom we call "walk-ons"). Thus we can deal directly with the extent to which it is the recruitment/admissions nexus that has created the academic-athletic divide. A pivotal question, which no one has been able to answer to date because the data did not exist, is to what extent *recruited* athletes perform differently, relative to their formal academic credentials, than other students—including walk-on athletes.

Fourth, in this study we probe much more deeply the causes of academic underperformance by athletes; in our view, this systematic under-performance is the most troubling aspect of the academic-athletic divide.

Colleges and Universities Included in the Study:

Ivy League universities
Brown University
Columbia University
Cornell University
Dartmouth College
Harvard University
Princeton University
University of Pennsylvania
Yale University

UAA universities
Carnegie Mellon University
Emory University
University of Chicago
Washington University in St. Louis

Women's colleges
Bryn Mawr College
Smith College
Wellesley College

NESCAC colleges
Amherst College
Bates College
Bowdoin College
Colby College
Connecticut College
Hamilton College
Middlebury College
Trinity College
Tufts University
Wesleyan University
Williams College

Coed liberal arts colleges (other)
Carleton College
Denison University
Kenyon College
Macalester College
Oberlin College
Pomona College
Swarthmore College

Key questions include: Are problems of academic performance concentrated at the bottom of the SAT distribution, or do they extend more broadly? How do recruited athletes fare if they stop playing intercollegiate sports? How much attrition is there, and how does it correlate with performance? How did recruited athletes and walk-ons perform academically in years when they were *not* playing—as compared with how they did in years when they were competing?

Fifth, in this study we present a far more "textured" explanation of processes such as recruitment and the role of coaches. Through conducting interviews, commissioning papers by athletic directors, and reviewing internal self-studies at specific colleges we have been able to gain a more nuanced understanding of both the dynamics of the present-day process of building intercollegiate teams, including the forces responsible for the steady widening of the athletic divide, and the consequences of the athletic divide.

Sixth, this study is more prescriptive than its predecessor: we include an extended discussion of why we regard the present "divide" as unacceptable from the standpoint of educational values, the kinds of reform efforts at both conference and national levels that seem to us especially promising, and the lessons about process and leadership that can be gleaned from recent experience. A frequent reaction to *The Game of Life* by college and university presidents, as well as by others, was: "All right. It is clear that there is a problem, but what are the main choices we have in considering what actions, if any, to take?" "What are the implications of just 'staying the course'?" "Is it possible to sustain—and even enhance—the positive value of college sports without paying a large academic price?"[11]

Frequently used terms:

Athlete:	Any student who was listed on the roster of an intercollegiate athletic team at any point in his or her college career.
Student at large:	Any student who was *not* listed on an athletic roster.
Recruited athlete:	A student who, as an applicant, was included on a coach's list submitted to the admissions office.
Walk-on athlete:	An intercollegiate athlete who was not included on the coach's list submitted to the admissions office.
High Profile sports:	Football, basketball, and men's ice hockey—the sports that have historically received the most attention at many of the schools in this study.
Lower Profile sports:	All men's sports other than the High Profile sports.
Admissions advantage:	The likelihood of admission for a recruited athlete (or another type of student) relative to the likelihood of admission for a student at large with the same credentials.
Underperformance:	The phenomenon of a group's having a lower GPA or rank-in-class than would be predicted on the basis of pre-college achievement and other observable characteristics.
Athletic divide:	The tendency for recruited athletes to differ systematically from students at large in academic credentials (such as SAT scores), in academic outcomes (such as majors chosen and rank-in-class), and in patterns of residential and social life; sometimes also referred to as the "academic-athletic divide."

HOW HAS ALL OF THIS BEEN ALLOWED TO HAPPEN?

The interest of college and university presidents in exploring a reform agenda leads directly to one of the questions we have been asked most frequently by commentators surprised by the present-day extent of the academic-athletic divide: "How has all of this been allowed to happen? Many of these colleges and universities have had excellent leadership, committed to educational values, and yet that leadership appears to have been able to do little to stop this drift. Why?"

Any full answer to this intriguing question would require an analysis of decision-making processes in colleges and universities that is well beyond the scope of this study. But we can hazard a few thoughts (which are discussed more fully in Chapter 13).

- Lack of data has been a huge problem. Until now there has been no systematic evidence to demonstrate that there is a serious academic-athletic divide or to allow anyone to understand the factors at work—such as the consequences of allowing coaches to play such a large role in identifying recruited athletes, who enjoy a substantial advantage in the admissions process. Absent data, one person's anecdote is as good as another person's.

- Because of the intensity of competitive pressures among schools, no one school can act alone. Collaboration is essential (and ideally collaboration that extends beyond a single conference or league), and it is notoriously difficult for college and university presidents and trustees who value institutional autonomy to act forcefully together. There is a reluctance to probe inside another institution, a desire to be "collegial," and a constant temptation to seek a kind of lowest-common-denominator consensus. There is also an endemic fear that change of any kind will give an untoward advantage to a traditional rival or lead to humiliation on the playing field.

- College and university presidents are very busy people, and yet it is difficult in this sensitive area to find anyone other than the president who can provide the leadership needed to bring about real change. This problem is compounded by the need to take a holistic approach to reform; past efforts have generally been limited to specific issues and referred to committees.

- Athletic establishments at both conference and national levels are very good at resisting change—and they have the incentives, the knowledge, and the time to be effective in pointing out the problems with any reform proposal, insisting on the need to "keep up with the Joneses" and, at a minimum, to maintain the status quo.

- Loud voices and the fear of unpleasant if not dangerous conflicts with key trustees and active alumni/ae can discourage "getting out front." The fact that many faculty and alumni/ae favor "reclaiming the game" may count for relatively little in the political calculus involved in leading an institution.

• Inertia is a powerful force, and there are always more pressing problems. It is just easier to look the other way.

WHY STUDY ATHLETICS OUTSIDE DIVISION IA PROGRAMS?

We are also often asked why we have spent so much time and energy studying athletics at colleges such as Carleton, Colby, Kenyon, Macalester, Smith, Swarthmore, and Williams, as well as at universities such as Carnegie Mellon, Columbia, Dartmouth, Harvard, Princeton, the University of Chicago, Washington University in St. Louis, and Yale. The public at large is much more interested in what goes on at athletic powerhouses such as Duke, Maryland, Michigan, and Stanford than it is in the athletic programs of the schools in our study. And yet athletics and athletics programs have a far greater impact on the composition of the entering class (and perhaps on the campus ethos) at an Ivy League university or a small liberal arts college than at most Division IA universities. To many people, this was one of the most revealing findings of *The Game of Life.*

Whereas a large university can field many teams with only a tiny percentage of its students, a small liberal arts college or a university with a modest-sized undergraduate college cannot. The Ivies, the NESCAC schools, and the other small, academically rigorous liberal arts colleges, with their commitment to broad participation in athletics, often field more teams than a big-time Division IA university even though class size is much smaller. For example, the Ivies field an average of 31 teams and the NESCAC colleges field an average of 27, as contrasted with an average of 23 for a select set of Division IA universities (Duke, Northwestern, Rice, and Stanford). (See Figure 1.1.)

College athletes (defined throughout this study as students who, at one time or another during their college careers, have been on the roster of a team that has participated in intercollegiate competition) can easily comprise anywhere from 25 to 40 percent of the class at a Division III college and 20 to 30 percent of the class at an Ivy League university—as compared with under 5 percent of all undergraduates at a school such as the University of Michigan.[12] The percentage of athletes in any entering class depends, of course, on both the scale of the athletics program and the overall enrollment at the school. While the Ivies have by far the most athletes in their entering classes—183 men and 132 women on average in the 1995 entering class—they also have the largest entering classes, averaging nearly 1,500 students. The UAA universities such as the University

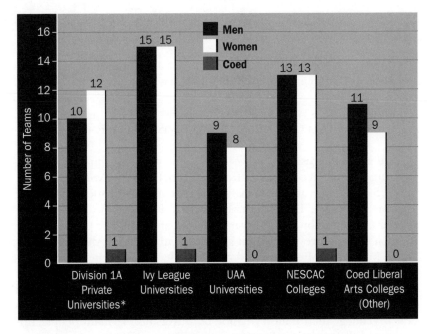

Figure 1.1. Numbers of Teams, by Gender and Conference, Academic Year 2001–02

Source: Individual school athletics Web sites.

*Division IA Private Universities included are Duke University, Northwestern University, Rice University, and Stanford University.

of Chicago and Washington University have undergraduate enrollments that are only slightly smaller, but they have much smaller intercollegiate athletics programs and thus appreciably lower percentages of athletes in an entering class (roughly 10 percent, on average). The real contrast is provided by the coed liberal arts colleges, and especially by those in NESCAC. They average only about 500 entering students each year, and yet they have more intercollegiate athletes—an average of 200 per class— than do many far larger universities. At NESCAC colleges such as Colby and Wesleyan, more than 40 percent of men play intercollegiate sports. (See Figure 1.2 for the percentages of athletes in the entering classes and Appendix Table 1.1 for class sizes.)

The decidedly above-average number of intercollegiate athletic participants in the Ivies and in the NESCAC colleges is consistent with the stated educational philosophies of these schools and is regarded as a mark of pride. (The differences between these schools and Division IA schools in numbers of athletes are even greater than the differences in numbers

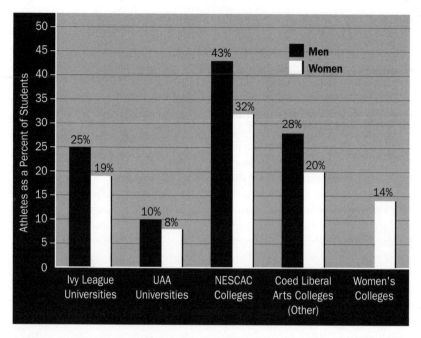

Figure 1.2. Athletes as a Percent of Students, by Gender and Conference, 1995
Entering Cohort
Source: Expanded College and Beyond database.

of teams, which indicates that typical squad sizes tend to be larger—a
reflection of these schools' emphasis on broad participation in intercollegiate sports.) Surely one of the attractions of these excellent schools
is that they offer the possibility of combining demanding academic programs with abundant opportunities to play on varsity teams. For this
reason, the more strictly educational issues associated with college sports
today affect extremely large percentages of students at the selective colleges and universities outside Division IA (though they are hardly absent
at the more selective Division IA private universities such as Duke, Northwestern, Notre Dame, and Stanford).[13]

This study focuses on academically oriented colleges and universities
outside the Division IA category for another reason. Some of the problems faced by the schools we are studying are, without doubt, similar to
those faced by the big-time Division IA universities (e.g., academic underperformance by athletes), and the evolution of big-time athletic programs has stimulated some of the issues that now appear at the Division
IAA (Ivy) and Division III levels.[14] Nonetheless, it is important to recog-

nize that the schools with big-time athletics programs face a host of other issues and pressures that are related to their use of athletic scholarships and to the array of commercial, political, and historical forces that swirl around them. Other commentators have elected to focus on these highly volatile issues, which require different kinds of specialized knowledge.[15]

One of the many ironies is that the evident problems of commercialization, low graduation rates, and blatant disrespect for academic values in many of the most visible big-time programs engender a false sense of comparative well-being, and therefore complacency, elsewhere. The "success-by-invidious-comparison" syndrome ("We can't be so bad; just look at what is going on over there") is a real problem.[16] To our way of thinking, each set of institutions needs to look hard at how its own athletics program is functioning in relation to its own mission, and to apply its own standards in evaluating these programs. Expectations should be different (higher, in our view) at academically rigorous colleges and universities that do not face the political pressures from governors and legislators to appear in bowl games and on national television.

There is also a greater possibility for constructive change at the institutions we are studying than there is for change at the schools with big-time programs that are driven so powerfully by commercial and political considerations. One factor inhibiting adjustments within Division IA is the complex and restrictive set of NCAA regulations (related to control of the massive television revenues from "March Madness," in particular) that make it difficult in the extreme for Division IA institutions to moderate their commitment to scholarship-driven, recruitment-intensive programs in even the least visible of the Lower Profile sports. As a practical matter, colleges and universities that operate outside the Division IA framework have much more opportunity to decide which schools they will play against in which sports, how much they will spend on athletics, how aggressively they will recruit talented athletes, what compromises they will make in terms of academic qualifications for admission, what they will expect of recruited athletes in the classroom, and how they will select and reward coaches. Finally, as we point out in Chapter 13, dollar signs point in exactly opposite directions: they encourage reform in the institutions we are studying at the same time that they are a major stumbling block to reform within Division IA.

It is important to recognize that, just as there are major differences between the schools in this study and Division IA schools, there are also substantial differences among the colleges and universities we study here. Although all of the liberal arts colleges and universities in our study place a high value on academic rigor, there is significant variation in the number of applications the schools receive and in the number of applicants they accept. As a result, topics such as the recruitment of athletes and admissions advantages—in particular, the concept of "opportunity cost" discussed later—are more relevant to some institutions than to others. However, the major themes of this book are relevant, we believe, to *any college or university that places a high value on its academic mission and reputation.* The evolving characteristics of athletics programs and the present-day intensity of intercollegiate competition, including the pressures exerted by participation in postseason competition, have far-reaching effects on institutions that differ from each other in selectivity, geographical location, and many other respects.

ASSESSING THE EFFECTS OF ATHLETICS PROGRAMS

Colleges and universities are, at the end of the day, *academic* institutions. They are chartered to serve educational purposes, and surely the bottom-line test of how they do is their success in educating the young men and women whom they admit. To be sure, education takes many forms, and some of the most valuable learning experiences occur outside the classroom, laboratory, and library. But that hardly means that academic rigor and intellectual excitement are anything less than central to the academic enterprise. There should never be reason to apologize for looking closely at the academic performance of athletes who have been admitted to these highly selective institutions, for celebrating the achievements of those who have excelled academically, and for being disappointed when scarce places in an entering class are filled with students who seem not to appreciate fully the exceptional educational opportunities they have been given.

Places in the entering class are extremely valuable in the most selective colleges and universities, and the wise rationing of academic opportunity is a major challenge faced by all of them. Vivid testimony to the importance attached to admissions decisions is provided by the notes sent and phone calls made to these schools by hordes of disappointed applicants, parents, and guidance counselors. The weight attached to athletic talent in crafting a class demands urgent attention precisely because there are so many talented young people who want to attend the leading colleges and universities, including many who present exceptional qualifications outside of athletics that do not translate into anything like the same advantage in the admissions process. At these schools, the cost of admitting Jones is the inability to admit Smith, and this basic concept of "opportunity cost" (what an institution is giving up by following one path) is a central concept to which we will return throughout this study.

The performance of athletes in the classroom *relative* to the performance of their classmates (and, by inference, to the presumed performance of more or less equally talented candidates who were denied admission on the margin of the admissions process) is one key benchmark in assessing the opportunity costs associated with intensive recruitment of athletes. This is why we attach special weight to what we call "academic under-performance." Comparisons of performance on an "other-things-equal" basis, holding constant factors such as SAT scores, high school grades, and socioeconomic background, are useful indicators of the extent to which students classified in one way or another are taking full advantage of the scarce educational opportunities that they have been given.[17]

As any teacher will attest, how well students perform academically depends on a host of factors, including their backgrounds, motivations, and priorities. Admissions officers are expected each year to make hard judgments not only concerning what a particular applicant is capable of doing, but of what the applicant is in fact likely to do—how hard the student will work, how adventuresome the student will be, with what zeal he or she will pursue a new subject, how much real pleasure the student will derive from making the extra effort required to turn a solid B into an A.[18] The ever more intensive recruitment of athletes enters the admissions equation at precisely this point.

The academic underperformance of athletes as a group is also relevant to another disturbing problem that has been called to our attention: the stigma that can be felt by an athlete at an academically selective college or university *even if the athlete in question is a dedicated student who performs as well in the classroom as on the playing field.* Results that hold for a group may not apply at all to particular individuals within the group. It is patently unfair to stereotype students, and every student should expect to be judged on his or her merits. But we know that stereotyping occurs and surely exacerbates the academic-athletic divide. Stereotypes often derive, at least in part, from some underlying reality, and an important reason for addressing the academic performance of athletes as a group is to diminish any basis that may exist for presuming that an offensive lineman is necessarily less interested in doing well in a literature course than a classmate who plays the oboe.

We want to re-emphasize, as we did in the preface to the paperback edition of *The Game of Life,* that we are writing about *policies,* not about people. Students who excel in sports have done absolutely nothing wrong, and they certainly do not deserve to be "demonized" for having followed the signals given to them by coaches, their parents, admissions officers, and admiring fans. In our view, there are real problems with the direction in which college athletics is moving, but attention should be focused on the underlying forces and on the relevant policies, not on the particular individuals caught up in a process not of their own making.[19]

In thinking about the proper rationing of places in academically selective colleges and universities, we also need to think about the rationing
of *athletic* opportunity. Another recurring refrain in discussions of trends
in athletics is that it is so much harder these days for students with broad
interests in academics *and* athletics to be admitted (a question we examine in Chapter 3). Moreover, once such students are admitted, it has become much harder for them to be able to compete. They may be accomplished athletes who want badly to play, but they may lack the raw
talent, or may have failed to specialize sufficiently in one sport (or even
in playing one position), to win a place on a team that has taken on a
"quasi-professional" tone. These may be some of the students for whom
the experience of playing intercollegiate sports would be especially valuable, but they may no longer have that opportunity.

We are often asked to speculate on whether the impressive achievements of athletes who attended these colleges and universities in earlier
days can be used to predict the after-college outcomes of those being admitted today. In doing the research for this study we have collected new
data only on recent matriculants and therefore have no basis for answering this question; it is best left—necessarily—to subsequent research. But
it is important to note that the experiences *in college* of the graduates of
earlier days contrast in many ways with the experiences of today's athletes;
for example, the appearance of systemic underperformance is a relatively
recent phenomenon. This we do know, and we also know that, contrary
to much popular mythology, how one does in college is of more than passing relevance to how one does later in life.[20] Studying in-college experiences is relevant for this reason, but it is, of course, important primarily
as a guide to assessing how well colleges are doing in their most essential
task: providing the best possible education for their students.

ORGANIZATION OF THE STUDY

A rough "reader's guide" is implicit in what has already been written. A
somewhat more organized outline may nonetheless be useful. This study
has three parts. We are concerned with the academic-athletic divide as it
exists today (Part A), the more or less inexorable forces that have been
widening it (Part B), and what might be done in order to "reclaim the
game" (Part C of the study). Following Part C is a brief summary of the
study including key findings and recommendations for reform.

Part A, "Athletes on Campus Today," is a blend of descriptive and analytical materials. Throughout we present detailed comparisons of academic outcomes in different sports—with special attention given to dif-

ferences between the so-called High Profile men's sports (football, basketball, and ice hockey), the Lower Profile men's sports (such as soccer, track and field, swimming, and tennis), and women's sports.[21] We also compare outcomes in different conferences and associations, noting in particular the similarities between the Ivy League universities and the NESCAC colleges and the differences between these two conferences (where substantial academic-athletic divides are evident) and the experiences of the UAA universities and the other liberal arts colleges.

The first chapter in this part of the study (Chapter 2) contains a discussion of the evolution of recruiting practices, with special emphasis placed on the roles played by coaches. Chapter 3 discusses admissions policies (including the increasing importance of Early Decision programs) and documents the substantial admissions advantage enjoyed by recruited athletes in most settings. In Chapter 4 we detail the incoming academic credentials and other characteristics of athletes compared with both walk-ons and students at large—examining SAT gaps, socioeconomic backgrounds, attrition from athletics programs, and the effects of athletics programs on campus ethos and campus culture. Chapter 5 presents our findings on the characteristic academic choices made by athletes (fields of study, in particular) and on their academic performance (graduation rates, rank-in-class, and honors). Chapter 6 addresses the endemic problem of academic underperformance by students involved in athletics and examines in detail the factors that may be responsible for it. A key finding is that the time commitments required by athletics can explain only a modest part of the underperformance that is observed; selection criteria (including motivation and priorities) appear to be far more important.

Part B, "Forces Creating the Athletic Divide," begins with a discussion (Chapter 7) of the pronounced differences in outcomes associated with the conferences in which schools compete. The histories of the conferences, which are summarized in the addendum to this introduction, provide the raw materials used to consider the lessons that can be learned about the effects of different kinds of groupings. Chapter 8 summarizes the evidence on the extent of the present-day athletic divide in different settings and how the divide has widened over time. We discuss in detail the broad societal forces internal to athletics that are responsible for what has transpired: increased specialization among athletes, the specialization/professionalization of college coaching, the allure of participation in NCAA national championships, and the rather subtle and complex role of Title IX. We then attempt (Chapter 9) to put the athletic divide in context, first by examining forces from within higher education that have widened it—especially the increasing stratification of higher education, with the most prominent schools (as defined by national rankings) attracting larger and larger numbers of the most academically talented applicants, and the increasing emphasis on independent work. We conclude with a detailed examination of how the academic-athletic divide for recruited athletes compares with the experiences of minority students and legacies, who also receive special consideration in admissions, and with the experiences of other students (orchestral musicians) who devote large amounts of time to extracurricular activities.

Part C, "The Higher Ground: A Reform Agenda," contains five chapters. Chapter 10 begins with an examination of the benefits of intercollegiate competition and the growing "costs" (mostly non-financial) of the academic-athletic divide. We then list the principles that we believe should guide reform efforts and discuss the need for a nuanced perspective on "winning" and the "pursuit of excellence in all things." Chapter 11 considers ways in which the recruiting-admissions-coaching nexus might be altered within individual institutions and conferences. Chapter 12 continues the discussion of reforms at the institutional/conference level by examining "program definition," by which we mean season length, off-season activities, postseason play and national championships, program scale (including the special case of football), club sports, and possibilities of altering the "athletic culture." Chapter 13 shifts the focus of the discussion to the national level and considers ways in which a new national structure or division (within or without the NCAA) might reinforce reform efforts at the conference level. We conclude (in Chapter 14) by considering the process of achieving change: barriers to be overcome, the importance of leadership from various quarters, and the need to orchestrate a sound process. A recurring theme is that reform needs to be undertaken "holistically," not piecemeal.

STATISTICAL METHODOLOGY AND THE UNDERLYING DATA

This is a data-driven project, and the empirical findings are central to the work. Most of the data used in this book are new and were assembled by the schools participating in this study working in collaboration with The Andrew W. Mellon Foundation. Some parts of the text refer to findings reported in *The Game of Life* or depend on data from the original College and Beyond (C&B) database. More information about such data is available in both *The Game of Life* and *The Shape of the River*. The bulk of the analysis, however, is based on the new data that collectively are referred to in the text and in figures and tables as the "expanded College and Beyond database."

The main set of new data, which consists of detailed records for the cohort of students that entered college in the fall of 1995, was collected for all 33 schools in the study in a way designed to ensure consistency. "Raw" data for individual students were sent to the Mellon Foundation from the schools, and Foundation staff then checked, cleaned, and organized the data prior to making summary calculations of one kind or another; the anonymity of individuals was carefully protected. Building the data presented in the book in this way—from "the ground up," as it were, by starting with data for individual students—has enormous advantages: it protects against inconsistencies that otherwise might be present if individual institutions calculated their own "averages," and it allows us to combine and analyze the data in any number of different ways.

Records for a total of 27,811 students are included in this part of the analysis. These records include demographic and pre-collegiate information (gender, race, and SAT scores), college grades, fields of study, graduation status and graduation dates, and athletic participation. "Tags" were used to identify students who were on a coach's list that was submitted to the admissions office, a procedure that allowed us to make detailed comparisons of recruited athletes and other students that were not possible in previous studies. We also collected elaborate data indicating the sports in which students participated, the years they played, and whether they participated at junior varsity or varsity level. Some schools were able to provide additional data, such as information on financial aid, graduation honors, and participation in other extracurricular activities.

In addition to the data for the 1995 entering cohort, detailed data on the entire 1999 admissions pool were also assembled so that we could study the probability of admission of recruited athletes and other groups of students. These data were collected early in the study and were not collected for schools added to the project later (in contrast with the records for matriculated students, which we obtained for all schools in the study). Thus these data are available for four of the Ivy League universities, nine of the NESCAC colleges, seven coed liberal arts colleges outside NESCAC, and two women's colleges. These admissions data were taken from 132,301 applications and in general include more limited information than what is available for matriculants: usually SAT scores, recruit status, race or ethnicity, legacy status, and whether an applicant was offered admission.

Finally, records were obtained from the Educational Testing Service (ETS) for 21 of the schools in the study and matched to the institutional records using social security numbers. These records contain both students' testing histories (SAT I and SAT II scores) and students' answers to the questions on the Student Descriptive Questionnaire. The Student Descriptive Questionnaire is completed by students registering for the SAT I and contains information about high school classes and activities, parental education and income, and college plans. This source of data has been particularly useful as a way of identifying high school athletes.

For the most part, the findings presented in this study are simple tabulations, such as the average number of athletes, the percent of athletes who are recruited, the average SAT scores of recruited athletes, percentages of athletes and other students majoring in different fields, and average rank-in-class. Many of these numbers are presented graphically, and still others are in tables or in the text. All averages are "school-weighted." That is, we calculate the measure separately for each school and then average across all schools in the group (such as the Ivies, the NESCAC schools, or the UAA universities). This approach has the advantage of preventing the averages from being dominated by the larger schools.

There are places in the book where, in addition to tabulations, we present the results of regresion analysis. The use of such analysis is described in detail in both *The Game of Life* and *The Shape of the River;* Appendix B in *The Shape of the River,* in particular, gives step-by-step descriptions of regression analysis. The advantage of regression analysis is that it allows us to compare "like with like." Rather than simply comparing the chance of admission or the academic performance of recruited athletes to that of all other students (who may have different academic credentials and so on), regression analysis allows a comparison of the performance of recruited athletes to that of others with the same characteristics.

We employ a fairly sophisticated regression technique to calculate the "adjusted admissions advantage" in Chapter 3. We use separate logistic regressions for men and women at each school that control for SAT scores, minority status, legacy status (where available), and recruit status to predict the probability of admission. A logistic regression is used rather than an ordinary least squares (OLS) regression because admissions decisions are categorical (yes or no). But because the coefficients of a logistic regression are more difficult to interpret than those produced by an OLS regression, we present the results as an "adjusted admissions advantage." We use the coefficients from the logistic regression for each school to estimate the average probability of admission across all applicants to the school as if all applicants were athletic recruits and the average probability of admission across all applicants as if all applicants were not recruits, regardless of the actual recruit status of each applicant. The difference between these two averages is the adjusted admissions advantage (of recruits over other students) for the school; averaging this value for all schools in a group (the Ivy League, NESCAC, etc.) gives us the adjusted admissions advantage for the group. This method is discussed in more detail in Chapter 3, which addresses in particular the somewhat complex question of how to interpret the adjusted admissions advantage and whether (and how) it is affected by "pre-screening" on the part of coaches.

In Chapter 6 we use an OLS regression to compare the academic performance of athletes, those who were recruited and others, to what might be expected of them on the basis of the academic performance of students at large with similar incoming credentials. The regressions control for race, field of study, individual SAT scores, and the average SAT score of the institution; in this way, they allow us to estimate the effect on academic performance of being a recruited athlete, holding these other factors constant. This basic model is altered slightly to look at specific questions, such as whether athletes on financial aid have particular trouble academically, whether underperformance varies by SAT levels, or whether recruited athletes underperform in years when they are not participating in athletics. One particular technique, discussed in more detail in the chapter, is the use of interaction models. In order to assess the joint impact of, for example, being a recruited athlete and being on financial aid, we use a model that estimates the (additive) effects of being a recruited athlete, being on financial aid, and being both a recruited athlete and on financial aid. The essential purpose of the analysis—which is to compare the academic performance of athletes to that of other students who are similar in relevant respects—remains the same.

In many of the figures in Chapter 6, we show bars designating the 95 percent confidence intervals around the point estimates generated from the regression. One way of thinking about this presentation is that there is a 95 percent chance that actual underperformance falls somewhere on the bar in the figure. If the bar crosses zero, the estimate is "not significant" in the sense that there is more than a 5 percent chance that the true value is equal to or greater than zero (no underperformance). In addition, the bars can be used to determine at least roughly whether separate estimates for two or more groups are statistically different from each other. When two bars on the same graph overlap, the implication is that the estimates are not significantly different; the more the bars overlap, the more likely it is that the true underperformance of the two groups is the same.

In the text we rely mainly on the point estimates, in part for the sake of simplicity. There is, however, also a statistical reason for regarding the point estimates as particularly reliable in this case. Statistical methods of estimating significance assume that one is working with a limited and random sample of an infinite population. Measures such as the 95 percent confidence interval discussed earlier are used to indicate what values of the "true" measure for the underlying population are consistent with the observed estimate from the sample. In this study we are dealing with a finite population—all the freshmen who entered the study schools in the fall of 1995—and we have data on the *entire* population for each of the schools in the study. Thought about this way, whether our findings are "statistically significant" is an irrelevant question. The results we present, such as the average SAT score for recruited female athletes at coed liberal arts colleges or the percent of male athletes in High Profile sports in the bottom third of the class, are not estimates based on a sample from a larger population; they are the actual values for the defined population.

We are, however, interested not only in the freshmen who entered the study schools in the fall of 1995, but in a slightly larger population. We would like the results to generalize to years in the same time frame (1995 was chosen only because it would allow a full five years for students to graduate) or, in the case of the UAA, to the other schools in the association. If the relevant population is more broadly defined—all freshmen entering these and other similar schools in the 1990s, for example—we only have a portion of a finite population. There are methods for adjusting tests of significance when the sample is a known part of a finite population, and these have the effect of making the test for significance "easier to pass." However, we decided to use the traditional methods because they *are* the traditional methods (and thus will be familiar to many readers) and because they will, if anything, *underestimate* the statistical significance of the findings.

ACKNOWLEDGMENTS

As a former collaborator of one of us (William Baumol) used to say, "The Acknowledgments is where we wash our clean linen in public." In this case, the size of the wash is enormous. No project of this scale could possibly have been completed without the active involvement of a veritable army of colleagues and friends.

We begin by thanking our collaborators, James Shulman, Colin Campbell, Susanne Pichler, and Martin Kurzweil.

James Shulman pioneered work on this subject. He led the building of the C&B database, developed a clear conceptual framework for investigating the ways college sports do and do not comport with educational values, and had the courage (as well as the skill) to raise issues that many did not want to confront. At one point we hoped that James would be a co-author, but his current commitment to create "ARTstor" (a massive electronic database of art images and associated scholarly records) made this unrealistic. Nonetheless, we have benefited more than we can say from his earlier work, his continuing interest in the issues, his wise counsel, and his friendship.

Colin Campbell, who was president of Wesleyan University in the early days of NESCAC, has been a second key ally. We would also have liked Colin to be a co-author had his duties as president of the Colonial Williamsburg Foundation permitted him to assume that role. He was able, nonetheless, to contribute significantly to the framing of this new study. In addition, he interviewed presidents, faculty, and others on several college campuses and was a thoughtful (and forceful) participant in discussions of the findings and their implications for policy.

Susanne Pichler is the extraordinarily able librarian of the Mellon Foundation. Her work on this project, however, has gone far beyond the contributions that could be expected of a person with such responsibilities. To be sure, Susanne has worked tirelessly to find key reports, articles in campus publications, and other information that we would have missed; she has also assumed full responsibility for checking the accuracy of citations. But she has done much more than that. She has read the manuscript with a keen intelligence, made many substantive suggestions for improvements, and drafted some sections.

Martin Kurzweil joined the Mellon Foundation and began work on the project in the summer of 2002. Martin exemplifies the meaning of the phrase "a quick study." Within days of arriving he had taught himself many of the intricacies of working with the expanded C&B database and—miraculously—made a more or less immediate finding concerning the "macro" relationship between the size of the admissions advantage enjoyed by recruited athletes and the degree of underperformance on various campuses (reported at the end of Chapter 6). Since then he has made many other consequential contributions to the study as well as drafting and editing text, reanalyzing data, and working with those who contributed quotes to be sure their views were represented accurately.

We mention next other colleagues at Mellon who have been important contributors. Cara Nakamura, a research associate in the Foundation's Princeton office, worked with participating institutions to add their institutional records to the expanded C&B database; she also took direct responsibility for gleaning information from the "High Test-Takers Database" that permitted the first estimates of the pool of academically and athletically talented high school students interested in attending the schools in the study (see Chapter 3); finally, she took the lead in working with ETS to link their background information on matriculants at these schools to the expanded C&B database. Susan Anderson, who also works in the Foundation's Princeton office, wrote several valuable background papers, including an informal history of the Academic Index in the Ivy League; in addition, she succeeded in unraveling some of the intricacies of NCAA regulations and in tracing the history of debates within the NCAA over the "non-traditional" season. Pat Woodford, senior administrator in the Foundation's New York office, has done her usual superlative job of keeping track of all the pieces of the puzzle and (working with Martin and Susanne) preparing the manuscript for submission to Princeton University Press. Pat McPherson and Harriet Zuckerman, two senior officers of the Foundation who have spent their lives in the worlds of the liberal arts colleges and research universities (McPherson as president of Bryn Mawr College for 19 years and Zuckerman as a leading sociologist at Columbia University), read and commented on the entire manuscript and made innumerable suggestions for improving the analysis and the exposition. Lisa Bonifacic, assistant librarian, cheerfully tracked down esoteric references and compiled information that went into a number of the appendix tables.

We decided early on that this study would benefit from much more "texture" than we were able to include in *The Game of Life,* and we were able to enlist four experienced athletic directors to prepare commissioned papers, which we cite frequently in the pages that follow. We learned a great deal from these carefully crafted accounts, replete with personal observations, of subjects such as increasing specialization in athletics and the pros and cons of competing for national championships. These authors also commented extensively on early drafts of the manuscript and saved us from countless errors. For providing such valuable commentary, we thank John Biddiscombe, director of athletics and chair of physical education at Wesleyan University; Amy Campbell, director of athletics and physical education at Bryn Mawr College, formerly a senior associate director of athletics at Princeton University and a coach and administrator at Connecticut College; Robert Malekoff, director of physical education, athletics, and recreation at the College of Wooster, formerly director of physical education and athletics at Connecticut College, associate director of athletics at Harvard University, and a coach and administrator at Princeton University; and Richard Rasmussen, executive secretary of the University Athletic Association. James Litvack, former executive director of the Council of Ivy Group Presidents, also prepared an excellent paper on the history of efforts at reform in the Ivies during his period of service.

We are also indebted to an extremely able group of "vetters," who read the manuscript carefully and with critical eyes. This group includes distinguished social scientists (who were especially helpful in reviewing the statistical methodology and the handling of data), college and university presidents and other senior officers, and faculty members at several of the colleges and universities included in the study. We are able only to list their names, but we hope they know how much we appreciate all of their help: William D. Adams, president, Colby College; Jonathan Cole, professor of sociology and provost, Columbia University; John Emerson, professor of mathematics, Middlebury College; Alan B. Krueger, professor of economics, Princeton University; Richard Levin, professor of economics and president, Yale University; Stephen Lewis, professor of economics and former president, Carleton College; Michael MacDonald, professor of political science, Williams College; Nancy Malkiel, professor of history and dean of the college, Princeton University; Michael S. McPherson, president, Macalester College; W. Taylor Reveley, dean of the Law School, College of William and Mary, and former trustee of Princeton University; John Schael, athletic director, Washington University; Sarah E. Turner, associate professor of economics and higher education, University of Virginia; Thomas H. Wright, esq., vice-president and secretary, Princeton University; Mark S. Wrighton, professor of chemistry and chancellor, Washington University; Richard Zeckhauser, professor of political economy, Harvard University.

In addition to Richard Rasmussen of the UAA, Jeffrey Orleans, executive director of the Council of Ivy Group Presidents, and Andrea Savage, administrative director of NESCAC, provided much valuable information about their conferences. William Adams was helpful not only as a particularly insightful commentator, but also as the chair of the NESCAC presidents' group during most of the course of this research. Norman Fainstein, president of Connecticut College, has succeeded President Adams as chair of NESCAC and has been equally helpful. Many other NESCAC presidents have taken an active interest in the research, and we would mention particularly Douglas Bennet at Wesleyan, Tom Gerety at Amherst, and John McCardell at Middlebury. In the Ivies, Hunter Rawlings, president of Cornell, was unfailingly supportive and helpful as chair of the Council of Ivy Presidents, and Lawrence Summers at Harvard and Shirley Tilghman at Princeton asked a number of stimulating questions, as did Richard Levin at Yale (already listed among the vetters). Derek Bok, a former president of Harvard University, has also exchanged ideas with us on this subject over several years. Alfred Bloom, president of Swarthmore, and Michael McPherson of Macalester provided very useful perspectives by discussing the reviews of athletics that were carried out at their colleges during the course of this study. Henry Bienen, president of Northwestern, and James Delaney, commissioner of the Big Ten Conference, contributed yet other angles of vision, based on their knowledge of the NCAA. Daniel Dutcher, chief of staff for the NCAA's Division III, provided much valuable information about Division III.

We also acknowledge the contributions to our thinking of two leaders of Yale University in earlier days: A. Bartlett Giamatti, now deceased, a former president who gave an exceptionally eloquent talk on our subject back in 1980 (well ahead of his time), and James Tobin, one of the country's great economists, who wrote perceptively about issues linking athletics to admissions, in particular, and who sent us materials from his personal files shortly before his death.

We also thank (without listing them by name) the large number of coaches, athletic directors, admissions deans, faculty members, and others who arranged visits to their schools and who took time to talk with us candidly about their own experiences, perspectives, and concerns. These interviews were invaluable, and we have cited many of them in the text of this book. In some cases we have quoted individuals by name; in others we have understood and respected preferences for anonymity—which in itself is a commentary on the highly sensitive nature of these issues, and on worries about maintaining friendships and effective working relationships.

Looking back to the creation of the C&B database and now to its extended version, special thanks are due to the institutional researchers and others at the participating colleges and universities who worked so hard to be sure that this research would be based on reliable data, which had to be assembled painstakingly. This group includes Russell Adair, Yale University; Lawrence Baldwin, Wellesley College; Daniel Balik, Macalester College; Elena Bernal, Bryn Mawr College; Becky Brodigan, Middlebury College; Aileen Burdick, Connecticut College; Barbara Carroll, Harvard University; Christine Brooks Cote, Bowdoin College; David Davis–Van Atta, Carleton College; Marne Einarson, Cornell University; William Elliot, Carnegie Mellon University; Richard Fass, Pomona College; James Fergerson, Bates College; Joseph Greenberg, Princeton University; Harrison Gregg, Amherst College; Andrea Habbel, Hamilton College; Andrew Hannah, University of Chicago; David Jones, Colby College; Jean Jordan, Emory University; Bernard Lentz, University of Pennsylvania; Katherine Lewis, Brown University; Larry Litten, Dartmouth College; Lynn McCloskey, Washington University; Richard Myers, Williams College; Brenda Olinski, Smith College; Marian Pagano, Columbia University; Ross Peacock, Oberlin College; Stephen Porter, Wesleyan University; Jacqueline Robbins, Kenyon College; Patricia Ruess, Denison University; Robin Huntington Shores, Swarthmore College; Kent Smith, Trinity College; Dawn Geronimo Terkla, Tufts University; Lew Wyman, Barnard College.

In the final stages of working on the manuscript, we were aided greatly by Robert Durkee, vice-president for public affairs at Princeton, who made an heroic effort to strike redundant passages, clarify the argument, improve the organization of the study, and in general make the book much better than it would have been otherwise. Similarly, we are indebted once again to Walter Lippincott, director of Princeton University Press; our editor, Peter Dougherty; and their associates at the Press and at Princeton Editorial Associates, including Neil Litt and Peter Strupp. Finally, it is our pleasure to thank the trustees of The Andrew W. Mellon Foundation for their steady support of our work, and for once again allowing us to come to our own conclusions. On a more personal note, Sarah A. Levin thanks, for their support and encouragement, her parents, Jon, Amy, Daniel, Becca, and Christian; and William G. Bowen thanks both his "family at home" and his "family in the workplace" for their understanding of the demands of this project and for putting up with the behavioral consequences (the occasional outrage).

It is customary to end by excusing all those who talked with us and contributed ideas and criticisms from any responsibility for what we have written and for the conclusions we have reached. We embrace this custom wholeheartedly, since we would regret it greatly if an erroneous attribution of "guilt by association" were to plague any of those who shared ideas with us (including contrarian views). We alone are responsible for the shortcomings of the study. It has been our great pleasure to work together on a fascinating project for which we take "joint and several responsibility."

Principal Conferences and Associations

ATHLETICS PROGRAMS can be understood only within the broader organizational structures that define their common boundaries. The conference, association, or league to which an institution belongs establishes rules for its members, largely determines their competitors, and provides a "mirror" in which schools view their athletic successes and failures. The National Collegiate Athletic Association, the national umbrella organization that encompasses the schools in this study, does much the same thing on a larger scale through its divisional structure.

THE NATIONAL COLLEGIATE ATHLETIC ASSOCIATION

The athletics programs at the schools in this study are governed by the National Collegiate Athletic Association (NCAA), an organization composed of about 1,200 institutional members. The NCAA was founded in 1906 under the name of the Intercollegiate Athletic Association of the United States and was charged with the responsibility of regulating college sports and minimizing the dangers they entailed, particularly in football. By 1921 the organization had assumed its current name and sponsored its first national championship—in track and field.

The association was divided into three legislative and competitive divisions in 1973 (Divisions I, II, and III), based on the scope and missions of members' athletics programs. There was a change in the governance structure in 1997 that provided more autonomy for each division and, in principle at least, more control by the presidents of the member colleges and universities.[1] A principal driving force behind this change was the determination of the big-time programs to make their own rules, according to their own preferred governance principles, without interference from the large number of other programs. Television contributes nearly 90 percent (or $370 million in 2002–03) of all NCAA revenue, and control over budgets and allocation of funds rest firmly in the hands of the Division I leadership—whose programs are of course the source of the television revenue as well as the great bulk of the rest of the revenue stream.[2] For what are largely historical reasons, the Ivies belong to Division I (IAA for football), whereas all of the other schools in this study, colleges and universities alike, belong to Division III.[3]

The stated differences in philosophy between Division I and Division III are as profound as the differences in their respective economic models. Among other things, a member of Division I (see Addendum Table 1, at the end of this addendum, for the full statement):

Strives in its athletics program for regional and national excellence and prominence. Accordingly, its recruitment of student-athletes and its emphasis on and support of its athletics program are, in most cases, regional and national in scope;

Recognizes the dual objective in its athletics program of serving both the university or college community (participants, student body, faculty-staff, alumni) and the general public (community, area, state, nation);

Sponsors at the highest feasible level of intercollegiate competition one or both of the traditional spectator-oriented, income-producing sports of football and basketball;

Believes in scheduling its athletic contests primarily with other members of Division I, especially in the emphasized, spectator-oriented sports, as a reflection of its goal of maintaining an appropriate competitive level in its sports program;

Strives to finance its athletics program insofar as possible from revenues generated by the program itself.[4]

In contrast, the Division III statement of philosophy says (among other things, see Addendum Table 2, at the end of this addendum, for the full statement) that its members:

Place special importance on the impact of athletics on the participants rather than on the spectators and place greater emphasis on the internal constituency (students, alumni, institutional personnel) than on the general public and entertainment needs;

Award no athletically related financial aid to any student;

Encourage participation by maximizing the number and variety of athletics opportunities for their students;

Assure that athletics participants are not treated differently from other members of the student body;

Assure that athletics programs support the institution's educational mission by financing, staffing and controlling the programs through the same general procedures as other departments of the institution;

Give primary emphasis to regional in-season competition and conference championships.[5]

These contrasting philosophies translate into a number of practical requirements. For Division I programs, they include commitments to sponsor at least seven sports for men and seven for women (or six for men and eight for women), mandated minimum attendance levels at football games, minimum as well as maximum numbers of athletic scholarships to be provided, and stringent scheduling requirements. (Outside football and basketball, Division I schools must play 100 percent of the minimum number of contests in each sport and 50 percent of anything over the minimum number against Division I opponents.) Division III institutions, on the other hand, are required to sponsor only five sports for men and five for women; there are contest and participant minimums for each sport, but otherwise they have reasonably wide latitude.[6]

ATHLETIC CONFERENCES, LEAGUES, AND ASSOCIATIONS

The three athletic "groupings" (variously called conferences, leagues, or associations) upon which we focus in this study are the Ivy League, the New England Small College Athletic Conference, and the University Athletic Association. More than two-thirds of the schools in this study (23 out of 33) belong to one of these three sets of schools, and in this addendum we present brief histories of each of the three. In Chapter 7 we look again at these conferences in order to assess how closely they have adhered to their founding principles and to see what lessons can be learned from their experiences. The other liberal arts colleges that we have studied (both the women's colleges and those that are coed) have their own conference affiliations, which are of course very important to them. However, because these schools are scattered among a number of different conferences, and because the other members of these conferences are not included in our data, these affiliations receive less attention in this study. (See Addendum Table 3, at the end of this addendum, which shows the conference affiliations of all schools in this study.)

Ivy League

The Ivy League (or "Ivy Group," as it was self-styled) was founded in 1954, when presidents of the Ivy institutions extended to all sports a 1945 agreement that had applied only to football. Members of the Ivy League are Brown University, Columbia University, Cornell University, Dartmouth College, Harvard University, Princeton University, the University of Pennsylvania, and Yale University. It was created to resist precisely the tendencies so evident in the world of big-time sports today.[7] At the most general level, the Ivy presidents were concerned about pressures to allow athletic interests to dominate (or interfere with) educational purposes. It is revealing that the Original Agreement of 1954 begins by "reaffirm[ing] the principle that in each institution *the academic authorities should control athletics* [our emphasis]."[8] The evident concern was that alumni/ae and other outside actors might have too much influence, including influence over the appointment of coaches and the admission (and eligibility) of players.

In addition to being concerned about governance, the Ivy presidents were also concerned about the conduct of intercollegiate athletics on their campuses. Thus, the second proposition in the Original Agreement begins as follows: "The [members of the Ivy] Group affirm their conviction that under proper conditions intercollegiate competition in organized athletics offers desirable development and recreation for players and a healthy focus of collegiate loyalty."[9] The qualifying phrase "under proper conditions" alerts the reader to the presence of worries of various kinds. The paragraph immediately goes on to address the concern that has been referred to ever since as "representativeness." The actual language used in 1954 (and retained in today's Revised Agreement) is unambiguous: "These conditions require that the players shall be truly representative of the student body and not composed of a group of specially recruited athletes."[10] The Agreement next addresses how sports are to be played and how athletics must be seen as an integral part of a larger educational mission: "They ['the proper conditions'] further require that undue strain upon players and coaches be eliminated and that they be permitted to enjoy the game as participants in a form of recreational competition rather than as professional performers in public spectacles. In the total life of the campus, emphasis upon intercollegiate competition must be kept in harmony with the essential educational purposes of the institution."[11] The Agreement then becomes somewhat more specific: "The Group conclude that these conditions and requirements can best be fulfilled by denying to the fullest extent possible external pressures for competitive extremes. To this end, the Group will foster intra-group athletic competition in all sports. No member institution, however, shall necessarily field a team in every sport. The Group approve a round-robin schedule in football and the principle of round-robin schedules in as many sports as practicable."[12]

Eligibility rules are discussed at some length in the Original [1954] Agreement, and two points stand out. First, the Group reaffirmed its prohibition of athletic scholarships: "Athletes shall be admitted as students and awarded financial aid only on the basis of the same academic standards and economic need as are applied to all other students." The refusal to award athletic scholarships remains a distinguishing characteristic of the Ivy League (essentially alone among Division I conferences),[13] as it does of all Division III colleges. Second, the Ivy presidents ruled out freshmen eligibility ("No student shall be eligible for a varsity team until he has completed satisfactorily an academic year's work at the institution he is to represent") and limited the number of years a student could compete ("No student shall be eligible for a varsity team in more than three different academic years . . . [, and] a year in which a student is ineligible for scholastic or disciplinary reasons shall nevertheless be counted"). These provisions do not appear in the current Revised Agreement; they were subsequently deleted when, through a series of decisions in the 1970s and 1980s, the Ivies allowed freshmen to compete on varsity teams (freshmen were first eligible to play varsity football in 1991).

The Ivy League sponsors competition in 33 sports. In a number of sports, Ivy teams have high national rankings and win national championships.

New England Small College Athletic Conference

The New England Small College Athletic Conference (NESCAC) has 11 member institutions that are located in or close to New England— Amherst College, Bates College, Bowdoin College, Colby College, Connecticut College, Hamilton College, Middlebury College, Trinity College, Tufts University, Wesleyan University, and Williams College. It was founded in 1971, the year when the original "NESCAC Conference Agreement" was adopted following extensive conversations going back to 1967, informal discussions of one kind or another dating back to 1939, and a "Four College Joint Agreement" drawn up by Amherst, Bowdoin, Wesleyan, and Williams in 1955.[14] This agreement has much in common with the Ivy Agreement. Most fundamentally, the NESCAC colleges shared with the Ivies pride in their strong academic programs and a determination to pursue athletics within the framework of their educational missions. The NESCAC colleges differed from the Ivies in having joined Division III of the NCAA (after it was formed in 1973) and in having styled themselves from the start as a somewhat looser "conference" of 11 institutions rather than a tighter "league" of 8 institutions committed to round-robin play.

The evolution of NESCAC is of considerable interest from the standpoint of this study, because this Conference reflects, throughout its history and especially in the present day, a tension between two conflicting desires: (a) to embrace a rather low-keyed "amateur" approach to athletics, based on broad participation and an emphasis on educational values rather than on "winning," and (b) to offer opportunities for athletically talented students to "test themselves against the best" and to have visibly successful programs. A key question is whether a conference structure such as NESCAC restrains competitive pressures or escalates them. Some of those involved in the founding of NESCAC realized at the time that this was an open question—and it still is.

The discussion preceding NESCAC's establishment reveals much more clearly than the early history of the Ivy Agreement that the presumed benefits of an organization of this kind were seen by some as carrying with them real worries about longer-term effects on the intensity of competition. Such concerns do not appear to have been present at all in the Ivies. The debate over whether to have a "league" or a looser "conference" was really about this issue. Ted Etherington, president of Wesleyan, stated his strong preference for a "conference" in these terms: "The league idea has at least superficial appeal, and appears to have support among some of our athletic directors, but seems not to be practical or wise for at least two reasons: (a) It would be impossible to form a small league (eight schools) without excluding some that ought to be logically included; and (b) the formation of a league might be misinterpreted as a new point of emphasis on intercollegiate athletics, especially football, in spite of the fact that the true purpose would be to keep football and other sports in proper perspective."[15] Lee Levison, an historian of this early period, sums up the case for the conference this way: "A league arrangement would be too narrow and constrained and it stressed the wrong thing—winning. . . . The conference structure would allow for maximum flexibility. The number of member institutions could vary without upsetting the conference; schools could either join or drop out without disrupting the standing relations of member institutions."[16] An explicit statement of the opposing point of view (which eventually was rejected overwhelmingly) was provided by the head coach of football at Union, George Flood: "My objective of a conference would be as a controlling organization that would have as its goals improvement of competition among the schools and the production of a competitive drive toward a championship."[17]

The person who expressed the most serious reservations about the whole concept of an athletic organization at the small college level was John Chandler, then president of Hamilton College (later president of Williams): "I would wonder if it would not generate a set of pressures and problems which would make it extremely questionable as an enterprise of a group of educational institutions which now command great respect for the clear-cut priority which they assign to educational programs and goals."[18] Chandler was not enthusiastic about "keen" competition and league championships. According to Levison, he "argued that striving for league championships would 'place undue pressure on both coaches and players to win.' A non-title year would be considered a failure. And in order to bolster the performance of the team, the criteria for admissions would be stretched to admit those students with 'special' athletic talents. Chandler could envision the double standard in admissions spreading like a cancer in the league."[19]

Also present at the founding of NESCAC was a strong positive sense of what the new conference might accomplish, not just practically in terms of making it easier to schedule contests and to regulate the "rules of engagement," but also philosophically in terms of the values it might promote. President Jacobs of Trinity argued that "the increased professionalization of the national athletic scene worked against small liberal arts colleges, and some form of athletic organization between these schools would provide a necessary counterbalance to preserve small sports programs."[20] Others at NESCAC colleges agreed that an organization of this kind was necessary to protect their interests—*to advance their values.* This is another argument for conferences such as this one: they can serve as both a visible expression of a set of values and a political instrument to be used in the defense of these values.

In expressing NESCAC's values, the 1971 Conference Agreement lists just three principles (see box), which are an even more succinct statement of the intended place of athletics within the educational enterprise than the principles embodied in the Ivy Agreement.

NESCAC founding principles:

   I. The program in intercollegiate athletics is to be kept in harmony with the essential educational purposes of the institution.
   II. Competing players are to be representative of the student body.
   III. The academic authority in each college is to control intercollegiate athletic policy.[21]

The Agreement also contained a number of regulations governing recruitment (which are more restrictive than those adopted by other conferences and leagues in that they prohibit off-campus recruiting in homes and permit visits to secondary schools only on invitation), schedules, practice dates, and out-of-season practice (which was banned). Two other regulations, governing conference championships and postseason competition, are especially noteworthy in light of subsequent events. Rule IIB was a straightforward prohibition of conference championships: "There are to be no conference championships or rankings in any team sport." Postseason competition was permitted only for individual performers, not teams or relay teams, and it was not to conflict with examination schedules. (See the vignette about women's lacrosse at Williams in the prelude to *The Game of Life* for a vivid illustration of the difficulty of maintaining this policy.) Section V reads: "Post-season competition, even in the modest forms allowed below, is not to be understood as automatic. Postseason competition is to be understood as exceptional and the decision on whether to participate lies wholly within each institution."[22] The emphasis on institutional autonomy, self-regulation, and no bureaucracy is another recurring theme of this document and of the deliberations that led to its adoption.

NESCAC today sponsors 23 sports, and some NESCAC teams are among the strongest in the nation at the Division III level.

University Athletic Association

The third and last athletic "conference" to be considered in some detail is the University Athletic Association (UAA). The UAA took pains, at its inception, to characterize itself as an "association" rather than either a "conference" or a "league," and we apologize for our occasional use of the more generic term. Younger than either the Ivy League or NESCAC, the UAA was launched in June of 1986 by representatives of eight private research universities of national standing: Carnegie Mellon University, Case Western Reserve University, Emory University, Johns Hopkins University, New York University, the University of Chicago, the University of Rochester, and Washington University. Brandeis joined the UAA a year later, and the membership remained at nine universities until John Hopkins decided to leave at the conclusion of the 2000–01 academic year. These schools are all members of the Association of American Universities (AAU), an organization composed of 62 of the most prominent research universities in the United States and Canada. They all offer extensive graduate and professional programs, they are highly selective at both undergraduate and graduate levels, 8 of the 9 are among the 50 most highly endowed colleges and universities in the United States, and they are all located in major urban areas in a geographic region stretching south from Boston to New York and Atlanta, and west to Pittsburgh, Cleveland, St. Louis, and Chicago.[23]

During the 1980s a number of the universities that later joined the UAA were conducting studies of the role of athletics on their campuses, and there were a number of informal meetings and conversations among representatives of some of these schools. Harry Kisker, a dean at Washington University, is given credit for having visualized the potential of a different kind of association, reaching across a broad geographic area, and he visited a number of campuses to explore the interests of others in participating in such an effort. In the fall of 1984, William Danforth, chancellor of Washington University, and Dennis O'Brien, president of

Rochester University, began talking in earnest about "starting a national Division III intercollegiate athletic association based on academic similarities instead of athletic comparisons." The Danforth-O'Brien conversations took place at a meeting of the AAU, and to this day the presidents of the UAA universities hold their meetings in conjunction with meetings of the AAU.[24]

Everyone with whom we have spoken about the UAA has emphasized how important it was that leadership in forming the Association came "from the top." (In addition to Danforth and O'Brien, Jay Oliva at New York University and Hanna Gray at the University of Chicago were very important in this process.) As Jay Oliva put it: "It was understood from the beginning that the presidents were going to run the UAA." Richard Rasmussen, executive secretary of the UAA, noted: "It would be difficult, if not impossible, for such a movement to originate among coaches and athletic administrators and work its way through the administrative hierarchy of a single institution, much less ten."[25] Crucial to the formation of the UAA was both a strong consensus on what its guiding principles should be (described later) and a set of circumstances and concerns that were shared by the founding members.

At the time the UAA was formed, each of the member schools was playing in what Oliva called "the neighborhood." The opponents were generally local or regional teams, and they often represented institutions that were radically different from the UAA universities.[26] In the case of New York University, Oliva did not think that the schools they were playing "in the neighborhood" were "appropriate." Andy Schaffer, general counsel for the university, added that their students derived a lot of satisfaction from playing against academic peers rather than against students who might be more talented athletically but attended institutions with different missions that were less selective. One of the problems faced by most of the UAA universities was that they were "'one-of-a-kind' institutions within their respective geographic regions." One of the appealing aspects of the Association for the presidents was that "they would be associated with institutions they respected and whom their faculties respected."[27]

There were some differences among the presidents as to how closely they should be linked, and for what purposes. The term "association" was chosen rather than "conference" because it was felt that "association" suggested a "continuum of relationships rather than the more threatening notion of structure and control often identified with the concept of a conference."[28] John Schael, director of athletics at Washington University, emphasized (in an interview) that "the success of the UAA is due in part to the fact that it is an 'association' not a 'conference.' Conferences tend to want to regulate their members in intrusive ways, and the association is simply looser and yet offers a necessary structure."

Another major theme running through the discussions that led to the formation of the UAA was an increased interest on almost all of these campuses in improving the quality of student life. In his capsule histories of the individual schools that joined the UAA, Rasmussen makes this point over and over. For example, we are told that senior administrators at Carnegie Mellon felt that their school had "developed an overemphasis on research at the expense of students, particularly undergraduate students and undergraduate education." At Emory a blue-ribbon committee appointed by President Laney concluded that "more attention needed to be given to programs, activities, and services directed to undergraduate students." President Muller at Johns Hopkins saw the UAA as a way of reinvigorating undergraduate life. And President O'Brien at Rochester was focused on developing strategies to ensure that Rochester would attract sufficient numbers of highly qualified undergraduate students. Dean Kisker's primary task at Washington University was "to remedy a serious deficiency in the quality of student life on the campus; athletics was a large part of the picture."[29]

These concerns about student life were given special force by demographic projections. According to Rasmussen, when the UAA was formed "colleges and universities across the nation were facing the prospect of a major decline in the number of high school graduates entering the traditional pool of prospective college applicants. The forecast decline in the applicant pool ran as high as 20% to 30% in some states. . . . [It was felt that] supporting athletic recruitment could be an effective means of maintaining and increasing the take of prospective students from a shrinking pool. Increased attention to the recruitment of qualified student-athletes thus became part of a larger admissions effort on these campuses."[30] More generally, Rasmussen observes: "During the post World War II period, the attention of these campuses was focused on the development of academic and research programs and the movement of these institutions from the role of prominent regional universities to that of national research universities. . . . By contrast, the 80s brought dismal forecasts of declining undergraduate populations and the urgent need to focus on ways to attract prospective undergraduate students to campus."[31]

These shared circumstances and concerns would not, however, have produced the UAA had there not also been a strong agreement on the kind of athletics program these institutions wanted to support. The most basic decision was to embrace the philosophy of Division III of the NCAA, not Division I—a decision that appears to have required essentially no discussion, almost to have been taken for granted. At the time of its founding, all members of the UAA were members of Division III, and, in Rasmussen's words, "planned to continue to compete in Division III."[32] From the start, the leadership of the UAA was concerned to establish "what might be termed a proper athletic emphasis." The UAA universities declared themselves from the start "committed to the NCAA Division III philosophy." For them, "Division III is an approach to athletics—not a synonym for third-rate."[33] With the exception of Emory, all of the UAA universities had at one time or another in their histories participated in "big-time" athletics (most notably Chicago in football and New York University in basketball), and "at some point in their histories, they all made considered decisions regarding the direction of their athletics programs. In every case that decision recognized a very basic principle—that intercollegiate athletics provides a unique means of educating undergraduate students, but only when its programs complement the academic experience; when the academic interest is compromised by athletics, the value of athletics is inevitably compromised as well."[34]

In a statement of principles released at the time of the announcement of the formation of UAA, the members of the association identified four themes, which they continue to stress today (see box).

UAA principles:

First, athletics is integral to the overall educational process of the institution and should be conducted in a manner consistent with the institution's central academic mission.

Second, student athletes shall be measured against the same standards as other students in admissions, financial aid, and academic programs.

Third, the chief executive officer at each university shall be ultimately responsible for the control of athletics at each institution.

Fourth, equal opportunities shall be provided for men and women.[35]

The UAA sponsors 22 sports. UAA schools play every other UAA school in at least one men's sport and one women's sport, and they participate in at least three UAA "festival" sports (with tournament formats) for men and for women. In 2001–02, 10 UAA teams finished in the top 10 in their sport, and 12 more finished in the top 20 national (Division III) rankings.

Women's Colleges and Women's Athletics

The women's colleges in this study have long been associated with one another in the informal grouping known as the "Seven Sisters." This group was seen as the women's analogue to the Ivy League before the Ivy universities became coeducational institutions. Unlike the Ivy League schools, however, the Seven Sisters are not grouped together for purposes of athletic competition; the association is based on academic caliber, reputation, and mission. The women's colleges belong to various athletic conferences, based primarily on their location.

Smith and Wellesley both compete in the New England Women's and Men's Athletic Conference (NEWMAC), which began as a conference for women only in 1985 (called the New England Women's 6, or NEW6), but started sponsoring men's sports in 1999. Bryn Mawr is a member of the Centennial Conference, which includes Mid-Atlantic schools such as Dickinson, Franklin and Marshall, Johns Hopkins, Swarthmore, and Ursinus. The three women's colleges in our study also engage in limited competition with the Seven Sisters, excluding Barnard (which competes with Columbia in the Ivy League) and Radcliffe (which has recently become an Institute for Advanced Study). Vassar, an original member of the Seven Sisters that is now a coeducational college, continues to participate in these competitions, which generally involve one major tournament per season in each relevant sport.

It was this type of competition, and not round-robin-style conference play, that dominated intercollegiate athletics at women's colleges until relatively recently. The Northeastern women's colleges have always emphasized fitness and athleticism; as early as the 1870s, many women's colleges had physical education requirements, whereas these activities were voluntary at most men's schools.[36] The focus was on health and fitness, and participation was more important than competitive success. According to Gertrud Pfister, a sport historian, the motto for women's college athletics in the first half of the 20th century was "A girl for every sport and a sport for every girl."[37]

To achieve this end, the women's colleges sponsored mostly intramural sports. Occasionally, however, several colleges would offer "play days" during which "fun and recreation, cooperation and togetherness took the place of competition and record breaking."[38] It was only with the advent of Title IX in 1972, which compelled coed colleges to bolster their women's athletics programs, that the competitive structure of intercollegiate sports at the women's colleges began to resemble that of men's sports. As we noted in *The Game of Life*, women's sports at coed colleges prospered in imitation of the male model;[39] consequently, athletics programs at women's colleges had to move in the same direction in order to be competitive. Even today, women's colleges have been more reluctant than coed colleges and universities to embrace the "male model."

These changes were not instantaneous, however. The Association for Intercollegiate Athletics for Women (AIAW), formed by women athletic administrators in 1971, organized the national structure for women's intercollegiate athletics for the first 10 years of Title IX. The AIAW initially banned athletic scholarships, and when, in 1973, the Association yielded to complaints that this policy prevented female athletes from receiving the same benefits as male athletes, its leaders still insisted that the scholarships be for four years instead of requiring yearly renewal. The AIAW also instituted a number of other policies that set women's sports apart from the NCAA male model. Transfer students did not have to sit out for a year, but instead could play immediately; all teams were invited to participate in national championships; and academic eligibility criteria were stricter than the NCAA's.[40]

For most of the 1970s, the NCAA struggled against Title IX, while the AIAW continued to exercise oversight of women's college sports. At its peak, the AIAW had a membership of 974 colleges and universities and supported 41 championships in 19 different sports.[41] But in 1980, perhaps because its leaders realized that Title IX was "here to stay," the NCAA voted to sponsor championships in women's sports for the first time. In 1982, unable to compete with the far wealthier NCAA, the AIAW went out of existence.[42]

Other Coed Liberal Arts Colleges in This Study

The coed liberal arts colleges included in this study (aside from those in NESCAC) compete in several different conferences. Both Carleton and Macalester compete in the Minnesota Intercollegiate Athletic Conference (MIAC). Denison, Kenyon, and Oberlin are members of the North Coast Athletic Conference (NCAC). Swarthmore is in the Centennial Conference (with Bryn Mawr), and Pomona, our only West Coast school, plays in the Southern California Intercollegiate Athletic Conference (SCIAC).

As is apparent from their names, these conferences generally have regional memberships. Perhaps because of this, they are populated by a wide variety of schools. Most are private, but school size, mission, religious affiliation, and academic quality differ enormously within conferences. Some of the problems that this diversity raises will be addressed in Chapter 7.

The histories of these conferences are rich in detail. We have space here only to note that the principles behind their foundings differed markedly. Groups such as the SCIAC and the MIAC were founded early in the 20th century on the basis of proximity. The Centennial Conference and the NCAC, on the other hand, were formed in 1981 and 1983, respectively, through the initiative of liberal arts colleges seeking to support their educational missions and to reinforce their academic standards by aligning themselves with like-minded institutions—which meant, in some instances, distancing themselves from historical rivals that were less strong academically.

ADDENDUM TABLE 1
Division I Philosophy Statement

In addition to the purposes and fundamental policy of the National Collegiate Athletic Association, as set forth in Constitution 1, members of Division I support the following principles in the belief that these statements assist in defining the nature and purpose of the division. . . . A member of Division I:

(a) Subscribes to high standards of academic quality, as well as breadth of academic opportunity.

(b) Strives in its athletics program for regional and national excellence and prominence. Accordingly, its recruitment of student-athletes and its emphasis on and support of its athletics program are, in most cases, regional and national in scope;

(c) Recognizes the dual objective in its athletics program of serving both the university or college community (participants, student body, faculty-staff, alumni) and the general public (community, area, state, nation);

(d) Believes in offering extensive opportunities for participation in varsity intercollegiate athletics for both men and women;

(e) Sponsors at the highest feasible level of intercollegiate competition one or both of the traditional spectator-oriented, income-producing sports of football and basketball. In doing so, members of Division I recognize the differences in institutional objectives in support of football; therefore, the division provides competition in that sport in Division IA and Division IAA;

(f) Believes in scheduling its athletic contests primarily with other members of Division I, especially in the emphasized, spectator-oriented sports, as a reflection of its goal of maintaining an appropriate competitive level in its sports program;

(g) Strives to finance its athletics program insofar as possible from revenues generated by the program itself. All funds supporting athletics should be controlled by the institution; and

(h) Understands, respects, and supports the programs and philosophies of other divisions. . . .

Source: 2001–02 NCAA Division I Manual, Section 20.9.

ADDENDUM TABLE 2
Division III Philosophy Statement

Colleges and universities in Division III place highest priority on the overall quality of the educational experience and on the successful completion of all students' academic programs. They seek to establish and maintain an environment in which a student-athlete's athletics activities are conducted as an integral part of the student-athlete's educational experience. They also seek to establish and maintain an environment that values cultural diversity and gender equity among their student-athletes and athletics staff. (Revised: 1/10/95)

To achieve this end, Division III institutions:

(a) Place special importance on the impact of athletics on the participants rather than on the spectators and place greater emphasis on the internal constituency (students, alumni, institutional personnel) than on the general public and entertainment needs;

(b) Award no athletically related financial aid to any student;

(c) Encourage the development of sportsmanship and positive societal attitudes in all constituents, including student-athletes, coaches, administrative personnel, and spectators;

(d) Encourage participation by maximizing the number and variety of athletics opportunities for their students.

(e) Assure that the actions of coaches and administrators exhibit fairness, openness, and honesty in their relationships with student-athletes.

(f) Assure that athletics participants are not treated differently from other members of the student body;

(g) Assure that athletics programs support the institution's educational mission by financing, staffing, and controlling the programs through the same general procedures as other departments of the institution;

(h) Provide equitable athletics opportunities for males and females and give equal emphasis to men's and women's sports;

(i) Support ethnic and gender diversity for all constituents; (Adopted: 1/12/99);

(j) Give primary emphasis to regional in-season competition and conference championships; and

(k) Support student-athletes in their efforts to reach high levels of athletics performance, which may include opportunities for participation in national championships, by providing all teams with adequate facilities, competent coaching, and appropriate competitive opportunities.

Source: 2001–02 NCAA Division III Manual, Section 20.11.

ADDENDUM TABLE 3
Conference Affiliations of Schools Included in the
Expanded College and Beyond Database

Ivy League
  Brown University
  Columbia University (and Barnard
    College)
  Cornell University
  Dartmouth College
  Harvard University
  Princeton University
  University of Pennsylvania
  Yale University

*New England Small College Athletic
Conference (NESCAC)*
  Amherst College
  Bates College
  Bowdoin College
  Colby College
  Connecticut College
  Hamilton College
  Middlebury College
  Trinity College
  Tufts University
  Wesleyan University
  Williams College

University Athletic Association (UAA)
  Brandeis University
  Carnegie Mellon University
  Case Western Reserve University
  Emory University
  New York University
  University of Chicago
  University of Rochester
  Washington University, St. Louis

*Minnesota Intercollegiate Athletic
Conference (MIAC)*
  Augsburg College
  Bethel College
  Carleton College
  College of St. Benedict
  College St. Catherine
  Concordia Moorhead College
  Gustavus Adolphus College
  Hamline University
  Macalester College
  St. John's University
  St. Mary's University
  St. Olaf College
  University of St. Thomas

*Southern California Intercollegiate
Athletic Conference (SCIAC)*
  California Institute of Technology
  California Lutheran University
  Claremont McKenna—Harvey Mudd–
    Scripps Colleges
  Occidental College
  Pomona—Pitzer Colleges
  University of La Verne
  University of Redlands
  Whittier College

Centennial Conference
  Bryn Mawr College
  Dickinson College
  Franklin and Marshall College
  Gettysburg College
  Haverford College
  Johns Hopkins University
  McDaniel College
  Muhlenberg College
  Swarthmore College
  Ursinus College
  Washington College

*New England Women's and Men's
Athletic Conference (NEWMAC)*
  Babson College
  Clark University
  Massachusetts Institute of Technology
  Mount Holyoke College
  Smith College
  Springfield College
  U.S. Coast Guard Academy
  Wellesley College
  Wheaton College
  Worcester Polytechnic Institute

North Coast Athletic Conference (NCAC)
  Alleghany College
  College of Wooster
  Denison University
  Earlham College
  Hiram College
  Kenyon College
  Oberlin College
  Ohio Wesleyan University
  Wabash College
  Wittenberg University

Source: Conference Web sites.
Note: Schools in **bold** are included in the study.

Athletes on Campus Today

CHAPTER 2

Recruitment of College Athletes

COACHES ARE teachers, and many teach very, very well. But coaches are the first to emphasize that in almost every collegiate sport today, the success of a team depends much more on the athletic talent available to it than on how well that talent is nurtured. "Among the many things I can't teach a kid," one basketball coach was heard to lament, "are how to jump higher and run faster." The former coach of women's swimming at Harvard, Maura Costin Scalise, put it this way: "In the sport of swimming, I'm only as good as the athletes I bring in; 95 percent of my success is due to recruiting."[1] As another commentator put it, "The best way to assure competitive success is to attract great players."[2]

THE EVOLUTION OF RECRUITING PRACTICES

Recruitment of college athletes is hardly new. In his history of football at the University of Chicago, Robin Lester writes that "the period from 1895 to 1905 saw student-players become player-students." There was widespread recruitment of schoolboy athletes. Dr. Joseph Raycroft, a member of the University of Chicago's Board of Trustees, provided this rationale: "The university, to protect itself, must engage actively in a canvass for new students. Others did it, and we must do it, too." Legendary football coach Amos Alonzo Stagg organized interscholastic track meets at Chicago as an important part of the recruitment process. Secondary school leaders resented this practice, and the Chicago superintendent of schools, Edwin G. Cooley, described the Chicago-Michigan approaches to Chicago schoolboys as "practically stealing boys out of high school for athletic purposes before their high-school courses are completed. . . . There are in the University of Chicago three pupils who are on the team who did not complete their high-school course."[3]

If the rationale for recruitment of "player-students" sounds similar to what we hear today, so too do proposals for reform—and the responses to them. President Charles R. Van Hise of the University of Wisconsin proposed that "all athletes should spend a year in residence before competing in intercollegiate athletics." President Harper of the University of Chicago dismissed the proposal on the grounds that "the inevitable re-

sult will be to send all men who are interested in athletics to eastern colleges." The Intercollegiate Conference (the forerunner to the Big Ten)
"passed a resolution in 1912 that neither [athletic] directors nor coaches
were to 'initiate correspondence or interviews' with high school athletes,"
but these rules proved difficult, if not impossible, to enforce. Lester provides a telling example of detailed instructions Stagg wrote out for an
alumnus to pass along to a prospect, telling the prospect to arrive at
school early so that he could get the best jobs, and so on.[4]

What has changed over the past 75 years or so? At its extreme edges, recruitment of high-school superstars in sports such as men's basketball has
become so aggressive that not even lip service is paid to educational values. The recruitment of Dajuan Wagner, who was famous for scoring 100
points in a game for Camden (N.J.) High School, by John Calipari at the
University of Memphis is a case in point. Recruiting Wagner involved hiring his father as an assistant coach and providing a basketball scholarship
for Arthur Barclay, Wagner's best friend and high school classmate. When
asked about the propriety of hiring the recruit's father, R. C. Johnson, the
athletic director, said: "I was O.K. with people saying we got him only because of his son. I think that's part of recruiting, and it's not illegal." At
the start of the school year, a reporter asked Wagner what courses he was
going to take. Wagner replied: "Man, I don't even know. Wherever they
tell me to go, I go."[5] In his one year at Memphis, Wagner led Memphis
to the National Invitational Tournament title; he then announced (to no
one's surprise) that he would leave college and participate in the National Basketball Association draft.

This is truly recruitment "at its extreme edge," and it is impossible to
imagine any of the schools in this study going to anything like such
lengths—even if they awarded athletic scholarships, which none of them
does. Still, there are connections. First, because the stakes are so high,
and the temptations to cross boundaries are so great, the NCAA now has
in place unbelievably complex regulations that govern recruiting at the
Division I level.[6] Even the *2001–02 Division III Coaches Recruiting Guide* is
17 pages long and includes, for example, three pages of instructions concerning "Tryouts" and "Tryout Exceptions." The *Division I Coaches Recruiting Guide (Sports Other Than Football and Basketball)* is 31 pages long
and includes, for example, a three-page section of regulations concerning telephone contacts, which begins with a long paragraph that defines
a telephone call (see box).[7] The timing and frequency of telephone contacts are regulated in excruciating detail, as are all other forms of contact. The Ivies, like all other schools that compete at the Division I level,
are subject to these regulations as well as to other self-imposed rules of
their own. Compliance officers are now common in essentially all conferences, and "following the rules" can be a very demanding activity.[8]

NCAA definition of a phone call:

"The definition of a telephone call does not include a facsimile or other electronically transmitted correspondence (e.g., electronic mail). Pre-arranged electronically transmitted correspondence between an authorized institutional staff member and one or more prospects and any electronic correspondence sent by 'instant messenger' or similar means shall be considered a telephone call. The use of a pager to contact a prospect is considered a telephone call. If a pager permits a text message to be displayed, an institutional staff member who leaves a message in excess of a greeting is considered to have made a telephone contact."

Within the Ivies, Bob Blackman at Dartmouth is widely credited with having introduced in the 1950s the highly organized recruiting machinery that is found throughout the Ivy League today.[9] It was not always this way. Writing in the *Harvard Magazine,* Craig Lambert begins a lengthy account of "The Professionalization of Ivy League Sports" with a vivid portrait of the "then-and-now" change that has occurred in racquet sports:

> In the fall of 1965, at freshman registration, Jack Barnaby, '32, then head coach of tennis and squash, sat behind his table in Memorial Hall, hoping to interest these freshest of freshmen in racquet sports. A young man who had come to Harvard from Bombay, India, approached and greeted Barnaby politely in British-accented English: "My name is Anil Nayar and I would like to try out for your squash team." The coach learned that Nayar had played squash, and invited him to Hemenway Gymnasium to hit a few balls and talk further. At the gym, Barnaby asked Nayar if he had played competitively. The freshman said yes, so Barnaby inquired, "How did you make out?" "I won," was the simple reply. "Oh—were you the junior champion of India?" Barnaby asked. "I have been the men's champion of India," Nayar explained, "for the past two years." . . . Nayar . . . went on to play at number 1 for Harvard's squash team and won the national intercollegiate singles championship three times. . . . Later, Barnaby asked an admissions officer why they had kept the young champion a secret. "We thought you'd find it a very pleasant surprise," was the answer.[10]

The days of such surprises are over. Today squash coaches would spot an athlete of Nayar's caliber years before he applied to college, and all American schools with varsity squash programs, including Harvard, would vigorously recruit him.

PRESENT-DAY RECRUITMENT IN THE IVY LEAGUE

In this same article, Lambert provides a good description of the way that Harvard football coach Tim Murphy and his staff recruit football players in today's environment:

> Because NCAA rules forbid coaches to go on the road recruiting until December 1, when the high-school football season is over, college coaches cannot see their prospects play "live." Instead, the Harvard football staff begins with a database of 4,000 videotapes, dossiers, and transcripts, which they winnow down to the top 1,000 prospects who may have a chance of admission. They apportion these among the five-man staff and narrow the pool to 100 by the Christmas break. Between then and March 1, Murphy tries to meet all these boys in person. For those winter months, his family sees little of him. "I'm on the road five days a week—and even on weekends, I'm here at Harvard, seeing student-athletes who are visiting the campus," he says. The football staff submits its final list of prospects to the admissions office, identifying the athletes they like who appear to be academically qualified.[11]

A recurring theme in talking with coaches is that, in the words of Armond Hill, head coach of the men's basketball team at Columbia, "recruiting is just a never-ending cycle; once the letters go out to seniors, you have to start looking at the next class. It's a part of the job." John R. Thompson III, head coach of men's basketball at Princeton, confirmed that "recruiting has become a larger piece of the job." Under the NCAA guidelines, coaches in Division I are allowed to travel off campus for "recruiting opportunities," either to meet with athletes or their families or to evaluate an athlete's athletic or academic qualifications. A school may devote as many as nine of these recruitment opportunities to each football prospect, as many as five to each basketball prospect, and as many as seven to each player in all other sports. A coach may also telephone each potential recruit once a week. Recruitment opportunities and telephone calls are further governed by an NCAA timetable of "contact, dead, evaluation, and quiet" periods. High school athletes also must follow NCAA guidelines for their visits to colleges, which are classified as either official (paid) or unofficial (at the student's own expense). A student may make as many as five official visits, each to a different school, during his or her senior year. Students may visit schools "unofficially" before their senior year, and as many times as they like.[12]

The head coach of field hockey at Columbia, Susan Eichner, told us that the number of potential recruits she deals with prior to July 1 is also in the 200–250 range. She winnows the list down to about 30 by July 1, but she has to use highly subjective means since, unlike swimming and tennis, field hockey does not have "times" and tournament rankings. A key aspect of this coach's recruiting is her work at a summer camp in Virginia; she will have worked with players in this camp for a number of years before they are ready to enter college, and perhaps a third of her team comes from this one camp. She also relies on her network of associations in the sport. After July 1, Eichner starts making phone calls to all of the 30 people on her initial list, and she tries to call them every other week. Some will select themselves out by committing to scholarship schools. She then focuses on 12 to 15, working closely with the admissions office. She will end up with 8 to 12 potential recruits by mid-February and can expect to admit and matriculate 5 to 8. Recruiting is a draining process, and coach after coach has said that it can take fully 80 percent of their time.[13]

In a widely discussed speech he gave to the Alumni Association at Yale in 1980, President Giamatti decried the emphasis on recruiting in the Ivy League at that time and observed: "I believe it must be widely acknowledged . . . that recruiting is not coaching." Giamatti predicted that budgetary realities would mean that "coaches will have to teach in the future in more than one area [and presumably recruit less]." He also advocated "restricting recruiting by coaches to on-campus conversations and visits."[14] Needless to say, events have taken the Ivy League (and all of college sports) in precisely the opposite direction, with much more time devoted to recruiting and with fewer and fewer coaches responsible in any way for more than a single sport.

One of the most important recent developments in recruiting is that, as one coach put it, "everything is happening sooner." According to Andy Katz, a senior writer at ESPN.com, the acceleration of recruiting schedules has made official paid visits to campuses in the fall of a student's senior year "nearly history." The pressure is growing for applicants to scholarship schools (Division I programs other than the Ivies) to make "unofficial" self-financed visits before the end of their junior year and, in effect, to commit to a school before the end of the summer before their senior year.[15] One article reported that 60 of the 100 top high school basketball players who were rising seniors had made commitments to schools before the start of September.[16]

When this happens, the pressure to decide early trickles down to schools in the Ivies and elsewhere, which may not be competing for these top players but are competing for the next group. Players and their parents call coaches and say, in effect, "Please tell me if I fit into your plans." Scholarship schools in which a prospect is interested will not hold a scholarship unless the prospect is willing to make some kind of commitment. The NCAA has adopted a "National Letter of Intent" early signing date in mid-November, when a student can formally commit to a scholarship program (with informal commitments often coming much earlier).

The result is a kind of "squeeze play" in which, as Coach Thompson puts it, "We can't promise, and they won't wait."

Athletes at Brown University benefit from what the Office of Financial Aid calls its "Early Athletic Reading Process," which starts in August and provides an initial financial aid estimate in the month of September. Director of Financial Aid Michael Bartini is quoted as saying that it "helps them make some of their decisions earlier."[17] As we will see later, one consequence of the early matching of athletes to schools is that the yield on admitted athletes (the percentage of those admitted who elect to enroll) has gone way up. In the Ivy League, coaches are strongly inclined to put on the lists that they submit to the admissions offices only those candidates whom they know, with some certainty, will matriculate. And, as we show in the next chapter, the "everything happens sooner" syndrome plays directly into pressures to admit more and more students (not just athletes, but athletes in large numbers) through Early Decision programs.[18]

What are the criteria used by coaches in deciding which candidates to push for in the admissions process—which ones to put on the all-important "coach's list" (submitted to the admissions office) that has such an important effect on who is admitted? The answers given to this question were highly consistent. First, coaches certainly do not want to waste a spot on a candidate whose academics are so questionable that admission is unlikely. Nor do they want to waste spots on candidates who are not likely to enroll. The athletic ability of the candidate is of primary importance, and as one experienced athletic director put it: "Increasingly, the goal has been to recruit students who can compete at the national level." Also important is the "fit" between the candidate's skills/position and the needs of the team. In an era of increasing specialization, one swimmer may be more attractive than another because the team is thin in the event he or she swims, a hockey team may have a special need for a center, a basketball team may need a point guard more than it needs another power forward, and so on.

Finally, a number of the coaches we interviewed emphasized the importance of focus and commitment to the sport. We asked one coach if he would have to think hard about a *very* promising athlete who also had other interests and wasn't entirely sure about his priorities. The immediate answer: "No, I wouldn't spend one minute thinking about that kid." The field hockey coach quoted earlier distinguishes potential recruits who want to go to a good school and think playing field hockey would be a bonus from those who know that they would be coming to college to play field hockey on her team. Not surprisingly, it is the latter group that ends up on the coach's list.[19]

The burden of this ever more intensive recruiting process on the coaches is captured by Lambert's description of the activities of two head coaches at Harvard: "Men's soccer coach Steve Locker sees 1,000 players per year, watching up to six games in a day: one format is the 'showcase,' which might mean traveling to Cincinnati, Ohio, to spend a Saturday watching soccer from 8:00 A.M. to 7:00 P.M. with 150 other coaches. Diving coach Keith Miller monitors about 75 recruits with a software program that is designed for people in sales. In fact, the process of identifying and qualifying prospects, retrieving information, and logging the results of contacts closely parallels a sales relationship—in essence, it is one."[20] And of course the prize recruits see the same process from the proverbial other end of the telescope. Lambert reports that Emily Stauffer, one of the most dominant soccer players in the history of the Ivy League, found 24 messages from soccer coaches on her answering machine when she returned from a trip on July 2.[21] Some recruits commit early precisely because they want all the telephoning to end.

The recruitment process has recently become even more complicated because of the growing emphasis on recruiting foreign athletes. In earlier years, the all-American squash teams were almost all U.S. athletes. "Now," according to Harvard squash coach Bill Doyle, "you'll see a minimum of 70 percent foreign players."[22] Several coaches observed that the Internet has made it much easier to contact foreign athletes, and the strength of the American system of higher education, combined with opportunities to compete at what is really an international level, encourages athletes from many countries to seek opportunities to compete in the United States. The first chapter in the latest edition of *Inside Recruiting* is titled "Recruiting the Foreign Athlete."[23]

A related trend is the recruiting of athletes in sports such as ice hockey who have had extensive experience playing on club teams or even national teams, often honing their athletic skills after graduation from secondary school. The result is a roster that contains a number of somewhat older, more experienced players. The Princeton ice hockey program now lists both the hometown and the "last team" of each team member. On the 2001–02 roster, there were only four players (all juniors and seniors) who listed their secondary school as the last team for which they had played. The recruitment of talented foreign students and the increasing tendency to recruit athletes who have had experience playing on a serious team after secondary school remind us that these college teams are increasingly open only to the most highly skilled athletes, who have trained for years for the opportunity to play "college sports." This professionalization of intercollegiate athletics is real, and it has major implications for the onetime "walk-ons," who are more and more relics of history.

RECRUITING IN DIVISION III

The NCAA rules governing recruiting in Division III differ in a number of respects from those that apply to the Division I Ivy League programs.

In general, they are less restrictive. Coaches in Division III do not have to wait until July 1 to contact a prospective player; in fact, contact by mail or telephone is permitted any time after the student enters ninth grade. Also, there is no limit in Division III on the number of contacts that coaches and others are permitted to make. Historically, there seemed to be less need for detailed regulation in a division that stressed broad participation rather than achieving competitive success at the highest level (see the Division III principles in the addendum to Chapter 1).

But make no mistake. Recruiting is a serious and extremely important aspect of intercollegiate athletics at the coed liberal arts colleges such as Amherst, Colby, Middlebury, and Wesleyan in the New England Small College Athletic Conference (NESCAC); at the urban research universities such as Washington University and the University of Chicago that have chosen to play at the Division III level within the University Athletic Association (UAA); at the other coed colleges, such as Macalester in St. Paul, that play in other conferences or as independents; and, increasingly, at women's colleges such as Bryn Mawr and Smith. There are far more similarities than differences between recruiting in the Ivy League and recruiting at these academically selective Division III colleges and universities.

NESCAC is interesting in that it tried for years to avoid the "professionalization" pressures in recruiting that were so evident elsewhere. Influenced by the Ivy Agreement of 1954, the NESCAC founding credo represented, at least in part, a statement of that conference's approach to recruiting.[24] Systematic efforts to identify and recruit student-athletes began only in the late 1970s, well after they were common in the Ivy League. Coaches have never been allowed to recruit off campus, as coaches do in essentially all other settings. But, as one wag put it, this means primarily that their phone bills are higher. Also, as John Biddiscombe, long-time director of athletics at Wesleyan University, has explained: "Coaches typically work two to four summer sports camps, not for the opportunity to make extra income, but more to observe talented, soon to be, senior prospects"[25] —surely a variant of off-campus recruiting.

In September of 1999, the Faculty Committee on Admission and Financial Aid at Amherst College released an extensive report titled "Admission to Amherst" that contains a succinct summary of today's recruiting process within, we believe, most of the NESCAC colleges.[26] After first noting the many things that Amherst does not do to attract athletes, the report explains:

> Nevertheless, our coaches do make strenuous efforts to encourage applications from promising student athletes, within the constraints imposed by the NCAA and NESCAC rules. Coaches are allowed to solicit or accept video

recordings of a student's performance on the field and, depending on the sport, each coach will review between 200 and 600 such tapes a year. Some coaches organize or participate in summer camps for high school players. All make use of networks of high school coaches and alumni in the effort to identify and attract talented student athletes. The Athletics Department invites applicants with marked athletic ability to visit campus, at the students' expense, for tours and overnight stays. Coaches also maintain contact with prospects by telephone, and often invest long hours in cultivating students whom they believe to be both academically admissible and athletically outstanding.[27]

The report goes on to describe a rating system used at Amherst that may or may not be comparable in its detail to systems used elsewhere in NESCAC:

In the late 1980s, the Athletics Department and the Admission Office developed a systematic method of rating the athletic promise of applicants and the special needs of teams that is still in use. Working through a committee composed of senior coaches, the Athletics Department assigns prospective student athletes, identified either by their own efforts or through the regular admission process, two ratings: one an assessment of the candidate's athletic ability and the other an assessment of the College's need for a competitor in the student's sport and position. Applicants judged to have sufficient athletic ability to flourish in Division III play are typically assigned an "ability" rating of 1 or 2 on a scale of 1 to 5. At Amherst, as at other colleges in NESCAC, competitiveness at the intercollegiate level depends on a steady supply of such "highly rated athletes." Recruiting them has become a major concern of coaches over the past two decades, in both male and female sports.[28]

This picture is consistent with the impressions we gained from interviews at Tufts, another NESCAC member, and from recent reports prepared by faculty committees at Middlebury and Williams. The director of athletics at one NESCAC school was quick to agree that "recruiting has become much more significant as a coaching responsibility and that this is not necessarily a good thing." The 2002 *Report of the Ad Hoc [Faculty] Committee on the Future of Athletics* at Middlebury says succinctly: "All the members of the athletics staff we interviewed pointed to recruiting as the single biggest change in their jobs over the last 10 or 15 years."[29]

Some of the pressure also flows from the bottom up, in that high school students and their parents have become very sophisticated about the admissions process and put pressure on the coaches to use the students' athletic talent to leverage spots at their schools. Amy Campbell, who has had a wide range of experiences in NESCAC, in the Ivies, and now at Bryn

Mawr, writes: "Sports specialization has had a dramatic effect on the burgeoning pre-college athletic opportunities for both genders and on the culture of youth sport. As families' expectations of sport shifted from a form of free play, self-initiated play, playing sports because it was fun, to a more formalized culture of play, including lessons, camps, clinics, and competition of all sorts, the expectations for more organized activity have grown. The heightened level of activity feeds into the expectation of an athletic scholarship or at the very least substantial leverage in the college admission process."[30]

Recruiting practices in the UAA can be considered something of a hybrid. The process remains somewhat less professionalized than what one finds in the Ivies (where one athletic director describes it as "more science than art") and, for that matter, at some of the NESCAC colleges. In interviews, a number of UAA coaches and admissions officers emphasized that their recruitment processes are much more informal than those found in either the Ivies or the most selective NESCAC colleges. At the same time, coaches in the UAA are permitted to recruit off campus as well as on campus, in contrast to the practice in NESCAC.

Still, by any definition, recruiting in the UAA, as elsewhere in Division III, is very important. Richard Rasmussen, executive secretary of the UAA since its founding, writes: "Recruiting has become every coach's second and third sport."[31] John Schael, director of athletics at Washington University in St. Louis, described the stages of the recruitment process at Washington University in much the same terms as those used by other athletic directors: coaches identify prospective students, they review tapes and other materials during the student's junior year in high school, they check the student's academic credentials to be sure the student is above threshold, and they build relationships with their recruits, arrange visits, and so on. Coaches then give lists of prospective athletes to admissions, but the lengths of the lists can vary greatly, and there appears to be less focus on the precise characteristics of "the list" than there is in some other settings.

At the University of Chicago, Athletic Director Tom Weingartner described the importance of recruiting in one word: "Enormous." The head coach of women's soccer, Amy Reifert (who was described by several of her colleagues as the best recruiter at the University), said that she keeps two lists of candidates: "my list," which she has built from her own sources, and the "admissions list," which contains the names of students who have contacted the University and indicated some interest in playing soccer. There is some overlap, but not much, between the lists. Reifert refines her own list by the beginning of June, and she uses the fact that she can contact students during June (when Division I schools cannot) to gain "a little bit of an edge." At this stage she will be working with a list of 50 or 60. The next step is for her to find out "who really wants Chicago," and the first questions she always asks students are: "What do you want to study?" "What courses are you taking?" Students who are interested in fields such as engineering that Chicago doesn't offer are not pursued; similarly, students with undemanding academic programs are discouraged. Reifert looks for students who want to study the core arts and sciences, who have taken Advanced Placement courses, and who are potentially good "fits" with the rigorous undergraduate curriculum for which the University of Chicago is known.[32]

Reifert emphasized that recruiting is a highly personal activity, and that she enjoys making real friendships with the individuals she recruits. She contacts her recruits by phone some 15 times and also writes to them. She tries hard, she said, to "avoid recruiting prima donnas." Her goal is to recruit students who can get in and who will enjoy studying at the University of Chicago. She recognizes that she will lose a considerable number of her recruits during the recruitment/admission process, and she may well end up enrolling only about a quarter of the recruits who are offered admission and in whom she is interested. Others at Chicago, including the men's basketball head coach, Mike McGrath, presented a very similar picture of a recruiting process that seems to fit the culture of that university very well.

The director of athletics at one UAA school, Jeff Cohen at Brandeis, said that while his coaches do not have trouble identifying athletes who are of the appropriate academic caliber, they do face great challenges convincing those students to come. Brandeis is competing, he said, with the Ivies, some of the strongest NESCAC colleges, and the other UAA institutions. Financial aid is a major issue in recruiting at many of the UAA universities, as well as at liberal art colleges that have limited financial aid budgets. Another UAA athletic director, Chuck Gordon at Emory, after covering many of the same points, emphasized the importance of a campus visit. Gordon views the willingness of a prospective student to travel to Emory, at the family's expense, as a good test of the student's real interest in Emory and of whether the student will be willing to pay to come.

The circumstances of the coed liberal arts colleges outside NESCAC vary so much that we are unable to provide a capsule summary—except to say that, in general, recruitment at these colleges seems less intense than it is in NESCAC. Perhaps it is best simply to describe the situation at Macalester in St. Paul, which, although an excellent school, does not have the same pulling power (especially for male students) as a number of other colleges and universities in our study. The recruitment/admissions process at Macalester is an interesting contrast to many that we have described in that there are no real coaches' lists of recruits. Rather, athletes are rated, and this information is used, along with other information, in making admissions decisions.

Administrators and coaches at the women's colleges in our study describe a recruitment process that is still relatively informal but is steadily becoming more structured and intense. At Bryn Mawr, coaches find out about high school athletes in three different ways: through athletes who contact the admissions office, through athletes who contact the coaches, and through coaches' scouting and contacts in the world of high school sports. According to Amy Campbell, Bryn Mawr's athletic director, the first group tends to contact the admissions office the summer after their junior year; the coaches generally know about the latter two groups by the end of the students' junior year or the fall of their senior year. Campbell believes that most coaches have a good idea of who is interested in playing a sport at Bryn Mawr by December of the students' senior year, but because very few will apply Early Decision, they maintain a long list of prospective students.

To trim their list, the coaches attempt to assess whether the candidates meet the school's academic profile based on the previous year's admitted class, their desire to attend a women's college, and the nature of their interest and ability in athletics. By January, each coach submits a list of prospective student-athletes to the admissions office. The athletes are ranked by potential contribution to the team, as well as by other criteria that the coach believes will help the admissions office. Campbell notes that even though the end result is a small coach's list, every student who expresses interest in athletics to the admissions office or a coach is tagged in the admissions database.

To construct their original list of athletes, coaches at Smith College rely on the same channels of communication as do those at Bryn Mawr. One of Smith's coaches explained that she assigns priorities through a process that begins with a list of approximately 300 high school athletes, about two-thirds of whom are juniors and seniors. Between 30 and 50 of these athletes are those whom the coach saw play at a "showcase" event or who were referred to the coach by a scouting service, and it is on these athletes that the coach focuses her attention. She winnows this group down to 10 or 15 based on their transcripts and their interest in Smith, and encourages these students to apply early. In a recent year, 8 of the 12 athletes on the list that this coach submitted to the admissions office were accepted, and five of those admitted enrolled.

Audrey Smith, the director of admissions at Smith, points out that although athletic recruitment in the women's colleges has become more structured, it is still very different from the process at most other schools: "We have seen a change in the recruiting by coaches in recent years. In the 1980s, Smith coaches were hired to coach more than one sport and many of these multi-sport coaches had a physical education background.

As a result of their professional background and the lack of time they had to devote to recruiting for two teams, they did not recruit off campus. Today's coaches at Smith must be more intense in their recruiting, oftentimes traveling to prospects' competitions in order to evaluate talent and encourage applications." However, Smith notes that many sports provide opportunities for varsity participation to students with less experience than that required at other schools. Recruitment at the women's colleges, though more formal than in the past, is still—in the words of Karen Tidmarsh, dean of the undergraduate college at Bryn Mawr—focused on athletes who are interested in the college, are reasonable candidates, and have athletic ability.

To obtain another, very different, perspective on athletic recruiting, we visited MIT—a university that was invited to join the UAA but declined (for reasons discussed later). MIT currently ranks near the top of American universities in the number of varsity teams that it supports—41. But its sports program has other distinguishing characteristics: there is very little recruitment of athletes, there is no recruiting budget, and there is only the most tenuous link between admissions and athletics.

The athletics department at MIT has a card that goes in the admissions packet to identify athletes, and coaches are able to follow up on students who look promising. Coaches also send lists of candidates to admissions, and students who are on a coach's list are identified by a colored sheet in their files. According to the director of athletics, Candace Royer, there is a broad spectrum of interest in recruiting on the part of the coaches. Some are active in trying to identify high-achieving students who are also good athletes, while others spend very little time on this. One MIT coach who was at a NESCAC college previously said that, whereas at the NESCAC college she would get her top recruits (presuming that they were reasonable candidates academically), at MIT she is not even sure that submitting recommendations is a good use of her time. MIT coaches have a broader array of coaching and teaching responsibilities than coaches elsewhere—a pattern that is workable precisely because so little time goes into recruiting.

The considerable variation in recruiting practices, even among these academically selective institutions that are similar in many ways, is a reflection of the fact that recruiting operates within the context of institutional objectives and constraints. MIT is an outlier in many respects, and its academic characteristics (as one commentator put it, "you can teach Lagrangeans in Econ 101") both restrict the pool of candidates it can consider and free it from some of the competitive pressures that affect other schools. At all of the schools in our study, athletic recruiting has become an ever more intense activity. Variations in rules, conventions, and practices should not be allowed to obscure this central point. There is no counterpart, outside of athletics, to the time and other resources devoted to recruiting athletes.

CHAPTER 3

The Admissions Advantage

IT IS NOT surprising that some coaches have been heard to refer to the admissions office as "heartbreak house" (sometimes smilingly, sometimes not!). At the academically selective schools in this study, how the admissions office views recruited athletes has profound implications for the institutions' intercollegiate sports programs. Coaches have to rely heavily on understanding, if not sympathetic, colleagues in admissions.

Aggressive recruitment of athletes affects the overall pool of candidates, so even in the absence of any advantage granted to athletes in a selection process, recruitment would matter. At enrollment-driven colleges and universities, where the challenge is not to ration spots but to fill all of the places in an entering class with reasonably well-qualified candidates, recruitment by coaches can be an important part of the process of meeting enrollment targets.[1] The schools in this study, however, are in the fortunate position of having a plethora of well-qualified candidates. In a recent front-page story subtitled "Finding the Key to College," the *New York Times* commented on the intense competition for places: "Harvard had 19,605 applications this year for 1,650 spots, versus 13,029 a decade ago. At Pomona College in Claremont, Calif., the most recent applicant pool was 4,229 for 390 spaces, contrasted with 2,883 in 1992. And at Washington University in St. Louis, 19,512 applicants competed for 1,280 places in the freshman class, up from 8,329 a decade ago."[2] In these settings (and it is pure coincidence that all three of the schools chosen by the *Times* to illustrate its point about selectivity are included in our study), the question of who gets in matters greatly.

As we show in the first part of this chapter, the nature of the interaction between recruitment and admissions varies considerably within even the relatively narrow confines of the academically selective schools in our study. Part of the explanation is the different aspirations of schools and groups of schools in terms of athletic achievement (a focus on winning national championships or the Sears Cup versus a focus on being competitive within the conference itself);[3] part is different conference histories—the Ivies are unlike the schools of both the University Athletic Association (UAA) and the New England Small College Athletic Conference (NESCAC), and the women's colleges are distinctive, too;

and part is different degrees of selectivity (enrolling athletes who are "representative" of their classes is harder when the average SAT score is 1350 than when it is 1200). The depth of the applicant pool and the degree of selectivity of the college also determine the "opportunity cost" of favoring athletes in the admissions process. One school may find itself turning away candidates with truly superb academic and other qualifications in order to admit a top-notch swimmer with so-so SATs, while another may find that the difference in academic (and other) qualifications between the swimmer and the candidate consigned to the waiting list is barely perceptible.

The different expectations and circumstances of the schools, including the degree of selectivity, lead, naturally enough, to different degrees of preference for recruited athletes. The most striking new data presented in this chapter show just how big an advantage it is, in the intense competition for admission to the most selective of these colleges and universities, to be a "listed recruit" on "the coach's list."[4] In the last part of the chapter we present new data that help answer another frequently asked set of questions concerning the underlying pools of high school athletes. "I keep being told," one president explained, "that if the coaches recruited less aggressively, we would be left with an entering class composed solely of 'nerds.' Is this true?" he asked. "How big is the pool of athletically talented applicants who also have high test scores?"

RECRUITED ATHLETES IN THE ADMISSIONS PROCESS

The admissions processes at the schools in this study are, in many ways, models of professionalism. In our interviews we were told repeatedly—and emphatically—that there is one admissions process for all students, including athletes; that all final decisions rest with the admissions office, not with the coaches; and that all admitted applicants have to be above a single, high, academic threshold. Karl Furstenberg, Dartmouth's longtime dean of admissions, recently emphasized that athletes go through the same admissions process as everyone else and then added: "Coaches have input into admissions decisions. . . . But all the decisions are made entirely in the admissions office."[5]

To be sure, there is no lack of stories of what "other schools" do.[6] Still, overall, we find the standard pronouncements about the probity of the admissions process convincing. There are real issues in admissions—serious issues, we believe—but they have to do with policies and priorities, not, except in rare cases, with deceit or underhandedness.

Ivy League Admissions

In the Ivies, in particular, the process of admitting recruited athletes has become much more regularized over time (much more "efficient," as Fred Hargadon, dean of admission at Princeton, puts it). There are well-defined channels of communication—which, of course, vary in their detail from one school to another; there is a great deal of pre-screening designed to weed out at an early stage prospective athletes who have no chance of being admitted; determined efforts are made to control the overall number of recruited athletes; and there is careful monitoring by the Ivy League Office of both numbers of recruits and their academic qualifications. The Ivy League differs from the other conferences in our study in that it uses a formal method of assessing the academic qualifications of admitted athletes (an "Academic Index," based in part on SAT scores and in part on high school grades, which is calibrated for each member school to reflect the average test scores and grades of all matriculants).[7]

This "more regularized" approach has been driven by the increased pressures on admissions from all sides. Columbia University is an interesting case in point. Over the past 10 to 15 years, the school's enrollment has increased, but applications have increased even faster, with the result that Columbia is now much more selective; in 1989 Columbia admitted about 30 percent of its applicants, and it now admits about 12 percent. Efforts to enroll an ever more diverse student body continue. In athletics, the number of teams at Columbia has gone way up, in large part because of the admission of women in 1983 and Title IX; Columbia now supports 28 teams, and some of those added recently, such as field hockey, have done very well competitively.

Deciding how best to allocate scarce spots in the entering class is an issue for all Ivy League universities. The problem of fitting obligations to field larger numbers of teams into this framework is compounded by the need to "overadmit" because of the absence of athletic scholarships; even the most assiduously recruited players may play for only a couple of years (see the discussion of attrition in Chapter 4). At the same time, as we showed in the previous chapter, there has been a definite increase in the importance attached to recruiting students who can compete at the national level. As a result, the admissions office faces increased pressure to admit the most talented athletes.

The growing emphasis on admitting highly talented (and highly specialized) athletes must also be understood in the context of a profound change in admissions philosophies that goes back to the 1960s. Mark Bernstein, in his history of football in the Ivy League, describes what transpired in the 1960s through the words of a Harvard dean at the time, F. Skiddy von Stade, Jr.: "What we're after is not the well-rounded boy but the lopsided boy who will make up a well-rounded class." Bernstein goes on to observe: "Though little appreciated at the time, lopsidedness was also a recognition of the continuing American trend toward specialization. If excellence, whether or not tempered by balance, was the ideal, it invited separation of athletes from the rest of their class. The implication of this change in philosophy would become more apparent over time."[8]

It would be a mistake to attribute this shift in thinking about admissions to forces within athletics; at Princeton, it was the mathematics faculty who objected vehemently to the rejection of candidates who had extremely high math aptitude but were not impressive in other respects. And today "generalists" of all kinds may feel that they are at a disadvantage in the admissions process. The director of college guidance at the Collegiate School is quoted in the *New York Times* as telling a student interested in Yale: "You're a white upper-middle-class generalist; I don't think you'll get in." The reporter goes on to observe: "In the lingo of the trade, Jed [the student being profiled] had no hook, unless they [the people at the Collegiate School] could parlay his theatrical talent."[9] But it would also be a mistake, as we argue later in the book, to equate the arguments for admitting a super mathematician with the arguments for admitting a nationally regarded volleyball spiker, given the educational missions of these universities.[10]

The Ivy League has been trying to control the number of recruited athletes in several ways. The Council of Ivy Group Presidents announced in June of 2002 that the number of football players each school recruits will drop from 35 to an average of 30 starting with the 2003 entering cohort.[11] More generally, admissions deans have been trying, in the words of one, "to keep the numbers of recruited athletes as low as possible— to take as few places as possible from others in the class—while still fielding teams that have a chance of competitive success." At Princeton, Dean Hargadon is proud of the progress he has made in reducing the number of recruited athletes at the same time that more teams have been competing.

There are, however, real trade-offs associated with reducing the number of athletes admitted. For example, a school that is eager to keep down the number of admission "slots" assigned to athletes may tell its coaches, in effect: "We are going to give you fewer admits, but we will pay especially close attention to your preferences in deciding which prospective athletes to admit." Placing more emphasis on the coach's view of which applicants will do the most for the athletics program is likely to lead to admitting not only the most athletically gifted applicants but also those who are the most dedicated to the sport. Thus we suspect that reducing the number of recruits has generally led to a purer distillation of "athleticism" among those who are admitted and enrolled.

The increasingly evident aspirations for competitive success at the national level have also led to more vigorous competition of Ivy League schools with scholarship-granting Division IA schools. The operative timetable (which is driven by the National Letter of Intent day in mid-November)[12] puts great pressure on coaches to seek "early indications" of who will be admitted and fuels the desire to have a large number of athletes admitted through Early Decision programs. Because spots are at such a premium and because of the need to clarify expectations as soon as possible, coaches and prospective players are more and more inclined to "bond" early in the admissions process. Later in the chapter we show that yields (the percentage of those offered admission who enroll) of recruited athletes have continued to rise and are now very high at many schools.[13]

It is understandable that coaches do not want to "waste a place" on their list by pushing for the admission of someone who decides not to come. Admissions deans also like high yields, in part because they make it easier to manage the size of the incoming class and in part because of the weight placed on high yields (and low admit rates) by *U.S. News & World Report* in ranking schools. Whatever the wisdom of putting so much emphasis on a high yield (and we have real doubts that this is wise),[14] it is clear that the combination of better communication all around and the growing desire to regulate numbers of admits results in the placement of more and more emphasis on the "fit" between a coach's needs and the attributes of a prospective recruit.

Another question to ponder is how the emphasis placed today on admitting the most sought-after athletic recruits affects the chances for admission of high school athletes who are not on the coaches' lists. Do athletically inclined students who do not make the coaches' lists get any kind of break in the admissions process? Or, alternatively, are such applicants at something of a disadvantage compared with the prospective musician or physicist (on the grounds that the athletes have already been taken care of and that there are other constituencies that also need to be considered)? We asked this question of one dean from an Ivy League school, and he said that the second interpretation is much more accurate—that is, this dean tends to favor candidates other than athletes after he has dealt with the coaches' lists.

This point was reinforced by a vignette contributed by the Columbia head field hockey coach, Susan Eichner. Eichner recalled that a year or two ago she was in contact with a very strong student academically who was a "reasonable" field hockey player. Eichner thought that because of this combination of qualities the individual would probably get in (though she was careful never to promise her that she would). It didn't turn out that way. The admissions office wanted to know which of the field hockey players on Eichner's list would have the most impact on her team, and this candidate was not one of them. The admissions office was able to take only four or five recruits from her list, and it honored her rank ordering. The result was a highly disappointed applicant, who then launched a lengthy correspondence with Coach Eichner and Columbia, believing that she had been dealt with unfairly. Not an easy situation for anyone.

NESCAC and the Other Liberal Arts Colleges

The NESCAC colleges are more like the Ivies in terms of numbers of teams, academic selectivity, and their general approach to athletics than are any of the other groups of schools included in this study. As we have shown, the NESCAC colleges offer almost as many sports as the Ivies (an average of 27 versus an average of 31) in spite of being, on average, about one-third the size (enrolling roughly 500 students per class versus nearly 1,500).[15] The Ivies are more selective, in spite of being larger, and have an average admit rate of 18 percent versus an average of 29 percent for the NESCAC colleges; average SAT scores are a little more than 100 points lower in NESCAC schools than in the Ivies. One other difference is that the NESCAC colleges are a somewhat more heterogeneous group than the Ivies, in that the ranges of admit rates and SAT scores are wider.[16]

The actual workings of the admissions processes at these colleges vary considerably from school to school (or at least between groups of schools). The most detailed explanation is provided by the 1999 report of the faculty committee at Amherst that was cited in the previous chapter. It reports:

> Formal contacts between the staff in Athletics and Admissions occur in three ways. An Athletic Liaison Committee brings together three senior coaches, representing the views of the Athletics Department, and two senior members of the Admission Office. It is in this committee that the coaches make a case at the beginning of the admission cycle for a target number of "highly rated athletes" and inform the Admission Office of special needs—a pitcher, a quarterback, a stronger defensive line. A tentative "target number" and a list of priorities emerge from discussion in this committee. The "target number" is not a formal quota, but rather a shared judgment regarding the number of talented student athletes necessary to maintain competitive teams and build up weak squads. It may be met, or not, depending on the strength and depth of the applicant pool.

Later in the admission cycle, the Athletics Department sends "rating sheets" on individual applicants to the Office of Admission. These sheets assess an applicant's ability and a team's need for that ability and supply such other information as coaches believe may be useful in making an admission decision. . . .

The academic strengths of applicants with high athletic ratings are evaluated in the same way as those of other applicants during the weeks when folders are read. . . . Applicants whose reader rating falls below a certain minimum are not considered for admission regardless of their athletic achievements or potential. Those candidates deemed admissible on academic grounds are then referred to broader committee meetings at which admission decisions are made. It is in these meetings that athletic ability and the needs of teams become factors, much as do considerations of racial diversity, disadvantaged background, familial connection to Amherst, and special artistic ability. In principle, therefore, unusual athletic ability is but one among many factors affecting admission decisions.

In practice, however, the sheer numbers of students involved in athletics and the constant anxiety on the part of teams and coaches to ensure the viability of their sports generate pressure within the admission process to give priority to athletic ability in a disproportionate number of individual admission decisions.[17]

The report then presents carefully considered data demonstrating the changes over time in the preference given athletes at Amherst. In essence, the odds of being admitted for athletes are compared with the odds of being admitted for other candidates with the same academic ratings—essentially the same approach that we use later in this chapter to calculate the admissions advantage enjoyed by athletes at all of the schools in our study. There was obviously a big drop in the standard applied to athletes (relative to other applicants) in the mid-1990s, and the principal explanation given is concern at the time for the disheartening won-lost record of the football team. The report also pointedly notes that decisions in those years concerning priorities and criteria for admission were made without consulting the faculty or its representatives.

In an interview, John Servos, a professor of history at Amherst who served on the faculty committee, reports that substantial changes have now been made—in part because of the publication of the report and also because of the arrival of Tom Parker (formerly dean of admission at Williams) as dean of admission and financial aid at Amherst. The admissions system has been made more transparent, and the number of targeted athletes has been reduced. An important procedural change is that the faculty admissions committee now has to vote to "ratify" the class that is to be admitted—a step that may well have a prophylactic effect.

The evolution of the processes used to admit athletes at Williams is also instructive. Richard Farley, the highly successful football coach at Williams, recalls that a major change was introduced in the early 1980s when admissions officers said that they did not want to be the ones making decisions about how to measure athletic accomplishments. Coaches were also frustrated, Farley said, by having spent months recruiting prospects only to have the candidates turned away in April. The Williams athletic director at the time, Bob Peck, came up with a new way of doing things. Each coach got a certain number of athletes that they could designate as being worth admitting ("tips"), even if they did not quite measure up academically. "Until they put in the tip system, it was tough sledding in football and ice hockey," Farley is quoted as saying. "Why should the admissions guy be in the position of having to evaluate goaltenders?" The reporter writing this story goes on to note that "the football team gets 14 tips, while most other squads get two or three. . . . In the 2001 academic year, . . . 72 players were tipped. 'If we are going to give any admissions advantage because of athletics, it's going to have to be for someone who would really have an impact,' says Richard Nesbitt, Williams's admissions director."[18]

Several presidents and deans of admissions have told us that football poses a particularly difficult problem for two reasons: first, squad sizes are exceptionally large; second, there is a sense that the football players the NESCAC colleges want are often taken by the Ivies. As an illustration of the seriousness of the problem, Tom Parker provided this account:

> Williams rates its applicants 1–9 and can comfortably build a class with those rated 1 or 2. In a recent analysis of 4,900 applicants, a sort was done to determine how many applicants were rated either 1 or 2 and (a) had earned football letters for two years in high school and (b) intended to play in college. The result: only 9 were in that group, 7 were admitted, 2 attended Williams and 1 played football. The rest of the football cohort for that year had to be selected from below the 1 or 2 rated group. [The number of football-playing students at Williams in the cohort used in the study was 16, so the "rest-of-cohort" group was 15 students.]

All of the deans of admission in NESCAC contend with the challenging problem of how to admit athletes who will compete successfully at a time when the admissions standards for all students continue to rise. After reporting that the same general process is followed at Wesleyan as elsewhere (final authority rests in admissions, there is one process, and so on), the dean of admission and financial aid, Nancy Hargrave Meislahn, told us that the root of the admissions dilemma is that "the overall profile of applicants has gotten much stronger and the athletic profile has stayed about the same." Her position is that the bar has to be raised for athletes, as it has been for the rest of the students. But, as we know, this is far from easy to accomplish, and substantial changes may be possible only through concerted action. Meislahn also notes that the most selective of the NESCAC colleges have "trade-off" problems (turning down large numbers of superb candidates to take additional athletes) that are not present to the same degree at less selective colleges.

This last observation about trade-offs provides a good transition to a consideration of the situation at the other coed liberal arts colleges in our study. Those with more modest average SAT scores and somewhat higher admit rates (such as Denison and Kenyon) have less of a problem justifying the admission of an athlete because their opportunity cost is lower; the hypothetically displaced non-athlete is less likely to be an outstanding applicant than his or her counterpart at the more selective colleges. Our group of coed colleges outside NESCAC also includes some highly selective institutions (such as Pomona and Swarthmore, two of the most selective schools in the country), and at these places the trade-off issues are very much the same as at an Amherst or a Yale.

Admitting enough football players whose academic credentials overlap somewhat with a school's regular academic profile is a challenge at all of these schools. Swarthmore, for all of its attractiveness as an excellent liberal arts college, has faced the same conundrums described above by Tom Parker in talking about the pool of football recruits available to Williams. In fact, Swarthmore's problem with football was even more serious because it enrolls such small entering classes (about 350)—at a time when specialization has been requiring ever larger squads. The widely publicized decision by Swarthmore to terminate its football program was driven in part by its desire to devote more resources—both places in the entering class and financial resources—to other sports.[19]

Macalester has the advantage of a somewhat larger entering class (almost 450), but it has to contend with the offsetting problem of difficulty attracting male applicants; and it, too, has high academic standards, though not as high as those at Swarthmore. Macalester also has suffered from being "stuck" (in the words of one Macalester official) in the Minnesota Intercollegiate Athletics Conference, or MIAC, which includes schools that are less selective academically and recruit large numbers of very good football players. People with whom we met at Macalester were candid in saying that, not surprisingly, admissions makes much more of a "reach" for football players than for athletes in any other sport. Macalester has no fixed number of slots for athletes, but uses a rating system: highly rated athletes are assigned scores of either 1 or 2, and it is only in football that athletes rated 3 are actively sought. The problem of building a competitive football team is further compounded by the low yield on admitted candidates. According to the dean of admissions and financial aid, Lorne Robinson, in a recent year Macalester enrolled only 3 of 24 rated football players. In contrast, the yield for men's soccer players was 43 percent—much better, but still a far cry from the nearly 100 percent yields at some of the Ivies and some of the NESCAC colleges. It is not hard to see why President McPherson agonized over the future of the football program before deciding to make a renewed effort to compete, but outside the MIAC.[20] The survival of football at Macalester and its demise at Swarthmore are discussed in more detail in Chapter 12.

The women's colleges do not face the problems posed by football, but they, too, have had to incorporate athletic recruitment into their admissions practices in new ways. The relationship between staff in athletics and in admissions at the women's colleges is now very close, and the director of admissions at Smith College reports that the full athletics and admissions departments meet twice a year to enhance communication. The admissions office has a full-time admissions officer who acts as a liaison to the athletic department. This liaison acts as an advocate for athletes in the admissions process and as a source of information for coaches. This close relationship undoubtedly smoothes the admissions process for athletes, but Audrey Smith, the director of admissions, stresses that the primary benefit is that it helps coaches to understand the decisions—welcome and unwelcome—that the admissions office makes.[21]

Bryn Mawr also has a liaison system in place. However, in this instance it cuts both ways: the athletics department has a staff member who is the primary liaison with the admissions office, and the admissions office has designated a staff member who communicates with the coaches. At the end of the admissions process, the athletics department receives two lists: one shows the prospective students who were "listed" by coaches and whether or not they were admitted, and the other shows the admitted students who expressed an interest in athletics or indicated that they played a sport at some time during their four years in high school. Coaches use the second list to try to entice admitted students to attend by encouraging their interest in athletics, and letters are sent to the matriculating students who have played a fall sport, inviting them to pre-season tryouts. Through this highly unusual practice, potential walk-ons are targeted by the admissions office and pursued by coaches.

Amy Campbell concurs that different coaches have different levels of success in having their recruits admitted. She feels, however, that this has more to do with how sophisticated the coaches are in identifying the students to recruit and "list" than with personal influence in the admissions office. Campbell notes that there has been improvement in this area and that most coaches are beginning to identify prospective students who have the appropriate academic credentials and are also athletes. Although the admit rate of recruited athletes has been reasonably good, Bryn Mawr has lost athletes to other schools in recent years because, Campbell suspects, they received merit aid elsewhere.

The UAA and MIT

The UAA universities are quite different from the Ivies and the NESCAC colleges in their admissions practices; in some ways they are more like the other coeducational liberal arts colleges. One clear difference is that the relations between coaches, athletic directors, and admissions officers seem less structured, more informal, and more "personal" in the UAA. This is in part because the UAA offers fewer sports and has fewer full-time head coaches. The situation is also eased by the fact that athletes comprise a much smaller share of the student bodies at these universities than they do in either the Ivies or NESCAC (roughly 10 percent in the UAA, versus an average of more than 20 percent in the Ivies and nearly 40 percent in NESCAC). For all of these reasons, the UAA universities do not have "slots" reserved for athletes and are more relaxed about the entire process of enrolling enough good athletes to compete successfully within their own orbit.

The University of Chicago may be the most extreme example. Although the dean of admissions, Ted O'Neill, was very eager to cooperate with our study, he was unable to comply with our request that he "tag" recruited athletes so that we could compare them with the walk-ons and the students at large (as we do in detail for almost all other schools in the study). At Chicago coaches vary greatly in how they interact with admissions. Some submit no lists at all, while others are very aggressive recruiters. The basketball coach, Mike McGrath, does submit names, but they may be the names of 40 or 50 students. Football recruiting is more organized, with relatively long lists, more ratings, and so on. As O'Neill put it, "the football coach is really asking for help in enrolling students who can play."

More generally, O'Neill described admissions at Chicago as "homemade." There are no directives from "on high" as to how he should view athletes, and he has considerable flexibility. One thing is clear, however: "the admissions office is in the driver's seat and makes the choices; no coach gets to have a heavy say in which particular students will get admitted." The head coach of women's soccer at Chicago, Amy Reifert, corroborated this view of how things work. She told us that she is "very honest in her letters to the admissions office about students, and she will not hesitate to say when she is uncertain whether the 'fit' is right for a particular student." Reifert also recognizes that the admissions office has to look at all applicants in terms of the high school context. If one of her potential recruits ranks something like twelfth in a good school and Chicago may be turning down the fourth- and fifth-ranked students, they are unlikely to take her candidate. She is, as she put it, entirely "content with a situation in which it is admissions, and not the coaches, who make the real admit decisions." The flexibility of the admissions process at Chicago can also benefit coaches in that admission may be offered to someone whose paper credentials are questionable if the coach knows the student well and is really willing to "go to bat" for him or her. But then the burden is on the coach to be right in his or her prediction!

Conversations with representatives of other members of the UAA (Emory, New York University, Rochester, and Washington University) provided a generally consistent picture of a set of admissions processes that, while they differ in their detail, reflect a mindset in which admissions offices are clearly cognizant of the needs of their schools' athletic teams but seem to feel less pressure (less "obligation"?) than they do in many other settings to meet the specific requirements of coaches. To repeat a point made earlier, the relatively small number of athletic recruits, in relation to the size of the typical student body, plainly makes a difference, and so does the clearly stated "education-first" philosophy of this relatively new association (which we described in the addendum to the introduction and discuss in great detail in Chapter 7).

We conclude this narrative account of admissions processes by once again briefly mentioning MIT, a university that has long supported an extensive athletics program (which includes 41 intercollegiate teams), but operates very differently from any of the schools in this study. We noted in the previous chapter the lack of recruiting budgets at MIT and, in large degree, the lack of recruitment. In admissions, there is little if any preference given to athletes, and coaches mainly work with players who were admitted according to exactly the same criteria as their classmates. Larry Bacow, president of Tufts, who was chancellor at MIT with oversight of athletics, told us that "the link between admissions and athletics is practically nonexistent at MIT." Bacow went on to explain that this approach is consistent with the generally egalitarian emphasis throughout MIT; for example, little if any preference in admissions is given to legacies. This tradition, combined with the required math, physics, and chemistry courses, would make the more typical approach to athletics impractical. MIT is a very unusual institution, and we are certainly not suggesting that what works there would work at colleges and universities with different objectives and different histories. Nonetheless, as an academic institution of the first rank that marches to a different drummer, it serves as a useful reference point.

THE ADMISSIONS ADVANTAGE ENJOYED BY RECRUITED ATHLETES

Describing recruitment and admissions processes in qualitative terms, and conveying the impressions of the people involved, day by day, in recruiting and admitting athletes, provide a much-needed texture for understanding the trade-offs that confront the academically selective schools in this study. But there is no substitute, finally, for careful examination of quantitative data that provide a more precise sense of present-day realities.

On the use of statistics:

In their book on Early Decision / Early Action programs in admissions, *The Early Admissions Game: Joining the Elite,* Avery, Fairbanks, and Zeckhauser write: "Some observers complain that we cannot capture all relevant factors about an applicant with a finite set of numerical variables. For this reason, some admissions deans have told us that they do not believe that any statistical analysis of admissions decisions can produce convincing results." After describing the methods they use to get reliable results, the authors end by quoting Damon Runyon as having observed: *"It may be that the race is not always to the swift, nor the battle to the strong—but that is the way to bet."*[22]

One key definition must be kept in mind: *when we speak of "recruited athletes," we refer to those applicants who were on a coach's list at the time admissions decisions were being made.* We do not include other applicants who may have played sports intensively before applying to college and who may well have been in active contact with the coaching staff but did not—for whatever reason—make the coach's list. Some of these students may regard themselves as having been recruited, but in our parlance they were not. Of course not all recruited athletes end up playing intercollegiate sports (though the vast majority do, as we show in Chapter 4), and some students who were admitted without having been on the coaches' lists (a group we define as the "walk-ons") compete on the same teams as the recruited athletes. Later, in Chapters 5 and 6, we compare the academic outcomes in college of enrolled students who were recruited athletes, walk-ons, and the rest of the students (who did not play intercollegiate sports). But our focus in this chapter is on applicants, not matriculants, and our goal is to understand how an applicant's fate in the admissions process depends on whether the applicant was or was not on a coach's list. To carry out this kind of probabilistic analysis, it is necessary to have complete data on *everyone* who was in a college's admissions pool—

whether or not the applicant was admitted, and whether or not those applicants who were admitted decided to enroll. Data sets of this kind are hard to obtain and very rare. Fortunately, 23 of the schools in this study were able to supply such data for their 1999 pools of applicants.[23]

A simple way to begin is by asking how the overall admit rates for recruited athletes compare with those for all other students. The four Ivy League universities for which we have the needed data offered admission to 59 percent of athletes on their coaches' lists, as compared to 16 percent of all other applicants. The NESCAC colleges accepted just under two-thirds of their "tagged" athletes, as compared with 31 percent of all other applicants. Both the coed liberal arts colleges outside of NESCAC and the women's colleges also accepted around two-thirds of the recruited athletes in their applicant pools, as compared with just under half of all other candidates. *In short, being on a coach's list certainly appears to have been a tremendous advantage in competing for a scarce place at these academically selective schools.*

Before coming to any stronger conclusion, it is necessary to ask how these simple comparisons may have been affected by the pre-screening of potential athletes. As we heard many times in our interviews, and as we reported in the first part of the chapter, athletes who ended up on the coaches' lists were often culled from a much larger pool of potential recruits, and serious efforts were made by coaches and members of the admissions staff to assess the likelihood that individuals with athletic talent had a good chance to be admitted and to succeed academically at the college in question. Jeff Durso-Finley, associate director of admission and liaison to the athletic department at Brown, has explained that "most of the narrowing down of the pool [of recruited athletes] happens before applications are even filed. . . . Coaches may mention the academic qualifications of the targeted students early in the school year and, 'I'll screen them out right there. We do very little late saying no, and more early saying no.'"[24]

Close inspection of the entire distribution of SAT scores for the Ivies and the NESCAC colleges reveals that this culling process did indeed ensure that recruited athletes, male and female, were no more heavily represented at the very bottom of the SAT distributions than were all other applicants (Figures 3.1a, 3.1b, 3.1c, and 3.1d).[25] In the Ivies, only about 2 to 3 percent of each group had SAT scores below 1100; in NESCAC, only about 2 to 3 percent were below 1000.[26] However, once we move above these bottom categories, we find that recruited athletes were more heavily represented than other applicants in each 100-point range until we reach SAT scores of 1400 in the Ivies and 1300 in NESCAC. The relationship reverses sharply thereafter, with recruited athletes less frequently represented in each of the higher SAT categories. In the Ivies, for example, about three-quarters of male recruits in the applicant pool had SATs

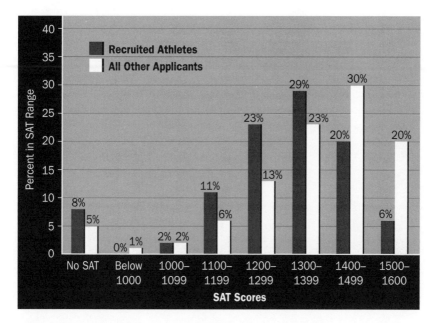

Figure 3.1a. SAT Distribution of Male Recruited Athletes and All Other Male
Applicants, 1999 Applicant Pool, Ivy League Universities
   Source: Expanded College and Beyond database.

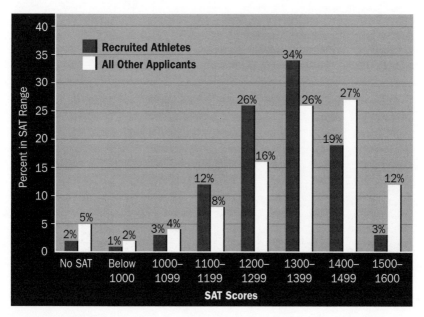

Figure 3.1b. SAT Distribution of Female Recruited Athletes and All Other
Female Applicants, 1999 Applicant Pool, Ivy League Universities
   Source: Expanded College and Beyond database.

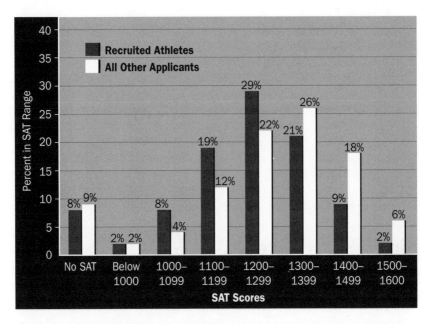

Figure 3.1c. SAT Distribution for Male Recruited Athletes and All Other Male Applicants, 1999 Applicant Pool, NESCAC Colleges
Source: Expanded College and Beyond database.

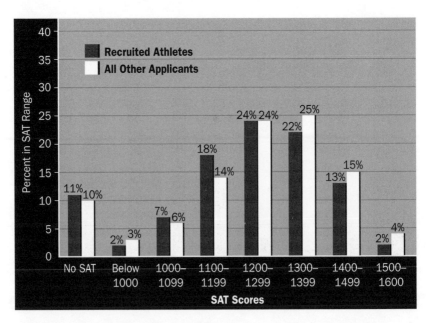

Figure 3.1d. SAT Distribution for Female Recruited Athletes and All Other Female Applicants, 1999 Applicant Pool, NESCAC Colleges
Source: Expanded College and Beyond database.

below 1400, as compared with exactly half of all other male applicants. The picture is similar for female recruits in the Ivies and for male recruits in NESCAC. On the other hand, while female recruited athletes in NESCAC are also more likely than all applicants to be in the lower SAT categories, the distributions for recruited athletes and all other applicants are much closer together (see especially Figure 3.1d). The corresponding distributions for other coed colleges and for women's colleges (not shown here but presented in Appendix Table 3.1) are roughly similar to those for the NESCAC colleges.

We conclude, first, that the pre-screening of recruited athletes has indeed limited the number of recruited athletes at the very bottom of the SAT distribution. Pre-screening serves mainly to set a floor that keeps off the coaches' lists candidates whose test scores are clearly below threshold. But above this floor, there is no evidence that pre-screening by coaches occurs to any great extent. Much more pre-screening is done, de facto, by the broad set of non-recruited potential applicants (acting on their own, and with the advice of school counselors). That is, many members of the general population of potential applicants to these highly selective schools will understand, or be told, that the odds of getting in are low unless they have truly excellent credentials. This knowledge may cause a number of those with modest SATs (by the standards of these elite schools) to self-select out of these applicant pools and apply elsewhere.

In any case, the recruited athletes as a group clearly have lower test scores than applicants in general. If recruited athletes were given no preference in admissions, they would be expected to have appreciably lower admit rates than applicants in general. For this reason, the simple differences between admit rates of recruited athletes and other applicants (pronounced as they are) *understate* the advantage that recruited athletes enjoy in the admissions competition. *In short, the existence of some degree of "pre-screening" at the lower end of the SAT distribution does not account for higher admit rates for athletes on the coaches' lists.*

The key empirical question has to do with how the admissions offices treat the various sets of applicants that end up in the applicant pool. At these academically selective schools there are, needless to say, large numbers of candidates whose test scores are well over the threshold to be realistic competitors for a place in the class. Within these large pools of qualified candidates, how big an advantage did the applicants on the coaches' lists have over others—including other aspiring athletes as well as academic high achievers and those applicants with extracurricular interests of other kinds? One way of illustrating the degree of advantage enjoyed by those on the coaches' lists is by plotting the acceptance rates of both recruited athletes and all other applicants *within each SAT range* (Figures 3.2a, 3.2b, 3.2c, and 3.2d).

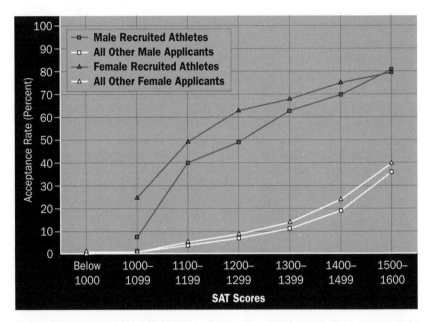

Figure 3.2a. Acceptance Rates of Recruited Athletes and All Other Applicants,
by Gender and SAT Group, 1999 Applicant Pool, Ivy League Universities
Source: Expanded College and Beyond database.

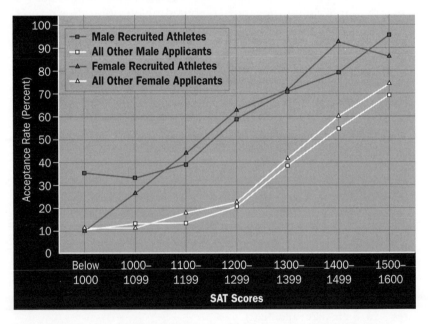

Figure 3.2b. Acceptance Rates of Recruited Athletes and All Other Applicants,
by Gender and SAT Group, 1999 Applicant Pool, NESCAC Colleges
Source: Expanded College and Beyond database.

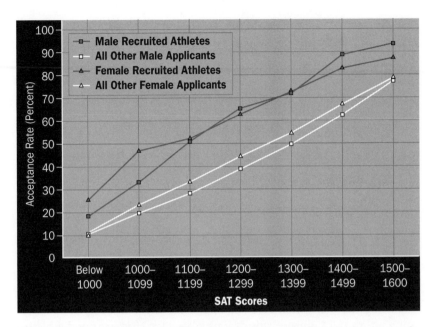

Figure 3.2c. Acceptance Rates of Recruited Athletes and All Other Applicants, by Gender and SAT Group, 1999 Applicant Pool, Coed Liberal Arts Colleges (Other)
Source: Expanded College and Beyond database.

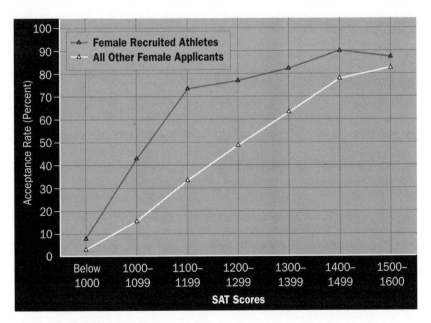

Figure 3.2d. Acceptance Rates of Recruited Athletes and All Other Applicants, by Gender and SAT Group, 1999 Applicant Pool, Women's Colleges
Source: Expanded College and Beyond database.

As one would expect, acceptance rates rise with SAT scores for all groups of students, however categorized. Noteworthy, however, is the substantial gap at each SAT level between the acceptance rates for the recruited athletes and for all other students. In the 1300 to 1399 SAT range in the Ivies, for example, the probability of being admitted for a male athlete on a coach's list was over 60 percent, as compared with a probability of about 10 percent for all other male applicants (Figure 3.2a). The congruence between the plotted figures for the men and women is striking; the corresponding probabilities of admission in the same SAT range for recruited female athletes and for all other female candidates are just under 70 percent and roughly 15 percent, respectively. Gaps are also sizable in NESCAC—with the differences in the admissions probabilities in this conference greatest in the 1200 to 1299 SAT range (Figure 3.2b). Gaps are somewhat less pronounced and more regular in size over the entire SAT distribution in the coed liberal arts colleges (Figure 3.2c). In the women's colleges, the gap is greatest in the 1100 to 1199 range, where recruited athletes have more than a 70 percent chance of admission, as compared with about 35 percent for all other applicants (Figure 3.2d).

A straightforward method of summarizing these findings is by calculating an overall "adjusted admissions advantage" for recruited athletes, men and women, at each group of schools in the study. This summary measure estimates the *difference* between the "average" admission probability for a recruited athlete on a coach's list and the "average" admission probability for any other candidate *after controlling for differences in SAT scores and other variables.*[27]

This is one instance in which the results (shown in Figure 3.3) really do speak for themselves. We see that the typical recruit in the Ivies enjoyed an admissions advantage of more than 50 percentage points over other applicants, and that the admissions advantage enjoyed by female recruits was actually slightly larger than the advantage enjoyed by their male counterparts. Since the "base" probability in the Ivies (the odds of getting in for all applicants other than recruited athletes, averaged across SAT categories, taking account of race and legacy status) was roughly 15 percent, it follows that the typical male recruit had an overall probability of admission of 66 percent (the base admissions probability of 15 percent plus the 51 percentage point admissions advantage); that is, *he had more than four times as good a chance of being admitted as did the comparable male applicant not on a coach's list.* The odds of admission for the typical female applicant on a coach's list were more favorable yet.

The results for the other groups of schools can be interpreted analogously. The most important point is that all groups of recruited athletes enjoyed a substantial admissions advantage over other applicants.[28] Also, we see again that there are striking similarities in the findings for male and female recruits. The *absolute* degree of admissions advantage enjoyed

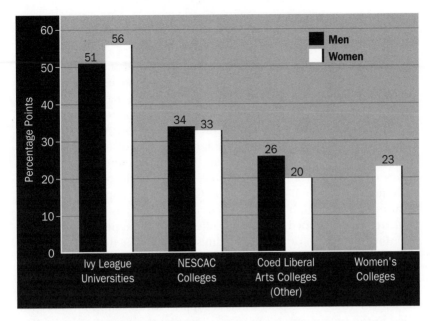

Figure 3.3. Adjusted Admissions Advantage for Recruited Athletes, by Gender and Conference, 1999 Applicant Pool
Source: Expanded College and Beyond database.

by recruited athletes is seen to be quite similar across these sets of Division III schools (averaging around 30 percentage points). The *relative* degree of advantage, however, is appreciably greater in NESCAC than elsewhere outside the Ivies because of NESCAC's lower "base" probability of admission (roughly 30 percent versus 45 to 50 percent). Thus the typical recruited athlete in NESCAC had slightly more than *twice* as good a chance of getting in as did other NESCAC applicants with similar credentials; for the other coed colleges and the women's colleges, the typical recruited athlete's odds of being admitted were roughly 1.5 times greater than the odds enjoyed by other applicants.[29]

We believe that the greater selectivity of the Ivies is one reason that the admissions advantage conferred on recruited athletes is greater in the Ivy League than it is in the other conferences we are studying. If this line of reasoning is correct, we might also expect to find that the size of the admissions advantage varies somewhat according to the selectivity of individual institutions *within conferences*. And this is in fact the case. In general, the more selective the school, the greater the admissions advantage enjoyed by its recruited athletes. The common-sense interpretation of this pattern is that schools that are less selective need not give as much of a "special break" to athletes in the admissions process in order to recruit enough athletes to be competitive.[30]

A second factor that we suspect affects the degree of admissions advantage conferred on recruited athletes is the number of teams that a school supports and the way that coaches' lists are formed. Again, the Ivies define one end of the spectrum. They support more teams than any other conference in our study (an average of 31). Moreover, as we saw in the first part of the chapter, they have made determined efforts to limit the overall number of recruited athletes by reducing the lists of athletes given special consideration by admissions—on the understanding that they will make extra efforts to admit those athletes judged by the coaches to be critically important to their programs. NESCAC does not appear to have gone as far down this path, but it is surely more like the Ivies in these respects than are the other coed liberal arts colleges or the women's colleges.[31]

Unfortunately, we do not have admissions files for the UAA universities and so cannot calculate admissions advantages for them. We are confident, however, that if the data were available they would show that the admissions advantage is much smaller in the UAA than in either the Ivies or NESCAC. Strong indirect support for this supposition is provided in the next chapter, where we show that there is much less difference in SAT scores between the recruited athletes and their classmates in the UAA than there is in the Ivies and in NESCAC. Earlier we noted that longer coaches' lists are common in the UAA and that UAA admissions officers appear to exercise more discretion in deciding which athletes on the lists should be admitted—two related characteristics of the recruitment/admissions process that would suggest a smaller admissions advantage for listed athletes.

It would be interesting to know how the admissions advantage varies by sport. No systematic evidence is available because the admissions files available to us show only whether an applicant was a tagged athletic recruit, not the sport for which the prospective athlete was being recruited. However, seven liberal arts colleges[32] were able to identify tagged football players, and it turns out, as we would have expected, that in every case the admissions advantage enjoyed by the football players in the applicant pool was greater than the admissions advantage given to other recruited male athletes. The average admissions advantage for football players at these seven colleges was 37 percentage points, whereas the average advantage for all recruited male athletes was 29 percentage points. These data offer quantitative reinforcement for the comments reported earlier concerning the greater difficulty experienced by essentially every college in enrolling football players. In fact, they may understate the problem in that two of the colleges that have faced the greatest problems recruiting football players—Macalester and Oberlin—are not among the seven included in these statistics.

An even more important question has to do with trends. The testimony of everyone with whom we have spoken suggests that the admissions advantage enjoyed by recruited athletes has grown markedly over time. While the lack of data for earlier years prevents us from measuring the changes that have occurred with any precision, we are able (thanks to the efforts of a dedicated archivist) to track trends at one representative university. The admissions advantage for male recruits increased from 23 percentage points for the 1976 entering cohort to 30 points for the '89 cohort and to 48 points for the '99 entering cohort. The admissions advantage for female recruits over this same period of time increased even more rapidly: from 15 percentage points in the case of the 1976 entering cohort to 26 points for the '89 cohort and then to 53 points for the '99 cohort.[33] By the time of the '99 entering cohort, the women's colleges were also paying special attention to recruited athletes, and we saw earlier (Figure 3.3) that the admissions advantage for women recruited to play sports at these schools was at the same level as the admissions advantage for women at the NESCAC colleges (and greater than at the other coed colleges). As one commentator put it, "The women have certainly caught up with the men!"

EARLY DECISION PROGRAMS AND YIELDS

The intensification of recruiting and the increasing admissions advantages enjoyed by recruited athletes are both related to the increased popularity of "Early Decision" programs—"whereby a student applies early to a single school, receives an early answer, and promises to attend if accepted."[34] Early Decision is a complicated subject all its own, which others are both studying and debating.[35] It has direct relevance for college sports because it both fuels and responds to all the pressures to "get it done sooner." Coaches are eager to "lock in" their most prized recruits, and admissions staffs are often just as eager to reduce the uncertainty associated with multiple applications and delayed decision-making by applicants accepted at several schools. Avery, Fairbanks, and Zeckhauser provide this example: "A student at Princeton summarized her experiences as a recruit for the golf team: 'Coaches prefer for you to apply early to demonstrate interest; if you apply early, they might move you up on the list of their preferred applicants. Potential teammates will emphasize this if they want you to attend.'"[36] There is also, as always, the question of a "competitive edge": if School A does not encourage an applicant to apply early, School B may, thereby preventing School A from having any chance to enroll the student in question.

There is quantitative support for the widely held assumption that applying early increases an applicant's chances of admission, and especially the chances of a recruited athlete. The adjusted admissions advantage for recruited athletes at one representative Ivy League university, which was large for recruits in the regular admissions pool, was appreciably larger for those who applied early: 65 points versus 46 for male recruited athletes and 65 points versus 51 for the women (comparing the left and center panels of Figure 3.4). These data also show (right panel of Figure 3.4) that all other applicants who applied early enjoyed a smaller, but still clear, advantage over candidates in the regular pool who had similar qualifications and attributes. As Avery, Fairbanks, and Zeckhauser document at length, many deans of admission seem to be in denial when responding to questions about the degree of preference given to applicants who apply early; the publication of their study should lead to considerably more "truth-telling" on this sensitive subject.

One surprising finding is how much the reliance on Early Decision programs for athletic recruitment increased over just the four years between 1995 and 1999. In the 1995 entering class, 38 percent of male recruited athletes (at the university for which we have the most complete data) were early admits. In the 1999 entering class, 55 percent of the recruited male

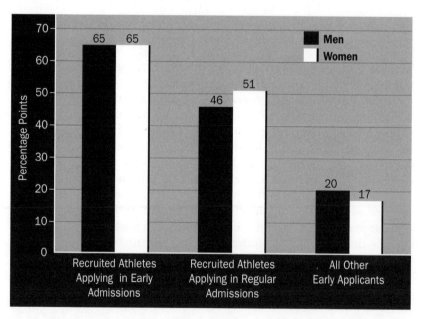

Figure 3.4. Adjusted Admissions Advantage for Recruited Athletes Applying in Early and Regular Admissions and for All Other Early Applicants, Controlling for SAT Score, Race, and Legacy Status, 1999 Admissions Pool, Representative University

Source: Expanded College and Beyond database.

athletes had been admitted through an Early Decision program. The reliance on Early Decision programs was even greater among the female recruited athletes: in the '99 entering class, 62 percent of them were admitted early. To be sure, there was some increase in the fraction of all enrolled students who had gained admission through an Early Decision program, but it was much more modest (about 4 percentage points) for the general population than for recruited athletes. Early Decision programs have clearly become crucial components of athletic recruiting and admissions. It is impossible to know whether this trend will plateau, continue, or be reversed—as it would be if the concerns expressed by President Richard Levin of Yale and others lead to a rethinking of the wisdom of this approach to admissions.[37]

The use of Early Decision programs affects yields since, by definition, the yield on Early Decision admits is close to 100 percent; anyone who is accepted through an Early Decision program is obligated to enroll (except if financial aid issues arise). Yields for recruited athletes in the Ivies are now often above 80 percent—for this and other reasons, including the generosity of their need-based financial aid programs, the prestige of the schools, and the informal commitments to attend often obtained by coaches before they put a prospect high on their admissions lists. Yields for recruited athletes in NESCAC appear to average around 50 to 60 percent, but to be nearly 80 percent in some schools; as in the Ivies, yields for recruited athletes are considerably higher than yields for all admitted applicants.[38]

The situation is quite different at some of the coed liberal arts colleges outside NESCAC and in the UAA universities. At Macalester, for example, the yield on highly rated athletes has hovered in the 25 to 30 percent range for the past five years. Limitations on the availability of financial aid and competition from less expensive schools are major considerations. In the UAA, coaches at the University of Chicago told us that they sometimes end up enrolling only 25 percent of the recruited athletes who are offered admission. The biggest problem at Chicago is, in the words of one person with whom we spoke: "We often get outpackaged"—that is, potential recruits may be offered better financial aid packages elsewhere. Similar comments were made by representatives of a number of other UAA universities. The wealth of a school and particularly the generosity of its financial aid program obviously matter, as do prestige and other factors that affect a school's overall ability to attract students. Also, while no college or university in Division III is allowed to offer athletic scholarships, there is a recurring suspicion that the presumed "leadership qualities" of highly talented athletes are sometimes used to justify giving them merit awards. As one athletic director put it: "Merit aid awards are beginning to feel like athletic scholarships."

Later in the book we show that the greater the degree to which schools give recruited athletes special treatment in the admissions process—by admitting large numbers of them through Early Decision programs and by granting a greater role to coaches in selecting those admitted (as their lists are compressed to include only their highest-priority candidates)—the greater the impact on how recruited athletes fare as students on campus.

HIGH SCHOOL POOLS OF ATHLETES

We return now, in the last section of this chapter, to the question posed by several college presidents about the sizes of the pools of high school athletes who had high test scores *and* participated actively in high school sports.[39] Thanks to the availability of a new database, we are able to answer this question for both the '89 and '95 cohorts of students and to refine the analysis further by looking specifically at those high school students who indicated they were likely to apply to the kinds of schools in our study.[40]

The results of our analysis should be very reassuring to those who worry that the most academically gifted students are less and less likely to be interested in sports. Of all men taking the SAT in 1995 who had a combined SAT score of 1200 or higher, 62 percent of those intending to apply to a NESCAC college had played high school sports. Moreover, 22 percent of these prospective applicants had played high school sports for four years or more. The corresponding percentages for the female test-takers are only slightly lower (53 percent and 19 percent, respectively). These percentages are considerably higher than the same figures for the '89 cohort; indeed, the percentage playing for four years almost doubled over this four-year interval. Interest in playing sports among academically high-achieving high school students has increased markedly (Figure 3.5). Similar calculations for high-scoring students who expressed interest in attending an Ivy League school or another school included in the original *Game of Life* study produce nearly identical results (see Appendix Table 3.2 for detail).

These findings are supported by data from an entirely different survey of top-ranking high school seniors carried out by scholars at Harvard.[41] Among the carefully culled group of students in the Harvard survey, who were randomly selected from the "top portion of their senior classes" by counselors in more than 400 of the leading public and private secondary schools in the country, 13 percent listed a major athletic accomplishment as one of their top three accomplishments. These "major accomplishments" in athletics usually involved having been the captain of a team or having won a special award. This standard of athletic accomplishment

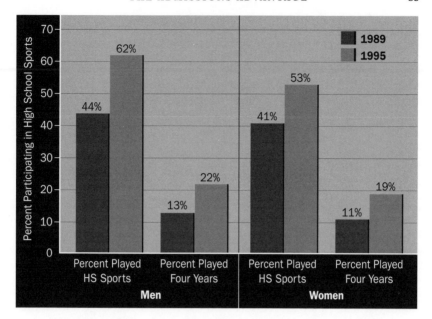

Figure 3.5. High School Athletic Participation, by Gender, High-Scoring Takers of the SAT (SAT > 1200) Intending to Apply to NESCAC Colleges, 1989 and 1995 Test-Takers
Source: High Test-Takers database.

presumably outranks having played for four years as a mark of athletic prowess, so the slightly lower percentages for this measure seem consistent with the other findings.

Middlebury has collected data on its own student body that further reinforce these findings: "In 2002, 905 of the 1617 students we admitted hope to play an intercollegiate sport. Among these, just 260 are athletes who were rated by a Middlebury coach. . . . The extent of student interest in competitive sports is great."[42]

Still another source of corroborating evidence, albeit impressionistic, is the experience at MIT. As we saw earlier, MIT does not recruit athletes and gives little weight to athletic achievement in admissions. Chancellor Phillip Clay of MIT was surely guilty of understatement when he observed in an interview that "the MIT culture is not one that puts athletics first. We value all evidence of high achievement—athletics, music, arts, as well as science, mathematics, or writing." Nonetheless, he reported that an increasing number of MIT applicants have played on varsity teams in high school. The high level of participation in intercollegiate sports at MIT demonstrates that an active program of college sports can be carried out in one of the most academically demanding environments, with "regular students" playing on the 41 teams MIT sponsors.

Nancy Malkiel, Princeton University's dean of the college, made a special point of saying what a pity it was that her school had to turn down so many fine candidates who had both superior academic credentials and considerable athletic talent because the coaches preferred other applicants who might make an even stronger—or more focused—contribution by filling specific positions on teams. Seeking the left outside linebacker who can blitz or the field hockey player especially skilled in setting up a corner shot plainly affects recruiting regimes and admissions policies—but the alternative is not a student body bereft of outstanding students who are also fine athletes.

The high priority (near-obsession, in some cases) given to gaining admission to an academically selective college or university quite naturally causes many parents, as well as their children, to ask probing questions about fairness. In a featured series on the travails of college admissions, a *New York Times* reporter provides this account: "After the make-it-or-break-it tests, Ms. Dancik [the mother of a student at the Collegiate School in New York who had wanted to go to Yale but had been turned down] found herself voicing the persistent complaint of the privileged classes: that scores mattered so much for boys like Jed [her son], while minority applicants had slack. 'You have had every privilege,' she said, 'and in a way it's a disadvantage.'"[43]

Innumerable court cases remind us that there is a widespread tendency to blame minority students, or affirmative action programs based on race, for disappointments in the admissions process. But these days there are far more recruited athletes than there are students from underrepresented minority groups enrolled in the colleges and universities in this study. It is surprising that there is not more questioning of what "affirmative action for athletes" means for the admissions chances of other highly talented applicants. A recent conversation with the grandparent of a disappointed applicant to an Ivy League school (who was a legacy with 1600 SATs) suggests that attitudes may be changing, perhaps in part because there is more discussion of the issue.[44] This grandparent clearly saw the implications of having admitted a large number of recruited athletes for the chances of other applicants, and he was not reluctant to express his feelings to anyone who would listen. It is actual situations like this one that make the concept of opportunity cost come alive.

Athletes in College: Academic Credentials, Athletic Participation, and Campus Culture

THE RECRUITED athletes—who, as we saw in the previous chapter, enjoy a substantial advantage in the admissions process—make up a very large fraction of their class at the schools in our study (Figure 4.1). Because recruited athletes are both more likely to be accepted and more likely to enroll than are other applicants, their share of the incoming class at all of the institutions studied is far greater than their share of the applicant pool or even the admit pool. At the coed liberal arts colleges, both in the New England Small College Athletic Conference (NESCAC) and outside NESCAC, roughly a *quarter* of the men and a *sixth* of the women are recruited athletes. Even at the Ivy League schools, with their larger student bodies, roughly 1 in every 6 men is a recruited athlete. On the other hand, recruited athletes are a much smaller fraction of the student body (less than a tenth) at the University Athletic Association (UAA) universities and the women's colleges.[1] This is due to differences in both the scale of the athletic enterprise—as reflected especially in the smaller number of teams that are supported—and the emphasis given to recruiting.

In this chapter we examine the relative numbers of recruits versus "walk-ons," the academic credentials of athletes, attrition among athletes (including years played on varsity teams), the effects of athletic recruitment on diversity, and, finally, the question of whether there is a separate "athletic culture."

"RECRUITED" ATHLETES VERSUS "WALK-ONS"

The percentage of all athletes who were "recruited" (by our definition of having been on a coach's list submitted to the admissions office) ranges from a high of 82 percent in the High Profile men's sports of football, basketball, and ice hockey at the Ivies to a low of 41 percent in the Lower Profile men's sports in NESCAC colleges (Figure 4.2). Although we suspect many of our readers will be surprised to find that the percentages of athletes who were recruited are so *high,* many of the coaches, athletic directors, and presidents with whom we spoke were surprised to find them

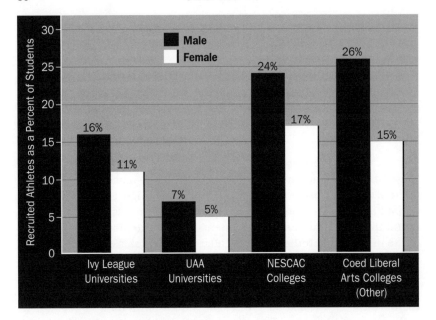

Figure 4.1. Recruited Athletes as a Percent of Students, by Gender and
Conference, 1995 Entering Cohort
  Source: Expanded College and Beyond database.

so *low.* Quite a few presidents asked if it could be right that there were *any*
walk-ons in the High Profile sports. Coaches of many teams (women's as
well as men's, Lower Profile as well as High Profile) said that they could
recall only a handful of walk-ons in recent years.

There is an important definitional question: who counts as a walk-on?
In our terminology, the walk-ons are those athletes competing on intercollegiate teams who were *not* on the coaches' lists. Today's typical walk-
on is an accomplished athlete who has been in contact with the coach
throughout the admissions process. In all likelihood, this student followed the advice of parents, secondary school coaches, and even media
such as *U.S. News & World Report* and initiated contact with the coach, perhaps even providing a video highlighting his or her skills.[2] Nonetheless,
the coach decided not to include this applicant on his or her admissions
list—perhaps judging that the student is not talented enough athletically,
not dedicated enough to the sport, or not interested enough in the
school.[3] Louise Gengler, the head coach of women's tennis at Princeton,
says there are always many strong tennis players who apply to Princeton

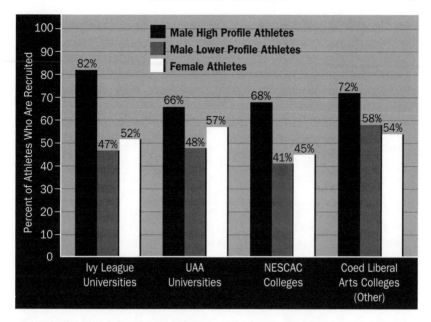

Figure 4.2. Percent of Athletes Who Are Recruited, by Gender and Conference, 1995 Entering Cohort
Source: Expanded College and Beyond database.

that she does not include on her list because she does not envision their having an impact on the varsity squad. Sometimes these "unlisted" players do get in, and in any given year one or two might move up from the junior varsity (JV) team to the 12-person varsity squad. Other coaches related similar experiences. Each year some talented athletes who were not included on a coach's list make their way onto campus and onto the school's intercollegiate teams.

These walk-ons may be quite different from the walk-on athletes some might remember from days gone by. Only in a very few sports is it still possible for a student to enter college having never played the sport ("novices" as they are sometimes called) and go on to become a member of the varsity team. This was not always the case. Anita L. DeFrantz, bronze medalist and two-time Olympian in crew, saw her first shell walking to class at Connecticut College. She recalls, "I went over to inquire, and there was a man standing there. I didn't know he was the coach, but he said, 'This is rowing and you'd be perfect for it.' Since I'd never been perfect at anything, I thought I'd give it a go."[4]

Some teams still do "recruit" outside classroom buildings and in dining halls, especially if they are looking for players to fill specific positions, such as that of a rowing coxswain or sailing crew. In a recent four-year period, Harvard's sailing team had six All-American crews, four of whom were recruited out of the freshman lunch line. But such opportunities do not extend to all participants even in this most "amateur" of sports; in the same four years, the team had six All-American skippers, all of whom were accomplished sailors before college. Moreover, there is reason to believe recruiting will only intensify in the future. According to a recent article in *U.S. News & World Report,* "Even fencing [at Harvard] . . . is becoming more of a blood sport. 'This is the last year as far as Harvard fencing being a walk-on sport,' says head coach Peter Brand. Of the current squad, two of nine female starters and one of nine male starters were recruited. Next year, six of nine men will be recruits."[5] Opportunities to "pick up" a sport in college or join a team on a whim are increasingly limited to the club sports—ultimate Frisbee and rugby teams are often populated with high school athletes who started those sports in college—and to special places on the varsity squad in a few relatively uncommon sports.

Robert Malekoff, director of athletics at Wooster, explains the pronounced decline in walk-ons in the Division III colleges and universities as well as in the Ivies in part in terms of what has happened at the secondary school level. He notes, for example:

> Lacrosse twenty years ago was primarily a regional game played in the northeastern part of the country. College coaches actively recruited walk-ons from football and soccer teams at their schools because these young men had strength and speed and could develop enough stick skills to contribute to the team . . . in some cases even to go on to play a starring role. In essence, not enough good high school players existed to fill the rosters of college teams. Today, lacrosse has become much more of a national sport at the youth and high school levels. Consequently, college lacrosse coaches can find more than enough experienced and highly skilled high school players to fill their rosters.[6]

Not only are more highly skilled players graduating from high schools; coaches have become increasingly sophisticated at identifying these players. John Biddiscombe, Wesleyan's athletic director, observes: "In the 1980s most Division III coaches learned about prospective players through alumni contacts, listings of All-State / All County teams, and informal and formal input from scouting contacts. . . . A number of potential prospects fell through the recruiting cracks and might show up on campus with a legitimate chance of making a team, even becoming key contributors." This is much less likely today.[7]

ACADEMIC CREDENTIALS

The recruits and the walk-ons constitute two reasonably distinct sub-groups of athletes, and throughout the book we compare these two groups both to each other and to the remainder of the student body ("students at large"). The degree to which recruits and walk-ons are distinct sub-groups depends a great deal on the recruiting and admissions processes described in the previous chapters. We might expect that at the Ivies and the NESCAC colleges, where the recruiting process is more formal and the advantage given to athletes in admissions is greater, the sub-groups differ more than they do in settings where recruitment is less intensive and the admissions advantage is less pronounced. Inspection of the incoming academic credentials of athletes, as measured roughly by SAT scores, demonstrates that this is indeed the case.[8]

At both the Ivies and the NESCAC colleges, the relationship between athletic recruitment and lower SAT scores is striking (Figure 4.3a). In

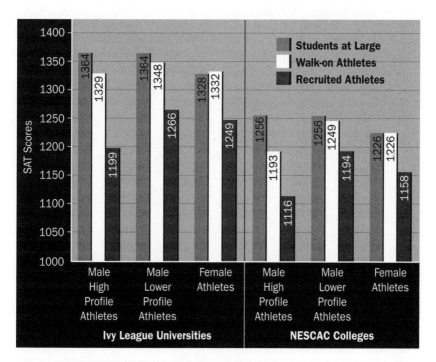

Figure 4.3a. SAT Scores, by Recruit Status and Gender, 1995 Entering Cohort, Ivy League Universities and NESCAC Colleges
Source: Expanded College and Beyond database.

both of these settings, recruited athletes have substantially lower average SAT scores than *both the students at large and the other athletes.* This important finding is entirely consistent with the picture of the admissions process presented in the previous chapter: athletes on coaches' lists are given substantial preference in admissions, but other high school athletes are not. While the gaps are largest in the High Profile men's sports— roughly 150 points separate the average for recruited athletes from the average for students at large (165 in the Ivies and 140 in the NESCAC colleges)—they are by no means limited to these sports. The gaps in SAT scores between recruited male athletes and students at large are also sizable in Lower Profile male sports (nearly 100 points in the Ivies), and female recruited athletes have average SAT scores more than 65 points below the average for female students at large. Walk-ons in women's sports and in men's Lower Profile sports have average SATs that are essentially the same as those of other students. Only in the High Profile men's sports is there a pronounced gap between the SAT scores of walk-ons and the scores of students at large (over 60 points in NESCAC); even so, the scores of walk-ons are still significantly higher than the scores of recruited athletes.[9]

At the other Division III schools, both colleges and universities, the relationship between recruitment and SAT scores is much looser (Figure 4.3b). In the coed liberal arts colleges outside NESCAC, recruited female athletes and recruited male athletes in the Lower Profile sports actually have slightly higher SAT scores than walk-ons. In these colleges, it is only in the men's High Profile sports that athletes—both those who were recruited and walk-ons—have average SAT scores that are markedly lower than those of the students at large. In the UAA as well, it is only the athletes in the High Profile men's sports who have lower average SATs than students at large—although, surprisingly, at these schools in these sports it is the walk-ons and not the recruited athletes who have lower average SATs. In women's sports, the UAA universities have succeeded in recruiting teams whose SAT scores are close to indistinguishable from those of their classmates. The less well-defined relationship between recruiting and SAT scores at the UAA universities and liberal art colleges, compared to the Ivies and NESCAC colleges, is most likely due to the differences in the approaches taken to recruiting and admissions discussed in the previous chapters. These numbers indicate that at the UAA universities and the coed liberal arts colleges outside NESCAC, only High Profile athletes have been given some break in admissions—regardless of whether they were on a coach's list.

The contrast between recruited athletes and students at large in the Ivies and the NESCAC colleges is dramatic, as looking at the gaps in SAT scores between these groups by sport confirms. Some of these gaps are substantial; the gap between students at large and recruited athletes in

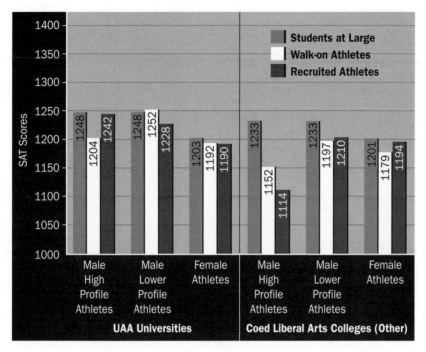

Figure 4.3b. SAT Scores, by Recruit Status and Gender, 1995 Entering Cohort, UAA Universities and Coed Liberal Arts Colleges (Other)
Source: Expanded College and Beyond database.

men's ice hockey in the Ivies is 177 points.[10] Athletes in the Ivy League sports of wrestling, men's baseball, women's basketball, and women's ice hockey join those in the High Profile sports of football, men's ice hockey, and men's basketball in having SAT "deficits" of more than 100 points; athletes in soccer, men's swimming, and softball are close behind (Figures 4.4a and 4.4b). The differences at the NESCAC colleges are smaller in general, but the pattern is no less consistent. Only athletes in a handful of "low-recruit" sports such as cross country, crew, and sailing have average SAT scores similar to or better than those of the students at large (Figures 4.4c and 4.4d).

The significance of these gaps can of course be misinterpreted. We are certainly not suggesting that the recruited athletes enrolled by these schools were poor high school students. The recruited High Profile male athletes in the coed liberal arts colleges have a mean SAT score of 1114, which is the lowest score for any of the groups in our study, yet above the 75th percentile nationally.[11] Nor are we suggesting that coaches (or admissions offices) are purposely looking for applicants with weaker cre-

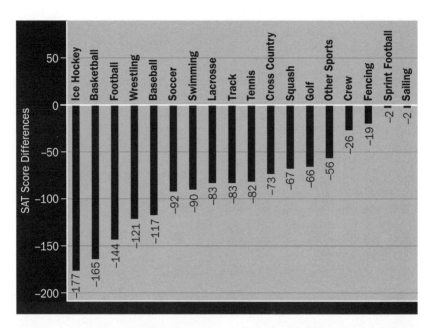

Figure 4.4a. SAT Scores: Differences between Male Athletes and Male Students at Large, by Sport, 1995 Entering Cohort, Ivy League Universities
Source: Expanded College and Beyond database

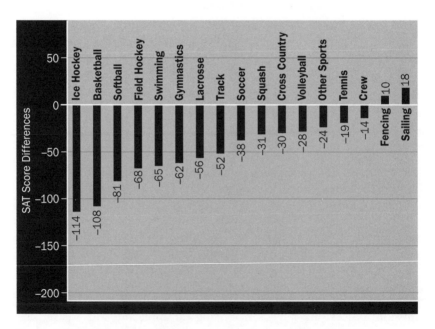

Figure 4.4b. SAT Scores: Differences between Female Athletes and Female Students at Large, by Sport, 1995 Entering Cohort, Ivy League Universities
Source: Expanded College and Beyond database.

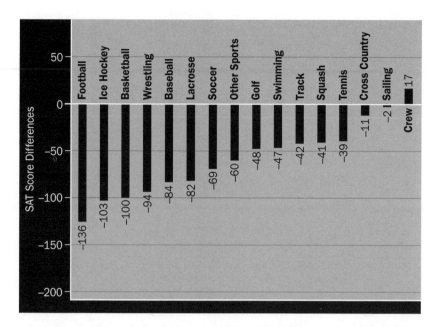

Figure 4.4c. SAT Scores: Differences between Male Athletes and Male Students at Large, by Sport, 1995 Entering Cohort, NESCAC Colleges
Source: Expanded College and Beyond database.

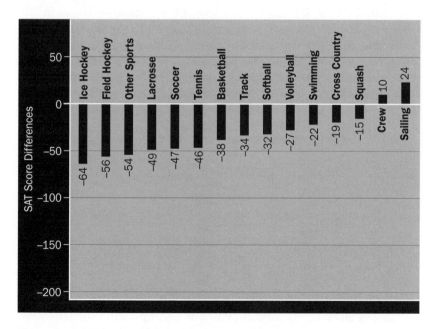

Figure 4.4d. SAT Scores: Differences between Female Athletes and Female Students at Large, by Sport, 1995 Entering Cohort, NESCAC Colleges
Source: Expanded College and Beyond database.

dentials. Of course not. We know from many interviews that coaches are seeking the best athletes they can recruit for their teams *subject to the constraints of the academic standards at their school.* But the reality is that the qualities the coaches are looking for—athletic talent, dedication to the sport, teamwork—are unlikely to be highly correlated (positively) with SAT scores; therefore, selecting on these qualities, even subject to satisfying the criterion of being above an academic threshold, necessarily produces a group of individuals with lower average SAT scores than the students at large, who are selected on the basis of other (more strictly academic) criteria.

Put another way, there are only so many high school seniors who have SAT scores above 1300, and there are only so many high school seniors who have the athletic talent necessary to play in the Ivy League; only a very small number meet both of these tests. In sports that require only a few key players, this is not too serious a problem, as these highly regarded schools can attract the needed handful of multi-talented seniors. However, the more players a coach must recruit (20 or more in a sport like football), the greater the chance there will not be enough students who meet both academic and athletic criteria. As any number of athletic directors said to us, football, in particular, is a numbers game. Fielding respectable teams, especially in an era of two-platoon football and high degrees of specialization, requires a large intake of players each year, and it is hard to fill such a large complement of places without dipping down academically.[12] As Richard Rasmussen, the executive secretary of the UAA, explains, "You cannot just recruit from the [right-most] tail of the curve [the bell-shaped curve of academic credentials]; you have to go into the middle of the curve to get enough football players." The data support this proposition: in the UAA, football is the only sport whose players have an SAT gap of more than 50 points.

PARTICIPATION BY SPORT AND LEVEL OF PLAY

There are also important differences in the athletic participation of recruits and walk-ons, starting with what sports they play. Of the walk-ons—many of whom were at least partially "recruited" in the sense of having had extensive contact with the coach before matriculating and most of whom are accomplished athletes—a large number are concentrated in certain sports. In the Ivies roughly a third of all male walk-ons row crew, and in Division III roughly 20 percent run track. Football is the counterpoint to these sports. Because, like track and crew, it has large squads but, unlike track and crew, it relies almost exclusively on recruits, the percentages of all male recruited athletes who play football at the schools in this study are very high: nearly 30 percent in the Ivies and between 30 and 40 percent in the UAA universities, NESCAC colleges, and coed liberal arts colleges outside NESCAC (Figure 4.5). The corresponding percentages of walk-ons who play football are 10 percent or below in the Ivies and the NESCAC colleges, and under 20 percent in the UAA universities and the coed liberal arts colleges outside NESCAC.

There is no equivalent to football in women's sports, and thus the female recruited athletes tend to be more evenly distributed across sports. There is still some concentration by sport among the walk-ons, however. At the Ivies and in NESCAC, most female walk-ons are found in crew, fencing, and sailing and, in NESCAC, in squash, cross country, and golf. At the other Division III schools, which field fewer teams, the walk-ons are concentrated in the more traditional sports of track, soccer, and tennis. Some sports, like tennis and squash, are viewed very differently in the Ivies than in the Division III schools. Women's tennis, for example, is much more dependant on recruits in the Ivies (more then 70 percent recruited) than in the Division III schools (fewer than 50 percent recruited).

Even with fewer than 50 percent of the players recruited, the reliance on recruiting in sports like tennis at the Division III level is more pro-

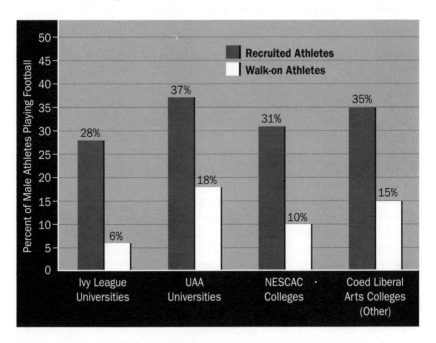

Figure 4.5. Percent of Male Athletes Playing Football, by Conference and Recruit Status, 1995 Entering Cohort
Source: Expanded College and Beyond database.

nounced than many would have believed it to be. It is clear that recruiting is no longer limited to the High Profile men's teams. With the exception of a handful of sports in the Ivies and the NESCAC colleges—crew, sailing, sprint football, and, in the case of the NESCAC men's sports, tennis—more than a third of the athletes participating in every men's and women's sport are recruited (Appendix Table 4.1). At the UAA universities and the coed liberal arts colleges outside NESCAC, the patterns are very similar. In *every* sport, more than a third of the athletes were recruited, and the percentages of recruited athletes are most commonly in the 50 to 70 percent range.

Recruits and walk-ons differ in the persistence of their participation in athletics, and this may help explain why some coaches found the number of walk-ons reported here so surprisingly high. In every type of sport and at every type of school, the recruited athletes play, on average, appreciably more years than the walk-ons (Figure 4.6). Thus, the fraction of athletes playing *at any given time* who were recruited is higher than the fraction of athletes who *ever* play who were recruited. We present the "ever play" comparisons. A coach, on the other hand, will most likely be answering the question "how many members of my current squad were recruited?" not "how many of the players over the past four years were recruited?"

Moreover, recruits are far more likely to play at the varsity level—and to do so for their entire playing careers. Many coaches note that the walk-ons they do have will work their way up from the JV team or from the bench and become varsity players only in their senior years, if then.[13] Recruits, on the other hand, are expected to contribute from the beginning. Ninety-three and 95 percent of male and female recruited athletes who play in the Ivies play at the varsity level; the corresponding percentages for men and women in the NESCAC colleges are both 89 percent (Figure 4.7).[14] More than half of the walk-ons at the Ivies and more than two-thirds of the walk-ons in NESCAC play varsity *at some point* in college, but walk-ons are also more likely to play for some time at the JV and freshman levels. Only about 20 percent of recruited athletes (men and women in both sets of schools) ever play JV sports, and even fewer receive freshman letters; recruits are clearly more likely to spend their entire college careers playing on the varsity squad. This pattern further inflates the recruit percentage on a varsity team at any given point in time.

Not only do recruited athletes play more years and at a higher level of play than walk-ons; they are also more likely to be the "key players" on a team and thus to feature more prominently in a coach's mind. For five of the Ivy universities—Brown, Dartmouth, Penn, Princeton, and Yale—we were able to identify athletes who started in football.[15] Being in the starting line-up is relatively rare—only 32 percent of the football players at these schools were starters—but recruited athletes were far more likely to

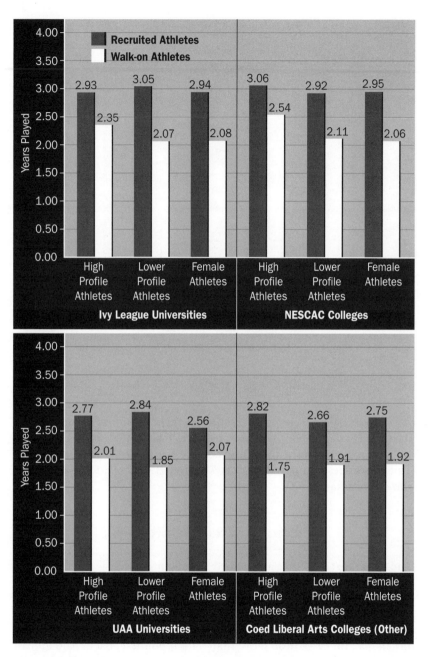

Figure 4.6. Years Played, by Conference, Type of Sport, and Recruit Status, 1995 Entering Cohort

Source: Expanded College and Beyond database.

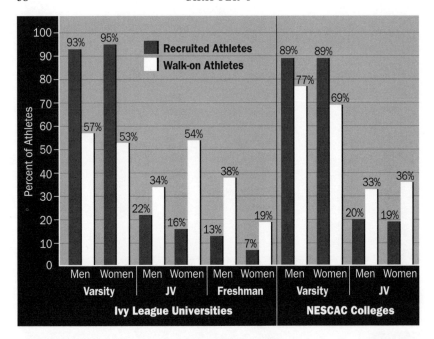

Figure 4.7. Level of Play, by Conference, Gender, and Recruit Status, 1995
Entering Cohort
   Source: Expanded College and Beyond database.

make the cut than were walk-ons. Over a third of the recruited football
players started at some point, compared to just over a tenth of the walk-
ons. Put another way, over 90 percent of the football starters were recruited athletes compared to only 78 percent of those football players
who did not start.

ATTRITION OF RECRUITED ATHLETES

One of the first decisions a recruited athlete must make is whether to follow through with an implied commitment to the coach and participate
in athletics. Unlike the situation at the big-time Division IA schools, where
an athlete is likely to lose his or her scholarship by choosing not to play,
at the Ivies and Division III schools recruited athletes are free to make
this choice; they risk little more than a disappointed coach. And at least
some of the athletes who are recruited will never play intercollegiate athletics; others will quit the team after one or two years. This phenomenon
of athletic "attrition" has a significant impact on the athletics programs

at these schools and on admissions more generally, because it has clear implications for the numbers of athletes who are recruited and for the experiences on campus of recruited athletes who matriculate.

There are many reasons why recruited athletes choose not to play. Sometimes, it is alleged, applicants leverage their considerable athletic talent to receive the coach's endorsement in the admissions process (no small advantage, as we have seen), and yet have no intention of ever playing. Others are no doubt far less calculating, but arrive on campus and find that with the myriad other options available, from singing groups to political clubs to intramural and club sports, not to mention academics, they would rather not devote themselves to a varsity sport.[16] There is also the problem of "burning out." After years of playing a sport year-round, as some have done since they were young children (in an era of increased athletic specialization), some college freshmen say that they have, as one coach put it, "lost their love of the game." In still other cases, an injury may cut short the athletic career of a promising recruit. Athletes who are not getting much playing time may be more likely to quit a team than the regulars, and decisions of this kind can be related to all sorts of factors beyond an athlete's control, such as the success of the team. John Thompson III, the head coach of the men's basketball program at Princeton, reports that he rarely has problems with attrition. But then again, he notes, "The overall success of the program is probably a factor in the lack of attrition."

For whatever combination of reasons, a non-trivial percentage of recruited athletes never play the sports for which they were recruited. At the Ivies and in the UAA universities, around 10 percent of those students who were on the coach's lists at admissions time never play intercollegiate sports (Figure 4.8). This percentage is much higher for the liberal arts colleges outside NESCAC, where between 20 and 25 percent of recruited athletes never play. We suspect that the somewhat less intensive recruitment process at this set of schools gives those athletes who are recruited less of a sense of obligation to their coaches.

Never playing is by far the most severe form of attrition, but certainly not the only kind. Most recruited athletes play for at least a year or two, but fewer than half play a full four years. Between two-thirds and three-quarters of recruited athletes at the Ivies play at least two years, but only 40 to 50 percent play all four years (Figure 4.9).[17] An Ivy League coach can expect less than three years of play from a recruited athlete and so may feel compelled to recruit and enroll three athletes for every two spots on the team.

To a coach making crucial decisions about which applicants to endorse, the presumed dedication of an athlete can thus be as important as his or her athletic talent. One Ivy League coach with whom we spoke prefers to recruit students from public schools and those who need finan-

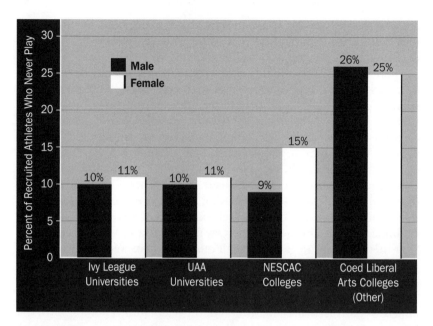

Figure 4.8. Percent of Recruited Athletes Who Never Play, by Gender and Conference, 1995 Entering Cohort
Source: Expanded College and Beyond database.

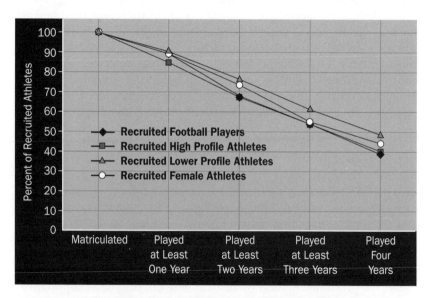

Figure 4.9. Attrition of Recruited Athletes, by Type of Sport, 1995 Entering Cohort, Ivy League Universities
Source: Expanded College and Beyond database.

cial aid rather than the privileged students from preparatory schools who are more typically found in the sport. These less traditional prospective students are more likely to feel grateful to the coach for helping them gain a spot at such an elite school and are less likely to quit the team. Many coaches echo the sentiment expressed by the basketball coach quoted in Chapter 2 who said he would not spend any time thinking about a student with broad interests outside sports. Throughout our conversations it has been clear that, especially as admissions offices have been working to lower the numbers of recruited athletes (as we were told they have at Columbia and Princeton, among other schools), coaches have felt compelled to look more and more for athletes who will stay with the program for all four years. As we noted earlier, we do not think it is a coincidence that the percentages of recruited athletes who never play are highest at the coed liberal arts colleges outside NESCAC, where the admissions advantage is smallest and the coaches' lists are longest.[18]

That coaches are disappointed to lose a player is entirely understandable. It is also easy to understand why admissions officers and deans see athletic attrition as leading to a misallocation of scarce places in a class. Jonathan Cole, the provost at Columbia, comments: "At the end of the day, we have large numbers of recruited athletes who are given significant advantages in the admission process, who take up spots in the class, and who don't play." Given that most of those who quit teams are not playing anyway, he argues for lowering the number of recruited athletes. We consider the implications of this approach in more detail later when we focus on policy choices. However, it is worth repeating here that limiting the number of recruits puts more pressure on the coaches not to "waste a spot" by recruiting an athlete who also has other interests and may not be totally dedicated to the team. Recruiting more and more narrowly focused athletes is not necessarily a good thing at schools that pride themselves on offering a wide range of opportunities for students and on attracting students who will take full advantage of the variety of learning experiences that are available. We are left with a conundrum. We do not want to bemoan a student's decision to shift gears and pursue new interests, and yet we recognize that the student may have been admitted in preference to another student solely because of his or her athletic prowess.

MULTI-SPORT PARTICIPATION AND SPECIALIZATION

Whether an athlete plays all four years is not the only way of characterizing a student's commitment to athletics. The frequency with which college athletes concentrate on a single sport, rather than play two or more sports, is a measure of the degree of specialization within athletics. To some, including many who have spent their lives guiding athletic programs, one of the most troubling trends in athletics is increased specialization at all levels. Fewer and fewer athletes participate in more than one sport while in college. And many athletes are specializing far earlier than that. Summer sports camps and youth travel teams with year-round schedules are standard in many sports well before high school. "'There's this thrust towards specialization at all levels,' says [Harvard] men's basketball coach Frank Sullivan. 'Parents feel that their children have to specialize, or they won't be as good as the rest of the kids. So they wind up playing soccer all year, or basketball all year. There are loads of clinics and camps, run by entrepreneurs.'"[19] Bob Malekoff elaborates: "Where 20 years ago a youth soccer program would consist of a fall league through September and October, far more is expected of today's elementary school-aged players. They are expected to play in a fall outdoor league, a winter indoor league, a spring outdoor league, and to attend a variety of soccer camps in the summer. In addition—if the youngster is deemed to be talented enough—he or she will participate on a variety of traveling teams that may compete against teams from other states and regions."[20] The pressure to compete at an early age, and to specialize, surely contributes to the "burn-out" problem noted earlier.

Consistent with trends in youth programs, collegiate seasons have also lengthened, activities in the non-traditional season have increased, and the level of play has improved markedly. According to former Harvard athletic director Bill Cleary, who played hockey for Harvard and the U.S. Olympic team, "All sports are being extended. When I played, we didn't start until December 1. Now, practice starts October 15—and we [the Ivies] are the last ones [to start practice]."[21] Not only have the official seasons gotten longer; the non-traditional season now includes workouts, practices, and, increasingly, contests with other schools. These factors combine to make it difficult to juggle more than one sport, and few athletes even attempt it. For both the men and the women at the Ivies for whom we have data for earlier days, multi-sport participation has steadily declined (Figure 4.10).[22]

Today in the Ivies, the UAA universities, and the women's colleges, only 6 to 7 percent of athletes play more than one sport; at the coed colleges in and out of NESCAC, the percentages are much higher, with roughly 20 to 30 percent of athletes playing more than one sport (Figure 4.11). Multi-sport participation has always been higher at the colleges; at the seven coed liberal arts colleges where we can make these comparisons, the relative numbers of multi-sport athletes today are roughly the same as for the 1976 entering cohort.[23] The NESCAC colleges, which sponsor so many sports with such small student bodies, must (and do) rely on second-sport athletes to fill out the squads. At the other coed liberal arts

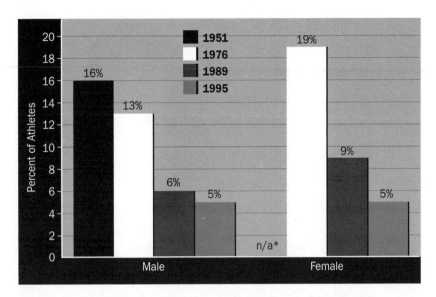

Figure 4.10. Percent of Athletes Who Compete in More Than One Sport, over Time, 1951, 1976, 1989, and 1995 Entering Cohorts, Ivy League Universities
Source: Expanded College and Beyond database.

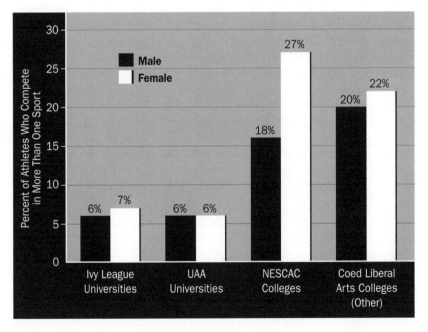

Figure 4.11. Percent of Athletes Who Compete in More Than One Sport, by Gender and Conference, 1995 Entering Cohort
Source: Expanded College and Beyond database.

colleges, the multi-sport athletes may be concentrated in a few common combinations. Indeed, 57 percent of the male multi-sport athletes at these schools play football and 44 percent run track (many of the same students compete in both of these sports).

That more athletes are able to compete in two or even three sports at the liberal arts colleges may well be a reflection of differences in the level (and intensity) of play. Susan Eichner, who coaches field hockey at Columbia, notes that competition in the Ivies is far more intense. When we spoke to her, her team had recently scrimmaged with a Division III squad, which she described as "fast, maybe faster than my girls, but not as well conditioned." Time in the weight room, and time spent conditioning, affect the range of other activities that a student can contemplate. In all conferences, recruits are more likely than walk-ons to participate in more than one sport, and this pattern is especially evident in the colleges, where (among recruited athletes) more then 20 percent of the men and 30 percent of the women do so. Perhaps talented athletes with interests in more than one sport choose to attend colleges (rather than universities) in part because they know they will have more opportunity to play several sports there.

The degree of specialization of athletes is also clearly related to the degree of specialization of coaches. Robert Malekoff provides a "family vignette" that makes this point clearly:

> As a high school student my brother, Andy Malekoff, was no different from many high school athletes in the 1970s in that he played more than one interscholastic sport. Andy was a three-sport athlete, participating in football, wrestling and lacrosse. He went on to Rutgers University . . . and continued to participate successfully in all three sports. . . . Nine members of the Rutgers football team were also members of the school's lacrosse team. . . . One reason that nine members of the Rutgers football team also chose to play lacrosse was because the defensive coordinator of the football team also served as head coach of men's lacrosse. That coach had a vested interest in seeing these students participate in two sports.

Malekoff goes on to note that today few, if any, Division I assistant coaches take on a second sport and that while Division III coaches once routinely coached two and sometimes three sports, they are now often responsible for only one team.[24]

In reflecting on the meaning and consequences of the increased specialization within athletics, it is of course important to remember, as John Biddiscombe reminds us, that "specialization in college sports has followed the same path as all of education. . . . Twenty years ago Wesleyan had a Biology Department, then Molecular Biology and Biochemistry became a major and now we have also added a Neuroscience and Behavior major."[25] Also, it is entirely appropriate to ask at what stages in a student's life he or she should begin to specialize. Rasmussen draws a clear distinction in this regard between the pre-college "growing-up" stage and life in college: "While I would argue strongly that specialization of athletes at the youth and scholastic levels is inappropriate for a variety of reasons . . . I do not make that same argument at the college level. College students are assumed to be young adults. . . . They should have the freedom to direct their own athletic experience."[26]

Dedication to any goal requires trade-offs, and Rasmussen also notes that playing several sports at the collegiate level today imposes heavy time demands on a student and makes it harder to pursue other (non-athletic) interests. We agree with Rasmussen that the decline in the number of multi-sport athletes is not in itself to be deplored; it is, however, another indication of the major commitment required today to be competitive in intercollegiate athletics.

Whatever one may think about the implications for the individual athlete of the increasing tendency to concentrate on one sport, the implications for collegiate athletics programs (and admissions) are clear-cut. The decline in the number of multi-sport athletes has a big impact on the number of recruits that a college like Swarthmore needs to enroll in order to be competitive in a wide variety of sports. If the same athlete cannot be expected to play on several teams, many more recruits are needed, and the pressures on admissions are that much greater.[27]

DIVERSITY

The set of qualities that coaches seek—which may or may not correlate with the qualities important to the admissions office—can have other implications for the composition of a class. One important potential side effect of athletic recruiting is related to the diversity of the student body. More specifically, it is sometimes suggested that the recruitment of athletes contributes substantially to racial and socioeconomic diversity.[28]

In investigating this issue, we made two somewhat surprising discoveries. First and most important, *recruited athletes in the schools in our study are in general appreciably less likely than students at large to be from underrepresented minority groups* (Table 4.1).[29] The most notable exception to this generalization occurs in the High Profile men's sports. At the coed colleges outside NESCAC a quarter of the recruited athletes playing High Profile sports are underrepresented minorities, compared to less than a tenth of the students at large. On the other hand, at *every* group of schools, fewer than 10 percent of recruited Lower Profile male athletes and no more than 5 percent of recruited female athletes are minorities. At the Ivies,

TABLE 4.1
Percent of Athletes and Students at Large Who Are
Underrepresented Minorities, by Conference, Type of Sport,
and Recruit Status, 1995 Entering Cohort

	Ivy Universities	*UAA Universities*	*NESCAC Colleges*	*Coed Liberal Arts Colleges (Other)*
High Profile Male Athletes				
Students at large	12%	7%	9%	8%
Walk-on athletes	16%	24%	12%	35%
Recruited athletes	16%	6%	6%	25%
Lower Profile Male Athletes				
Students at large	12%	7%	9%	8%
Walk-on athletes	14%	13%	9%	9%
Recruited athletes	5%	9%	3%	7%
Female Athletes				
Students at large	18%	10%	14%	10%
Walk-on athletes	12%	11%	9%	6%
Recruited athletes	5%	4%	2%	5%

Source: Expanded College and Beyond database.

just 5 percent of recruited Lower Profile male athletes come from minority groups, and just 5 percent of the recruited female athletes are minorities. The corresponding percentages of minorities among students at large in the Ivies are 12 percent for the men and 18 percent for the women. Only at the coed liberal arts colleges outside NESCAC does athletic recruitment increase the proportion of minorities on campus. In general, the fraction of minority students represented in the student bodies of the Ivy League universities and the NESCAC colleges would have been slightly *higher* if recruited athletes had been replaced by other matriculants with the same racial mix as the current population of students at large; in the UAA universities, the fraction would have been unchanged. Thus, as a statistical proposition, recruitment of athletes cannot be said to have contributed to increased racial diversity on these campuses.[30]

The second finding is even more surprising: *recruited athletes are consistently less likely than walk-ons to come from minority groups* (see Table 4.1 again). In the case of the female students, the percentage of minority students among the walk-ons is often twice and sometimes three times as high as the percentage of minority students among recruits (Figure 4.12).

We have no full explanation for the relatively low numbers of minority students recruited to play most of these sports (the High Profile sports of football and basketball are the major exceptions), and we certainly do not mean to suggest that coaches discriminate against minorities when recruiting. One commentator has suggested that high-talent athletes from minority groups are especially likely to accept athletic scholarships at schools that offer such aid. Others have wondered if coaches leave minority students off their lists because they think they will be admitted anyway through affirmative action programs.

Recruiting networks may also tend to produce disproportionately large numbers of white recruits, especially in traditionally "white" sports. Reliance on certain feeder schools, and on sports camps, may be part of the explanation. Or it may be that there are not many minority athletes, especially female minority athletes, in the recruiting pools for some sports. According to Tina Sloan Green, the president and executive director of the Black Women in Sport Foundation, few minority women have access to the facilities or coaching necessary for these sports as children.[31] Even in sports that are available to them at early ages, minority students may lack access to high-quality athletics programs at the secondary school

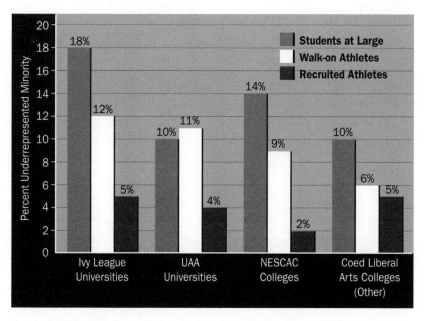

Figure 4.12. Female Percent Underrepresented Minority, by Conference and Recruit Status, 1995 Entering Cohort

Source: Expanded College and Beyond database.

level. A deeper look at the interplay of race in America and access to athletic opportunities is beyond the scope of this study, but the current pattern is clear.

Although recruited athletes as a group do not contribute substantially to racial diversity, they may contribute to other forms of diversity, such as socioeconomic or geographic diversity. For nearly all of the colleges and universities in our study, we know which students received need-based aid.[32] Need-based aid serves as at least a rough proxy for socioeconomic status, and we find that recruited High Profile athletes are consistently more likely than students at large to receive need-based financial aid. While between 40 and 50 percent of male students at large received need-based financial aid, the percentages of recruited High Profile athletes qualifying for need-based awards were 64 percent at the NESCAC colleges and the UAA universities, 74 percent at the Ivies, and 78 percent at the other coed liberal arts colleges (Figure 4.13). Two commentators from NESCAC colleges (William Adams at Colby and John Biddiscombe at Wesleyan) emphasized that athletic recruiting in football and basketball, in particular, has a beneficial "social class" component, in that it at-

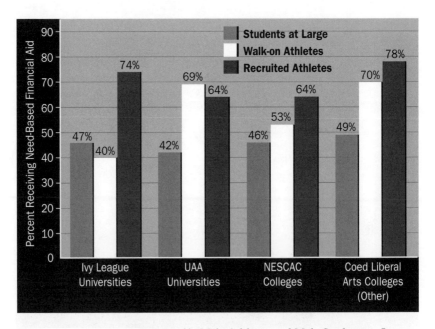

Figure 4.13. Percent of High Profile Male Athletes and Male Students at Large Receiving Need-Based Financial Aid, by Conference and Recruit Status, 1995 Entering Cohort

Source: Expanded College and Beyond database.

tracts students from communities that differ from those that produce most of their applicants. The pattern is more mixed for other male athletes; but in no case are recruited athletes substantially less likely to receive aid than students at large (Appendix Table 4.2). On the other hand, the walk-ons in Lower Profile men's sports and in women's sports are generally less likely to receive aid than students at large.[33]

These findings are driven by the demographics of the pools of talented athletes, and should not be read as reflecting on the values or attitudes of coaches. Many are surely as conscious as other faculty and staff of the importance of a diverse campus population, while others may attach less weight to this objective. In any event, coaches should be expected to feel a primary responsibility to their teams—especially at a time when, as we have been told repeatedly, coaches are judged more and more on achieving competitive success.

CAMPUS CULTURE

Athletes—men and women, recruits and walk-ons alike—do far more in college than participate in athletics. First and foremost, they of course go to class. They are students like their classmates, and the next two chapters are concerned with the fields in which athletes major and how they perform academically—both in absolute terms and relative to their classmates. But residential universities exist because of the belief that much education occurs in myriad informal ways outside the formal curriculum. A question of interest to many involved in thinking about college sports is how well recruited athletes fit within, and contribute to, the overall life of the colleges or universities in which they are enrolled.[34] Stated more narrowly, the question to be considered here is, to what extent is there a separate "athletic culture"? And, if there is such a thing, what are its implications for the institution and for the present directions in which intercollegiate athletics is tending? Does this question have greater significance for liberal arts colleges than for the larger universities?

On the most basic question of whether athletes tend to have a kind of separate identity, there seems to be considerable agreement, at least at most of the liberal arts colleges. One experienced administrator at a NESCAC college spoke of an "athletics sub-culture" and said that the hockey team had become a "mini-fraternity." Similar references were made to football and swimming teams at other schools. The same language keeps being used. Student leaders at one NESCAC college described some teams (especially men's teams) as "reincarnations of fraternities" and noted that team-based "clannishness" is particularly troublesome in athletics because of "the problem of numbers"—athletes are the largest sub-group on campus. Several faculty at this same school said that "the division between athletes and non-athletes is *the* 'great divide' on campus."[35] A *Report on Varsity Athletics* recently issued at Williams College is, if anything, even more emphatic about the pervasiveness of "something akin to a culture of athletics" on that campus: "Athletes, who often are drawn and brought to Williams because they are athletes, feel comfortable here socially. They do not think they preside over social life, but other students believe that they do. Athletes live and socialize together. Moreover, a majority of non-athlete students feel defined as non-athletes, over half of non-athlete students feel athletics is too pervasive here, and over half of our non-athlete students feel too much importance is attached to belonging to teams."[36]

These patterns may be most pronounced at small residential colleges, but they are also present at some universities. The former master of one of the residential colleges at Princeton, Professor Charles Berry, provides this account of the pervasiveness of the athletic culture:

> One of the things that I noticed first when I got to Rockefeller [College] was the degree to which the "high profile" athletes were segregated from other students, and the rapidity with which that happened. I noticed also that the effect was to make the other, non-athlete students uninterested in varsity sports. They were not involved. Their friends were not involved, and there was no reason for them to be interested. . . . The non-athlete student body no longer identifies with the high profile athletes. The two groups are different. They have different interests. At [my residential college] we tried to counter this. . . . We spent hours attempting to rig freshman room assignments. . . . We tried to rig it so that the roommates—athletes and non-athletes—would become interested in each other, and in each other's activities. And it worked, but only for a month or so. After that the athletes were eating by themselves, playing by themselves, partying by themselves.[37]

It is hardly surprising that large numbers of athletes spend lots of time with each other, living, eating, studying, and partying together. After all, they spend a great deal of time practicing, traveling, and competing, and strong bonds are naturally likely to form between teammates, who then, more or less inevitably, also choose to spend a great deal of informal time together. We know from several studies that, at both colleges and universities, intercollegiate athletes spend far more time on their sports than members of other extracurricular groups spend on their activities. Athletes spend around 20 hours a week on athletics; the closest extracurricular activities in terms of time spent are the performing arts (orchestra, theater, singing groups) and media (student newspaper, radio), which require on average under 10 hours a week.[38] Thus, athletes spend *more than twice as much time* on their primary extracurricular activity than even those students participating in the most time-intensive other extracurricular activities.

Equally important is the consistency of time spent on athletics by every member of the team. While the editor of the student newspaper surely spends well over 20 hours a week working on the paper, other students may participate by writing one article a week. Not so in athletics. Every player, from the bench-warmer to the super-star, attends the same regularly scheduled practices. Moreover, much of the formal time athletes spend together is spent away from campus and other students. All teams travel for games. At many schools, athletes arrive on campus earlier than their classmates for pre-season practice and spend vacations together on training trips.

Studies of informal interactions yield a similar picture. According to Cantor and Prentice, athletes may spend as much as an additional 10 hours a week with teammates outside formal group activities; more than 40 percent of the time they spend attending parties and eating and hanging out with others is spent with teammates. These numbers are similar to data for members of social groups such as fraternities, but much higher than the corresponding numbers for members of performing arts organizations.[39]

Housing patterns are also relevant. The Amherst Special Committee report on athletics notes:

> Athletic self-segregation is reflected somewhat in housing patterns. . . . Of the 188 football players between 1996 and 2000, 56% lived in a room group consisting exclusively of football players. Of the 428 non-football male athletes, 27% lived in room groups consisting of athletes from the same sport. . . . This concentration . . . is far different from the housing patterns among female athletes. . . . [Of] 431 female athletes, . . . only 6% . . . lived in room groups consisting solely of athletes in the same sport. These housing patterns lead to upper class dorms with high concentrations of athletes and other dorms with very low concentrations of student athletes. For example, during academic year 2000, the percentage of varsity athletes in seven of the 28 upper-class dorms exceeded 50%, and in five dorms was below 10%. The concentration of athletes in selected dorms is more prevalent among men than women athletes, but in two dorms, over 30% of the residents were female varsity athletes.[40]

A similar picture is presented by the faculty report on varsity sports at Williams: "Team membership plays a major role in organizing housing choices. 61% of our varsity athletes met some of those they plan to live with next year on a team."[41]

Rewarding friendships are undoubtedly formed as a result of opportunities to spend time together, but a price is also paid for this focus on

a close-knit group of fellow students who share a strong interest in playing varsity sports. Athletes at Amherst (which has made a particularly detailed study of these patterns) reported less involvement in other types of
activities than other active students: "In each of their four years, athletes
reported that being a member of their group made it significantly more
difficult to attend cultural events than did other active students."[42] Participation on an athletics team also seems to make it more difficult to
meet new people; by contrast, other students feel that participation in
their primary extracurricular activity helps them meet new people.[43]

Another factor that may contribute to this perceived difficulty in meeting new people is the stigma sometimes associated with athletic participation. In earlier days male athletes, in particular, were often regarded as
"big men on campus" who were cheered on by their fellow students and
welcomed in any setting. Times have changed. To cite what may be an extreme case, one person at the University of Chicago notes that athletes
are often viewed with some hostility by other students and are asked questions like "Why are you here?" and "Why would anyone want to play football at the University of Chicago?" Not surprisingly, athletes develop a tendency to, as this person puts it, "circle the wagons." An Amherst faculty
report notes with concern that "[The 'dumb jock'] stereotype, in conjunction with a tendency among members of many athletic teams to socialize together, may be contributing to divisions within the campus community that diminish the social education of all of Amherst's students."[44]

A faculty member at another NESCAC college, who is also a high-
ranking administrator, echoed this concern and went on to express
disappointment that the hope of creating a campus environment in
which "terrific athletes can interact with others in a very healthy way" is
not realized because "in fact, they don't." In her view, the current situation creates a "truth-in-advertising issue" for the college. Put another
way, the "tighter" the athletic culture, the greater the risk of losing many
of the benefits associated with a residential setting peopled by an array of
interesting individuals.

There is another kind of "missed opportunity" that some believe is associated with the trend toward a more professionalized, more intensive
mode of athletic competition. Ideally, competing against athletes from
similar schools, with similar educational as well as athletic goals, should
add a valuable dimension to college life. And we were told that spirited
competition does just this in many settings. Seven Sisters' weekend tournaments are said to have precisely this effect. The UAA seems to have
been especially successful in fostering an atmosphere in which players
from competing schools come together after a game to share a pizza and
to make or renew friendships that cross institutional lines. For example,
Amy Reifert, the women's soccer coach at Chicago, told us how much she

and her team enjoy traveling to New York to compete against New York University. But in the Ivies, for example, we were told that athletes in sports such as men's ice hockey commonly arrive for a game, play, dress, and then get back on the bus as quickly as possible—suggesting a more "professional" approach to competition. The coach of one Ivy team, who had previously worked at the Division III level in the Midwest, said that she missed the easy colleagueship among coaches in her sport that she had known before. It is unfortunate, in our view, if "friendly rivalries" (with an emphasis on "friendly") become transformed into competition of a different kind.[45]

Another concern expressed by faculty members and deans at a variety of schools is that the athletic culture is associated with atypically heavy use of alcohol and a variety of behavioral and disciplinary problems. A vice-president at Wesleyan referred specifically to a "disproportionate number of honor code violations which are demoralizing and time-consuming." We attempted to collect data from the full range of institutions participating in this study that would permit a more rigorous test of such propositions, but we were unsuccessful—because of a combination of issues related to record-keeping practices and proper concerns for the privacy of certain kinds of records. We have learned, however, of several internal studies that validate the concerns expressed about disciplinary problems. Most recently, the faculty committee at Williams studying varsity athletics reported that it reviewed recent data on disciplinary incidents and honor code offenses and found:

> The numbers of incidents are small, and must be approached cautiously. Nevertheless, certain patterns emerge. First, disciplinary actions in general at Williams overwhelmingly involve male students; this pattern holds for athletes as well. Second, 56% of the disciplinary actions taken against students with the A attribute [a code assigned after admissions to students expected to have a major impact in athletics] were directed towards the members of two teams. . . . Third, athletic admits were about twice as likely as the student body as a whole to receive "discuss/warnings," and were more likely than the student body to be found culpable of multiple offenses, and receive probation, suspension, or expulsion. Finally, athletic admits were three times as likely to be found to commit honor code violations than the student body as a whole.[46]

Although it would be a mistake to exaggerate the significance of what is fortunately a small absolute number of infractions, the pattern is clear.

From the perspective of faculty members, in particular, the most troubling aspect of the so-called athletic culture is how it interacts with a school's academic mission. Peter Patton, professor of earth and environmental science at Wesleyan, said that in the past decade he and many faculty members have felt that there has been a shift in attitude on the part of students and coaches: "In an earlier time, there was no question but that academics came first. That is no longer the case. There appears to be a constant debate between students and faculty members about being away from classes and even exams, not meeting deadlines, etc., because of athletic schedules." The Williams faculty report also expresses special concern for scheduling issues and devotes an entire section to what it calls "the recurrent problem of scheduling."[47]

Other faculty members at a variety of colleges (where these issues often seem to be seen differently than at many of the universities) consider, in the words of one of them, "the major issue to be the impact on the classroom of academically disinterested athletes. . . . Faculty are upset by the athletes' lack of preparation for classes, their underachievement, and their tendency to register in large classes and sit in the back row and do nothing." This individual went on to point out that "as teaching has become more interactive, one-fifth of the student body cannot seem to interact, and this affects everyone's experience." The Amherst Special Committee report contains an extended discussion of an "anti-intellectual 'culture'" associated with athletics, and the report quotes one student leader as saying: "It is demoralizing to the academic students that there are some athletes, especially on a few teams, who don't care about academic work."[48] Similarly, the Williams faculty report notes: "The greatest concern of the faculty in the Economics and History Departments [where many athletes enroll, as we show in the next chapter] is evidence of anti-intellectualism, of clear disengagement and even outright disdain, on the part of varsity athletes, again in particular sports. . . . Such an attitude is especially troubling because it affects the entire chemistry of a class. . . . One faculty member was sufficiently discouraged by the impact of athletes that she had come to feel it is sometimes better if athletes skip class. Then, at least, they do not taint the rest of the class with their attitude of disdain."[49]

Needless to say, not everyone will agree with such assessments (at Amherst, Williams, or anywhere else), and the true picture is bound to be a complex one.[50] Some have suggested that faculty may be prejudiced against athletes, assuming that they are not serious students. One athletic director opined that some faculty are "mean-spirited" and that athletes, particularly larger male athletes, are given a hard time. Melissa Hart, the coach of women's basketball and women's soccer at MIT, says her students sometimes complain that professors are not supportive of athletes, but she adds that of course she hears about professors only when her students are having problems. Athletes report that being an athlete makes it more difficult to be taken seriously by professors, and such feelings, justified or not, can affect academic performance.[51] Needless to say, the problem of professors' buying into a "dumb jock" stereotype can only be exacerbated by actual differences in academic outcomes, which we examine in the next chapter.

In concluding this discussion, we want to reiterate that the presence of an "athletic culture" is perceived to be much more of an issue at some institutions than at others. In general, the smaller the school and the more intimate the setting, the greater the importance of these questions. Similarly, the higher the fraction of recruited athletes in a class, the more important it is to assess the effects of their presence on campus life writ large. It is no accident that the issues we have just been discussing receive a great deal more attention in, for example, the NESCAC colleges than they do in the UAA universities.

In the next two chapters we show that academic outcomes also differ considerably by conference. There is reason to believe that "culture and outcomes" influence each other and are, ultimately, interdependent. There is even stronger reason to believe that the twin processes of recruiting and admitting highly specialized and dedicated athletes drive both culture and academic outcomes.

CHAPTER 5

Academic Outcomes

STUDENTS WHO have been recruited by coaches and given special consideration in the admissions process enter college, as we saw in the previous chapter, with somewhat less imposing academic credentials than their classmates. The far more important question, however, is how recruited athletes actually perform in the classroom after they arrive on campus. Test scores and high school grades are far from perfect predictors of college performance; much depends on interests, motivation, time-management skills, creativity, and other late-developing qualities that no battery of tests captures well. Conventions, norms, social groupings, and a host of other factors can either encourage or discourage academic achievement. The presence of a strong "athletics culture" is, we believe, an important consideration in some settings.

In this chapter, which is the first of two on academic outcomes, we begin to fill the "fact gap" by examining the major fields of study chosen by both recruited athletes and walk-ons, graduation rates, grades (measured by rank-in-class), and academic honors. When we consider the phenomenon of underperformance in Chapter 6, we compare these academic outcomes to the outcomes we would expect based on the entering qualifications of the students in question; in this chapter we present the basic descriptive statistics, which are themselves very revealing. Of particular interest are differences in outcomes across sports, genders, and conferences. Do the academic outcomes of athletes participating in High Profile men's sports such as football differ systematically from those of athletes in Lower Profile sports such as tennis and crew? Are the results for recruited women athletes and recruited male athletes alike? Are there consistent differences across groups of schools—between the Ivies and the University Athletic Association (UAA) universities, between both groups of universities and the liberal arts colleges in and out of the New England Small College Athletic Conference (NESCAC), and between the women's colleges and the coed colleges and universities? The short answer is that there are many such differences, some quite pronounced, which appear to relate quite directly to the characteristic patterns of recruitment, admissions, and campus life described in the past three chapters. To the best of our knowledge, this is the first time that it has been possible to make such detailed comparisons by sport, gender, and type of school.[1]

Few will be surprised to learn that, in most settings, recruited athletes *as a group* do less well academically than their classmates. But this is of course a generalization, and there are many exceptions to it. It is gratifying to see that outstanding individuals continue to excel academically as well as athletically. This has long been the case, as the records of many distinguished graduates of the schools in this study demonstrate. What has changed, and changed dramatically, is the overall pattern of academic performance. The Middlebury Ad Hoc Committee observed: "That some of the less academically talented athletes turn out to be Phi Beta Kappa graduates is inspiring, but such anecdotes do not represent the broader reality."[2] Exemplary performance in the classroom has become exceptional for athletes, where once it was more typical. The trajectory over time is as worrying as the gaps in performance that are evident today.

Academic outcomes matter, we presume, to the athletes themselves. But other groups also have a legitimate interest in these findings: disappointed applicants and their parents, other students, faculty members, college and university presidents and deans, trustees, and even the public at large have a stake in how effectively these institutions use their academic resources. We certainly are not suggesting that colleges and universities should be concerned solely with academic performance. Attendance at college, and especially at a residential institution, is meant to provide a much broader and deeper "education" than grades alone can ever measure. That said, rigorous pursuit of things academic is surely a touchstone of selective colleges and universities. The degree to which students are truly engaged intellectually is a cardinal indicator of an institution's allegiance to its basic purposes.

FIELDS OF STUDY: MAJORS

Since many teams get organized even before classes start, commitments to coaches and teammates are among the first decisions made by recruited athletes (and also by other classmates who want to try out for a team that has early fall practices); similarly, representatives of many other extracurricular activities contact prospective students before they arrive on campus and seek to engage their interest as early as they can. But most students, recruited athletes and others, recognize that their most important early choices have to do with their course programs. All of the schools in our study require that undergraduates not only fulfill a set of general requirements, but also structure their course selections so that they end up "concentrating" or "majoring" in a particular discipline or interdisciplinary field of study.

As far back as the early part of the 20th century, accounts of "jock majors" have been common. It was Robert Hutchins's refusal to have a physical education major at the University of Chicago that is said to have ruled out "the one alternative that might have enabled Shaughnessy [the football coach who succeeded Amos Alonzo Stagg] to produce stronger teams." In his history of football at the University of Chicago, Lester goes on to point out: "The use of the physical education major (or other majors, such as business administration in the 1950s, communications in the 1970s, and sports management in the 1980s) . . . [to attract athletes and keep them eligible] meant that even comparatively rigorous institutions could file their athlete-students in a safe and non-threatening place."[3] In its 2002 special report on college sports, *U.S. News & World Report* attributes to John Cooper, a former football coach at Ohio State, the observation that graduation rates for football players would have been higher "if Ohio State had not eliminated some classes and raised the standards for majors like sport and leisure studies."[4]

The range of majors at the colleges and universities in this study is much narrower than the range one would find at a large state university that puts more emphasis on professional programs. Moreover, since one of the stated objectives of the Ivy League, NESCAC, and the UAA is to field intercollegiate teams that are "representative" of their student bodies, we should be surprised to find that athletes choose different majors than students at large. Nonetheless, athletes in these schools do tend to be concentrated in certain fields. Even more surprising, at least to us, are the pronounced differences in the extent of "bunching" by sport, gender, and conference. (NESCAC and the Ivies differ markedly in this regard from the UAA, the other coed liberal arts colleges, and the women's colleges.)

We begin by examining choices of majors made by recruited athletes in the High Profile men's sports of football, basketball, and ice hockey, seen in relation to the choices made by male students at large (Figure 5.1a).[5] In all four sets of schools shown in the figure, the recruited High Profile athletes are more likely than students at large to major in the social science and business cluster of departments and less likely to major in the humanities or the science cluster.[6] In the Ivies, the NESCAC colleges, and the other coed liberal arts colleges outside NESCAC, *over half* of all recruited High Profile athletes in the 1995 entering cohort majored in the social sciences or business (as contrasted with about a third of male students at large). This general preference for the social sciences and business fields was reported and discussed at length in *The Game of Life*, where it was attributed in part to the greater interest of athletes in business careers.[7]

The large "surplus" of recruited High Profile athletes in the social sciences was offset, as it had to be, by "deficits" in the other fields of study.

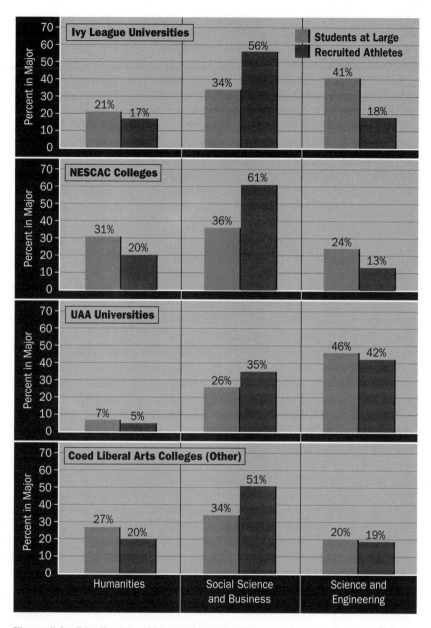

Figure 5.1a. Distribution of Majors for Male Students at Large and High Profile Recruited Athletes, by Conference, 1995 Entering Cohort
Source: Expanded College and Beyond database.

Particularly noteworthy is the relatively small number of recruited High Profile athletes who majored in fields in the science cluster (here defined to include math, the natural sciences, computer science, and engineering). This pattern is especially evident in the Ivies, where the typical male student at large was about two and a half times more likely to major in one of the science departments than was his classmate who had been recruited to play one of the High Profile sports (41 percent versus 18 percent). While the actual percentages varied, the pattern was consistent across all eight Ivies. In the NESCAC colleges, male students at large were nearly twice as likely as recruited High Profile athletes to major in the sciences.

The "bunching" of course majors among High Profile athletes appears to have been much less pronounced in the UAA universities.[8] The gap between these athletes and students at large in the relative number of social science and business majors was smaller, and the fraction of recruited High Profile athletes majoring in the sciences was nearly as high as the fraction of male students at large (42 percent versus 46 percent). The recruited High Profile athletes in the other liberal arts colleges were as inclined to study science as were their classmates.

The general picture for the recruited athletes in the Lower Profile male sports is essentially the same as it is for the High Profile athletes (Figure 5.1b). Over half of these athletes in the NESCAC colleges majored in the social sciences or business, and the science "deficits" at both the Ivies and NESCAC continued to be large. The contrast with the UAA universities and the other liberal arts colleges in the interest of recruited athletes in the sciences is even sharper here than it was when we looked at the High Profile sports.

Female recruited athletes in all four sets of schools chose majors in roughly the same proportions as did female students at large (Figure 5.1c). Only in the Ivies were the recruited female athletes less likely to major in the sciences than female students at large. The strong pro–social sciences inclination demonstrated by male athletes shows up among the recruited female athletes only in NESCAC. Data for athletes at the women's colleges show a similarly "representative" pattern: in fact, women athletes at these colleges were somewhat *more* likely to major in the sciences than were women students at large (18 percent versus 13 percent) and somewhat *less* likely to major in the social sciences (32 percent versus 38 percent).[9]

Examining the majors chosen by male walk-ons, compared to majors chosen by both recruits and students at large, adds another dimension to this picture (Appendix Table 5.1). Again, it is instructive to concentrate on the social sciences and business and the science cluster and to distinguish the male athletes playing the Lower Profile sports from the High Profile athletes.

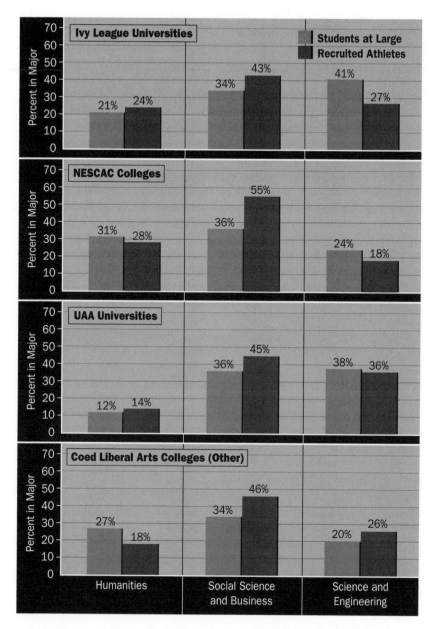

Figure 5.1b. Distribution of Majors for Male Students at Large and Lower Profile Recruited Athletes, by Conference, 1995 Entering Cohort
Source: Expanded College and Beyond database.

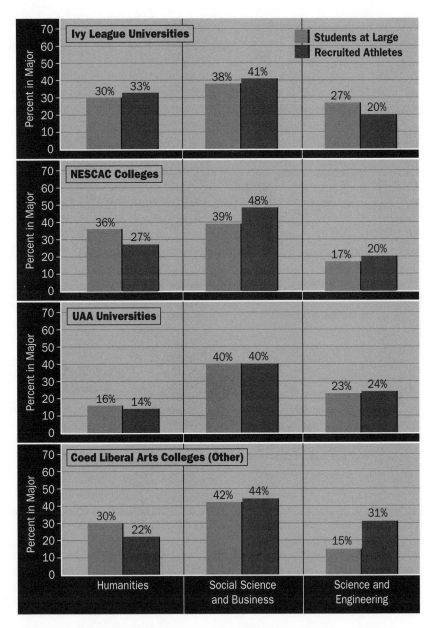

Figure 5.1c. Distribution of Majors for Female Students at Large and Female Recruited Athletes, by Conference, 1995 Entering Cohort
  Source: Expanded College and Beyond database.

In the case of the Lower Profile athletes, *the walk-ons were more like male students at large than they were like recruited athletes in their choice of major.* The walk-ons in these sports were both more likely to major in science and less likely to major in social sciences and business than were the recruited athletes. Their choices of majors were very similar to the choices made by male students at large. To cite just two examples from the table: 38 percent of the walk-ons playing Lower Profile sports in the Ivies majored in science, as compared with 27 percent of the recruited athletes and 41 percent of the male students at large; 38 percent of the walk-ons playing Lower Profile sports in the NESCAC colleges majored in the social sciences and business, as compared with 55 percent of the recruited athletes and 36 percent of the students at large.

In the case of the High Profile athletes the picture is only slightly more complex, and the tenor of the results is the same. Male walk-ons in the High Profile sports were more inclined to study science than were the recruits: in the Ivies, for example, 36 percent of the male walk-ons concentrated in science as compared with 18 percent of the recruits and 41 percent of the students at large; in two of the other three sets of schools, the walk-ons in the High Profile sports were as inclined or even more inclined to study science than were the students at large. Walk-ons in the High Profile sports were less likely than recruits but more likely than students at large to major in the social sciences and business.[10] Overall, the walk-ons consistently differed from the recruited athletes in having a distribution of majors that was more like what we found for male students at large.[11]

These findings regarding the concentration of athletes (especially recruited athletes) in certain fields of study are directly related to the discussion of an "athletic culture" at the end of the previous chapter. The tendency for athletes to live together and to spend social time together is plainly reinforced by a tendency to take the same courses. A number of the patterns noted earlier for the NESCAC colleges are underscored by the Williams Ad Hoc Committee's report on athletics. It notes that "at least 66 percent of students who were flagged as athletes . . . are Division 2 majors [social sciences]." Even more dramatic is the fact that 78 percent of the members of the three men's teams at Williams with the weakest academic records majored in Division 2 fields.[12] This is concentration with a vengeance! It is not surprising that the Williams faculty who teach in Division 2 fields are the most concerned about the effects of athletic recruitment on the overall culture of the college, especially on intellectual values (Chapter 4).

We are unable to say with confidence to what extent this "bunching" of athletes in certain fields is due to attitudes and interests that athletes bring with them when they matriculate, to differences in academic preparation, or, rather, to peer group pressures and an understandable desire to "bond together" academically as well as socially. One commentator suggested that the low proportion of athletes in science and engineering majors may be related to the difficulty of reconciling laboratory and practice schedules. The data on differences in attitudes and interests assembled in *The Game of Life* are, at the least, suggestive of a tendency for many male athletes to elect social science and business majors because of their above-average interest in pursuing business careers and being "very well off financially."[13] Unfortunately, our data do not allow us to compare the attitudes and interests of recruited athletes with those of walk-ons, so we cannot fully explain the greater concentration of recruited athletes in social science and business majors. One possibility is that dedication to one's sport and competitive drive are highly correlated with market-focused attitudes and interests. Presumably all college athletes are dedicated and competitive, but because coaches select for these attributes in the recruiting process, they may be strongest among recruits.

One other credible explanation for these outcomes is that group dynamics of teams in sports like football and hockey (that are composed almost entirely of heavily recruited athletes) play an independent role in encouraging teammates to take the same courses and major in the same fields.[14] From this perspective, it is not surprising that the "bunching" of majors is most common among athletes in the High Profile sports (where there are the most recruits and team ethos is presumably the strongest), next most common among the recruited male athletes in the Lower Profile sports, less common among the male walk-ons in the Lower Profile sports, and hardly present at all among the women athletes—who are widely perceived to be the most fully integrated into the broader campus culture of any group of athletes.

Nancy Hargrave Meislahn, dean of admission and financial aid at Wesleyan, said in an interview that she is concerned that at Wesleyan athletes are urged by peers to take the same classes, sometimes in fairly large numbers. The Williams Ad Hoc Committee reports: "Some team members take courses in packs, adopting 'tag-team' approaches for attendance and assignments. Such problems alter the role of teaching, some faculty noted: professors must police students, making assignments for the sole purpose of making sure students do work. One senior professor noted, for example, that some—mostly male—athletes do not do assigned work unless policed, and the need for policing casts a pall over the course."[15]

As the Williams Ad Hoc Committee was careful to make clear, there are many other situations in which athletes are engaged and effective participants in the academic enterprise, and a major task of the rest of this chapter is to document as carefully as we can how athletes do academically in terms of graduation rates, grades and rank-in-class, and the pursuit of academic honors. Vivid accounts of particularly troubling problems are never a substitute for data, as everyone recognizes. Still, comments of experienced observers do provide insight into why patterns revealed by "dry statistics" may be of real concern. For example, we were told pointedly by a faculty member in economics at Williams that a heavy concentration of certain groups of male athletes in a field like economics can discourage other students (especially women students, it was claimed) from choosing that major. More generally, colleges have a proper interest in the balance among fields of study, since too many majors in any discipline, whether the students are athletes or not, can cause real problems for teaching and the allocation of educational resources (quite apart from effects on the "chemistry" of classes). Although it is impossible to know exactly what is cause and what is effect, the concentration of athletes in already large departments further complicates the problem of staffing overenrolled courses and providing proper supervision for independent work.[16]

GRADUATION RATES

Since athletes at many Division IA schools have extremely low graduation rates, especially those participating in men's basketball, much of the national debate on the academic performance of athletes focuses on graduation rates. According to the most recent data, only 43 percent of men's basketball players who entered Division I schools in the 1995–96 academic year graduated in six years.[17] To be sure, these depressing statistics are driven in part by the fact that, as Myles Brand, former president of Indiana University and now president of the National Collegiate Athletic Association (NCAA), put it, "Some Division IA basketball players attend college primarily or exclusively to position themselves for a professional career . . . and have no plans to graduate."[18] Robert Hutchins saw this problem back in the 1930s and in his usual trenchant prose proposed this solution: "Since the primary task of colleges and universities is the development of the mind, young people who are more interested in their bodies than in their minds should not go to college. Institutions devoted to the development of the body are numerous and inexpensive. They do not pretend to be institutions of learning, and there is no faculty of learned men to consume their assets or interfere with their objectives."[19]

The academically selective schools in this study face issues and problems aplenty, but this is not one of them. In these schools, graduation rates are exceptionally high for both athletes and students at large (generally over 90 percent in the Ivies, over 80 percent in the UAA universities and the NESCAC colleges, and in the 70 to high 80 percent range at the other liberal arts colleges). Athletes attending these colleges and universities—both recruited athletes and walk-ons—generally graduate at *higher* rates than their peers (Appendix Table 5.2).

These gratifying results are consistent with other data on graduation rates at academically selective institutions. Athletes at the full range of colleges and universities in the original College and Beyond database (including the Division IA universities) have consistently graduated at higher rates than their classmates in every cohort for which we have data, from the '51 cohort through the '89 cohort.[20] In *The Game of Life* we suggested that "part of the explanation . . . is surely that playing a sport . . . helps to keep students on track" (p. 61). Data we collected for students who participated in other time-intensive extracurricular activities show that they, too, graduated at exceptionally high rates—at even higher rates than the athletes—so it appears that active involvement in many kinds of group activities is associated with above-average graduation rates.

Our new data for the 1995 entering cohort suggest that this positive association between athletic participation and high graduation rates is still present, at least at the UAA universities and the liberal arts colleges. For the recruited High Profile male athletes in the Ivies, however, the rela-

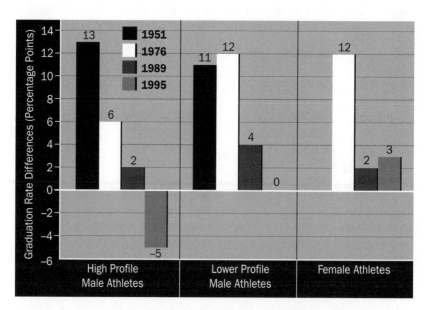

Figure 5.2. Graduation Rates: Differences between Athletes and Students at Large, by Cohort, 1951, 1976, 1989, and 1995 Entering Cohorts, Ivy League Universities

Source: Expanded College and Beyond database.

tionship appears to have changed. In the '95 cohort, these athletes graduated at a somewhat lower rate than did male students at large (86 percent versus 91 percent). At four of the Ivies, the graduation rate for recruited High Profile athletes was between 8 and 15 points lower than the graduation rate for their student-at-large classmates.[21]

This striking reversal of the usual pattern occurred after the time of the '89 cohort, because High Profile male athletes in the '89 cohort graduated at a higher rate than other students (89 percent versus 87 percent).[22] Most troubling is the trend: there has been a gradual erosion in graduation rates in the High Profile sports. Men playing these sports in the Ivy League in the early 1950s enjoyed a sizable advantage, 13 points, in graduation rates over their peers. This advantage declined markedly over the intervening decades; it has now become a 5-point disadvantage (Figure 5.2). The same general trend is evident in male Lower Profile sports and, to a lesser degree, in women's sports.[23] We have no way of judging whether this erosion will spread to the Division III schools, but the general tendency for trends in recruiting and admissions within the Ivies to influence, over time, what happens elsewhere makes it difficult to be sanguine.[24]

GRADES, RANK-IN-CLASS, AND HONORS

High graduation rates for athletes—which fortunately continue to be the norm in the schools that we are studying—are often cited, appropriately, as indicating that athletes attend these schools for reasons that transcend playing sports. This is surely true. "Getting by" is not, however, the appropriate standard. As the Amherst Faculty Committee on Admission said so well: "We expect not only competence but excellence and originality in our students."[25] With some notable exceptions, the athletes who attend these highly selective schools—especially those who were recruited, and especially those recruited athletes who play the High Profile sports—are not performing academically at the same level as their peers.[26]

It was not always this way. *The Game of Life* details the growing gaps between the grades earned by athletes and by students at large. In the 1951 entering cohort at the Ivies and the coed liberal arts colleges, athletes, including High Profile athletes, were academically indistinguishable from their classmates. By the time of the 1976 cohort, the male athletes were falling behind; by 1989 the gap had widened for men, and for the first time female athletes were doing less well than their peers.

What do the new data for the '95 entering cohort tell us? In general, they indicate that gaps in academic achievement for both male and female athletes at these schools have either stabilized at roughly the level of the '89 cohort or continued to widen and that, for the first time, modest achievement gaps are evident at the women's colleges, too. Athletes in the '89 cohort at the women's colleges did ever so slightly better academically than other students; athletes in the '95 cohort, on the other hand, ranked below their classmates at two of the three women's colleges we studied.[27] The differences were small, but the change in "sign" merits attention—both in and of itself and because it supports the thesis of a continuing "contagion" or "spread" of the problem of disappointing academic performance from, first, the big-time Division IA programs to the Ivies and then to the Division III colleges; second, from High Profile sports to Lower profile men's sports; third, from men's sports to women's sports; and, finally, from coed institutions to women's colleges.

Grade Inflation and Issues of Measurement

Efforts to calibrate differences in academic performance between athletes and their classmates are complicated by the effects of grade inflation, which tends to compress grades, fuzz over differences in achievement, and make it difficult to compare outcomes from one school (and one cohort) to another. As Henry Rosovksy and Matthew Hartley put it in their recent study of grade inflation: "Academics are only entitled to the respect they would like to command if they affirm some common standards. Among these . . . is the imperative for accuracy in evaluating their students' academic work. . . . Grades are intended to be an objective—though not perfect—index of the degree of academic mastery of a subject. As such, grades serve multiple purposes. . . . No one would claim that grades are a completely accurate index of the comprehension of subject matter, let alone a predictor of achievement in the world at large. Yet, they remain an efficient way to communicate valid information."[28]

Some argue that differences between athletes and other students in actual grades earned (a B or B-plus rather than an A) are in fact quite small and should not be regarded as consequential. Others point out that apparently small differences in letter grades, when they recur frequently (when the same students continue to get grades of B or B-plus, for example, at the same time that others score consistently in the A range), are indicators of real differences in academic performance. The Amherst Special Committee, for example, after acknowledging that apparent differences can be modest when looked at through the grade inflation lens, rejected the proposition that the remaining differences are unimportant:

> The College itself uses GPA [grade point average] as the basis for awarding
> various honors and prizes (such as election to Phi Beta Kappa and gradua-

tion honors). In addition, graduate and professional schools generally rely very heavily on grades as an important admission criterion. Responding to the widespread epidemic of grade inflation, graduate and professional schools are focusing increasingly on *relative* academic performance (rank in class) rather than absolute GPA. Law schools, for example, have largely abandoned absolute GPA in favor of a rank-in-class measure, either supplied by the undergraduate institution or constructed by the Law School Admission Council (which administers the LSAT [Law School Aptitude Test]).[29]

Our own analysis of actual GPAs at the schools in our study leads us to conclude that, grade compression notwithstanding, there are definite (and consistent) differences among groups of students in academic achievement.[30] To deal analytically with the problem of grade inflation, we follow the approach mentioned in the Amherst report and use percentile rank-in-class as a summary measure of a student's cumulative grade point average. This way of proceeding has the double advantage of making clear that there is a real difference between consistently earning a B or a B-plus rather than an A and ensuring that comparisons are not affected by differences between schools in grading systems or grading scales.[31]

Before presenting the detailed findings from our new research, we should note that the all-too-real problems of differences in academic performance between some athletes (by no means all) and students at large have often been obscured not only by grade inflation, but also by failing to distinguish between sub-sets of athletes. First, there is the distinction between recruited athletes and walk-ons. As we document shortly, the two groups perform very differently in the classroom. A second distinction is between participants in the High Profile sports of football, men's basketball, and men's ice hockey and male participants in the Lower Profile sports. Third, there are some differences in outcomes between men and women athletes (though this distinction is the least important). Finally, the conference in which the athletes compete turns out to be important. The key point is that disaggregation is essential to understanding what is going on. Grouping together disparate groups of athletes for statistical purposes can obscure important relationships by, in the language of a sports metaphor, "kicking up a cloud of dust around second base."

Average Percentile Rank-in-Class: Differences by Conference "Regime"

Figures 5.3a and 5.3b show the average percentile rank-in-class for students at large, walk-ons, and recruited athletes, with separate sets of bars for High Profile athletes, Lower Profile male athletes, and women athletes. The results for the Ivies, the NESCAC colleges, the UAA universi-

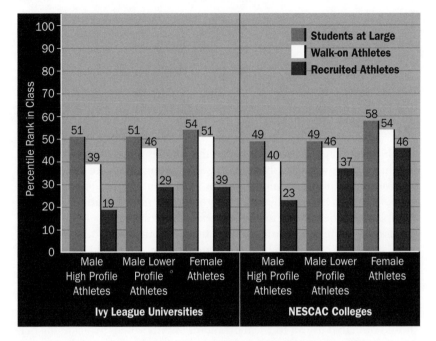

Figure 5.3a. Average Percentile Rank in Class, by Recruit Status and Gender, 1995 Entering Cohort, Ivy League Universities and NESCAC Colleges
    Source: Expanded College and Beyond database.

ties, and the coed colleges outside NESCAC are shown in individual panels.[32] There is, we recognize, a mass of data here, and the wealth of detail will be of more interest to some than to others. In general, three distinct conference "regimes" can be distinguished.

The Ivies and the NESCAC colleges constitute the first regime. The results for these two conferences are amazingly similar and can be discussed together (Figure 5.3a). The common features are:

1. These colleges and universities pay a very large academic price when they recruit High Profile athletes. Recruited High Profile athletes had a cumulative grade point average that put them, as a group, in the 19th percentile of their class in the Ivies and in the 23rd percentile in the NESCAC colleges.
2. The recruited athletes in the Lower Profile sports fared slightly better than those in the High Profile sports, but not that much better. Their cumulative GPA put them, on average, in the 29th percentile of the rank-in-class distribution (Ivies) and in the 37th percentile (NESCAC).

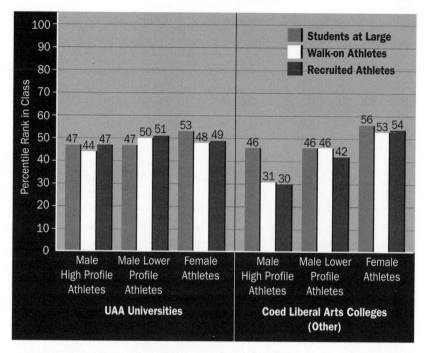

Figure 5.3b. Average Percentile Rank in Class, by Recruit Status and Gender,
1995 Entering Cohort, UAA Universities and Coed Liberal Arts Colleges (Other)
Source: Expanded College and Beyond database.

3. The recruited women athletes did somewhat better than the Lower
Profile men, but also earned grades appreciably below those of their
student-at-large classmates. Those in the Ivies ended up in the 39th
percentile (versus the 54th percentile for female students at large),
and those in the NESCAC colleges ended up in the 46th percentile
(versus the 58th percentile for female students at large).[33]

4. The average rank-in-class for the walk-ons was never more than
5 percentile points below the average for the students at large
except in the case of those in the High Profile male sports, where
the walk-ons ended up 10 percentile points or so below the students at large. Nonetheless, the walk-ons were closer to the students
at large in class standing than they were to their recruited teammates.

In short, in the Ivies and in the NESCAC colleges, being recruited and
playing a High Profile sport imply that a student is likely to earn a substantially lower grade point average. The recruited Lower Profile male

athletes and female athletes do better, but they, too, earn lower grades than the students at large.

The UAA universities operate under a different regime and occupy a space all their own (left side of Figure 5.3b). Overall, UAA athletes, recruited or walk-on, male or female, participants in High Profile or Lower Profile sports, earn grades that are, on average, essentially the same as those earned by their classmates. Put another way, the UAA "regime" differs dramatically from the other regimes in terms of the average grade point consequences (essentially none) associated with being an athlete.

The coed liberal arts colleges outside NESCAC constitute the third regime (right side of Figure 5.3b). Recruited athletes playing the High Profile sports (principally football at these schools) are like their compatriots in the Ivies and in the NESCAC colleges in that they do much less well academically than male students at large; even so, the gap for them is around 15 points in the rank-in-class distribution, as compared with 32 points in the Ivies and 26 points in the NESCAC colleges. Oddly, the walk-ons playing the High Profile sports at these colleges do as poorly as their recruited teammates—a phenomenon that we cannot fully explain, but we believe is related to the difficulty that many of these small schools have fielding football teams. Potential football players may get a break in admissions even if they are not on the coach's list; indeed, this supposition is consistent with the finding that walk-on High Profile athletes at coed liberal arts colleges outside NESCAC have SAT scores closer to those of recruits than to those of students at large (Figure 4.3b). In sharp contrast, the male Lower Profile athletes and the female athletes in these colleges do almost as well (but not quite as well) as the students at large. Outside the High Profile arena, academic outcomes for athletes at these colleges are the same as the impressive results achieved across the board in the UAA.

Bunching in the Bottom Third of the Class

An obvious next question is whether these average rank-in-class figures are driven by the very disappointing performance of a few people at the bottom of the scale or are more representative. Closer inspection of the data reveals that the low average rank-in-class of the recruited athletes in the Ivies and in the NESCAC colleges is not the product of just a few students' earning very low grades. Indeed, four out of five of the recruited High Profile athletes in the Ivies and nearly three out of four of those in the NESCAC colleges were in the bottom third of the class (Figure 5.4a). The corresponding figures for the recruited male Lower Profile athletes are only slightly less disappointing: about two-thirds of those in the Ivies

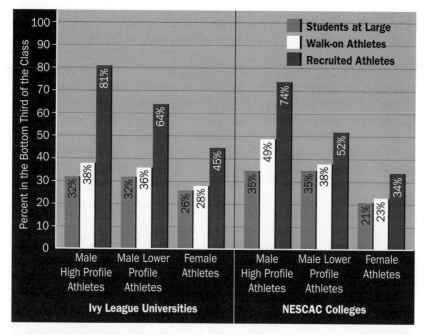

Figure 5.4a. Percent of Athletes and Students at Large in the Bottom Third of the Class, by Recruit Status and Gender, 1995 Entering Cohort, Ivy League Universities and NESCAC Colleges

Source: Expanded College and Beyond database.

were in the bottom third of the class (64 percent, to be precise), and over half (52 percent) of those in the NESCAC colleges were; and nearly half of the recruited women athletes in the Ivy League ended up in the bottom third of the class (45 percent), as compared with only a quarter of the female students at large.

The fractions of athletes and other students in the bottom third of their classes in the UAA universities and the other coed liberal arts colleges (Figures 5.4b) are also consistent with the relationships found by looking at average rank-in-class. In the UAA universities, only the female athletes (both those who were recruited and the walk-ons) were disproportionately represented in the bottom third of the class. In the other coed liberal arts colleges, the picture for the High Profile athletes is again distinct and roughly the same as in the NESCAC colleges, with over two-thirds of these students in the bottom third of the class. Otherwise, there were no major differences between the athletes and the students at large in either of these sets of institutions.

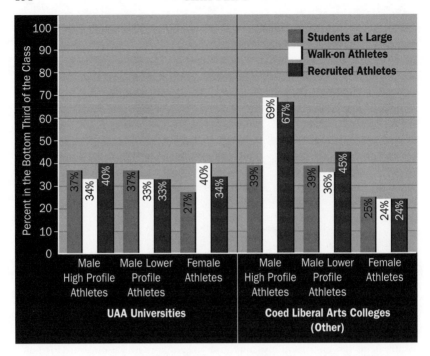

Figure 5.4b. Percent of Athletes and Students at Large in the Bottom Third of the Class, by Recruit Status and Gender, 1995 Entering Cohort, UAA Universities and Coed Liberal Arts Colleges (Other)
  Source: Expanded College and Beyond database.

Consistency of the Findings across Schools: No "Outliers"

These findings, whether stated in terms of average rank-in-class or in terms of percentages of athletes in the bottom third of the class, are highly consistent across institutions. In the Ivy League universities, the average rank-in-class of recruited High Profile athletes is in the 15th percentile at one university, the 16th percentile at two, the 20th or 21st percentile at three others, and the 23rd or 24th percentile at the final two. The percentage of these athletes in the bottom third of the class is in the 74–76 percent range at three of the universities, in the 81–83 percent range at three, and in the 87–89 percent range at two others. The same kind of consistency is found within NESCAC when the data are inspected on a school-by-school basis. The greatest dispersion in outcomes is found within the coed liberal arts colleges outside NESCAC, and this is what one would expect to find given the more heterogeneous nature of the group (in terms of selectivity and also in terms of the nature of the athletics programs that they offer).

It is human nature to believe that a widely perceived problem applies everywhere but "at home," and any number of individuals within both the Ivy League universities and the NESCAC colleges have expressed great concern over the general issues identified by our research but have gone on to assure us that no such problems exist at their own college or university. This tendency to "look away" is compounded by the fact that internal studies often lump together different groups of athletes (recruits and walk-ons, members of High Profile teams and those who row or sail, and so on), in part because on some campuses cohort sizes may be so small that it is hard to have enough data to do a finer-grained analysis. In any event, if progress is to be made in thinking through what are shared problems, it is important to move beyond the "not-at-home" mindset. The recent Amherst Special Committee report is notable for, among other things, explicitly acknowledging that "Amherst is no exception to these general findings."[34]

A memorable moment occurred at a meeting of NESCAC presidents to which we were invited. After we summarized some of our findings and presented data for individual colleges (with codes disguising the identities of particular schools), one president observed wryly: "The picture is very clear. There are no outliers—only liars!" This observation was followed by much good-natured bantering, and the process of moving ahead to confront these issues of academic outcomes as a group was helped greatly, we sensed, by the recognition that, in fact, there were no outliers.

The contrast between the general findings for the Ivies and NESCAC colleges, on the one hand, and for the UAA universities at the other end of the spectrum, enhances the importance of being sure about the validity of our UAA data. It should be recalled that our summary measures for the UAA are based on detailed student records obtained for only four of the eight UAA universities (whereas we have data for all eight Ivies and all eleven NESCAC institutions).[35] Fortunately, the UAA has kept excellent records for all of the universities in the Association, and the Presidents' Council agreed to provide us with detailed calculations of "Cumulative Grade Point Averages of Athletic Teams Relative to All-Campus GPAs" for three recent years. The highlights are summarized in Table 5.1.[36]

The over-riding conclusion is that there has been no noticeable difference (and often absolutely no difference at all!) between average GPAs for athletes and for the class as a whole. These data for all eight UAA institutions convey a message that is entirely consistent with the import of the somewhat more elaborate calculations that we presented for our subset of UAA universities in Figures 5.3b and 5.4b. There are, of course,

TABLE 5.1
Cumulative Grade Point Averages of Athletic Teams
Relative to All-Campus GPAs, UAA Universities,
1997–98, 1998–99, and 2000–01

	Academic Year 1997–98	Academic Year 1998–99	Academic Year 2000–01
Male student-athletes	3.06	3.14	3.15
Male undergraduates	3.06	3.13	3.18
Female student-athletes	3.16	3.21	3.28
Female undergraduates	3.15	3.20	3.29

Source: Reports provided by Richard Rasmussen, executive secretary of the UAA (with the authorization of the UAA Presidents' Council) based on data provided to him by the individual universities.

Note: According to Rasmussen: "The Average . . . is an average GPA for all students. . . . It is derived from the institutional team averages and numbers of participants on each team." Thus, it is participant-weighted rather than institution-weighted, as are our data. Also, athletes are not excluded from the all-male and all-female averages, as they are when we calculate figures for students at large. These are not, however, major differences in methodology.

some differences by institution. By good luck, the results for two of the four institutions in our sub-set tend to be slightly more favorable than the all-UAA norm (in the sense that the average GPA for athletes tends to be higher than the average GPA for all students), and the results for two of the four tend to be slightly less favorable (with athletes having an average GPA slightly below that for the class as a whole). The differences among institutions are not, in any case, pronounced. Again, there are no clear outliers.[37]

Differences in Rank-in-Class by Sport

We have already seen that the academic performance of athletes participating in the High Profile sports of football, men's basketball, and men's ice hockey, as a group, differs in almost every respect from that of athletes in the men's Lower Profile sports, also considered as a group. Examination of average rank-in-class on a sport-by-sport basis confirms that athletes in the three men's High Profile sports do in fact form a coherent group, judged in terms of grades earned by them, recruits and walk-ons alike. (Appendix Table 5.3 presents rank-in-class data for all participants in each sport, by gender and by conference.)

This is not, however, the full story, as there are some large differences among athletes in the men's Lower Profile sports (see Figures 5.5a and 5.5b for the Ivies and 5.5c and 5.5d for the NESCAC colleges). In the Ivies, the athletes on the wrestling, swimming, lacrosse, and baseball teams are all between the 24th and 30th percentiles in average class rank; at the higher end of the grade distribution among athletes, we find those in sailing (the only sport whose participants have an average rank-in-class above that of male students at large), tennis, squash, golf, sprint football (which used to be called light-weight or 150-pound football), fencing, and crew. Athletes in cross country, soccer, and track occupy intermediate positions. The general picture among participants in men's Lower profile sports in the NESCAC colleges tends to be similar, but the ranking of athletes in the individual sports varies somewhat (those in wrestling are, however, again at the bottom in terms of rank order). At the other liberal arts colleges and the UAA universities, the only Lower Profile men's sport to highlight is swimming, since swimmers have a surprisingly low average rank-in-class (only slightly above the comparable figure in the Ivies).

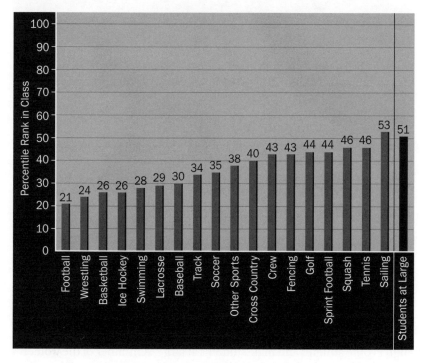

Figure 5.5a. Average Percentile Rank in Class of Male Athletes, by Sport, and Male Students at Large, 1995 Entering Cohort, Ivy League Universities
Source: Expanded College and Beyond database.

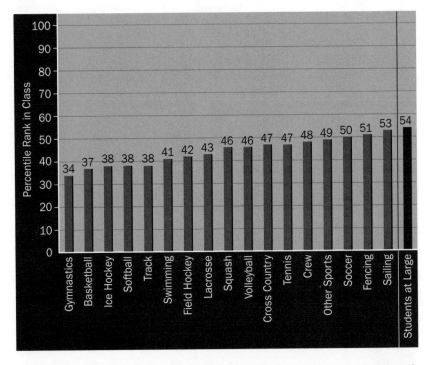

Figure 5.5b. Average Percentile Rank in Class of Female Athletes, by Sport, and Female Students at Large, 1995 Entering Cohort, Ivy League Universities
Source: Expanded College and Beyond database.

The grades earned by a small number of the women's teams are also worth noting. In the Ivies, the female athletes with the lowest average rank-in-class are those in gymnastics, basketball (which is rapidly moving toward "High Profile" status), ice hockey, softball, and track (all with average rank-in-class percentiles that are 16 points or more below those of women students at large). Again, as in the case of the men, participants in the racquet sports, fencing, crew, and sailing do better than those playing other sports—although *no* women's team has an average rank-in-class that meets the average for women students at large. The same statement holds for female athletes in the NESCAC colleges, with a single exception: those in cross country. It is worth noting that NESCAC women's ice hockey players have an average rank-in-class that is 23 percentile points below that of female students at large—a gap that exceeds that between NESCAC High Profile athletes and male students at large. A number of the women's teams in the other coed colleges and in the UAA universities, in contrast, meet or exceed the standard set by women students at large.

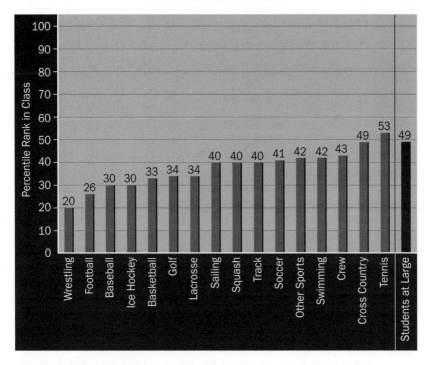

Figure 5.5c. Average Percentile Rank in Class of Male Athletes, by Sport, and Male Students at Large, 1995 Entering Cohort, NESCAC Colleges
Source: Expanded College and Beyond database.

We conclude that, especially in the Ivies and the NESCAC colleges, troubling issues of academic performance are not limited to the High Profile sports. Nonetheless, it is clear that it is in the High Profile sports, and especially in football, that almost every school in every grouping needs to be at least somewhat concerned about the academic performance of team members. In the Ivies and in the NESCAC colleges, this reality is well understood. The Williams Ad Hoc Committee was unequivocal in stating: "The mean GPA of the two [academically] weakest men's teams was much lower than that for male varsity athletes in general."[38]

The same problem is apparent at the coed colleges outside NESCAC, which, as in the cases of Macalester (discussed earlier), Swarthmore (which has now dropped football), and North Coast Athletic Conference schools such as Oberlin, find it very difficult to field football teams that both satisfy reasonable academic standards and can be competitive on Saturday afternoons. In the entire group of coed liberal arts colleges out-

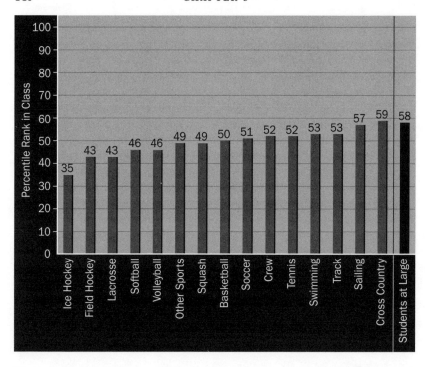

Figure 5.5d. Average Percentile Rank in Class of Female Athletes, by Sport, and Female Students at Large, 1995 Entering Cohort, NESCAC Colleges
    Source: Expanded College and Beyond database.

side NESCAC included in this study, the average rank-in-class of the football team was in the 25th percentile, a finding that mirrors the results in the Ivies and in the NESCAC colleges and speaks for itself.

In light of the excellent overall academic results achieved by teams playing within the UAA, it is especially noteworthy that the members of the football teams in our study have an average GPA that puts them in the 40th percentile—a better result than in any of the other conferences or groupings we have studied, but still cause for concern. The data for all eight UAA universities point to a similar conclusion: the average GPA of the football players has been consistently lower than the average GPA for all male athletes and for all male students.[39] As Rasmussen was quoted earlier as observing, football is "a numbers game," with obvious consequences for the academic qualifications and performance of the athletes recruited and admitted. It may also be true, as some have suggested, that the "culture of football" exacerbates the problem.

It would be wrong to end this discussion of grades and rank-in-class without noting one very important qualification to all that has been said thus far. Faculty members and administrators at several Ivy League universities suggested that the data available to us understate the true extent of disappointing academic performance by athletes. Their point is that we are unable to control adequately for the tendency (as they perceive it) of athletes to choose easier fields of study with less rigorous grading standards and, within these fields, to choose courses that are known generally to be easier than most.[40]

The Williams Ad Hoc Committee has made the most thorough effort of which we are aware to address this set of issues. The Committee tried hard to determine what *sorts* of courses varsity athletes take. First, they used student surveys to determine which courses students thought were relatively "hard" and which were relatively "easy." Then they found:

> The proportion of varsity athletes in hard courses was 23.4%; the proportion of varsity athletes in the easiest courses was 37.2%. . . . "Tipped" athletes [those given a special break in the admissions process because of their likely impact in athletics—analogous to recruited athletes on the coaches' lists] are 44% more likely than non-tipped athletes to take easy courses. . . . Members of some teams are more likely to take the easy courses than members of other teams. Football players, for example, are 47% more likely than students who are not football players to take easy courses, and men's ice hockey players are 93% more likely than other students to take easy courses. (Women's ice hockey players, on the other hand, are only 9% more likely than other students to take easy courses.)[41]

The Williams Committee also found that varsity athletes (especially football players) were more likely than other students to be in large classes, where they could "hide." Finally, the Committee found that in the 1999–2000 academic year, "4% of all varsity athletes and 13% of all other students took a tutorial [a learning experience closely identified with Williams that requires a major effort from students]."[42]

The Committee made no effort to quantify the effects of these patterns of course selections on rank-in-class. It seems evident, however, that the result was to inflate somewhat the reported academic accomplishments of athletes as a group.

Academic Success at the Highest Level: Honors and Phi Beta Kappa

Judicious selection of fields of study and of individual courses within fields may help any student, athlete or not, to meet basic requirements. It is much harder, however, to earn academic success at the highest level in such a fashion. For seven of the eight Ivies (all but the University of Pennsylvania), we were able to obtain data on the percentages of recruits, walk-ons, and students at large from the 1995 entering cohort who earned honors, high honors, or election to Phi Beta Kappa (Figure 5.6). The pattern is clear. Whereas 43 percent of male students at large earned honors, only 11 percent of recruited High Profile athletes and 19 percent of recruited Lower Profile athletes did so. Male walk-ons who played Lower Profile sports did appreciably better than either set of male recruits, and female walk-ons were almost as likely to earn honors as female students at large. But female recruited athletes were much less likely to earn honors (just 27 percent versus 45 percent of female students at large).

When we impose an even higher standard and ask who won highest honors ("summa" status) and who was elected to Phi Beta Kappa, the differences are even more striking. Only 1 percent of recruited athletes (men and women) earned highest honors—compared to 6 percent of male students at large and 4 percent of female students at large. The percentages elected to Phi Beta Kappa range from 1 percent of the recruited

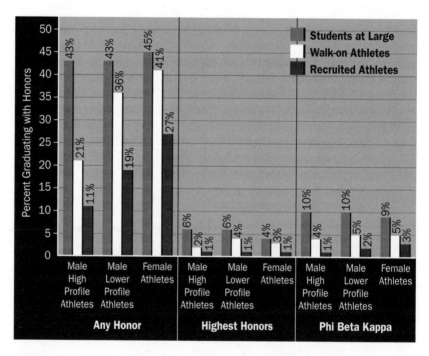

Figure 5.6. Percent of Athletes, by Type of Sport and Recruit Status, and Students at Large Graduating with Honors, Highest Honors, and Phi Beta Kappa, 1995 Entering Cohort, Ivy League Universities
Source: Expanded College and Beyond database.

High Profile athletes to 3 percent of the recruited female athletes. The fact that only 2 percent of the recruited Lower Profile athletes (versus 10 percent of the male students at large) were elected to Phi Beta Kappa reminds us that it is not only the High Profile sports that deserve attention. Moreover, the sharp differences in outcomes between female recruits and female students at large is further evidence that the relationship between athletic recruitment and academic outcomes is by no means a "male-only" issue in the Ivy League these days.[43]

Reviewing the results presented in this chapter inescapably leads to two large questions:

1. Has it always been like this?
2. What factors cause the athletes, and especially the recruited athletes, to earn grades that are appreciably lower than those earned by their classmates and to be found only rarely on the Phi Beta Kappa rolls and among the "summa" graduates?

In his recent article on athletics at Williams College, Welch Suggs notes that "S. Lane Faison Jr., Whitney Stoddard, and the other art historians who made Williamstown a launch pad for many of the top curators in the profession were athletes themselves. Mr. Stoddard, for example, had been a hockey goalie during his own college days." Suggs goes on to quote Kirk Varnedoe, a member of the Class of 1967 who was formerly senior curator at the Museum of Modern Art and is now a faculty member at the Institute for Advanced Study in Princeton, New Jersey, as recalling: "It's a work-hard, play-hard kind of place. It wasn't a place where categories were hard and firm—you didn't have to be an athlete *or* a student, and it was not considered unusual or weird to have a Phi Bet physics major playing football."[44] Obviously, times have changed.

In much of the rest of this study, we explore the national as well as the local factors responsible for the creation of today's "Great Divide," as the Amherst Special Committee described the situation. Our more immediate task is to disentangle the factors affecting the academic performance of the athletes recruited at the colleges and universities in this study. Some observers have emphasized a "disturbing professionalization of collegiate athletics" and attendant time pressures, which can affect all aspects of a student's life. Thus Harry Lewis, dean of the college at Harvard, was quoted as saying: "The seasons are too long, there are too many contests, there are too many travel dates, the off-season is too formal and there's too much training and practicing. All of the time and effort that intercollegiate athletes have to spend on their sports result in too often students having to make compromises between their athletic experience and their overall Harvard experience."[45]

Others focus on the initial admissions (selection) process and wonder if athletes are performing academically only as we should expect them to perform, given their test scores and previous academic records. Fortunately, we are able to make considerable headway in distinguishing between these "selection" and "treatment" effects. The next chapter is devoted to the important questions of whether, and to what extent, different groups of athletes "underperform" relative to how we should have expected them to do based on the academic credentials that gained them admission. Once again, we show that the answer is "It all depends" —on, among other things, whether the athlete was recruited or was a walk-on, on the sport in question, on the gender of the athlete, and on the conference setting.

CHAPTER 6

Academic Underperformance

As we showed in Chapter 4, athletes, and recruited athletes in particular, arrive on campus with weaker academic credentials than their classmates. Not surprisingly, then, athletes, and again recruited athletes in particular, do less well academically than their peers (see Chapter 5). As one dean put it, "We're accepting them at the bottom third of the class; of course they end up there." But this is by no means the full story, or even, from our point of view, the most troubling aspect of it. What is more surprising—and, we believe, of great concern—is the pervasive and persistent tendency for athletes at liberal arts colleges as well as universities *to underperform academically: that is, to do even less well in the classroom than one would expect them to do on the basis of their entering academic credentials.* Stated another way, athletes, male and female, are found, overall, to earn even lower grades than would be predicted by their SAT scores and high school grades, even after controlling for race, field of study, and institutional selectivity (measured by the mean institutional SAT score). The recurring presence of underperformance, defined in this way, was a major finding in *The Game of Life,*[1] and it is now reinforced by this more recent and more extensive analysis of academic outcomes.[2]

Why does academic underperformance matter? Some may feel that the actual grades earned are all that counts, that a B is a B, whether or not a student could have been expected to do better. But when some groups of students habitually underperform, and especially when they are blunt about their own (different) priorities, the combination of their attitudes and their performance can affect the campus ethos. One of the most striking findings in the Williams Ad Hoc Committee report is that "the longer students are here, . . . the more they detect a negative intellectual impact of athletics." Faculty in economics and history are concerned about "evidence of anti-intellectualism, of clear disengagement and even outright disdain, on the part of varsity athletes, again in particular sports. . . . The problem, it was stressed, is not the hard-working C student; it is the under-achieving C students."[3] Underperformance is a serious problem for reasons that have to do with educational values and with the optimal use of scarce educational resources; many students not admitted clearly could have used these resources to much fuller advantage than the students who significantly underperform.

The dispiriting effects of underperformance:

In *The Game of Life*, the argument is put this way: "Faculty often remark that the most discouraging aspect of teaching is encountering a student who just does not seem to care, who has to be cajoled into thinking about the reading, who is obviously bored in class, or resists rewriting a paper that is passable but not very good. Such students are failing to take full advantage of the educational opportunities that these colleges and universities are there to provide. . . . It is not good enough, we believe, just to get by. Respect for core academic values and the educational mission of these schools requires more than that. Otherwise, colleges and universities are failing to put their most valuable resources—their faculty and their academic offerings—to their highest and best use."[4]

To be sure, there will always be, by definition, students who underperform relative to the norm for their class (just as there will always be a bottom third of the class); and of course some athletes, in company with other students, overperform academically. But it is grounds for concern when a particular sub-group of students exhibits consistent and statistically significant underperformance.

OVERALL FINDINGS

Using a simple model that accounts for differences in race, field of study, individual SAT scores, and the average SAT score at the institution, we are able to estimate how athletic participation affects percentile rank-in-class while holding these other factors constant. Our most basic finding is that *in the Ivy League and in the New England Small College Athletic Conference (NESCAC), athletic participation has a substantial negative effect on rank-in-class, especially for recruited athletes* (Figures 6.1a and 6.1b).[5] Recruited athletes in the High Profile men's sports earned a percentile rank-in-class roughly 20 percentile points lower (19.0 in the Ivies, 20.4 in the NESCAC colleges) than students at large with the same race, field of study, and SAT score. But underperformance is not limited to the High Profile male athletes. In the Ivies and the NESCAC colleges, recruited athletes in both the Lower Profile men's sports and women's sports underperform by more than 10 points. Underperformance among walk-ons is also present at these schools, but it is substantially less pronounced (generally in the range of 3–7 points, except in the High Profile sports).

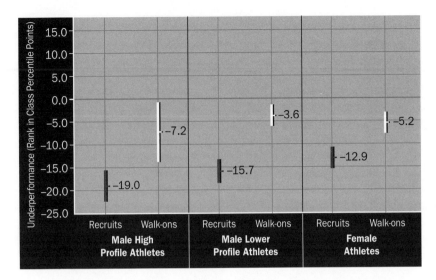

Figure 6.1a. Underperformance of Athletes, by Type of Sport and Recruit Status, Controlling for Differences in Race, Field of Study, SAT Scores, and Institutional SAT, 1995 Entering Cohort, Ivy League Universities
Source: Expanded College and Beyond database.

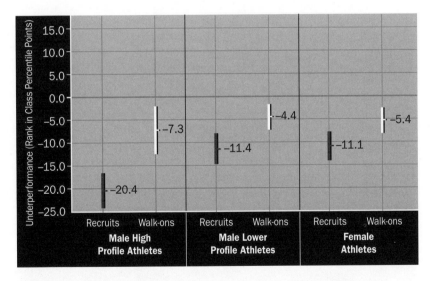

Figure 6.1b. Underperformance of Athletes, by Type of Sport and Recruit Status, Controlling for Differences in Race, Field of Study, SAT Scores, and Institutional SAT, 1995 Entering Cohort, NESCAC Colleges
Source: Expanded College and Beyond database.

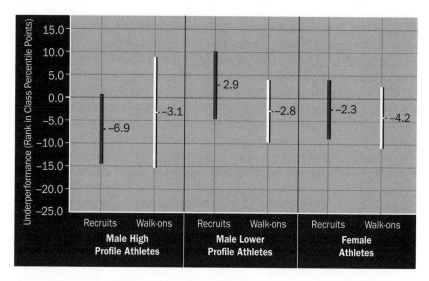

Figure 6.1c. Underperformance of Athletes, by Type of Sport and Recruit Status, Controlling for Differences in Race, Field of Study, SAT Scores, and Institutional SAT, 1995 Entering Cohort, UAA Universities
Source: Expanded College and Beyond database.

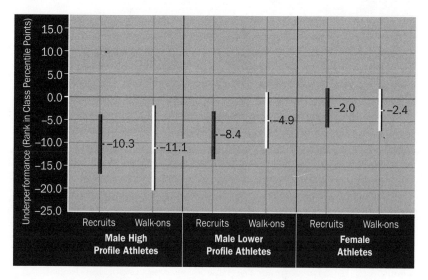

Figure 6.1d. Underperformance of Athletes, by Type of Sport and Recruit Status, Controlling for Differences in Race, Field of Study, SAT Scores, and Institutional SAT, 1995 Entering Cohort, Coed Liberal Art Colleges (Other)
Source: Expanded College and Beyond database.

An example may be helpful in illustrating what "underperformance" means. A white male student with a 1200 combined SAT score who is majoring in the social sciences at an Ivy League university where the average SAT score is 1350 can expect to have a grade point average (GPA) slightly below the middle of the class (in the 44th percentile). If that same student were a recruited High Profile athlete, he could expect to be in the 25th percentile of the class, 19 percentile points below what might otherwise have been expected.

Outside the Ivies and the NESCAC colleges the results are quite different. The sharpest contrast is with the UAA universities: there is no significant underperformance by any group of athletes at these universities (Figure 6.1c). At the coed liberal arts colleges outside NESCAC, there is significant underperformance, about 10 points, among the High Profile male athletes, both recruits and walk-ons, and also some underperformance among the recruited Lower Profile male athletes (Figure 6.1d). The walk-ons playing the Lower Profile sports and the female athletes at the coed liberal arts colleges outside NESCAC are like those in the UAA (and unlike those in the Ivy League and in NESCAC) in that they show no significant underperformance. Athletes at the women's colleges, on the other hand, show some underperformance, but not very much. (We cannot distinguish between the recruits and walk-ons at these schools, but athletes in general underperform by about 5 percentile points.)

These basic findings are clear, consistent, and thought-provoking. Any degree of underperformance in any setting is grounds for concern (especially if there is a trend moving in the wrong direction, as appears to be the case at the women's colleges). But the serious problems right now seem highly concentrated: (1) among recruited athletes in the Ivies and the NESCAC colleges and (2) among High Profile male athletes (principally the football players) in the other coed liberal arts colleges. Accordingly, we focus most of the rest of this chapter on recruited athletes in the Ivy League and NESCAC schools and on those playing High Profile sports at the liberal arts colleges outside NESCAC. The UAA universities appear distinctive in having largely[6] avoided this problem, and we return later to the intriguing question of how they have managed to do this.

MEASURING UNDERPERFORMANCE

Let us begin by considering briefly how underperformance is measured. Several commentators, admissions deans in particular, have questioned whether SAT scores are a valid and sufficiently sophisticated predictor of academic potential. Fred Hargadon, the dean of admission at Princeton, suggested that we may be "overpredicting" for athletes rather than measuring their "underperformance." There is a substantial literature documenting the validity of SAT scores as one predictor of academic performance in college, but of course any single measure has its limitations.[7]

To supplement our analysis based on SAT scores, we also used high school grades, the Ivy Academic Index, achievement scores, and self-reported intention to apply for Advanced Placement (AP) credit in college.[8] We have data on high school grades for all the Ivies and for seven NESCAC colleges.[9] If we add controls for high school grades, we see that they, too, are a significant predictor of college rank-in-class but that underperformance by all groups of athletes is only slightly reduced (Appendix Table 6.1). Even the largest change in the point estimate of underperformance (which occurs in the case of the High Profile recruited male athletes in the Ivies)—from –19.0 to –17.2—is less than 2 percentile points. In no case does adding controls for high school rank-in-class *significantly* change estimates of underperformance.

Using other controls, such as the Ivy Academic Index or special admissions ratings provided by an individual school, also fails to alter the basic results. Adding controls for SAT II test scores or the Ivy Academic Index (which includes SAT II scores in some cases) to the analysis made more of a difference than high school grades. Controlling for SAT II scores reduced underperformance coefficients by as much as 4 percentile points, but failed to eliminate statistically significant evidence of underperformance.[10] Use of the Ivy Academic Index had a similar effect. We also performed the analysis with a control for self-reported intention to apply for AP credit in college, which had a negligible effect on underperformance estimates. Since adding these more complex predictors does not change underperformance estimates appreciably, we use only SAT scores (which have the advantage of being readily available for all students and essentially all schools) in the rest of the analysis.

Other commentators, most commonly athletic directors, have questioned the use of percentile rank-in-class as an outcome variable. They suggest that the differences in actual GPAs are small and thus unimportant. As we suggested in the previous chapter, there are a variety of reasons, not least the effects of grade inflation and differences in grading standards across schools, for preferring percentile rankings to straight GPAs. However, in order to address this concern directly, we repeated the analysis, substituting cumulative grade point averages for percentile rank-in-class. Recruited male athletes playing both High Profile and Lower Profile sports, as well as recruited female athletes, in both the Ivies and the NESCAC colleges, continued to underperform significantly.[11]

The commentators are correct that the differences in GPA are not large in absolute value; the typical recruited female athlete in the Ivies, for example, pays a "price" of 0.14 points in cumulative GPA (compared to 12.9 percentile points in class rank). This is a difference equivalent to slightly less than half a grade change (where a grade change is a movement such as that from an A-minus to a B-plus). However, when one considers that nearly 40 percent of women in the Ivies have grade point averages *between* A-minus and B-plus, this modest difference does not seem irrelevant.

We should also recall the data in the Williams Ad Hoc Committee report showing that athletes, and especially male athletes in the High Profile sports, choose easier courses than other students.[12] We cannot control for such differences, and they clearly cause our estimates of underperformance to understate the true dimensions of the problem— conceivably by quite a bit.

UNDERPERFORMANCE OF RECRUITED ATHLETES

To return to the main story line: there is a consistent tendency for recruited athletes (in the Ivies and in the NESCAC colleges) to exhibit a much greater degree of academic underperformance than either walk-ons or students at large. This is the principal finding that stands out, and we have spent a great deal of time talking with deans, faculty members, athletic directors, and coaches in an effort to understand the roots of this pervasive phenomenon. In these discussions we were struck repeatedly by the degree to which those with whom we spoke were surprised ("astonished" would be a better word in many cases) both by the evidence of underperformance and by the degree to which it is concentrated among the recruits. For many, this was a new finding to contemplate, and many ideas were advanced to explain it. The most common hypotheses had to do with time commitments and levels of play, although it was also suggested that the "cultures" of certain sports might be relevant. Still other hypotheses focused on presumed relationships with socioeconomic status or on the extent to which recruited athletes might feel "tied" to coaches and therefore obligated to focus heavily on their sports. It was also suggested that we explore the relationship between underperformance and an athlete's SAT scores. And then, of course, there is the role played by the selection process itself and the degree to which recruited athletes, in particular, are less interested in academics than many of their peers.

We know from Chapter 4 that recruits and walk-ons differ in all sorts of ways, especially in the Ivies and the NESCAC colleges. Recruits not only have lower SAT scores than walk-ons (a factor taken into account in measuring underperformance), but they also are more likely to play certain sports, to play for more years, and to be varsity players and starters on their teams. Perhaps these (and other) attributes explain the greater relative underperformance of the recruited athletes. That is, perhaps recruits underperform more than walk-ons not because they are recruits, but because they are more likely to fall in some other category that is related to underperformance (such as athletes on financial aid, wrestlers, or athletes with low SAT scores). In order to understand better the roots of underperformance, we have tried to isolate the effects on rank-in-class of many of these differences between recruits and walk-ons.

Underperformance and Socioeconomic Status

Some have suggested that the underperformance of athletes is a "class" phenomenon. There are two separate arguments of this type. The first presumes that athletes are disproportionately from families with lower socioeconomic profiles and goes on to propose that, because students from such backgrounds tend to underperform, it appears that athletes are underperforming because they are athletes when in reality they are underperforming because they are from families with lower socioeconomic profiles. The second argument is that athletes from less affluent backgrounds are particularly pressed for time, as they participate intensively in athletics and also hold down jobs. The proposition is that this double time commitment is unique to athletes on aid because other students with work-study jobs can limit their extracurricular involvement to make time for jobs without unduly sacrificing study time.

The premise of the first argument is that the athlete is more likely to be less well-off (more likely to be on need-based financial aid) than the typical student at large—that being an "athlete" is in some measure a proxy for being "on aid."[13] But in fact, as we showed in Chapter 4, athletes as a group are not more likely to be on financial aid than are other students. Nonetheless, to be sure that we are not missing an important connection (especially in the case of particular sports like football, which are more likely to draw students from lower socioeconomic backgrounds), we added a control for "received need-based financial aid."[14] Receiving need-based financial aid does have a negative effect on grades at some institutions, but adding this control leaves the effects of athletic participation on rank-in-class essentially unchanged (Appendix Tables 6.2a and 6.2b). Were it the case that the athletic variable is "standing in" for socioeconomic status, we would expect to see a decrease in the size of the estimates of underperformance by the amount of the effect associated with being on financial aid. This is not at all the case, however, even for athletes in the High Profile men's sports, who are more likely than students at large to be on financial aid. For example, adding a control for receiving need-based aid reduces the underperformance measure for recruited High Profile athletes in the Ivies by only 1 point—from −19.0 to −18.0 (top panel of Appendix Table 6.2a).

To test the second hypothesis (concerning the possible combined effect of having time commitments related both to being an athlete and to being on aid) a slightly more complicated model is needed. The question is essentially whether there is some interaction between being an athlete and being on financial aid that causes athletes on financial aid to pay an academic price greater than the sum of the prices for being an athlete and being on financial aid. This does not appear to be the case. Appendix Table 6.3 presents both main effects (of being an athlete regardless of aid status and of being on aid regardless of athletic status) and interaction effects (of being both an athlete and on aid). Only one of these interaction effects is significant, and it contradicts the hypothesis; in the Ivies, recruited female athletes on financial aid do not pay the full price of being both recruited athletes and on financial aid.[15] In short, there is no evidence that athletes on financial aid are particularly hard hit by the double crunch of being on aid and being an athlete.

Underperformance and SAT Level

Several Ivy League university presidents asked if athletes' underperformance is related to the SAT scores of recruited athletes (or to the Academic Index used in the Ivy League). Do the athletes with the lowest SAT scores underperform the most? This question has direct policy relevance. If underperformance is concentrated among athletes at the lower end of the SAT distribution, the solution could be as straightforward as raising the minimum SAT score (or Academic Index) used as a threshold in setting admission standards. Unfortunately, it does not appear that such a simple solution will suffice. At the Ivies and the NESCAC colleges—where, as we have seen, underperformance is both most pronounced and most clearly related to recruiting—we divided the recruited athletes into three groups, those with low, mid-level, and high SAT scores. We set the cut-off for "low" SAT scores at about the 25th percentile for all students and the cut-off for "high" scores at about the 75th percentile.[16]

The clearest pattern that emerges is that recruited athletes with high SAT scores (above 1400 in the Ivies and above 1300 in the NESCAC colleges) do substantially better academically than other recruited athletes, even relative to the more impressive performance that can be expected of them because of their higher test scores (Figures 6.2a and 6.2b). In the Ivies, there is essentially no underperformance among recruited High

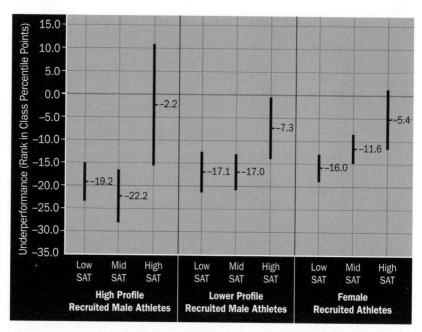

Figure 6.2a. Underperformance of Recruited Athletes, by Type of Sport and
SAT Level, Controlling for Differences in Race, Field of Study, SAT Scores, and
Institutional SAT, 1995 Entering Cohort, Ivy League Universities
Source: Expanded College and Beyond database.

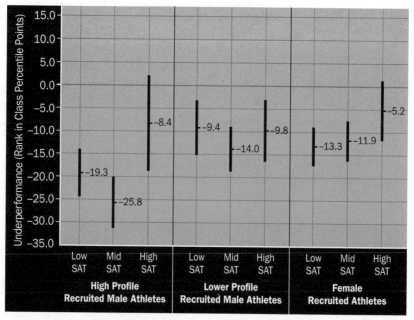

Figure 6.2b. Underperformance of Recruited Athletes, by Type of Sport and
SAT Level, Controlling for Differences in Race, Field of Study, and Institutional
SAT, 1995 Entering Cohort, NESCAC Colleges
Source: Expanded College and Beyond database.

Profile athletes with high test scores, and only among recruited athletes in the Lower Profile men's sports at the NESCAC colleges is there substantial and significant underperformance in the highest SAT range. This finding suggests that there is indeed some basis for thinking that raising the Academic Index (AI) threshold could alleviate the problem of underperformance. The difficulty with this proposition, however, is that the students in the broad middle SAT category (1250–1400 for the Ivies and 1150–1300 for the NESCAC colleges) have at least as serious a problem with underperformance as their teammates in the lowest SAT range. In the men's sports, particularly the High Profile sports, there is even some tendency for recruited athletes in the middle SAT ranges to have the worst problems with underperformance.

Thus in order to solve the problem of underperformance in the Ivies by raising the AI (or in the NESCAC colleges by instituting some form of academic index as a threshold requirement for admission), the bar would have to be set very, very high. In the Ivies, only 6 percent of the High Profile recruited athletes have SAT scores above 1400, and only 11 percent of the Lower Profile recruited athletes and 10 percent of the female recruited athletes meet this standard. The NESCAC schools fare only slightly better in this regard, with only 8 percent of the recruited High Profile male athletes, 23 percent of the recruited Lower Profile male athletes, and 14 percent of recruited female athletes entering college with SAT scores in our "high" range.

Since recruited athletes with the lowest SAT scores do not underperform the most, it is unlikely that the lower SAT scores of this group of athletes drive their persistent underperformance. Furthermore, the walk-ons in the Ivies do not even show the pattern we found for recruited athletes—namely, that those with the highest SAT scores do appreciably better, relative to their incoming credentials, than those with lower scores (Appendix Table 6.4). In fact, almost no group of walk-ons in the Ivies and the NESCAC colleges demonstrates large and significant underperformance—regardless of SAT score. *The clearest message to emerge from this analysis is that—except for the small number of recruited athletes with very high test scores—the degree of underperformance does not depend on an athlete's SAT score. Rather, underperformance among recruited athletes is largely an across-the-board phenomenon.*[17]

Underperformance by Sport

It is possible that certain sports interfere more than others with academic achievement. Different sports require different amounts of practice and travel. Schedules may differ and be more or less in conflict with academic commitments. Some sports may be more likely than others to foster cultural influences that do not value academic performance.[18] To test whether there are sport-by-sport differences, we looked first at the direct effect on underperformance of recruiting in general and then entered each sport into the regression separately, leaving in the control for recruiting. Were the underperformance of recruited athletes tied closely to the particular sports they play, we would expect the coefficient for the overall recruiting variable to be zero after adding the "sport dummies." For the Ivies and the NESCAC colleges, this is definitely not the case (Tables 6.1a and 6.1b). Being recruited is still a significant negative predictor of rank-in-class even after controlling for the sports played. In the

TABLE 6.1a

Underperformance of Male Athletes, by Sport and Conference,
Controlling for Differences in Race, Field of Study, SAT Scores,
and Institutional SAT, 1995 Entering Cohort

	Ivy League Universities	NESCAC Colleges	UAA Universities	Coed Liberal Arts Colleges (Other)
Recruit without sport variables	**−16.3**	**−13.8**	−1.7	**−7.4**
Recruit with sport variables	**−12.0**	**−9.7**	3.7	−2.9
Baseball	−2.5	**−7.1**	4.1	−5.4
Basketball	−1.5	−5.2	0.5	0.0
Crew	**−4.6**	**−5.6**		
Cross country	−0.6	1.8	5.5	5.1
Fencing	−5.0			
Football	**−9.1**	**−9.5**	**−11.6**	**−9.8**
Sprint football	−5.2			
Golf	1.3	−5.5		−8.5
Ice hockey	−3.3	**−7.8**		
Lacrosse	**−8.1**	−4.4		**−11.9**
Sailing	−1.7	−4.9		
Soccer	−2.4	1.2	−3.3	−2.1
Squash	2.5	−4.1		
Swimming	**−6.9**	−2.4	−9.2	**−8.9**
Tennis	4.3	5.9		−1.2
Track	−4.2	−3.2	−0.6	−2.6
Wrestling	**−7.8**	−11.6		
Other sports	−3.8	−3.6	3.5	−3.8

Source: Expanded College and Beyond database.

Note: Numbers in **bold** are significant at the .05 level.

TABLE 6.1b
Underperformance of Female Athletes, by Sport and Conference,
Controlling for Differences in Race, Field of Study, SAT Scores,
and Institutional SAT, 1995 Entering Cohort

	Ivy League Universities	NESCAC Colleges	UAA Universities	Coed Liberal Arts Colleges (Other)
Recruit without sport variables	**−11.6**	**−8.5**	−1.6	−1.7
Recruit with sport variables	**−8.0**	**−4.7**	−0.4	−0.3
Basketball	−2.8	−0.1	9.6	−5.5
Crew	**−5.7**	**−6.2**		
Cross country	2.9	3.8	4.9	3.2
Fencing	−1.7			
Field hockey	−4.5	−4.5		**−11.0**
Gymnastics	**−12.0**			
Ice hockey	−3.9	**−17.7**		
Lacrosse	−4.4	**−8.2**		−5.7
Sailing	−3.4	−5.0		
Soccer	1.2	−0.4	−7.8	−7.6
Softball	**−8.2**	−4.7		−7.5
Squash	−4.1	−5.0		
Swimming	−5.1	−2.3	−1.0	0.1
Tennis	−2.5	−1.4	−7.6	**15.7**
Track	**−7.1**	−2.6	−2.5	2.0
Volleyball	−3.6	**−7.9**	−7.1	0.2
Other sports	−5.1	0.4		12.1

Source: Expanded College and Beyond database.
Note: Numbers in **bold** are significant at the .05 level.

Ivies, for example, the underperformance coefficient associated with having been recruited falls only from −16.3 to −12.0 after the control variables for particular sports are introduced.[19]

Of the individual sports, only football and, somewhat surprisingly, crew, are consistently related to underperformance. In every group of schools—including this time the UAA universities—playing football is associated, on an "other-things-equal" basis, with a decrease in class rank of about 10 percentile points. This clear finding illustrates again why so many of the individuals whom we interviewed emphasized the difficulties posed by competing in this high-visibility sport. Surprisingly, crew is also related to significant underperformance for both men and women, around 5 percentile points. This pattern may be explained in part by the unique schedule of crew teams, which tend to practice year-round and in the early morning. Another possible explanation is that rowers, who tend to enter college with relatively high test scores and other academic credentials, would be predicted to do very well; for them modest academic success may translate into statistically significant underperformance. Finally, it may be that the very nature of the sport, with its intense focus on teamwork, helps create an environment that emphasizes rowing above all.

That football players consistently underperform cannot be explained by either season length or entering academic credentials. Football teams at the schools in our study play the shortest season, participate in the fewest contests, and have the most limited off-season commitments of any college teams; and we showed in Chapter 4 that football players tend to have the least imposing entering academic credentials of participants in any sport. It is possible, however, that the nature of the game itself hinders academic performance. Athletes in other sports with high levels of contact, like men's ice hockey, men's lacrosse, and wrestling, show signs of underperformance in some sets of schools. Perhaps such sports leave their students particularly exhausted, but we would guess that most swimmers and female lacrosse players would disagree. The large squad sizes required for football and the emphasis on teamwork (similar to that in crew) may enhance negative peer effects. Additionally, the historical role of football on college campuses and the culture surrounding it may lead some football players to feel differently about their academic commitments than other athletes.

The "How-Much-Time-It-Takes" Hypothesis

Many knowledgeable observers, on seeing the findings about academic underperformance in *The Game of Life* and in discussing our new findings with us, have suggested that the major difference between recruited athletes and other students is in the amount of time (and, some have said, the amount of energy) expended on extracurricular activities. The detailed studies quoted in Chapter 4 found that athletes spend, on average, more than twice as much time on their sports than do participants in even the most time-intensive of other extracurricular activities. In addition, the time demanded of athletes is often at inconvenient hours or requires travel. The recent Amherst report notes: "Some commentators suggest the problem is not so much the total amount of time required for athletic participation as the scheduling of that time. In too many cases, it is said, athletic participation conflicts with class time or laboratory time. Several science faculty specifically noted that athletes have difficulty fitting laboratory sessions into their schedules. Other faculty pointed out conflicts with classes occasioned by travel to away contests and post-season competition."[20]

In an earlier effort to disentangle various forces at work, a comparison was made in *The Game of Life* between athletes and other student "actives," those who were editors of the student newspaper, presidents of student government, or involved in the orchestra or the theater at a similar level of commitment. The "other student actives" are a good comparison group in that these especially involved students almost certainly devote the sort of time to their extracurricular activities that athletes devote to their sports, and they, too, often have difficult scheduling constraints. Yet these other student actives did not underperform academically—indeed, they *over*performed, relative to how they could have been expected to do.[21] This was true despite the fact that many of these "actives" were involved in their demanding activities at the same level of intensity for essentially the entire academic year, whereas some athletes are most fully engaged in their sports "in season."

Another challenge to the time hypothesis is the finding that underperformance, in those settings where it is most pronounced (the Ivies and the NESCAC colleges), is heavily concentrated among the recruited athletes. While the walk-ons are likely to have a less intensive athletic experience than the recruited athletes (refer back to Chapter 4 and see the later discussion in this chapter), it would be surprising if whatever differences there are in the amount of time that recruits and walk-ons spend in formal practice, competition, and travel are sufficient to explain the dramatic differences in their academic performance. The pronounced concentration of underperformance among the recruited athletes suggests that something more complicated than simply the allocation of time is involved.

Fortunately, additional data available to us for the Ivies permit a much more direct test of the "time commitment" hypothesis. We can compare the academic performance in a given year of recruited athletes who participated in athletics in that year to the academic performance of recruited athletes who did not participate.[22] We see that the "playing athletes" underperform to a slightly greater degree than other athletes for every situation in which comparisons are possible (Figure 6.3).[23] It seems that recruited athletes do a little bit better when not faced with the tremendous demands on their time and energy that playing entails—a finding that is hardly surprising, even though it does contradict the fre-

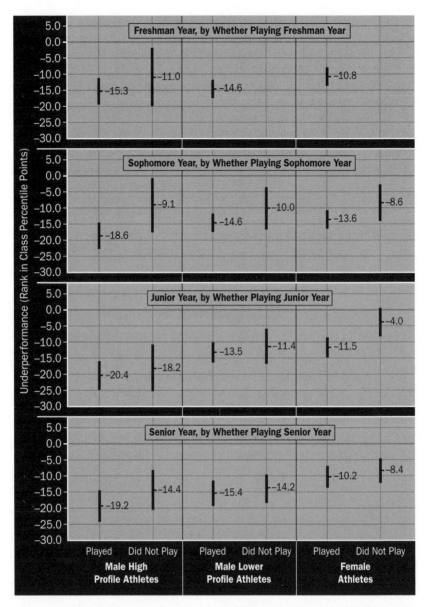

Figure 6.3. Underperformance of Recruited Athletes, by Year, Gender, Type of Sport, and Whether Playing, Controlling for Differences in Race, Field of Study, SAT Scores, and Institutional SAT, 1995 Entering Cohort, Ivy League Universities

Source: Expanded College and Beyond database.

quent comments to the effect that athletes manage their study time better when the demands of their teams are greatest.[24]

More surprising is the fact that *the difference is so very small and that, in almost every case, the recruited athletes who are not playing still show substantial and significant underperformance.* For example, in their sophomore year the recruited athletes who are not playing still have a percentile rank-in-class between 8 and 10 points lower than their credentials predict—a finding that holds for High Profile athletes, male Lower Profile athletes, and female athletes. In the case of the recruited High Profile athletes, the underperformance among those not playing doubles to 18 points in their junior year and is 14 points in their senior year. This is strong evidence that the time hypothesis can provide, at most, only a very partial explanation of the phenomenon of underperformance by recruited athletes.

A similar year-by-year analysis of playing and grades for the Ivy League walk-ons provides further evidence that time commitments alone do not explain underperformance (Appendix Table 6.5). There are not enough walk-ons in the High Profile men's sports to allow the comparison, but in the Lower Profile men's and women's sports, there is little evidence that walk-on athletes substantially underperform—whether or not they were playing! Thus, as we have found again and again, the underperformance of athletes is concentrated among those who were recruited and cannot be accounted for by any of the other differences between recruited athletes and walk-ons that we have examined thus far. The greater underperformance of recruited athletes, as compared to that of walk-ons, is not due merely to the fact that recruited athletes play more years, with time spent playing having a negative impact on grades. Recruited athletes underperform significantly even when not playing at all.

For four of the Ivies, we are also able to compare sophomore-year grades on a term-by-term basis.[25] We use these data to compare the grades earned by football players in the fall ("in season") to grades earned in the spring ("out of season"). Football is the sport best suited to this analysis because the Ivies limit the non-traditional season for football more than they do for other sports. The "time" hypothesis holds that underperformance would be largely limited to the fall, when the time demands of football are by far the greatest. Although it is the case that underperformance is most pronounced in the fall, it is present and substantial in the spring as well. Recruited football players who played in the sophomore year underperformed by 24 points in the fall and 20 points in the spring. In other words, football players underperform significantly even when their sport is not in season; therefore, the time demands of the sport can only partially explain underperformance.

The "Key Player" Hypothesis

There is another, related, proposition that needs to be considered: namely, that being a key player on a team affects academic performance in a variety of ways, not just through the ordinary time demands imposed on everyone who is on the team. Put another way, recruited athletes might underperform because they are so often the starters, and starting may be directly related to underperformance. As one observer surmised: "Perhaps non-recruited athletes are more spectators and cheerleaders than players. This would mean that they would not have to spend as much time or emotional energy on the sport as the core members of the squads. . . . The non-recruited athletes don't have to spend time showering after the games!" Surely the starters return from a game with less energy to study than the bench-warmers, and they may also be more driven to think about the team all the time.

The fact that recruited athletes underperform even when not playing at all contradicts the "key player" hypothesis as a complete explanation for underperformance, but this hypothesis can also be tested more directly. We showed in Chapter 4 that recruits are more likely to play at the varsity level than walk-ons and are more likely to do so all four years. Presumably those athletes who play only at the varsity level are more accomplished athletically than those who work their way up from the junior varsity (JV). For some of the Ivy League and NESCAC schools, we are able to distinguish whether students played JV or varsity and to compare the academic records of the two groups of athletes.[26] Only for the NESCAC men is there an additional underperformance penalty associated with playing solely at the varsity level (Appendix Table 6.6). In the Ivies the underperformance of recruited athletes changes *not at all* when controls are added for playing only on the varsity squad—a finding that holds for male and female athletes and for men who play the Lower Profile sports as well as for those who play High Profile sports. Even for the men at the NESCAC colleges, where playing only on the varsity does matter, the underperformance of the recruited athletes is significantly greater than the amount that can be explained by the "varsity-only" effect.

Level of play is not the only measure of whether an athlete is a key player, however, and for some of the Ivies we can test the "key player" hypothesis even more directly by looking at the results for football starters only.[27] One might argue that only those football players who are starters would exhibit underperformance, but this is not the case. The point estimate of underperformance for non-starters is –17.5, smaller than the point estimate for starters (−23.0), but still large and significant. The underperformance of recruited athletes is not limited to the key members of the team.

The "Athletic Culture" Hypothesis

Another possible explanation for underperformance is that there is an athletic "culture" that does not value academic achievement. Many team members live and study together, and it may be hard for an individual student to challenge the norms of the group. The facts that underperformance is concentrated among the recruited athletes and that recruited athletes underperform even when not participating on teams suggest that athletic culture is not the entire explanation. However, another fact—that walk-ons also underperform in the Ivies and in NESCAC (albeit to a lesser degree)—suggests that there is at least some "culture" effect.

Since there is a significant bunching of male athletes, and recruited male athletes in particular, in social science and business majors, athletes in these fields are most likely to take classes together and study together. In such situations "peer effects" may be most likely to have an impact on academic performance. Also, the athletes who choose to major in these fields may be more readily influenced by their teammates in academic matters (how much time to devote to preparing a paper, for example) than those who have chosen to "go against the grain" by majoring in another field. Thus we might expect there to be the most underperformance in the most widely chosen fields. This is not consistently true, but in the Ivies and the NESCAC colleges the athletes in the High Profile sports who major in the social sciences and business do demonstrate marginally higher levels of underperformance than their teammates who choose other majors (Appendix Table 6.7).[28] This pattern offers at least mild support for the culture hypothesis.

Another way of trying to get at culture or peer effects is by comparing athletes who are on teams dominated by recruited athletes with those who are on teams with large numbers of walk-ons. For the Lower Profile men's and women's sports, we designate teams that are more than 50 percent recruited as "high-recruit teams" and the others as "low-recruit teams." This is done on an individual team basis, so the men's cross country team may be a high-recruit team at one Ivy school and a low-recruit team at another. We then compare the underperformance of recruits on high-recruit teams and recruits on low-recruit teams, and similarly that of walk-ons (Appendix Table 6.8). For the most part, there do not appear to be substantial peer effects; the walk-ons on high-recruit teams do not do worse than those on low-recruit teams, and the recruits on low-recruit teams do not do better than those on high-recruit teams. The Lower Profile male walk-ons in the NESCAC colleges provide a slight exception, but overall there is little clear evidence of culture effects.

The "Stigma" Hypothesis

Another possible explanation for the underperformance phenomenon is that professors discriminate against athletes either directly, by giving them lower grades, or indirectly in ways that hurt academic motivation and interest. Particularly at the colleges, there is a sense that athletes are not taken seriously by professors. The Amherst report explains:

> [One] plausible explanation for academic underperformance is the discouragement and demoralization that athletes feel because of the way in which they believe themselves to be regarded by many faculty and students. We heard considerable testimony that a stigma does in fact attach to athlete status, or at least membership on certain teams. We heard from students, both team captains and non-athlete student leaders, that at least a few members of the faculty are widely known for their hostility to athletic participation or for their belief that certain athletes are academically inferior or unmotivated. . . . Whether this "stigma" actually affects academic performance is harder to measure, but it seems plausible to believe that, at the margin, it does.[29]

Work on the underperformance of minority groups indicates that academic performance can be negatively affected by stereotypes, a phenomenon referred to as "stereotype threat." It is possible that athletes as well are vulnerable to stereotype threat. However, it is hard to imagine that stigma and resulting demoralization can fully explain underperformance, especially at the larger Ivy League universities and in the men's Lower Profile sports and the women's sports, where it is not clear that professors would even know which of their students are athletes. In addition, male athletes in particular tend to have very high levels of academic self-confidence, higher in fact than their credentials might warrant, which should offer some protection against stereotype threat.[30]

UNDERSTANDING UNDERPERFORMANCE: BACK TO THE RECRUITMENT/ADMISSIONS PROCESS

If the underperformance of recruited athletes is explained only in part (and our evidence suggests only in relatively small part) by the time and energy they devote to their sports, what does explain this consistent and troubling finding? The peer effects of an athletic culture and the demoralizing effects of negative stereotyping by faculty may be part of the explanation, but again patterns of underperformance across conferences, sports, and genders are much too consistent to suggest that this is all that is going on.

Our central hypothesis is that, apart from the factors already discussed, underperformance relates primarily to the processes of recruitment and admissions at these highly selective colleges and universities. One way to conceive of this "selection" effect is to consider the criteria admissions officers use to make decisions. We know that recruited athletes receive a break on "observed" characteristics, as shown by the SAT score gaps between these athletes and other students and by the quantifiable admissions advantages these athletes receive. It may well be that they also receive a break on characteristics that are "unobserved" by us, such as intellectual interest and academic motivation. These characteristics, judged by admissions offices through essays, teacher recommendations, and high school curricula, are essential in translating formal academic credentials into performance. If recruited athletes receive a break on these "unobservables" as well as the "observables," this could explain the academic underperformance we see.

The recent faculty report at Middlebury College makes the important point that any negative consequences for the academic community resulting from the pursuit of athletic excellence are unintended.[31] Coaches are charged primarily (and increasingly) with organizing and leading successful teams, not with finding those students who will engage most actively in the academic and intellectual community of the school. To the contrary, in the pursuit of building the best *athletics* program that they can within the formal academic constraints of the school or conference (even if "best" is defined more broadly than just being successful competitively), they naturally seek to recruit those students who are not only talented athletes, but also dedicated athletes. Although academic and athletic interests, like academic and athletic talents, are far from mutually exclusive— as those exceptional individuals who excel in both areas repeatedly demonstrate—they are not likely to be highly correlated, either. The new— and very strong—evidence connecting underperformance among athletes to their active recruitment, coupled with the fact that by being on the coaches' lists recruited athletes receive special treatment in the admissions process at these highly selective schools, leads us to believe that *the interests and priorities of the recruited athlete are key factors in explaining underperformance.* It is hardly counter-intuitive to suggest that underperformance depends on the extent to which, as one president put it, "athletics is the focus of a student's life."

We are sure that recruited athletes who attend these schools, like their classmates, take pride in attending an excellent college or university. They graduate at high rates, and we know from evidence in *The Game of*

Life that former athletes, like other alumni/ae, go on to do well in their careers. But it seems reasonable to suppose that while they are on campus, the recruited athletes are more likely than other athletes (as well as other students) to focus on their sports and their teams. They are also much more likely than other athletes (and, again, other students as well) to feel a special tie to the coach who played such an important role in their admission, and to want to meet the coach's expectations. Richard Williams, associate dean of the college at Princeton, commented in an interview: "No other group [of students] is recruited in the same sort of individual way or automatically has such a close relationship with someone, like a coach, not directly connected to the academic center of the university; thus, from the very beginning, athletes are given a strong message that they are wanted at the school, but specifically in the capacity of athlete." As we have been told over and over by coaches and athletic directors, recruited athletes were put on coaches' lists in no small part because the coaches were convinced that they had dedication as well as talent—that they would devote a great deal of time, energy, and focus to their team.

Given their attachments and priorities, highly recruited athletes, selected largely on the basis of the talents and traits that make them exceptional athletes, may conceivably be more inclined than their classmates simply to "get by" academically; they may be less inclined (or even less able, recognizing the pressures and perhaps even the stress that their athletic commitments place on them) to make the extra effort needed to turn an acceptable performance in class into an exceptional performance. One experienced observer, Amy Campbell, comments that "the myth is that college athletes have to give up something in order to be successful athletes, and that they are thought to give up their social life. But, in reality, they give up opportunities to be more fully engaged in the broader life of the institution and the rigorous pursuit of their academics." Moreover, because the roots of underperformance may have more to do with priorities and motivation than with the time and energy athletics demands, substantial underperformance exists even when those students stop participating in athletics.

The nature of the recruitment/admissions process has carry-over effects after athletes arrive on campus. One commentator suggested that, having been instrumental in the admission of recruited athletes, coaches are likely to reinforce selection effects by encouraging "their players" to be dedicated to the team at the expense of extra study time. More generally, a strong athletic culture can reinforce selection effects through the close relations of like-minded people.

The seemingly substantial influence of the way in which athletes are recruited and admitted on their performance in college is corroborated by an examination of evidence at the institutional level. There is a "macro" correlation between underperformance by recruited athletes at particular schools and the weight given to coaches' preferences in deciding which athletes are admitted. One of the important findings of this study (which we certainly did not anticipate) is the pronounced difference in academic outcomes between athletes in the UAA universities on the one hand, and those in the Ivies and the NESCAC colleges on the other. It is no coincidence, in our view, that coaches in the UAA tend to give their admissions offices much longer lists of athletes (if any lists at all) and to expect their admissions offices to exercise much more discretion in deciding which athletes to admit. Differences in the incoming academic credentials of recruited athletes and students at large at the UAA universities are negligible; and, once admitted, the recruited UAA athletes do not, as a group, tend to underperform. Nor do we think it is a coincidence that there is less systematic underperformance in the liberal arts colleges outside NESCAC, where (with the possible exception of football) we observe less intensive recruitment of athletes and smaller admissions advantages.

More precisely, we find a decided correlation between the size of the admissions advantage given to athletes (the degree of preference extended to applicants on the coaches' lists) and the degree of underperformance. The correlations between the admissions advantage for recruited athletes and the underperformance of recruited athletes are around -0.5 for male High Profile, male Lower Profile, and female athletes (-0.51, -0.50 and -0.54, respectively).[32] This relationship is illustrated, for High Profile recruited athletes, in Figure 6.4. As the admissions advantage increases, the underperformance coefficients become more negative (indicating more underperformance). The corresponding pictures for male Lower Profile and female athletes are very similar.

The evidence we have examined—in its detail and especially in the clarity of its overall pattern—is consistent with the conclusion that, as one social science colleague puts it, this is a story about "selection, selection, selection." We keep being driven back to the effects on academic performance of the selection criteria employed in recruiting and admitting athletes in the Ivy League and in NESCAC. Here is why we come to this conclusion:

- Recruited athletes underperform significantly, whereas most walk-ons do not.

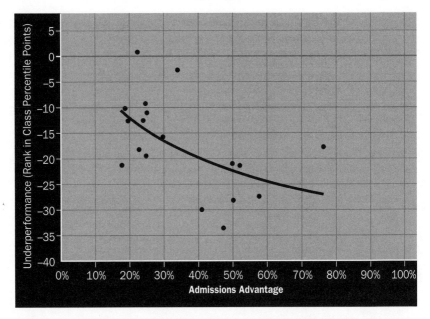

Figure 6.4. Admissions Advantage for Male Recruited Athletes versus
Underperformance for High Profile Male Recruited Athletes, 1999 Admission
Pool and 1995 Entering Cohort, Ivy League Universities, NESCAC Colleges,
and Other Coed Liberal Arts Colleges
   Source: Expanded College and Beyond database.

- Underperformance among recruited athletes is greater among men
  than among women, and more pronounced in the High Profile
  sports than in the men's Lower Profile sports, but it is ever-present
  in the Ivies and in the NESCAC colleges.
- All attempts to explain away this relationship between having
  been recruited and underperforming academically (within the Ivies
  and the NESCAC colleges) fall short: for example, recruit status
  is not "standing in" for lower socioeconomic status; taking account
  of the relationship between socioeconomic status and underperformance leaves the relationship between recruitment status
  and underperformance essentially unchanged.
- In these schools underperformance is related to recruit status on a
  more or less "across-the-board" basis. It is not restricted to recruited
  athletes with low SAT scores; on the contrary, it is present in large
  measure (if anything, even larger measure) among recruited athletes in the broad middle of the SAT range. Only those recruited
  athletes with *very* high SATs show little underperformance.

- One of the most telling findings is that highly significant degrees of underperformance persist among recruited athletes even when these athletes are not playing on intercollegiate teams; clearly, the time demands of the sports cannot account for this result.
- A parallel finding is that walk-ons show much less underperformance even when they *are* playing during a particular year. Again, what matters most is "selection" (whether an athlete was recruited) rather than "treatment" (whether the athlete plays a sport, and at what level).

To be sure, time spent on athletics does have some effect on under-performance, as do, we think, the culture of athletics and perhaps the attitudes of faculty toward prominent athletes (the "stigma" effect). But the best way of quantifying such relationships is to look at the degree of underperformance characteristic of walk-ons when they are playing on varsity teams—which is modest. Walk-ons in the Ivies and in the NESCAC colleges, where the admissions advantage is greatest, display at most modest underperformance, at all SAT levels and in all majors, whether they are playing or not playing, whether they are on high-recruit or low-recruit teams. Recruited athletes at these schools, in sharp contrast, display significant (and in most cases, substantial) underperformance across the board.

So, to repeat, the story line of this chapter on underperformance is "selection, selection, selection."

Forces Creating the Athletic Divide

CHAPTER 7

Orbits of Competition:
The Role of the Conference

OUR FOCUS in Part A of this study was on the college athletes—how many of them there are at these academically selective colleges and universities, how they are recruited and admitted, the academic credentials that they bring with them to college, which sports they play, how much attrition there is from teams, how much opportunity there is for walk-ons to compete, the extent to which there appears to be an "athletic culture," and how both recruited athletes and walk-ons fare academically. There are, as we have shown, important differences between High Profile and Lower Profile sports and between men's and women's teams. Still, a distinct overall picture emerges. Both statistics and informed testimony confirm that there is today a substantial "academic-athletic divide" on many of these campuses.

In Part B our focus shifts to the broad factors that have led to this present-day reality. We begin by looking at what has transpired through the prism of the different conference settings in which the schools in this study compete. The experiences and characteristics of the conferences themselves are an important part of the story.

*Inter*collegiate athletics is, by definition, an activity in which representatives of one school compete against representatives of other schools—not just against themselves and not just against classmates. In this crucial regard, there is an organized "external" aspect to intercollegiate athletics that is not present to anything like the same extent in other arenas of collegiate activity. To be sure, debate teams at one school compete against teams at other schools, and musical groups and student publications strive to be regarded as better than their counterparts elsewhere. Still, intercollegiate athletics is special, perhaps even unique, in the importance attached to direct year-after-year competition with traditional rivals and other conference members—and in the ease with which anyone can see which schools did better and which schools did worse.

In this chapter we have two related objectives. One is to clarify the roles played by specific conferences in either accentuating or retarding the development of the academic-athletic divide; the other is to explain, if we can, why athletes in different conferences show such pronounced differences in academic outcomes. Without question, the "divide" is most pronounced in the Ivy League and in the New England Small College Athletic Conference (NESCAC), and it is important to understand why these groups of schools have had difficulty honoring founding principles such as "representativeness." We also have an interest in understanding why the more youthful University Athletic Association (UAA) has been more successful (so far at any rate) in reconciling its academic and athletic objectives. In seeking to answer such questions, we will build on the early conference histories that were presented in the addendum to the introduction.

THE IVY LEAGUE

The philosophy and attendant policies enunciated so clearly at the founding of the Ivy League in the mid-1950s could not have been expected to solve all problems for all time, and they did not. The late 1970s were a time of particularly active debate over the course of Ivy League athletic programs. One concern was money, and a variety of actions were taken to reduce or at least limit the rate of increase in the costs of intercollegiate athletics (such as limiting numbers of coaches and travel squads, restricting overnight stays, curbing the costs of training tables, and restricting recruiting budgets). As James Litvack, then the executive director of the Ivy League, reports: "A number of the Presidents viewed the major problem with their intercollegiate athletics programs as financial, a problem that would grow as women's athletics increased in intensity and a number of Ivy schools adjusted to having recently gone coed."[1]

A more far-reaching set of concerns was expressed in the concluding paragraph of a letter sent by Martin Meyerson, then president of the University of Pennsylvania, on behalf of his fellow Ivy League presidents, to their Policy Committee: "More than anything, the presidents wanted to raise concerns over what seems to be a creeping intensification or professionalization of athletics in the Ivies, over the pressures this may be extending, particularly, to our admissions, and finally over the costs of our intercollegiate programs."[2]

A Twenty-Five-Year Anniversary Reformulation— and Subsequent Events

After many drafts and much editing and re-editing, the Ivy League presidents adopted, in July 1979, on the 25th anniversary of the Ivy Agreement, the following "Statement of Principles."[3]

1979 Statement of Principles (Ivy Group):

1. Intercollegiate athletics ought to be maintained within a perspective that holds paramount the academic programs of the institution and the academic and personal growth of the student-athlete.
2. The member schools are committed to equal opportunities in athletics for men and women.
3. The member schools ought to look primarily within the Group for standards of competitive excellence and, for most sports, ought to measure success or failure in competition with each other.
4. Each member school ought not merely to tolerate, but to value a balance of competitive success within the Group. Although schools may differ in those sports in which they excel, a reasonable competitive balance among institutions over time over all sports should be sought.
5. Wide participation in intercollegiate athletics should be sought. Although many of our student-athletes will have been at least recognized by alumni, admissions staffs, coaches, or faculty with athletic participation in mind, we should encourage non-recruited athletes to earn places on our teams.
6. Student-athletes should be generally representative of their class and admitted on the basis of academic promise and personal qualities as well as athletic ability.
7. Student-athletes must be admitted and notified of admissions status only by the admissions office, and must be awarded financial aid and notified of financial aid awards only by the office of financial aid. [Council; Spring 1999]
8. Financial aid for student-athletes must be awarded and renewed on the sole basis of economic need with no differentiation in amount or in kind (e.g., in packaging) based on athletic ability or participation, provided that each school shall apply its own standards of economic need.
9. The student-athlete should be held accountable to the same academic standards as other students.
10. Athletic participation ought never to interfere with or otherwise to distort normal academic progress toward the degree or post-baccalaureate plans for graduate work or employment.

This Statement of Principles was viewed as a "natural extension of the 1954 Agreement," and not a substitute for it. Thus the two documents coexist today in *The Ivy Manual,* even though there are differences in wording between them. Most notable is the shift from the wording in the Original Agreement that "the players shall be *truly representative of the student body and not composed of a group of specially recruited athletes*" to the statement in the 1979 principles that "student athletes should be *generally representative* of their class" (our emphasis), unaccompanied by any mention of specially recruited athletes. Also, the 1979 Statement of Principles is more guarded in its discussion of the primacy that should be accorded to intragroup competition. We do not want to exaggerate these differences in language, but they do reflect a heightened awareness of both the ways in which more aggressive recruiting was affecting the "representativeness" of athletes and the growing importance of national championships. In the words of one person who reviewed the history of the Ivy League, "Adherence to the spirit of the Agreement of 1954 was felt by some presidents to have gradually waned, until it was weak at most of the Ivy institutions."[4]

In a memo to the Policy Committee accompanying a draft of these principles, Meyerson asked directly: "What are the differences between the student athletes and their classmates? Are the athletes less representative of the class than earlier? How can institutions retain their necessary autonomy and still insure Ivy principles are respected?" Bowen, then president of Princeton, succeeded Meyerson as chair of the Council of Ivy Group Presidents and followed Meyerson's inquiry (in August 1979) with this formulation of the situation: "We are concerned . . . that a combination of circumstances and pressures has led us in recent years to accept somewhat too low an average level of academic qualification for athletes in the Ivy Group. We are even more concerned by the exceedingly low test scores of those at the bottom of the academic rank order, especially in some sports. Obviously, we are dealing here with a sensitive as well as difficult set of issues. Nonetheless, we are unanimous in believing that a determined effort must be made, effective with the Class of 1984, to begin to address these concerns."[5]

There followed, in the early 1980s, the introduction of the so-called Academic Index (AI), which was designed to reduce the number of athletes with very weak academic credentials and to ensure that athletes in general were more "representative" of their classes. We consider later (in Chapter 11) the lessons learned from this experiment with quantitative methods of regulating academic credentials; it is relevant here as an example of the need felt by the Ivy League members to regulate each other so as to protect the academic standards of the group and prevent member schools from enrolling academically marginal athletes. Because of the free flow of application and acceptance information among coaches, decisions to admit weaker candidates at one institution put pressure on the other institutions to admit similar candidates, thereby leading to a general, if gradual, lowering of standards throughout the League. The existence of the League provided a mechanism for addressing such concerns at the same time that vigorous rivalries among the members were part of the dynamic creating the issues that had to be addressed.

Another recurring (and related) problem was how to achieve the "balance of competitive success" within the League identified as an objective in the 1979 Statement of Principles. Bernstein describes in some detail the problems encountered by Ivy League football in achieving anything resembling competitive balance: "Some schools, such as Harvard and Yale, were more attractive than others, and efforts to balance things out were difficult." Also, Bernstein notes "a successful program's ability to perpetuate itself" and, conversely, the challenge of making an unsuccessful program competitive. Later he notes that the Ivy League presidents gave Columbia an exemption from the Academic Index in an effort to halt Columbia's long losing streak in football.[6]

Finding suitable opponents outside the League was also a problem, in part because of developments over which the Ivies had no control. For example, the Ivies were relegated to Division IAA by the National Collegiate Athletic Association (NCAA) in the fall of 1981 (because they could not meet the more stringent requirements for revenue and attendance imposed by the big-time programs), and this shift in their status affected the teams they could schedule.[7] It was shortly after this that the Ivy League launched an effort to help create the Patriot League in football—a set of Eastern schools not too dissimilar from the Ivies—which could fill out most of the non-Ivy football schedule. The Ivies also encouraged a recasting of the Eastern College Athletic Conference (ECAC) hockey league, so that the remaining non-Ivy schools would constitute the bulk of the non-Ivy hockey schedule.[8] In each of these efforts the non-Ivy schools were induced to change some of their athletic and financial aid policies to make competition more equitable. At more or less the same time, the Ivy League Policy Committee was proposing efforts to schedule more contests within the Ivy League and even proposed returning to a nine-game football schedule.[9]

Efforts to fine-tune various Ivy League regulations, such as specifying limits on the numbers of athletes in sports such as hockey, continued. The Academic Index was revised over the years in some technical respects, and its reach was extended beyond the High Profile men's sports; recently, consideration has been given to the inclusion of transfers within the measures. Most recently (June 2002), the Ivy League presidents acted to reduce the number of football players recruited each year from 35 to 30.[10]

A Balance Sheet Today

Stepping back from the manifold year-to-year changes in this or that regulation, what are we to conclude from the nearly 50 years of experience with the Ivy Group Agreement?

First, it is noteworthy that the membership of the group has stayed intact. In contrast to the experiences of many other conferences and groups, no members have left and none has been added. This is itself testimony to the coherence of the group and to the advantages that the members derive from associating with each other.

Second, the guiding assumptions and stated principles have stayed remarkably constant over half a century, which is a tribute to the initial conception of the founders and to the staying power of the basic ideas.

Third, the Ivy League Agreement has served as something of a model for other associations, most notably NESCAC and the UAA.

Fourth, looked at from the perspective of the broad changes that have occurred in intercollegiate athletics in the United States, the Agreement appears to have succeeded reasonably well in achieving its basic goal, which was to provide a framework that would make it at least somewhat easier for these universities to resist the "creeping intensification" of athletics than, in all likelihood, it would have been otherwise. (This conclusion assumes that moving to Division III was never an option for the Ivies, in part for historical reasons; certainly that idea never figured prominently in any of the internal discussions that led to the formation of the Ivy Group or to subsequent modifications in its policies.) The very different path followed by other leading private universities, such as Duke, Northwestern, and Stanford, that provide athletic scholarships and compete today in Division IA, illustrates an alternative, "more intense," model that at least some of the Ivies might have elected had they not been part of an organized group of institutions with its own stated principles and priorities.

Fifth, hard as it has worked to fend off external pressures and temptations, the Ivy League certainly cannot be said to have succeeded in keeping such forces entirely at bay. When the Ivy League members compete against other Division I programs for students with high levels of athletic talent, they have to respond to some, if not all, of the attractions that these programs offer, and the Ivies must compete with such programs if they are to have a realistic chance of succeeding competitively at the national Division I level. A closely related problem is that the pronounced success of some Ivies in winning national championships has unquestionably put pressure on others to recruit more aggressively, hire more specialized coaches, raise more money targeted to athletics, and improve facilities. It would be naïve to believe that the "arms race" so evident among big-time programs has not also affected the Ivy League.

In sum, the Ivies have succeeded in defending—and retaining—certain key principles, especially the prohibition on athletic scholarships. Beyond that, they have succeeded (with rare exceptions) in avoiding the behavioral excesses so often associated with big-time Division I programs.

The Ivy League has also avoided the worst forms of commercialization and has continued to regard expenditures on athletics as a proper charge against a school's general funds budget.

At the same time, the Ivies have not managed to prevent the development over time of the substantial academic-athletic divide documented in this study. The data in Chapters 4, 5, and 6 speak for themselves. It would be hard to claim that today's teams meet the first "proper condition" spelled out in the Original Ivy Agreement, namely, that they are to be "truly representative of the student body and not composed of a group of specially recruited athletes." Similarly, the heavy emphasis on recruitment today contradicts the notion that the Ivies would "encourage non-recruited athletes to earn places on our teams." More broadly, the Agreement states that "emphasis upon intercollegiate competition must be kept in harmony with the essential educational purposes of the institution." It is, at the least, debatable whether this overarching "condition" is satisfied today as fully as the founders intended it to be. The very fact that the Ivies compete in Division I of the NCAA (Division IAA in football) means that they are operating within an organizational structure shaped by a philosophy that is clearly at variance with their own. (See the full text of the Division I "Philosophy Statement" in the addendum to the introduction.)

THE NEW ENGLAND SMALL COLLEGE ATHLETIC CONFERENCE

President John Sawyer of Williams, the first chair of the NESCAC Presidents' Conference Committee when the Conference was founded in 1971, is credited with articulating the basic philosophy of the Conference in an oft-quoted one-sentence statement of objectives: "The largest feasible participation in a wide variety of sports well coached by high-quality people who remain genuinely interested in the students' personal growth and genuinely mindful of the educational goals of the enterprise."[11] Sawyer went on to suggest that there were three "checks" on adherence to this philosophy: prospective students would be "smart buyers" and would not participate in programs that did not have their best educational interests in mind; faculty would pay close attention to what was going on; and athletics would have to compete successfully for funding with other activities.

The internal reports recently released at Amherst, Middlebury, and Williams, which are cited frequently in this study, indicate the continuing involvement of faculty in assessing the health of the athletic program. Also, budgetary pressures are present everywhere. But only these two of Sawyer's three checks can be said to exist today. He was wrong in his assumption that student-athletes would themselves advocate, never mind "police," adherence to the original NESCAC philosophy. On the contrary, athletes at NESCAC colleges today strongly support many propositions that are directly contrary to Sawyer's thinking, including the importance of national championships and the need for organized out-of-season practice.[12] Sawyer and the other NESCAC presidents at the time did not anticipate, and probably could not have anticipated, the national trends that have produced the recruited athletes of today and that were, in some ways, to envelop both the Ivies and the NESCAC colleges.

One early conflict demonstrated that NESCAC could muster enforcement muscle when the need to do so was clear. Union College, one of the 11 original members of NESCAC, had a hockey coach and a hockey program interested in achieving national prominence. Accusations of recruiting violations kept recurring, and the NESCAC presidents saw no alternative to presenting Union with an ultimatum: "Remain in the conference and abide by *all* the principles and rules stated in the Agreement in *all* sports or leave." Subsequently, "it was decided by the Union Trustees and President that it would be in the best interest of the college to suspend its membership in NESCAC."[13] Union subsequently made inquiries about possible readmission but was turned down, as were a number of other institutions seeking admission. Connecticut College, however, petitioned for membership in 1982 and was accepted, bringing the number of NESCAC colleges back to 11.

Debates over Postseason Competition and the Regulation of Football

Without doubt, "the question of NESCAC team participation in NCAA Division III post-season competition is the issue which has provoked the most reviews and controversy in NESCAC history."[14] We reserve to Chapter 12 an examination of the pros and cons of postseason competition, and we have space here only to identify the main threads in this exceedingly complicated but revealing story. From the start, NESCAC permitted individuals to compete in national championships, but it precluded team participation. There were constant complaints of unfairness; for example, relay teams could not understand why they were denied this opportunity when individual runners could take part. The NESCAC presidents decided simply to accept this alleged inconsistency. They were also unmoved, at least for a time, by arguments that Division III (which did not exist when the initial NESCAC ban on postseason competition by teams was introduced in 1971) had a philosophy so similar to that of NESCAC that it would be possible to participate in Division III championships without any clash of principles.[15]

These arguments notwithstanding, the presidents decided in 1984 to continue NESCAC's traditional rejection of postseason competition by teams. But that decision by no means ended the debate. Pressure continued to mount, "coming to a head again in 1989 and 1990 with a letter-writing campaign from NESCAC coaches advocating a change." The coaches made a special point of arguing that postseason competition would help them greatly in recruiting. In 1990 the presidents mandated another year-long review of this issue and of related questions having to do with scheduling. In January of 1993, following further review, the Presidents' Executive Committee voted to allow NCAA team championship participation for a three-year experimental period beginning in the fall of 1993. This clear reversal of a "founding principle" appears to have been driven mainly by coaches and their worries about the effects of non-participation on the recruitment and morale of top athletes.[16] It was also justified in part by a desire to "showcase" NESCAC principles. One memo argued: "By participating in NCAA championships, NESCAC schools could demonstrate that institutions can sponsor nationally competitive athletics programs without sacrificing academic standards."[17] Large numbers of NESCAC teams participated in NCAA championships, and in 1996 the "experiment" was extended for another three years.

There were widely differing views among the NESCAC presidents on this (by now highly symbolic) issue, and there was a real risk that NESCAC would break up over it. There was a strong desire, however, to find some kind of common ground, and in 1998 a compromise was adopted. The presidents chose to "evolve into a qualified playing conference . . . (except football) . . . [and to] create appropriate mechanisms to determine a conference champion in all sports where it is practical." They also declared: "*We will allow only the conference champion to pursue post-season competition* [our emphasis] on one venue deemed appropriate—normally NCAA Division III."[18] This policy was scheduled to take effect in the fall of 2001.

Reaction from athletes to the one-school limitation was overwhelmingly negative. Forums were organized and student meetings held to protest this policy—which is related to the still broader issue of how the NCAA determines eligibility for its championships. In the NESCAC context, the obvious objection, which was raised by athletic directors and coaches as well as players, was that the one-school limit would exclude from postseason competition many teams in NESCAC that were among the best in Division III and therefore deserved a chance to compete.[19] The situation then changed in one major respect. At the time the NESCAC "compromise" was adopted, all conference champions did not automatically qualify for NCAA championships and there was considerable room for at-large qualifiers. In 1999 new selection principles were adopted by the NCAA that provided automatic qualification for all conference champions in all sports. Since field size was held constant, the opportunities for second- and third-place teams to qualify were sharply reduced. Thus it was no longer only NESCAC's own rule that limited championship opportunities for the NESCAC colleges. In part as a response to these new circumstances, the NESCAC college presidents have delayed, on a year-to-year basis, the implementation of the prohibition on accepting at-large invitations.[20]

The regulation of football has been troublesome for NESCAC from the very beginning. In this sport, and this sport alone, "the Presidents have adamantly remained true to the founding goal of prohibiting championships."[21] Even so, the intensity of play has continued to escalate, with growing squad sizes, pressures to add a ninth game, more aggressive recruiting, and serious worries about admissions policies. In December 1995 Robert Edwards, president of Bowdoin, prepared a report entitled "A Reflection about NESCAC Football: 1985–1994," in which he raised fundamental questions about where the sport of football was going and, more generally, about "competitive inequity" within NESCAC. In explaining why football is "special," Edwards observed: "It would be a mistake to underestimate the seductive power of winning football, still probably the largest and most visible campus sport." After producing a table showing changes in the average weight of linemen, Edwards went on to speculate "whether the changing character of the game itself—its emphases on uncommon strength, durability and speed—may be requiring more specialized physical types and self-selection at an earlier age." As a precursor to proposing that consideration be given to limiting squad sizes, Edwards noted that won-lost results in football had been very uneven in NESCAC. This observation led him to consider how the conference ought to view competitive balance. A related question was how to prevent traditional rivalries from taking on too much significance (note the Amherst Special Committee report, which bemoans the pervasive effects of the intense Amherst-Williams rivalry). Edwards used an African proverb, "When two elephants fight, the grass gets trampled," to call attention to the danger that rival schools may be "so intent on raising the competitive edge and taking each other out that they fail to notice that they have trampled the rest of the Conference."[22]

The NESCAC presidents took Edwards's report seriously, though they did not decide to limit squad size at that time.[23] But they did reject the proposal that they add a ninth game, and they began to consider a broader range of issues, including admissions practices. In the words of one commentator: "'Admissions' has become the most loaded word in current NESCAC conversations. It is often used to invoke an incomprehensible force which by definition does not tell the whole truth, and succumbs to all the societal influences NESCAC seeks to withstand. 'Admissions' loves overspecialized, unrepresentative athletes and active athletic recruitment, *especially if one is discussing the 'Admissions' of a rival institution* [our emphasis]. It is to be feared even more than football—in fact, it is entirely responsible for football, and has been insidiously feeding the growing competitiveness in NESCAC athletic programs."[24] Suspicions and lack of trust in what other schools are doing are problems in any setting. They certainly cut against the "reliance on mutual trust and confidence," achieved through informal ways of sharing information, which was another key principle at the founding of NESCAC. In today's world, there seems to be no avoiding a level of formal reporting and oversight that would have been unimaginable to President Sawyer and his colleagues in 1971. In 1999 the position of NESCAC conference coordinator was established.

Tensions Between Old Principles and Current Realities: Recent Actions

As we now look back on what has happened within NESCAC since its founding, there is no escaping the conclusion that it has failed to sustain its original emphasis on both avoiding national championships and ensuring that athletes are representative of their classes. Perhaps the original goals were impractical, or at least became impractical in the face of the broad currents in athletics that we describe in detail in the next chapter. It is, in any case, sobering to see that an idealistic conception of athletics as a part of education, imbedded in excellent colleges and supported by a series of able presidents, has fallen prey to the same pressures that have afflicted college sports generally. As our data make clear, *the academic-athletic divide is, without question, not just present but pronounced within NESCAC, as it is within the Ivies.* Recall, for example, that in the 1995 NESCAC entering cohorts 61 percent of male recruited athletes in the High Profile sports majored in the social sciences as compared with 36 percent of the other male students; that the average class rank of these athletes was in the 23rd percentile of the class; that 74 percent of them were in the bottom third of the class; and that they underperformed by an average of 20 percentile points.[25]

The far more heartening aspect of this history is that the NESCAC colleges have remained committed to each other and have used the mechanism of the conference to raise forthrightly fundamental questions about values and purposes that might have seemed out of place (if not downright odd) in most other settings in which athletic policy is discussed.[26] The 2001 "NESCAC Presidents' Statement on Athletic Review"

continues the tradition of hearkening back to first principles in that it begins by reaffirming a commitment "to establishing common boundaries
to keep athletics strong but in proportion to the overall mission of the
member institutions." The statement also repeats the NESCAC conviction that "students on intercollegiate teams are to be representative of the
overall student body" and publicly commits the presidents "to examine
our intercollegiate programs with the goal of assuring full conformity
with the core values of the Conference and our educational missions."[27]

In the fall of 2002, the NESCAC presidents adopted a formula for
limiting the number of "but for" athletic recruits (those who would not
have been admitted "but for" their athletic talents), and they also re-
emphasized their prohibition on any organized practice in the off-
season.[28] Moreover, as the discussion of reform proposals in Part C of
this study indicates, there is continuing discussion within NESCAC about
further ways to reduce the academic-athletic divide by working at both
national and conference levels. Perhaps the most important point is that
the NESCAC *presidents* have taken steps to reverse the direction in which
their athletic programs were taking them.

The question for the future is whether there are effective ways to arrest
the erosion that has taken place and set a different trajectory going forward. We believe that there are, and we believe as well that, in learning
from its history and seeking to address the real problems that exist today,
NESCAC can play a leadership role beyond its own boundaries.

THE UNIVERSITY ATHLETIC ASSOCIATION

The founding members of the newest of the three groupings of schools
that we study in detail, the University Athletic Association, had the advantage of being able, in the late 1980s, to observe the direction in which
big-time programs were moving and how these trends were affecting even
the Ivy League universities. They also had to address one highly practical
problem that was much more serious for them than for any of the other
sets of schools in this study: the costs, in dollars and time, of competing
across a broad geographical area.[29]

Implications of Scheduling Concerns for Costs and Competitive Alignments

The UAA universities' financially driven need to schedule carefully and
to be realistic about how much intra-association competition they could
afford meshed with an interest on the part of several members in retaining scheduling flexibility and continuing traditional ties to other schools

and even (in two cases in particular) to other conferences. The specific model adopted by the Association was a blend of round-robin competition and festival or championship competition. The UAA Bylaws required that, at a minimum, member institutions would compete annually in one round-robin sport for men, one round-robin sport for women, three festival-type sports for men, and three festival-type sports for women. This flexible policy allowed member institutions to determine their own levels of participation in the UAA.[30]

This pragmatic approach to scheduling led to manageable projections of travel costs that allowed the presidents to set aside the worry that finances alone would make the idea of the UAA unworkable.[31] At present, the yearly dollar costs of travel in the UAA average just over $500,000 per institution (around $27,500 per team). These are the *total* outlays for travel, not just the incremental travel costs resulting from current UAA scheduling, and are well within the range (in today's dollars) of the projections of *incremental* costs prepared more than 15 years ago. By way of comparison, travel costs in NESCAC average $335,000 per member institution per year (around $11,600 per team, because NESCAC schools sponsor many more teams).[32]

Quite apart from the dollars involved, extensive team travel has raised concerns about both the time commitment required and the possibility that the travel can reinforce the tendency of athletes to see more of one another and less of their classmates.[33] (Jay Oliva, former president of New York University, told us that some of the detractors of the UAA in Division III refer to it as "the airplane conference.") Nevertheless, team travel has permitted these leading universities to enjoy associations that would have been impossible had they chosen to compete only regionally.

Another concern throughout the life of the UAA has been achieving reasonable competitive equity. No conference (or association) wants one or two schools to win everything and another to be the perennial doormat. In this regard, as in others, the UAA has done reasonably well. Within six years of the formation of the Association, every school won a championship and every school had an athlete singled out as the best player in a given sport. This second measure, we should note, is a useful complement to the team measure, in that it allows excellent athletes—along with the universities they represent—to be recognized, even if they play on teams that do only so-so.[34]

Defections

Given this successful record of achieving goals set when the UAA was established, it is necessary to ask why one member, Johns Hopkins, left the

UAA entirely and another, the University of Rochester, will stop competing in the UAA in football in 2003 and has already withdrawn from UAA
competition in men's and women's indoor and outdoor track and field.
As best we can determine from conversations with a number of knowledgeable people, the answers are idiosyncratic. Hopkins was perceived by
the UAA as the most "marginally committed" of any member from the
start, as is reflected in the fact that Hopkins participated in only half of
the UAA-sponsored sports. Lacrosse (at the Division I level) has always
been paramount at Hopkins, and it is surmised that the university decided that competing within the UAA in other sports was just not worth
the cost. Hopkins continues to compete in the Centennial Conference.

Rochester is a different case. The new NCAA championship requirements may well have played an important role in leading Rochester to
conclude that its only realistic chance of qualifying for the NCAA Division
III football championships was to join a league that had enough members
to meet the NCAA criterion for automatic qualification. (The UAA does
not: seven is the NCAA minimum, and only five UAA universities, counting Rochester, play football.) This is a rather clear example of the way in
which NCAA rules affect conference affiliations. Rochester's decision to
cease participation in track and field may, in turn, have been driven by a
desire to reallocate dollars to the football program, which is now slated to
compete in the Upstate College Athletic Association.

In part as a consequence of these decisions by Hopkins and Rochester,
the UAA recently reconsidered how "flexible" it can be in allowing members to determine for themselves their degree of participation in the UAA.
At its April 2002 meeting, the presidents decided to "tighten up" somewhat, and from now on UAA universities will be required to participate in
at least seven sports for men and seven sports for women. Moreover, members must participate in two round-robin competitions in men's sports
and two round-robin competitions in women's sports (the previous requirement was one round-robin sport for men and one for women).
Furthermore, there is now a general expectation that every sport at a UAA
school will participate in UAA-sponsored competition. "Grandfathering"
arrangements have, however, been put in place to respect the situations
of the University of Chicago (which cannot participate in baseball without compromising its exam schedule) and the University of Rochester
(described earlier). We interpret these decisions by the UAA presidents
as reflecting a determination to give stability to the UAA while continuing to respect the special circumstances of founding members. A key question for the future is whether the UAA can attract a sufficient number of
members to sustain itself. The answer to this question could depend on
the outcome of discussions about new sub-divisions within the NCAA or
new entities outside it, which we consider in Chapter 13.[35]

Academic Outcomes: Why Has the UAA Done So Well?

The most basic question to be asked about the UAA is this: how has it managed to mount what is, by all signs, a successful intercollegiate program without paying the academic price that is so evident in the Ivy League and in NESCAC? To recapitulate results presented in detail in Chapters 5 and 6, we have found that:

- The "bunching" of majors in certain fields, so noticeable in both the Ivy League and NESCAC, is much less pronounced in the UAA.
- Overall, UAA athletes earn grades that are essentially the same as the grades earned by their classmates; only the football players do less well than other students, and the gap between their grades and the grades of other male students is much smaller than the corresponding gaps in the Ivies and in the NESCAC colleges.[36]
- In the UAA there is no significant academic underperformance by any group of athletes (again, with the possible exception of the football players), whereas underperformance is rampant among recruited athletes in the Ivy League and in NESCAC.[37]

In commenting on an early draft of this manuscript, Jonathan Cole, provost and dean of faculties at Columbia, observed: "One could use the [athletics programs at the] UAA schools *today* as a proxy for the Ivy League of *yesterday*" (while recognizing the very different histories of the two groups and without suggesting that the Ivies could or should return to some "golden past" that was far from ideal in many respects). One way of thinking about this comment is to ask to what extent the success of the UAA is mainly a product of its "newness" and whether in time it will come to resemble the Ivy League and NESCAC more closely. There are, as we have said, respects in which the "fresh start" of the UAA has helped produce the good academic results that we observe, and no one can rule out the possibility that an "aging" process will undermine what the Association has achieved. But we do not believe this is necessary or even very likely. There are other explanations for the present-day UAA success in balancing athletics and academics—in avoiding the "academic-athletic divide" that is so noticeable in other settings.

Of first importance is the clear determination of the UAA presidents to maintain a right sense of balance between academics and athletics and to put in place policies and practices that would sustain this balance. For example, from the beginning the presidents instructed the executive secretary of the UAA to monitor the academic *performance* of the athletes, not just their entering credentials. The active involvement of the University of Chicago, with its emphasis on core academic values, has without question been a help in achieving and maintaining this policy. At the same time, the UAA presidents have encouraged vigorous competition in sports—which has resulted in some success at the national level. However, although the UAA never tried to preclude national success, it has not emphasized it. Another critically important factor is that this guiding philosophy is shared by athletic directors and coaches (who seem to feel that they are more integral to the academic missions of their universities than do many coaches in different settings). In these key respects, the "mindset" within the UAA is the foundation on which all else has been built.

The translation of this mindset into the recruitment/admissions process has been, we think, of critical importance. Re-reading the discussions of recruitment and admissions in Chapters 2 and 3 reminds us that the UAA universities appear to have put strong emphasis on achieving a good "fit" between the programs of their institutions and the academic as well as athletic interests of their recruited athletes. The coaches have been aggressive recruiters (let there be no misunderstanding of this), but they have played much less of a *determining* role in admissions than has been the case at colleges and universities where "coaches' lists" are more consequential. We were told over and over that the coaches generally have little say over which of the prospective athletes they have identified will be admitted, and the fact that SAT distributions are so similar for recruited athletes and other students (see Figure 4.3b) seems to confirm this. Although we do not have direct measures of the advantage in admissions for athletes applying to the UAA universities (since we lack data on all applicants), it is highly unlikely that there has been a significant advantage, given the similar SAT distributions of matriculants. This is an important point because of the evidence presented in Chapter 6 showing that the degree of underperformance by recruited athletes at a given school is strongly correlated with the size of the admissions advantage enjoyed by recruited athletes at that school.

The percentages of admitted athletes who matriculate are also much lower in the UAA than elsewhere, which suggests that considerable self-selection by recruited students is going on and is affecting the patterns we observe. Recruited athletes who want a more intensive athletic experience may well turn down a UAA school for a scholarship-granting school or another school where athletics is more all-encompassing. In contrast, those students who want to go to the University of Chicago (to continue with that example) presumably know what kind of academic program they are choosing.

The operation of a UAA-type admissions process, in which coaches often give the admissions office long lists and do not expect the admissions office to defer to the exact rankings assigned by the coaches, is easier to manage in settings in which there are fewer recruited athletes in relation to the size of the student body. At small colleges that recruit for large numbers of varsity teams, admissions offices are naturally more concerned about the number of athletes proposed by coaches and are more inclined to give coaches "the athletes they really want" in exchange for tight controls on overall numbers. This is also the situation at many of the Ivies. The fact that recruited athletes comprise only about 6 percent of all students at the UAA institutions (7 percent of the men and 5 percent of the women) is obviously relevant.

It is probably also true, as a number of representatives of UAA universities suggested, that the relatively small number of recruited athletes, both absolutely and in relation to the size of the overall student body, diminishes the power of the kind of "athletic culture" that seems to be so much stronger at many NESCAC colleges and Ivy League universities. The absence of football at a number of the UAA institutions also makes a difference. William M. Chace, president of Emory, and Jay Oliva, former president of New York University, both told us emphatically that "no football helps a lot" or "no football is a huge plus." The athletic director at Emory, Chuck Gordon, added that "the culture of football could be contagious."[38] Having been at Wesleyan University before he went to Emory, Chace is in a position to compare the two situations: "The major difference is one of scale. The impact on the student body of the athletic program is much, much smaller at Emory because it does not field football and because it has a bigger student body [and also sponsors fewer varsity sports]. . . . At Wesleyan the athletes are more of a separate group, particularly culturally." Rigorous evidence is lacking, but qualitative accounts support the intuitively plausible idea that the extent to which there is an athletic culture affects underperformance.

The next factor to consider is the nature and intensity of athletic competition among the members of the various conferences and associations. There is no reason to believe that athletes at the UAA universities are any less interested in winning, or any less disappointed when they lose, than athletes anywhere else. Moreover, we know that the UAA universities have been successful in national competitions in some sports. Thus the UAA publication *Background Information, 2001–2002* contains this paragraph: "Teams throughout the UAA are perennial contenders for postseason play. In 2000–01, UAA teams were selected or qualified to compete in NCAA championship competition in men's and women's cross country, soccer, basketball, and tennis, as well as volleyball, baseball, softball, and golf. A UAA member team won [the Division III] national championship in women's basketball for the fourth consecutive year. In all, eleven UAA teams finished in the top ten in their national championships, and another nine finished in the top twenty."[39]

The most direct comparison for the UAA universities is with the NESCAC colleges, which also compete in Division III and have had even more success than the UAA universities in national competitions, despite their smaller size.[40] The differences in recruitment/admissions are, we suspect, at least part of the explanation. There may also be differences in expectations, at least in some sports. The UAA schools obviously care about national championships, but they have not made them an obsession. The head basketball coach at the University of Chicago, Mike McGrath, whose teams have done well in national competition, nonetheless told us emphatically that in his view: "National championships are not the 'be-all and end-all.'" He is much more focused on Association championships. The reason he does not want his students to focus on national championships is that he does not want them "to feel like failures if they do not get into the national championships." He added: "While we would love to win a national championship and we are striving for that, it is not a stated goal. I would like them to have aspirations that are challenging, but more readily achievable."

Differences in histories, in the expectations of alumni, and in competitive relationships within conferences and associations are also part of the story. McGrath told us that one reason intense competitive pressures are less of a problem in the UAA than in NESCAC or the Ivy League is because the UAA is so geographically dispersed: "We don't see ourselves as competing with each other every day in the way that Williams and Amherst do. There is just a different outlook." Close-knit conferences or leagues are more subject to "ratcheting" effects than is the UAA. When Williams has great success and keeps winning the Sears Cup, the bar is raised for everyone in NESCAC, and certainly for Amherst.

Hunter Rawlings, president of Cornell, says candidly that the exceptional successes in national competitions of Princeton (especially) and Harvard, and some of the other Ivies in particular sports, inevitably increase the pressure on recruitment and admissions all through the league. "Natural rivalries," heralded as a wonderful thing, can be engines of escalation. There is a case to be made for "looser" structures, or at least for structures in which winning and losing to particular schools is less consequential.

The final point to be made is that alumni exert quite different amounts of pressure in the various settings with which we are concerned here. Harold Shapiro, who was president of the University of Michigan and then president of Princeton, remarked that he spent far more time at Princeton on athletics than he ever spent at Michigan. Morton Schapiro, president of Williams, who has been forthright in acknowledging issues in NESCAC and at Williams that need to be addressed, is highly cognizant of the strong feelings among Williams alumni. In sharp contrast, Jay Oliva at New York University told us that he "gets no letters from alums or donors about athletics." "Athletics is fun," he said, "but not more than that." He added: "If for some reason NYU were to go back to Division I basketball, there would be a huge uproar from the faculty among others. The faculty would think the powers that be at NYU had gone insane— and the faculty would be right."

We have spent this much time on the history and characteristics of the UAA because the outcomes it has achieved are so very different from those at other schools in the study. Thus far, at any rate, the realities within the UAA comport with the principles enunciated at its founding, and there is little, if any, evidence of an academic-athletic divide. We do not mean to suggest that the UAA model is fully exportable. It may not be, certainly in its detail, but it is instructive nonetheless. At one important level, it represents a philosophy that many will applaud. At another level, the success of the UAA in blending academics and athletics is a product of a distinct set of circumstances and histories. For example, it is relevant that Warren Candler, president of Emory in the late 1800s, "established a firm policy against intercollegiate games."[41] Similarly, the University of Chicago and New York University, in very different ways, had "experienced" big-time sports and decided that they were better suited to another approach. There was no Division I nostalgia to tempt them.

LIBERAL ARTS COLLEGES OUTSIDE NESCAC

From the standpoint of having neighboring institutions with which they can compete comfortably in sports, geography has been kind to some of the liberal arts colleges in this study and unkind to others. History has located some of them in parts of the country—especially the Northeast, the Atlantic region, and parts of the Midwest—where there are a number of nearby liberal arts colleges of similar size, with similar aspirations. Others, such as Carleton and Macalester in Minnesota and Pomona in California, are more isolated. The search for suitable opponents is common to all, but it is a much more daunting task for a Minnesota college like Macalester than for an Ohio college like Oberlin or an Eastern college like Smith or Swarthmore—although the Kenyons and the Swarthmores have had scheduling problems, too, especially in football, and the women's colleges have conference-related issues that are in some ways peculiar to them.

The recent reviews of football programs at Macalester and Swarthmore illustrate well the tensions that a particular conference affiliation can create, and we return to these experiences in Chapter 12. The essential conclusion relevant to this discussion is that not even these leading colleges, with their less intensive athletics programs, have avoided the academic consequences of playing an ever more specialized sport that requires the recruitment of large numbers of players with special talents. This endemic problem is exacerbated when the college's conference includes schools able to field much deeper and stronger teams—such as football powers Allegheny in the North Coast Athletic Conference and St. John's in the Minnesota Intercollegiate Athletic Conference. "Uneven" conference alignments can clearly increase the pressure to allow a greater academic-athletic divide. But the NESCAC data remind us that colleges playing in closely knit conferences are subject to the same forces and are hardly immune from the nationwide trends within athletics described in the next chapter.

The women's colleges do not have the problems associated with football, but they face issues of their own that relate in part to the conferences in which they compete. Bryn Mawr is an interesting case in point. It competes in the Centennial Conference, which includes Dickinson, Franklin and Marshall, Gettysburg, Haverford, Johns Hopkins, McDaniel (formerly Western Maryland), Muhlenberg, Swarthmore, Ursinus, and Washington College. Bryn Mawr's main concerns with the Centennial Conference have to do partly with scheduling and partly with attitude. As Karen Tidmarsh, dean of the college, explained: "Bryn Mawr is the only women's college in the Centennial Conference. There have been times when the conference schedule has led to a feeling of marginalization among the players and coaches in those sports where there has been a desire to schedule men's and women's teams together. Lacking men's teams, we were asked to play with less rest between games and more frequently on Mondays, requiring Sunday practice, than were other schools."

There is also a more general problem related to differences in values and perspectives. According to Tidmarsh: "The Centennial Conference was founded on the idea that athletics came after academics, but the interpretation of this varies by school." Amy Campbell, Bryn Mawr's athletic director, believes that "the Centennial Conference has a strong history and mission which prioritizes the academic/athletic enterprise, but as institutions respond to changing priorities and pressures and the opportunities for national athletic recognition increase, the competitive gap among the schools has widened." Bryn Mawr, Haverford, and Swarthmore tend to view these issues very similarly and to vote together on issues that affect academic quality and reflect the increased specialization of sports programs. Campbell's straightforward conclusion is that "it makes sense to align with schools that have the same academic and athletic philosophy." But there are not always that many options.

Smith was strong in the New England Women's and Men's Athletic Conference (NEWMAC) until the mid- to late 1980s. Since then it has slipped in the standings, as other members have begun to recruit athletes much more aggressively. Smith is now taking steps to improve its program (doing more recruiting, raising money from friends groups, and so on).

Many of the pressures it faces can be traced to the growing competitiveness of women's teams at coed colleges, where Title IX, among other forces, has caused women's athletics to take on more and more of the characteristics of men's athletics. It is not a coincidence that the decline in the competitive fortunes of a college such as Smith came on the heels of the upgrading of women's athletics in, for example, the NESCAC colleges. This is an excellent example of how the "competitive dynamic" causes patterns in one set of schools to spread to others. Being in a conference such as NEWMAC makes invidious comparisons all too visible.

It is hard for us to judge to what extent the avowed increase in recruiting in the women's colleges has already created, or will create, an academic-athletic divide similar to what we see in many other settings. Our lack of data on recruited athletes at the women's colleges prevents the kinds of direct statistical comparisons that would help answer this question. But we do know that athletes in the 1995 entering cohorts at several of the women's colleges (those who were recruited and the walk-ons) had lost the academic "edge" over their classmates that athletes at these colleges enjoyed historically; the athletes in the '95 entering cohorts, unlike their predecessors in the '89 and '76 entering cohorts, showed evidence of underperformance (Chapters 5 and 6). It would be surprising if, over time, the national trends affecting all colleges and universities did not cause an academic-athletic divide, of at least modest size, to appear in these colleges as well as others. In the absence of broad changes in direction, it will be difficult for any set of schools that competes outside a tightly defined orbit to isolate itself from the all-too-real competitive pressures that are everywhere evident.

———————

Over histories that span decades, conferences have served various functions. Originally they were concerned mainly with defining eligibility and playing rules. The focus was on achieving "level playing fields" and completive balance. The emphasis then shifted to helping member schools manage what Rasmussen calls "the growing dichotomy between the academic mission of the institution and the pursuit of national prominence through athletic success." More recently, many conferences have focused on revenue generation. As Gordon White put it 20 years ago, "The moral seems to be: join a conference and make money; stay out of a conference and you better be as good as Notre Dame to keep your head above water."[42]

The conferences, leagues, and associations to which the colleges and universities in this study belong are all exceptions to White's generalization, since, whatever their idiosyncrasies, none is out to "make money." Our interest is in the question of whether, on balance, these conferences have retarded or accelerated the widening of the academic-athletic divide. Are they mere conduits for large societal forces, or do they (can they) exert independent effects? It is impossible to answer this question definitively, because so many powerful forces have been operating concurrently. But it seems that being a part of these groupings is both a help and a hindrance.

What can be said is, first, that founding principles matter greatly. The presidents of the Ivies and the NESCAC colleges are well aware of what their predecessors set out to do, and both groups of presidents are asking how they might move back in the direction of original commitments. No one could claim that these two conferences have succeeded in adhering to all of their founding principles, especially the principle of "representativeness"—or, as the Ivy Agreement put it, the "required condition" that "the players shall be truly representative of the student body and not composed of a group of specially recruited athletes." Nor have either the Ivies or the NESCAC colleges eschewed "national championships" or interest in national rankings, as the NESCAC founding principles called on its members to do. Still, the presidents of these colleges and universities are keenly aware of these tensions and are contemplating how best to address them in the present context. Insofar as they focus attention on founding principles, these conference mechanisms serve to retard the continuing widening of the academic-athletic divide. In the absence of these conference structures, established as they were in the 1950s and 1970s, it would be even harder for such highly competitive schools to stand against the forces that have steadily widened the academic-athletic divide—on their own campuses, as well as within higher education generally.

The UAA is an example of a conference that has succeeded in large part (remembering always that football is at least a partial exception) in being both athletically competitive and faithful to its stated principles of "representativeness" and "academics first." The UAA has been helped by the absence of intense rivalries among "close cousins" that so easily leads to a steady ratcheting up of the pressure to do what is necessary to meet the competition. The coed liberal arts colleges outside NESCAC, which also show smaller academic-athletic divides (excepting, yet again, football) have benefited in similar ways from the absence of the ratcheting effects that can follow from the exceptional success of a Princeton or a Williams in settings in which their principal rivals are keenly attuned to where each stands in the proverbial pecking order.

Reflecting on just these questions led Michael McPherson, who was at Williams before going to Macalester as its president, to wonder about the advantages of "floating conferences" in which schools might play different sets of opponents in different sports. It may not be best to play the same schools in everything, an arrangement almost certain to make it abundantly clear who is first, who is second—and who is last. At the same time, Macalester's own experience in football (see Chapter 12) vividly illustrates that it is also unhealthy to be compelled to play schools very different from your own. The ideal situation may be one in which a school competes with other schools that are similar in mission and philosophy, but does not have to compete every day in every sport with those schools that are its principal competitors in all other respects. There is much to be said for crafting orbits of competition that will encourage a certain degree of "murkiness" in outcomes; fine-grained hierarchies are problematic.

Tracing developments at the conference level helps to explain much of what has happened to the athletics programs at the schools in our study, and the lessons learned from these histories are invaluable in any attempt to envision an improved set of competitive structures. However, the conference story itself has to be seen within a still larger context. In the next chapter we broaden our perspective by examining the systemic forces within athletics—at both intercollegiate and pre-collegiate levels—that have had such pronounced effects on the athletics programs of conferences and their member institutions.

CHAPTER 8

The Widening Athletic Divide

THE CHANGES that have taken place in the conferences over their histories have undoubtedly had an impact on the athletic divide—which, to repeat, we define in terms of characteristics such as lower rank-in-class, "bunching" in certain majors, and social self-segregation that distinguish recruited athletes from students at large. But, in larger measure, the drifting from principles such as "representativeness" that has occurred most noticeably within the Ivy League and the New England Small College Athletic Conference (NESCAC) is the result of broader, deeper forces operating nationally. In this chapter we examine these forces in some detail, since it is important to understand why the "athletic divide" has become so pronounced on many of the campuses we are studying. First, however, we briefly review the extent of the divide and its "newness."

THE ATHLETIC DIVIDE TODAY

The athletic divide is seen most clearly in its academic manifestations. In choosing courses, athletes are much more likely to "bunch" in certain fields of study than are students at large. Also, we have shown that recruited athletes as a group do appreciably less well academically than their classmates. To recall just two statistics from Chapter 5, *over 80 percent* of recruited athletes playing High Profile sports in the Ivies graduate in the bottom third of their class, and these athletes are *one-tenth* as likely as their classmates to graduate with Phi Beta Kappa honors. An even more important finding (Chapter 6) is that differences in academic outcomes cannot be explained just in terms of differences in test scores and high school grades. Recruited athletes systematically "underperform" academically: they end up with lower grades than other students (walk-on athletes as well as students at large) who are similar in other respects— who have the same test scores, major in the same fields, and so on. Moreover, this tendency to underperform transcends the effects of the heavy time commitments associated with competing on varsity teams. In essentially all respects, then, recruited athletes on many of these campuses differ markedly from their classmates in the uses that they make of their academic opportunities.

But it is not only in terms of academic outcomes that recruited athletes are a "class apart" on many of these campuses. There is also evidence of a definite "athletic culture" (Chapter 4). The Amherst Special Committee report provides a vivid description of how other students see the situation: "The athletic/non-athletic division becomes, in the words of one commentator, the 'great social divide' at Amherst. . . . Several members of the faculty concurred that the division between athletes and non-athletes is *the* 'great divide' on campus."[1] At the same time, looking across the "divide" from the perspective of the athletes, this time at Williams, "almost half of varsity athletes . . . claim to experience discrimination 'sometimes' or 'often' from faculty in class."[2] An entire section of the Amherst report is devoted to "stigma and demoralization" among athletes.[3] So the existence of a divide is evident in the experiences and perceptions of both athletes and non-athletes—which makes it all the more real, and all the more consequential.

Amherst and Williams are, in many respects, special cases. They are small, highly selective colleges that historically have placed a heavy emphasis on athletics and have had, especially in the case of Williams, extraordinary success competitively. Still, the same issues presented so clearly and openly by the committees charged with studying athletics at these two colleges are present, in greater or lesser degree, at the large majority of other schools in our study, including some of the universities (recall the testimony of a former master of Rockefeller College at Princeton, reported in Chapter 4).[4]

The division between the athletic and academic sides of these colleges and universities is shaped, then, by both the academic profiles of the athletes and the kind of "athletic culture" that grows out of social interactions on campus. But it is not only students who create and define the athletic divide. It is also created and defined in the present-day relationship between coaches and the rest of the campus community—as well as in the steadily improving academic profiles of these institutions (discussed in Chapter 9). Richard Rasmussen, executive director of the University Athletic Association (UAA), speaks of the "decline of the 'physical educator-coach' and the evolution of the 'apprentice-coach'"[5]—who has a much narrower focus on his or her sport (a phenomenon that is discussed in detail later in this chapter).

It is hardly surprising that the newer type of coach is less caught up in the overall life of the college or university than his or her predecessors were. Coaches are separated from the faculty to a greater degree than used to be the case. A recent story in the *Chronicle of Higher Education* noted this reality even in the setting of small colleges that have much more modest athletic aspirations than the NESCAC schools: "On college campuses, professors and coaches walk across the same lawns and eat the same cafeteria food. They interact with the same students, but not often with each other. Coaches typically shun highfalutin academic presentations, and professors hardly ever attend superfluous athletic events—unless the team is good and they happen to be fans. The segregation arises from a culture clash that has made those in the academic and athletics worlds forget that whether they are teaching students how to throw a softball or analyze an ancient Greek text, they are doing the same thing."[6]

The attitudes of many coaches today toward "their players" have contributed to the athletic divide in another way. As Robert Malekoff writes from the perspective of his experiences as a coach and athletics administrator at a number of institutions: "Some coaches who have spent a tremendous amount of energy recruiting a student believe that this represents a kind of 'ownership' of their (the athlete's) time."[7] In his article on athletics at Harvard, Lambert observes: "The recruiting dynamic itself can also *segregate athletes* [our emphasis] and apply a lingering pressure on them after they matriculate."[8]

The resulting athletic divide is all too evident—and troubling—to many, especially those who think back on times when athletes were more like other students and when both athletes and their coaches were more integrated into the overall campus community.

EARLIER DAYS

We cannot date with anything approaching precision when this athletic-academic "divide" first became noticeable at the colleges and universities in this study. But both the data analyzed in *The Game of Life* and much testimony indicate that it did not exist in any marked degree in the mid-1950s. Academic measures are easier to chart than social-cultural patterns, and they provide some temporal markers. In the Ivies, the typical male athlete in the 1951 entering cohort had a cumulative grade point average (GPA) that placed him precisely in the middle of his class; in the coed liberal arts colleges, the typical male athlete actually ranked slightly higher than the average male student at large. There was no concentration of athletes in the social sciences in those days (in the Ivies, for instance, 21 percent of the athletes and 22 percent of the students at large majored in these fields).[9] Women's intercollegiate athletics programs were so limited in the 1950s that it was not even possible to gather data for women athletes at the coed institutions (and of course many of the Ivies and some of the NESCAC colleges were still all-male schools). Athletes in the 1950s were as likely as other students—perhaps more likely—to be campus leaders, not just team captains, and many of these former athletes went on to become prominent in their professions and key trustees of many of these schools. Their own positive experiences as athletes *and as students* on these campuses in earlier days can sometimes make it difficult for them to realize how much has changed.

By the late 1970s, when members of the 1976 entering cohort were enrolled, the picture was different. In the High Profile sports, in particular, gaps in academic performance were evident, and athletes were appreciably more concentrated than other students in certain fields of study (especially the social sciences).[10] Gaps in academic performance were also found among male athletes playing the Lower Profile sports, though they were smaller then, as they are today, than the gaps associated with athletes playing the High Profile sports. Women identified as athletes were now present in large numbers. However, they were indistinguishable from women students at large in their academic performance, and in this important respect they resembled the male athletes of the 1950s.

In the early 1990s, when members of the 1989 entering cohort were in school, the athletic divide was more pronounced. The academic performance of men who played both the High Profile and the Lower Profile sports was appreciably weaker than the performance of male students at large. Whereas women in the '76 entering cohort had done as well academically as other women, women athletes in the Ivies, in particular, now fell short of the standard set by their female classmates.

As we have shown, the academic outcomes for athletes in the '95 entering cohort (and especially for the recruited athletes, a category we cannot single out in earlier cohorts) have departed substantially from school-wide norms. The much more complete coverage of schools in the data for the '95 cohort, with all of the Ivies and all of the NESCAC colleges represented, makes it clear that, institutionally, there are "no outliers" today, whatever may have been the case in earlier periods. In addition, there is, for the first time, a gap in graduation rates between High Profile athletes and students at large in the Ivies. Finally, women athletes from the '95 entering cohort in both the coed liberal arts colleges and the women's colleges show—also for the first time—the beginnings of the problem of underperformance that initially appeared only among Ivy League women athletes in the '89 cohort.

The "drift" seems abundantly clear, and it is probably less important to try to date precisely when it started to appear (especially since the answer is sure to differ by type of sport, by gender, and by conference) than it is to recognize the unmistakable direction of movement. The Williams Ad Hoc Committee report calls attention to the importance of these "larger trajectories": "It is critically important for us to be at least conscious of the larger picture. To the extent that we make policy decisions solely on the basis of keeping up with or ahead of our comparison schools, such trends will clearly continue, and—and this is the key point—they will continue blindly."[11]

FORCES WIDENING THE DIVIDE FROM WITHIN ATHLETICS

We identify four developments within athletics that have widened the divide: the increased specialization on the part of the athletes, the professionalization/specialization of coaching, the growing allure of national championships, and some of the associated (albeit unintended) consequences of the interactions of Title IX with these trends.

Specialization among Athletes

Without question the increased specialization of athletes, starting from very young ages, has been one of the most important "drivers" of athletic intensity at the collegiate level. Jeff Orleans, executive director of the Ivy League, put it succinctly when he told us: "A lot of what has gone on [in college sports] is tied into major cultural changes. Particularly, athletes in high school and at even earlier ages increasingly see themselves as highly specialized and as wanting to compete in a single sport all year. They bring this mindset with them to college. Any college that does not offer them opportunities runs the risk of losing them."

Every one of the authors of the papers we commissioned emphasizes the extent to which sports specialization has affected every aspect of intercollegiate competition. Herewith, by way of recapitulation, two representative comments:

> *Amy Campbell, Bryn Mawr:* Time involved in sports before college has increased and become much more formal and structured. Sport structures more and more serve as marshalling agents, identifying and grooming the best athletes in a sport, training them year round, providing a significantly higher level of competition which enables the athletes to be noticed by college coaches or governing body coaches. Ultimately they hope to play on an intercollegiate team, on a US team, or professionally. This specialization has helped to re-enforce a sport culture at the collegiate level that is more intense, more specialized and more demanding than the programs of 15–20 years ago.[12]

> *John Biddiscombe, Wesleyan University:* Today, children are exposed to organized athletics at a very early age. Parents guide them into sports that have high visibility, or are the ones that they played in college. Frequently parents anticipate that sports will be a positive factor in their child's college admissions status or will provide a means to an athletic scholarship. Many parents

not only introduce their children to sports, but also become their personal coach. They arrange for the child to play the sport year around, get sophisticated coaching, and play on very competitive club travel teams. Club coaches are paid by the parents and, therefore, cater to the parents' expectations. The coaches justify their existence by arranging for more games and longer seasons. As well, the children are pressured to specialize in one sport by parents and coaches and as early as sixth grade the children begin to think of themselves as sports specialists.[13]

In light of this "sea change" in the way people think about sports, it is not surprising that recruiting practices at the college level have migrated to the secondary school level. After twice having its recruiting rules challenged before the U.S. Supreme Court, the Tennessee Secondary Schools Athletic Association (TSSAA) is engaged in a third lawsuit with Brentwood Academy, a private school that is a member of the TSSAA. Brentwood is challenging the validity of a TSSAA rule that bars high schools from recruiting junior high school students for athletic purposes.[14]

A CNN story titled "Toddler Athletes a Growing Trend" begins with this vignette: "Nicholas is trying to rush the net, but the net's a little taller than he is. Tatiana has her racket in the right position, but unfortunately she's looking at her father, not the ball, when it whizzes past her. And Noah might actually be able to hit the ball if he would only face forward instead of backward." The story goes on to say: "These tennis players are between two and three years old. They are part of the 'downward creep' in sports which has children playing organized sports at ages when their parents were still in sandboxes." One mother is quoted as saying that the competition, starting at age three, is a necessity: "I think you have an edge starting at three with all her [the daughter's] friends starting at four and five. It seems that it's gotten so competitive in this area that you have to start them younger. . . . We have her playing tennis every day now. She hits about 70 balls over the net. So maybe one day she'll be the next Venus or Serena, we're hoping."[15]

In reflecting on these same developments, one coach and athletic director with whom we spoke ties them directly into coaching requirements at the college level (our next topic): "Today's society breeds an environment in which parents and zealous coaches persuade children at earlier and earlier ages to specialize in one particular sport. . . . The athletes we admit come with high expectations in terms of continuing to develop their athletic skills and have been taught by much more advanced coaches than children in the 1960s. . . . Generally, today's student athletes are more sophisticated athletically and we must work harder to find them coaches capable of providing a satisfactory experience for them."

The Professionalization/Specialization of College Coaching

College coaching has become highly professionalized.[16] Specialist athletes require specialist coaches. The days are over when many college coaches, especially at Division III schools, either come from the regular faculty or have physical education backgrounds and see themselves as generalists, with a broad responsibility for "educating."[17] One current director of athletics, who spoke candidly with us on the condition that we report his comments anonymously, said that in his view "we need to return to a basic commitment to educational values." He bemoaned the fact that "fewer and fewer coaches have a real interest in education as broadly defined. . . . Not many have a background in educational methodology, and more and more of them are focused just on their own sport." Peter Slovenski, head coach of track and field at Bowdoin College, believes that "college athletics had far fewer excesses when teams were coached by faculty members hired into the department of physical education." In his view, "abolishing the physical education requirement left the business open to a new generation of coaches whose qualifications are evaluated by how well they will create winning teams with a small cadre of student-athletes rather than how they will teach college classes to the entire student body."[18]

We cannot assess the overall effects of reducing or eliminating physical education requirements (which obviously have to be judged according to a variety of considerations, including the demands placed on students by today's faculty). But we can report that several coaches we interviewed at the University of Chicago, which has maintained a phys-ed teaching requirement, reported that they enjoy their phys-ed classes in part because that experience allows them to get to know "the full range of students" at the university. Participation in the phys-ed program seems to engender a sense that athletics remains a part of the larger educational enterprise. Similar expressions of support for a phys-ed teaching requirement were voiced at MIT. Commenting from another perspective, Amy Campbell said that coaches' job descriptions changed in the early 1990s to give coaches more time to meet the increased demands of recruiting and practice during the non-traditional season. While this change better served the intercollegiate programs and met the needs of coaches who were more specialized in a particular sport, it also served to remove coaches from interactions with other students through the school's physical education/recreation offerings.

Nonetheless, phys-ed requirements are on the wane, so there is less need for coaches to teach these classes.[19] At the same time, the part-time head coach and the dual-sport coach are increasingly rare. One athletic director speaks from personal experience in describing the evolution of coaching responsibilities: "While coaching during the 1960s and 1970s, I was able to be a part-time coach and also maintain my position as a business professional. This situation became more difficult through the 1980s and it became apparent that a change needed to be made. When we hired my replacement in the 1990s it became a full-time position. Today, the complexity, competition, and demands of coaching are such that our head coaches increasingly depend on competent and more fully available assistants."

Amy Campbell also relies on her personal experiences at a variety of schools to describe the evolution of coaching in women's sports:

> As a new physical education teacher and coach at an independent school in the mid-70s I was assigned to coach both the varsity and junior varsity field hockey teams. No assistant, no additional practice time, just 30–35 girls with the ability difference from rank beginner to some who had gone to sports camps and were terrific athletes. This meant coaching the offense, the defense and the goalkeepers, trying to keep everyone busy, learning and becoming better players. This also meant coaching to the "mean"—coaching, teaching to the point where most all of the group was challenged. It meant more time with the less gifted to bring their skills up to the mean level and less time with the talented. While this proved to be the most efficient way to coach a large number of students with a broad range of skills and the need to learn the multiple disciplines of the game, it also meant an average or below average opportunity for the more gifted athletes to excel. Luckily, most teams were coached that way but the competitive balance shifted quickly and measurably when schools began hiring specialized coaches.[20]

Malekoff explains that, due primarily to specialization, recruiting demands, and pressure to win, "the two-sport coach is fast becoming the exception"—even in Division III. He goes on to point out:

> While some head coaches still serve as an assistant coach in another sport, we [at the College of Wooster] employ more full-time assistant coaches and full-time assistant coach interns than ever before. . . . Whereas Division III athletic departments once were staffed by "professional physical educators" who were accustomed to coaching a number of different sports and activities, today's coaches do not have such expectations. There was a time when Wooster's head men's basketball coach also led the men's tennis team despite a limited background in that sport. As late as 1993, our women's basketball coach coached the women's tennis team, our men's soccer coach coached the men's golf team, and our field hockey coach coached the women's lacrosse team. The two assistant football coaches served as head coaches of two spring sports—baseball and men's lacrosse. Today, six different coaches coach these six sports and the football team has two full-time as-

sistant coaches and two full-time intern assistants—none of whom have any
head coaching responsibilities.[21]

John Biddiscombe, writing from the perspective of Wesleyan University, paints the same picture, but in even brighter colors because of the
larger scale of the athletic enterprise in the NESCAC colleges than in
most of the coed liberal arts colleges, such as Wooster, that compete outside it: "Today, most college coaches do not come with professional
coaching training. Rather their coaching experience and philosophy is
only derived from being a player and from their early experiences as assistant coaches. . . . Today it is rare to find a person interested and/or
qualified to be a head coach in more than one sport. Also, today's Division III athlete is very skeptical of coaches lacking extensive experience
in a sport and often demand that their colleges hire coaches that are
[one-sport] specialists."[22]

This last sentence highlights one of the four recurring themes in the
comments we have read and heard about the factors responsible for an
ever more specialized (and "professional") coaching contingent. In brief:

1. Colleges and universities feel intense pressure to have coaching
   staffs that are able to meet the much higher expectations of today's
   recruited athletes for superior, specialized coaching (and instruction in skill enhancement) on a year-round basis. According to
   Malekoff: "Students who have specialized in one sport throughout
   high school do not want to be coached by someone who has a
   limited background in that sport."[23] From the coach's side of the
   conversation, Richard Rasmussen believes: "There is [today] an aspir-
   ation within the coaching profession [and he speaks from the
   perspective of a Division III coach and administrator] to the Division I model insofar as what is required for effective on-the-field
   coaching—that is to say 'I want to coach at a higher level of sophis-
   tication in my program' and that requires more coaches spending
   more time on the field with smaller numbers of athletes."[24] It has
   become essential to recruit a coaching staff with specialists "within
   sports" as well as by sports.[25]

2. As we showed in Chapter 2, the extraordinary increase in the emphasis placed on recruiting (an all-consuming pursuit in many programs today) has had profound effects on the lives of coaches and
   on the time they have available to do anything else. As Biddiscombe
   says: "Today the competitive nature of recruiting and the time it
   takes to recruit talented student-athletes makes it very difficult to recruit for two sports [at a Division III college like Wesleyan]."[26] As
   one experienced athletic administrator put it: "Recruiting has become every coach's second and third sport."[27]

3. The administrative and fundraising sides of coaching have become more complex and demanding. Rasmussen speaks in terms of the shift toward "the coach-administrator," and another athletic administrator has provided a lengthy list of activities and responsibilities that now fall on the coach. These include "issues and attendant paperwork due to the onset of compliance [with NCAA and other regulations]"; the need to be prepared to deal with a host of liability issues ranging from harassment to gambling to performance enhancing drugs; and safety and first-aid responsibilities. In addition, in the Ivy League in particular, there is more pressure "on the coaching staff to work with the Friends Groups to raise money."

4. Finally, we have been told over and over that, as Malekoff put it: "Increased pressure to win—and consequently to recruit successfully—has dramatically changed the life of the Division III coach. . . . Certainly more Division III coaches lose their jobs today because of a lack of competitive success than they did 15 to 20 years ago. . . . The Division I phenomenon of rewarding coaches who win and effectively punishing (by firing) coaches who don't win is more prevalent at the Division III level than ever before, particularly in the 'major' sports."[28] Irv Cross, the director of athletics at Macalester and a one-time defensive back for the Philadelphia Eagles, speaks eloquently about the "loss of balance" and about an obsession with won-lost records to the virtual exclusion of concern for the educational value of good coaching.

This combination of pressures has led, inescapably, to large numbers of full-time and part-time coaches, and also to what Rasmussen calls "a proliferation of part-time / volunteer assistant coaches who volunteer their time with no remuneration or who receive a very modest stipend."[29] The sheer size of the present-day coaching establishment is noteworthy: the number of full-time-equivalent coaches of men's and women's teams is, on average, about 60 in the Ivies and 25 in the NESCAC colleges—and these numbers do not always capture all of the "stipend/intern" coaches.[30]

Moreover, there are other specialized contributors to the athletics program. As one athletic director points out: "The current athletic environment requires strength training (a concept not in vogue 20 years ago) and individual skill work outside of the regular season." Nor is this just a Division I perspective: "Any Division III college that wants to field competitive teams has a full-time person responsible for strength training and fitness."[31] A recent article in the Wesleyan University alumni magazine brings to life the importance now attached to weight training and conditioning in general. The coach of the women's basketball team, Kate Mullen, reports: "The pre-frosh [who play women's basketball] weight train in high school, which was unheard of even just five years ago. They're playing year-round; they're playing AAU [Amateur Athletic Union] basketball, and they're also playing on their high school team summer league. . . . If you don't have a year-round program, high school students think you're not serious. . . . In the pre-season we do lifting, the kids run sprints twice a week, and they play together a few times a week. I never have to nag recruits about weight lifting. They get a look in their eyes; that's what they want."[32]

The financial cost to the institution of this level of commitment to intercollegiate athletics is discussed in Chapter 10. Here the point we wish to stress is that the shift in the character and thrust of athletics programs has been reflected dramatically in the *kinds* of coaches hired as well as in their numbers. The quality of play has certainly improved—as a result of higher skill levels at the time students enter college, more sophisticated coaching and training in college, and greater intensity and focus—and it would be unfair in the extreme to criticize these coaches (and players) for doing what they have been asked to do. But the combination of the specialized athlete and the specialized coach, both focused intensely on "their special role within their sport" and lacking much time (and, in some cases, much inclination) to pursue a broad range of activities, has contributed mightily to the athletic divide. Improved quality of play has come at a price.

The Allure of National Championships

The greatly increased importance of national championships is a third force from within athletics that has had a major impact on college sports. "March Madness" is the signature example within Division I, but it is not only in big-time basketball, and not only in Division I, that national championships have become measuring rods. In the words of some Division III athletic directors and administrators:

> *Robert Malekoff, director of physical education, athletics, and recreation, Wooster:* While the emphasis in Division III was once on conference championships, today some coaches and athletes view conference competition as little more than a means to an invitation to the NCAA tournament.[33]

> *Richard Rasmussen, executive director, UAA:* Where the baseline measure of success was once a winning season, it is now qualification for post-season play.[34]

> *Amy Campbell, director of athletics and physical education, Bryn Mawr:* Post-season bids have become the yardstick for identifying success.[35]

The carefully structured NCAA national championships as we know them today, organized mainly by division but also with some "national collegiate championships" open to schools from all divisions, are of relatively recent origin—even though the idea of the national championship predates the founding of the NCAA itself. The oldest intercollegiate championship is said to be the National Tennis Collegiate Championships, which were "first conducted in 1883 when Trinity College (Connecticut) hosted a tournament sponsored by the U.S. Lawn Tennis Association and held on the grounds of an insane asylum."[36] But the first "true" national collegiate championship (with a broader field of entrants) was an outdoor track and field meet that took place in 1921 at Stagg Field at the University of Chicago. (Recall from Chapter 2 that this meet was part of Coach Stagg's recruitment program for his football team.) Next came championships in swimming and diving (1924) and in wrestling (1928). Anticipating future developments, the committee that organized the swimming championships restricted eligibility to first-place winners in the various conferences and swimming leagues. Other championships were initiated in the late 1930s (in boxing, gymnastics, cross country, and basketball). Baseball, ice hockey, and tennis competitions were established under the auspices of the NCAA in the 1940s, with soccer following in 1959.[37] Needless to say, these championships, and all others prior to 1981, were for men only.

In the 1950s, national competitions for "College Division" institutions were instituted, beginning with a basketball tournament (1957). The representatives of the smaller schools within the NCAA had been frustrated by the difficulty they experienced in gaining opportunities to participate in national competition, which was, not surprisingly, dominated by the larger schools. At the same time, the larger schools that formed the "University Division" were concerned that the College Division schools had too much say in matters that had significant financial ramifications for them. These tensions eventually led to the establishment, in 1973, of separate Divisions I, II, and III. It was recognized at the time that "one of the points which should be underscored in reorganization is the creating of more championships."[38]

The national championship model was created initially by the big-time programs in what is now Division I, but the model was then adopted by Division III "with enthusiasm," as Amy Campbell puts it. As soon as Division III was formed, there was rapid growth in men's championships open only to their members. Between 1973 and 1976, Division III national championships were inaugurated in ten sports (baseball, basketball, cross country, football, golf, soccer, swimming and diving, tennis, outdoor track and field, and wrestling), with three more to follow in the early to mid-1980s (ice hockey, lacrosse, and indoor track).

The next milestone was the 1981 NCAA Convention, where—faced with the reality of the Title IX amendments to the Education Act of 1972 and the failure of efforts to weaken it—the members voted to conduct women's championships in all divisions. The Division I complement of women's championships was in place by 1983; Division III women's championships in 11 sports were initiated between 1982 and 1986, with some additional championships added subsequently (mostly national collegiate championships open to schools in all divisions).[39]

This bland mention of the assumption by the NCAA of responsibility for women's sports and women's championships utterly fails to capture the complex and contentious discussions at the time. Particularly relevant to our understanding of the forces leading to the intensification of college sports is the difference between the kinds of national championships that had been organized by the Association for Intercollegiate Athletics for Women (AIAW) prior to its demise and the NCAA men's model. The AIAW discouraged the awarding of athletic scholarships and, at the end of each season, staged national championships in which all teams were invited to participate—a practice intended to foster less of a winner-take-all attitude. There was, however, no stopping the momentum of the men's model, especially given the organizational power of the NCAA, the understandable appeal of scholarships and better-financed athletics programs to many women, and the prestige of men's athletics.[40] Also, the marked increase in the number of teams would make it impractical today, in any event, to invite "all teams" to participate in post-season championship competition.

In the intervening years, the NCAA has put more and more emphasis on national championships for both men and women. In 1999–2000, the NCAA membership instituted a new national championship selection model that allowed more conferences to receive automatic bids to national championship tournaments. As one athletic director explained: "The NCAA policies regarding national championships reflect the interests of the members. For the most part, the membership is fixated on national championships. Coaches want larger championship brackets so more teams can have the opportunity to participate."[41] Another person added: "The increased emphasis on winning and qualifying for postseason NCAA championship competition in Division III is reflected in the make-up of the NCAA Division III budget, in which approximately 85 percent of funds are earmarked toward the conduct of national championships. In the 2000–01 academic year, $9.8 million were spent on these post-season competitions."[42] Even the primary sponsors of national championships have begun to show some concern: in his farewell speech at the January 2003 convention, outgoing NCAA president Cedric Dempsey warned against this increasing emphasis on national championships in Division III.[43]

Another important development in the "nationalization" of competition in college sports was the establishment of the Sears Directors' Cup, a program managed by the National Association of Collegiate Directors of Athletics (in conjunction with *USA Today*) that "honors institutions maintaining a broad-based athletics program and achieving success in many sports, both men's and women's."[44] Begun in 1993–94 for Division I schools, it was expanded in 1995–96 to include other divisions. Amy Campbell observes:

> While there is limited media attention, schools use their ranking, eagerly publicizing their achievements. Athletic Directors at Division I and III schools have been known to suggest to their coaching staffs that placing in the top 25 or winning the Sears Cup is a goal for the department. Points are awarded through participation in post-season play, heightening the value of the post-season and winning national championships. [There is an elaborate scoring system, with points awarded for each sport based on national rankings and bracket sizes; the system has an egalitarian quality, in that first place in any sport receives 100 points.] The Sears Cup has become synonymous with achievement. When Williams College is ranked number one in the Sears Cup competition, . . . the rest of Division III take notice and use Williams as the standard, raising the bar for all others.[45]

Campbell does not exaggerate how well Williams has done. It has won the Sears Cup in six of the seven years that a Division III champion has been crowned. Other NESCAC teams have also fared well. Both Amherst and Middlebury ranked in the top 10 in 2001–02 (as they did in five of the seven years the cup has been awarded); two other NESCAC colleges joined these three in the top 50 (Bates and Bowdoin); and another three were in the top 60 (Colby, Trinity, and Tufts). There is no other Division III conference with as strong a record. But the UAA has done nearly as well. In 2001–02 Emory ranked 5th (right behind Middlebury), and Washington University ranked 17th. Four other UAA members (Brandeis, Carnegie Mellon, Case Western Reserve, and New York University) also ranked in the top 70 Division III programs out of the 277 schools included. At the Division I level, in 2001–02 Princeton finished 21st, Harvard finished 49th, and six of the other seven Ivies also finished in the top 80 (out of 261 schools)—a most impressive record of competitive success, especially in light of the fact that the Ivies are competing with many big-time programs that provide athletic scholarships and in general have less restrictive admission requirements. (See Appendix Table 8.1 for the Sears Cup data. Appendix Tables 8.2a and 8.2b provide tabular presentations of the success of the various schools in this study in reaching the final eight in the NCAA Division I and Division III championships in various periods.)

There is now yet another national survey of top collegiate programs that also pays attention to national championships (albeit to a lesser degree than the Sears Cup does). In March 2002, *U.S. News & World Report*, not to be outdone by *USA Today* (which publishes the results of the Sears Cup competition), initiated its own system for ranking just Division I college sports programs.[46] It identifies a group of top 20 programs and also identifies some of the worst programs, based on four categories of achievement: (1) gender equity; (2) competitive results, which are based on won-lost percentages calculated for all men's and women's school-to-school contests, as well as on the national ranking of schools in NCAA tournaments in such sports as gymnastics and swimming and diving; (3) the number of men's and women's varsity programs sponsored by the school; and (4) the graduation rate of athletes. In addition, the ranking system penalizes (by excluding from its honor roll) schools that have had major sanctions since 1992. Five of the Ivies were included in the top 20 honor roll in this initial survey.

While this *U.S. News* survey employs a somewhat mysterious methodology (with, for example, no explanation given of the weights assigned to the various criteria) and does not assign exact ranks, it is nonetheless another benchmark that schools will use to claim bragging rights. Nor is there an end in sight. *U.S. News* is now planning to create and publish rankings of Division III athletics programs, but we understand that at least one conference—NESCAC—has decided not to participate.[47] Other ways will also be found to publicize the success of the exemplar programs, and a plan has recently been announced to establish a new National College Sports Network, described as a "24-hour cable television network devoted to covering Division I, II, and III sports." Brian Bedol, one of the co-founders, is quoted as saying: "There are 25 great college sports, but only 2 are covered. . . . If you're a track and field, gymnastics, or lacrosse fan, this is stuff you can't get."[48]

The emphasis on winning at the national level has obvious implications. In the words of one commentator: "The organization of national championships in Division III has raised the stakes and taken the focus off the regular season and placed it in the post-season."[49] "Raising the stakes" in this way means, among other things, that colleges and universities aspiring to win national championships have to have objectives in recruitment and admissions that are consistent with this goal: they can not just find athletes who can pass academic muster, but they have "to recruit students who can compete at the national level."[50] More generally, in the words of another Division III athletic director: "The pressure to reach the postseason—and in some cases to compete for a national championship—often leads to many of our most serious problems: excessive practice time, missed class time, overemphasis on winning, limited time to pursue intellectual and/or other co-curricular pursuits."[51] As one Ivy League director of athletics put it (in off-the-record comments): "Success in national competition creates incentives, even pressures, to do the wrong things."

Participation in national championships naturally affects the aspirations of athletes and coaches—which can, in turn, lead to dispiriting assessments of how well they have "succeeded" or "failed" in their efforts to compete. Tom Parker, dean of admission at Amherst, describes national championships as "intoxicating." Biddiscombe comments: "For teams that have tasted the sweetness of placing in a national tournament, having a winning season is no longer a standard of success. I have observed talented, experienced teams that have reacted to an early season loss as if their season had no more meaning, knowing the loss would prohibit their return to the national championships tournament."[52] This same theme is echoed by Malekoff:

> Once a Division III team has tasted success at the national level, anything less becomes difficult to swallow. In 1997, the Wooster baseball team qualified for the NCAA Division III World Series (only eight teams in the nation qualify) and made it all the way to the national championship final game before being defeated. Some players who previously had hoped to win the conference championship and qualify for the NCAA tournament now claimed that their primary goal was to win the national championship. In the next three seasons the Wooster team compiled records of 40–6, 35–14, and 35–12, but failed to qualify for a return to the Division III World Series. Some followers of the program began to ask what was wrong with the team, and wondered why the program was "in decline."[53]

An example of how a "moment in the sun" can lead to the quick ratcheting up of expectations is provided by a letter sent by the director of the Blue and White Club at Hartwick College to a broad mailing list. Here is an excerpt:

> In just two short years of competition, the Hartwick Women's Water Polo team took the University of Michigan to triple sudden-death overtime before losing 7–6 in a game that would have meant an NCAA Final Four bid. . . . They [the team] have established themselves as a power in water polo and a contender for a Final Four appearance within the next two seasons. Now is the time to begin to make preparations to achieve that goal, and we need your help. . . . To be in a position to make the Final Four, coach Mike Maroney estimates that the team will need $50,000 of additional support. These funds will be used primarily for travel to the West Coast to play the top schools in Division I. . . . Equipment and off-season competitions will also be priorities to keep our team at a high competitive level.[54]

There are also spill-over effects, especially within conferences. When one school in a conference begins to have realistic (recurring) opportunities to compete for a national championship in a particular sport, other members of the conference feel great pressure to measure up to the standard set by the championship team or teams. Susan Eichner, coach of the field hockey team at Columbia, explained this dynamic very clearly when she told us: "My mandate is to be competitive in the Ivy League. But when the field hockey teams at Princeton and Harvard are regular contenders for national championships, I have to build a team that can play at that level if I'm going to compete against them." From this perspective, it is easy to see why the exceptional competitive success in recent years of schools such as Princeton in the Ivy League and Middlebury and Williams in NESCAC have led other schools to ask how they can play at the same level. Similarly, when access to places in the national championship competition depends almost exclusively on winning the conference championship, there are other unintended "social" effects, including (in the words of Rasmussen) "an increase in sensitivity over perceived advantages in scouting, schedule, recruiting, etc., more frequent departures from good sportsmanship, and a strained collegiality among coaches and administrators. This has not been a positive thing."[55] Finally, focusing so strongly on how to gain a berth in the national championships can distort decisions concerning conference membership and scheduling.

In considering the myriad interactions between the allure of national championships and how athletics programs are organized, carried out, and perceived, it is easy to understand why the steadily increasing importance of these competitions has become a matter of serious concern. In reviewing the history of the championships themselves, and in setting this history alongside the growth of the athletic divide, there is no mistaking the connections in time. As always, many forces have been operating (and interacting) concurrently, with changes in one domain both driving and responding to changes in another. However one wants to parse cause and effect, it is no accident that the growing professionalism of college sports in the Ivy League and in Division III has coincided with the growth in the number and importance of national championships. The two developments have been mutually reinforcing.

As we showed earlier in the chapter, today's "divide" in men's sports emerged sometime between the mid-1950s and the late 1970s, and it was over this interval, and especially in the early 1970s, that NCAA-sponsored national championships became important for the first time in Division III and had a greater impact than in earlier years on the Ivy League. The men's championships became increasingly important in both the Ivy League and Division III between the days of the '76 entering cohort and those of the '95 entering cohort, at the same time that the divide was becoming increasingly pronounced.

Similarly, we think it is no coincidence that the athletic divide for women first appeared later, in the data for the '89 entering cohort at the Ivies (and at the Division IA private universities such as Stanford included in *The Game of Life*) rather than in the data for the '76 entering cohort. After all, it was only in the early 1980s that the NCAA began to sponsor championships for women. Then, as more years passed, as more vigorous efforts were made to recruit women athletes, and as other forms of recognition such as the Division III Sears Cup awards became highly visible (with equal numbers of points awarded for championships won by women's teams), we see growing evidence of the spread of the academic-athletic divide to women's sports, particularly in the NESCAC colleges. The more aggressive recruiting of women athletes has unquestionably been stimulated by the national competitions and by schools' desire to excel at the national level.

There is, in our view, absolutely nothing wrong—in fact, there is everything right—with schools' wanting to measure up to the best of the best. This is, as one coach put it, "the natural progression in the competitive pyramid." The exhilaration and sense of accomplishment associated with having "won it all" can be more than satisfying; it can be a high point in the life of the athlete and the coach. The challenge, of course, is to compete on the right terms and without asking either the players or their schools to make the wrong kinds of sacrifices. Key requirements include getting the "rules of engagement" right and defining orbits of competition in the most appropriate way. We return to these issues in Part C of this study.

We want to make a last point about the protection of institutional values and institutional autonomy. In reflecting on her experiences at various Division I and III schools, Amy Campbell writes:

> What is troubling . . . is the post-season structure that skews the delicate balance of achievement, dedication, and sacrifice. The win-at-all-costs attitude and pressures can lead to crossing the line from supporting the institutional mission to an enterprise that functions *outside the primary institutional mission* [our emphasis]. The autonomy of institutions to define the appropriate athletic model, based upon the philosophy, the needs, and the desired outcomes of athletics for the college, is paramount. Just as schools decide what courses, majors, and concentrations to offer, so too should institutions carefully consider and determine the kind of athletic program offered students. What is difficult are the external factors governing competition that exist in athletics, by definition and purpose, that do not exist in academia. Academia is primarily an internal enterprise, the activity is within the institution and the measurement of success is between a student and her/his professor. . . . The activity of intercollegiate athletics is all about the external and very public measurement of success.[56]

This distinction between external and internal standards will be important to bear in mind when we consider possible modifications in both the "rules of engagement" and the most appropriate "orbits of competition."

Interactions of Title IX with the "Male Model" of Athletics

The athletic divide has also been affected by the passage in 1972 of Title IX, the gender equity amendments to the Education Act of that year, albeit in unintended ways. Our focus here is *not* on the broad effects of Title IX, which we regard as overwhelmingly positive; there have been dramatic improvements in athletic opportunities for women[57] and, more generally, in the subtle as well as overt ways in which boys and girls, and men and women, perceive each other. The continuing debates over how the law is (and should be) interpreted, and how colleges and universities should comply with it, cannot obscure the degree to which Title IX has changed permanently the "tilt" of the playing field for women, even if it is not yet level.[58] Our interest is in the much narrower question of how the implementation of Title IX has affected the athletic divide on the campuses of the colleges and universities in this study.

Title IX could have affected the athletic divide in quite different ways. Since the law mandated that colleges and universities offer to women whatever athletic opportunities they provided to men, it could have served as a signal to colleges and universities (and to the NCAA) that it was time to recalibrate the entire athletics enterprise so that it would be more congruent with educational goals. This would have entailed reducing the emphasis on recruiting, spending less money on athletic scholarships (if not eliminating them altogether), and in other ways carefully considering the adoption of other aspects of the model of athletics that was pioneered and developed by the AIAW.[59] This is not what happened— and, indeed, it would have been naïve to expect this path to be chosen, given the power of the NCAA establishment and the dominant concern for revenues associated with big-time men's sports. Instead, Title IX was, in effect, superimposed on the pre-existing "male model" of athletics. The key point is that it is not Title IX per se that has affected the athletic divide; rather, it is the way Title IX has interacted with policies already in place for men's sports. Seen in this context, Title IX served to magnify the effects of the national forces that were already operating to widen the divide. It did this in two ways: (1) by increasing the overall scale of athletic recruitment and the impact of related policies (including the conferring of admissions advantages on more students) and (2) by adding to "intensification" pressures, in large part through the pull of NCAA-sponsored national championships for women.

Title IX was not adopted in a vacuum, and the broader social and political currents that produced it would have had at least some effect on the scale of athletic opportunities for women in any case. At the schools in this study, the number of women's and men's teams is essentially the same today, although the number of female participants lags behind the number of male participants because of squad sizes in football (refer back to Figures 1.1 and 1.2).[60] All coeducational institutions have been under internally generated pressure to build up their women's programs. As more universities in the Ivy League and more colleges in NESCAC became coeducational, they committed themselves to providing excellent athletics programs for women students. From its beginning, the UAA has had as one of its founding principles "Equal opportunities in athletics shall be provided for men and women."[61] Commitments to fair play and equal opportunity at the collegiate level have, in turn, been reinforced by the burgeoning interest in women's sports in secondary schools (and earlier).

At the same time, it would be a serious mistake to think that Title IX has not been a consideration at the schools in this study. After all, it was a case involving an Ivy League school (Brown University) that led to the codification of rules for applying Title IX. The "substantial proportionality" test that grew out of the Brown decision is now seen as the only "safe harbor" for compliance with Title IX, and this test puts direct pressure on all schools that receive federal aid to see that the ratio of women athletes to all women students is roughly the same as the corresponding ratio for men.[62] One dean was clear in stating that "Title IX has clearly been the main driving force [in causing the addition of women's teams]." Scale alone is important, since it means that a school that formerly had, say, 300 (male) athletes playing intercollegiate sports now needs to have 600 (male and female) athletes, assuming that the proportions of men and women in the student body are roughly equal.

At the schools in this study, the effects on the athletic divide of the interaction between Title IX and other forces are seen even more clearly in the spread of "intensification" pressures. Even though these schools do not offer athletic scholarships, they are subject to "contagion effects" derived from Division I practices. Title IX is by no means concerned solely with numbers of participants (or teams), and questions are being raised with increasing frequency about parity in financial aid awarded by scholarship-granting schools, as well as parity in equipment and facilities, financial support for travel and expenses, assignment and compensation of coaches, and so on.[63] This close scrutiny of gender-related differences of every kind has meant that the athletic opportunities offered to women at the Division I level have come to resemble more and more closely the athletic opportunities offered to men by these big-time programs.[64] Because of the large overlaps in the pools of potential athletic recruits, this escalation in the competition to provide more and better coaching, improved facilities, and more extensive schedules has spread inexorably to the Ivies and to those Division III colleges that aspire to compete at the national level. Even the women's colleges have been affected, because they compete against the women's teams at coeducational colleges and universities and thus must take account of the increased emphasis placed on upgrading programs at these schools.

It is also clear that the interaction of Title IX with NCAA-sponsored national championships has had a major effect on the intensity of athletic competition. Title IX (and the associated attention given to women's athletics) was without doubt the major factor prompting the decision by the NCAA at its 1981 convention to embrace women's programs and to offer its own national championships for women.[65] The growth in the number and importance of national championships for women through the 1980s and into the 1990s has, in turn, been an important spur to the greatly increased emphasis on recruiting women athletes who could not just play, but also compete effectively at the national level. The impact within NESCAC has been particularly pronounced. As Karin Vélez points out in her history of the evolution of NESCAC:

> NESCAC did not anticipate the catalyzing effect that NCAA competition would have on its [highly successful] women's sports programs and also on men's sports programs by association. The success of NESCAC women athletes in NCAA competition has brought NESCAC institutions national visibility *and raised the expectations of the whole Conference* [our emphasis]. NCAA competition has become a standard measure for NESCAC's successful implementation of Title IX: it is proof that women student athletes are competitive not only with men's sports at their institutions but also with each other in the national arena. This has complicated the current question of NESCAC's participation in NCAA post-season competition.[66]

Some have argued that Title IX has also widened the athletic divide through its indirect effects on Lower Profile men's programs and on opportunities for walk-on athletes to participate. This is a highly contentious subject. Proponents of women's athletics resent claims by groups such as the wrestling coaches that it is Title IX that has led to the demise of their teams; rather, they say that athletic directors should confront directly the problem of huge football rosters and inflated football budgets, and cut back there in order to accommodate an expansion of opportunities for women.[67] Some college and university presidents agree that the issue here is not Title IX but principles of fairness. For example, the Reverend Donald Harrington, president of St. John's University, in announcing plans to eliminate five men's teams and one women's team, said:

> Many will say this was done due to Title IX. While Title IX is in the picture, we are looking at a broader picture. If a law is a good law, it has to be based on justice, and this was done as a matter of justice. Our demographics have shifted and 58 percent of our students are women. It would be very difficult

for me to explain to them why their tuition dollars were being used to support athletics programs that were made up of 65 percent men. If the Title IX laws were to change tomorrow, we would still have made the same decision based on what is just to our students.[68]

Whatever has happened (or one believes should have happened) at the national level, in the Ivies, the NESCAC colleges, the UAA universities, and the other coed schools in this study, the approach has been to add women's teams without eliminating men's teams.[69] In the main, these schools have been able to afford to support both.

There are, however, also less visible ways in which schools have chosen to comply with Title IX that have affected men's sports and, in the process, widened aspects of the athletic divide; we are referring to the elimination of separate freshmen and junior varsity (JV) teams and, in some instances, decisions by athletic departments to "cap" or limit the rosters of men's teams. Pressures to move in these directions are both directly related to Title IX (growing out of worries about how to achieve "substantial proportionality" in numbers of participants) and indirectly related (growing out of budgetary concerns). The Brown track and field coach quoted in Chapter 2 was clear in explaining that he welcomed new participants in the women's track and field program but discouraged male walk-ons.[70] The need to spend more money on women's teams inevitably constrains the funds available to support other activities, and budgetary concerns were directly related to decisions made by the Ivy League presidents to make freshmen eligible for varsity competition and to scale back JV programs.

The consequences are clear: opportunities for non-recruited athletes (walk-ons) to play are diminished, and recruited athletes increasingly dominate both men's and women's sports programs—for this and other, more far-reaching, reasons discussed earlier in the chapter. Such outcomes are, however, a consequence not of Title IX per se but rather of the way in which the legislation has interacted with broader policy choices that have been made concerning the nature of these athletics programs. Understood in this way, the overall impact of Title IX on the character of the athletics enterprise may exceed the sum of its separate effects. One commentator states her concerns for women's sports and educational outcomes very directly:

Sadly, this hubristic sports culture is entangling more and more women. The promise of Title IX, requiring equity among male and female college athletes, has given us Chamique Holdsclaw and Brandi Chastain. It's also given us an increasing number of female student athletes who are as academically weak and socially isolated as the men. Instead of moderating the role of athletics in higher education, Title IX too often has stimulated colleges simply to impose a flawed male model on women's sports. As female athletes get more and more heavily recruited for sports, their SATs, grades and academic performance start to lag.[71]

These consequences were never intended and cannot, fairly, be laid at the doorstep of Title IX. Taken on its own terms, Title IX has brought to the fore issues of fundamental fairness and has stimulated progress at many levels. The hard-to-suppress thought is that it nonetheless represents something of a missed opportunity: paired with an alternative model, Title IX might conceivably have led to a different athletic landscape than the one we see today. The question to which we return in Part C of this study is whether there are reforms that would both advance the cause of gender equity and narrow the athletic divide.

CHAPTER 9

The Athletic Divide in Context

"Divides," by their nature, have two sides. This study is concerned primarily with the athletic side of the divide, but broader trends within higher education have also contributed to the growing disjuncture between intercollegiate sports and the academic core of selective colleges and universities. The dramatic changes that have occurred in the shape and character of intercollegiate athletics have not taken place within a static, unchanging higher education universe. Powerful market forces have led to increasing stratification, with larger and larger fractions of financial resources, outstanding faculty members, and top students concentrated in the kinds of prestigious colleges and universities included in this study. Highly competitive markets for students and faculty members have become international in scope, and both student and faculty populations have become more specialized.

The driving forces are deep-seated. They are not random, do not represent passing shocks, and cannot be wished away. They are part and parcel of an American system of higher education that, shortcomings notwithstanding, is widely seen as the best in the world (in stark contrast to American elementary and secondary education). These forces should be expected to continue to distance the academic side of leading colleges and universities from the professionalized model of intercollegiate athletics that is so widespread today.

The first part of this chapter is devoted to charting these broad forces within higher education and describing their impact on the athletic divide. Then, in the last part, we consider other "divides." In particular, we ask whether some of the same trends and worries that are evident when we focus on recruited athletes are present when we examine other sub-groups of students, including those with particular talents in fields such as music and those who are legacies or minority students. The key questions addressed are only in part empirical; they are also profoundly value laden and philosophical. They compel us to confront the question of how paying special attention to various sub-groups does or does not relate to the core missions of the colleges and universities we are studying.

THE INCREASING STRATIFICATION OF HIGHER EDUCATION

If athletes, and especially recruited athletes, have changed in major respects over the past several decades—as they have—so, too, have their
classmates. Many faculty members, deans, high school counselors,
alumni, and prospective students (as well as their parents) share an in-
tuitive sense that it has become much more difficult for applicants to gain
admission to the most selective institutions. They are right. Admissions
deans readily cite evidence from their own institutions. In one striking
example, the admissions rate of Columbia College fell from 28 percent
in 1990 to 13 percent in 2000. The other Ivy League school that has become much more selective is the University of Pennsylvania, which admitted 42 percent of all applicants in 1990 but just 23 percent in 2000.
Five of the eight Ivies had admit rates at or below 16 percent in 2000.
Among the colleges in the New England Small College Athletic Conference (NESCAC), Middlebury admitted 40 percent of all applicants
in 1990 and just 25 percent in 2000; admit rates at 8 of the 11 NESCAC
colleges are at or below 30 percent. In the University Athletic Association (UAA), admit rates improved dramatically over the past decade at
Carnegie Mellon, New York University, and Washington University and
today are generally in the 30 to 50 percent range (as they are at a number of the liberal arts colleges outside NESCAC); see Appendix Table 9.1
for admit rates for all of the colleges and universities in this study in 1990,
1993, and 2000.

Admit rates are by no means an unambiguous indicator of selectivity,
however, since they tell us nothing about the quality of the applicant pool.
In addition, they are affected by yield, since when a high percentage of
those who are admitted matriculate, fewer candidates need to be admitted in order to fill a class—and yield is, in turn, affected by factors such as
financial aid and the use made of Early Decision programs (see Chapter
3). Average SAT scores of students at large—admitted applicants, other
than athletes, who actually matriculated—are somewhat more reliable indicators of selectivity, and we have these data, going back at least 20 years,
for a number of the schools in our study (Figures 9.1a and 9.1b).[1]

Here are some conclusions we have drawn from these data:

- Average SAT scores for male students at large in the Ivy League
  schools and for women attending women's colleges (the two groups
  of schools for which we have data going back to the 1951 entering
  cohort) have increased dramatically over this span of more than four
  decades. Athletes who matriculated in the Ivies in the 1950s, and who
  closely resembled their classmates, faced far less daunting academic
  competitors than do their counterparts today.

- We have data spanning the past two decades for more sets of schools, and the general picture is clear: test scores were not nearly as high in the 1976 cohort at the Division III universities as they are today; scores have also risen at the coed liberal arts colleges, although the change has not been as great in this sector.
- Test scores continued to rise somewhat between the time of the 1989 and 1995 cohorts, but the rate of increase appears to have slowed, and scores have essentially plateaued in the coed liberal arts colleges.
- These SAT scores are all the more impressive when we recognize that average test scores at *all* colleges and universities *declined* over this period. At the 731 private institutions in a panel of 1,121 baccalaureate-granting colleges created by Professor Caroline Hoxby at Harvard, the 50th percentile SAT scores were 1124 in 1966, 1100 in 1971, 1079 in 1981, and 1051 in 1991.[2]

The increased success of these highly selective colleges and universities in enrolling top students has not been due to happenstance. Philip Cook and Robert Frank, in a paper titled "The Growing Concentration

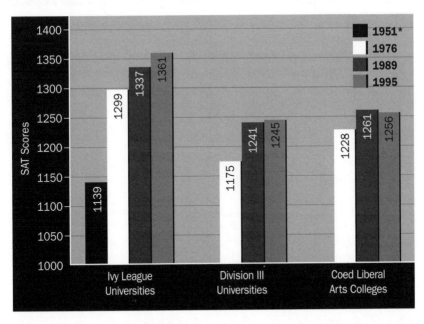

Figure 9.1a. Average SAT Scores for Male Students at Large, by Conference and Cohort

Source: Expanded College and Beyond database.

* Only for the Ivy League universities do we have data from 1951 for a sufficient number of schools to allow analysis.

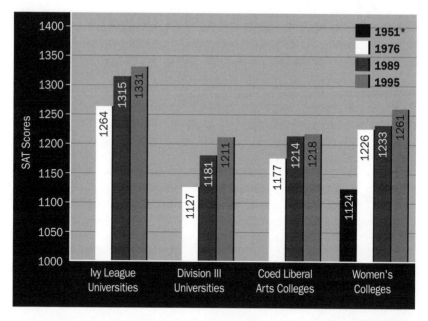

Figure 9.1b. Average SAT Scores for Female Students at Large, by Conference and Cohort

Source: Expanded College and Beyond database.

* Only for the women's colleges do we have data from 1951 for a sufficient number of schools to allow analysis.

of Top Students at Elite Schools," suggest that what we have here is an illustration of what is known in the economics literature as a "tournament," which is driven by a dynamic process and positive feedback and is, from their perspective, part of the "winner-take-all" behavior that they find in so much of society today.[3] They cite a variety of data to support (and explain) their claim that there is a greater concentration of top students at a relatively small number of schools, ranging from the distribution of Presidential Scholars and of finalists in the Westinghouse Science Talent Search, to growing preferences by applicants for "colleges that matriculate students whose SAT scores exceed their own," to an increase in the perceived value of top schools as pathways to the best jobs.

Similarly, Richard Spies found a dramatic increase between 1976 and 1987 in the percentage of students with given characteristics, including strong academic credentials, who chose to apply to elite private schools. For example, holding constant variables such as family income, race, geographical location, and high school grades, Spies found that the probability of applying to an elite private school for a student with combined SAT scores of 1400 rose from 50 percent in 1976 to 72 percent in 1987.[4]

By far the most careful analytical and empirical study of the changing structure of the market for college education has been done by Hoxby.[5] She demonstrates that "since 1940 . . . higher education has been transformed from a series of local autarkies to a nationally and regionally integrated market in which each college faces many potential competitors." The factors responsible for this transformation are important enough to highlight. According to Hoxby, they include:

- The advent of modern standardized admissions testing in 1943–48;
- The information exchange system among students, colleges, and scholarship donors that was initiated by the National Merit Scholarship program in 1956–58;
- The advent of standardized financial needs analysis (1956);
- Deregulation in the airline and telecommunications industries that resulted in substantially lower prices for long-distance travel and long-distance telephonic communication.[6]

One way of illustrating the effects of these forces is by noting that among applicants who scored at or above the 75th percentile on standardized tests, the percentage applying to at least one college outside their home state and its adjoining states increased from just under 40 percent in the high school class of 1972 to 43 percent in the class of 1980 and to nearly 70 percent in the class of 1992.[7]

Hoxby presents an elaborate model that demonstrates why, under reasonable assumptions, she would expect an integrated market to lead to increased stratification of colleges. Her model explains why we should expect to find both a growing concentration of the ablest students in what are perceived to be the best schools and an increasing tendency for the schools enrolling the ablest students to spend more per student on faculty, libraries, and laboratories (another form of stratification). Her model explicitly provides for peer effects and leads to a number of other propositions, including important ones related to tuition levels and financial aid, that are outside the purview of this discussion.

Over the period between 1966 and 1991, there has been a pronounced widening of the SAT gap between colleges at the top of the distribution and those at the bottom. For example, among the 731 private baccalaureate-granting colleges in Hoxby's panel of schools, the gap between the 5th and 95th percentiles widened from 361 points in 1966 to 452 points in 1991.[8] After demonstrating that measures of geographic integration are clearly related to the increased stratification of students by aptitude, Hoxby concludes: "The changes in market structure are due, at least in part, to fundamental changes in students' costs of geographic mobility and the amount of information that students and colleges have about each other. These changes are beyond the control of any individual college and they are unlikely to be reversed."[9] In short, Hoxby presents substantial evidence of the extent to which the "academic" bar (or standard) at these selective colleges and universities has risen, an elaborate explanation of why this has happened, and reasons to believe that *the forces increasing stratification are market-driven, impersonal, and here to stay.*

Most observers of American higher education would echo Hoxby's conclusions without being able to provide the analytical foundations that she has built so carefully. The greatly enhanced academic muscle of the leading universities, in particular, is reflected in their demonstrated ability to recruit and retain leading scholars, to attract the most promising candidates from all over the world to their graduate programs, and to produce scholarship and research that has led, in the sciences and engineering, to greatly enhanced patent revenues at universities such as Columbia and Stanford. These developments have, of course, reinforced the ability of these leading institutions to attract high-testing, high-achieving, high-aspiring undergraduates. The most selective of the liberal arts colleges have also become far stronger academically, and their resources, whether measured by endowments, success in recruiting faculty dedicated to teaching as well as to scholarship, or their state-of-the-art libraries and laboratories, have in turn stimulated their competitors to set new goals for themselves. This process of "ratcheting up," driven by the ready access to information, mobility, and competition, is evident among the coed liberal arts colleges and the women's colleges as well as the research universities.

These pronounced trends help us see why the athletes–whose precollegiate academic credentials have generally lagged behind overall improvements in standards—are more and more sharply differentiated from their classmates. This is particularly true of the recruited athletes in the High Profile sports at the most selective colleges and universities. In addition to sizable differences in test scores and high school grades, there appear to be widening differences in academic ambitions and interests. The increased stratification that Hoxby finds has obvious implications for athletes who have been recruited and admitted through processes that seem to be putting less emphasis on academic strengths and motivations. The resulting differences in "culture" as well as in academic performance that we have documented need to be understood in this context. The frustrations expressed by some faculty at colleges such as Williams (especially those teaching in the social sciences) surely reflect, to some significant degree, the contrast between the pleasure they take in teaching highly motivated, very well-prepared students at large and the less satisfying experiences they have with at least some students who are more focused on athletic achievement than on doing exceptionally well in writing papers or working in the lab.

FACULTY RECRUITMENT, INDEPENDENT WORK, AND ADMISSIONS

One highly experienced observer of the college and university scene, Taylor Reveley (a former chairman of Princeton's Trustee Committee on Student Life, Health, and Athletics who now serves as dean of the Law School at William and Mary), has observed: "In most spheres of life, specialization is the path to excellence."[10] Dean Reveley is referring to the effects of the vast proliferation of knowledge and the need to pursue topics in depth if one is to have any hope of mastering the relevant subject matter. Generalists are, of course, also needed—indeed, even more than in the past, because it is so important to be able to integrate the ideas generated by more accomplished specialists. But colleges and universities dedicated to the advancement of knowledge have no choice but to respect the worldwide trend toward increased specialization, which shows no signs of letting up. The Internet and digital technologies are just another set of forces breaking down national boundaries, increasing the speed with which new ideas are communicated, and raising the premium on staying ahead of the proverbial curve.

Reveley goes on to note: "The very selective, well-endowed U.S. colleges and universities have themselves elected to specialize in *academic* excellence." This implies a commitment to recruit outstanding faculty members from all over the world: individuals who have unquestioned scholarly credentials combined with a drive to learn, to discover, and to communicate new understandings and new discoveries. These individuals will often, though certainly not always, be gifted teachers as well as scholars—in part because the best scholars simply cannot help communicating their ideas, which is the essence of "teaching."[11]

What, more specifically, are the implications for the academic-athletic divide of this increase in faculty specialization and the attendant "ramping up" of institutional commitments to achieving academic excellence? First, the ability of these institutions to recruit highly talented faculty who are strongly committed to pushing out the frontiers of their own fields of knowledge inevitably affects the expectations of those charged with undergraduate instruction. Not surprisingly, these academically oriented faculty look for, and appreciate, undergraduates who are focused on academic achievement rather than on pursuing national championships in one or another sport. Some of these faculty may be less than welcoming to aspiring athletes, and in some cases may be guilty of stereotyping. The irritation with scheduling conflicts stemming from athletics that has been reported at Swarthmore (and elsewhere), and that is so evident in the Williams Ad Hoc Committee report, is an example of how this tension plays out on campuses where curricular and extracurricular aspects of student life are closely integrated.[12]

Another consequence of the upgrading of academic resources of all kinds, as a result of the stratification that Hoxby describes, is that there is more and more opportunity for gifted students to work with faculty (and, in the universities, with top graduate students) on a variety of research projects. As these colleges and universities attract better and better applicants, the students at large in incoming classes are increasingly individuals who arrive prepared to be challenged intellectually and who expect to take some considerable responsibility for their own education. It is natural, then, for these institutions to put greater and greater emphasis on independent work and seminar modes of instruction, which the scholarly resources at their command allow them to do.

A recent report by a national commission titled "Reinventing Undergraduate Education: Three Years after the Boyer Report" provides a wealth of information on progress made in creating research opportunities for undergraduates. In addition to a marked increase in opportunities to pursue laboratory research, the new survey found that "more than 80 percent of research universities that responded now offer some kind of seminar for first-year students. About 45 percent of the institutions enroll half or more of their freshmen in such courses. Almost all of the universities have increased their undergraduate writing requirements."[13]

This shift in pedagogy could be expected to have significant consequences for the athletic divide. An interactive approach to learning rewards the student who puts a high priority on working intensively on a research problem, and it inevitably raises the bar for other students, athletes or not, who have strong non-academic interests. Increased emphasis on independent work is unlikely to favor the recruited athlete, who has a practice schedule that is demanding, who may be less focused on academics than his or her classmates, and who is a member of a group with interests and priorities that are, in general, different from those of the aspiring engineer, computer scientist, or art historian.

Admissions officers are, of course, well aware of the greater and greater capacities of their schools to stimulate and take advantage of the interests of the intellectually focused student, and they pay close attention to evidence of exceptional talent in fields such as mathematics, music, and writing. In short, academic specialization as well as athletic specialization is rewarded in the admissions process. More generally, as we noted in Chapter 3, in choosing among the ever larger number of exceedingly well-qualified applicants who present themselves, admissions offices appear to be giving more and more weight to special, distinguishing qualities that candidates offer. As a number of people have put it, there has been a move away from an emphasis on admitting the "well-rounded individual" to the concept of building the "well-rounded class." This shift is also sometimes described as a move toward "categorization." A former dean of admissions and financial aid at Hotchkiss speaks from the perspective of someone working at the secondary school level:

> For years now, parents have heard college admission officers espousing the virtues of a well-rounded class over well-rounded students. Colleges believe that they can build a well-rounded class by assembling a group of students with particular talents in specific areas. These talents are often referred to as "hooks" and the students who possess them are called "spiky." The most visible evidence of this for many families is the admission of talented athletes to highly selective academically oriented colleges and universities. . . . And more and more students concentrate immediately and precisely on theater or music instead of experiencing the full range of artistic disciplines.[14]

Earlier we explored the implications of this way of approaching admissions for the recruitment of athletes with special talents (the left outside linebacker who can blitz). The point is that many of the linebacker's classmates will have their own specialties, whether they be in computer science or an exotic language. At the same time, these selective colleges and universities have been enrolling more foreign students, as well as more students from a wide range of racial and religious backgrounds. The challenge, in such a milieu, is to find mechanisms that will enable a wonderfully diverse set of students to benefit from one another's presence on the campus. This can certainly be done, and the results can be marvelously rewarding, but it is unquestionably more difficult today to discourage groups of students with particular backgrounds and interests from isolating themselves from their classmates than it was when classes were more homogeneous.

Thus in admitting all students, not just in admitting athletes, colleges seem to have become decreasingly interested in admitting individuals who offer mixed portfolios but are less outstanding than others in any one special "category" of interest to the college. As one dean explained, it is hard to find room in a class for the applicant who was both a good high school athlete and a promising scholar when he has already admitted a number of more skilled (and more dedicated) recruited athletes and now has to find places for the high-achieving physicist and the super-talented musician. Paying so much attention to these admissions "hooks" limits the number of "students at large" who might be especially inclined to cross the divide that often separates recruited athletes from other students. This tendency toward "specialized diversity," as we would term it, driven in large part by the increasingly focused academic talents and interests of many students at large, can make the campus of today a less friendly place than the campus of yesteryear for the nose tackle—who is also more specialized and more focused on his sport than was his counterpart of several decades ago.

OTHER DIVIDES

Musicians

Anecdotal evidence suggests that a number of the colleges and universities in this study have large numbers of students with a serious interest in music, and admissions officers have told us that they give special consideration to (for example) highly talented vocal artists and string players. It would hardly be surprising if some of the same tendencies to "hang together" noted in the case of athletes characterize this group as well. As Cantor and Prentice have demonstrated empirically, students with a strong interest in the performing arts do spend a great deal of time together (although less than athletes do).[15] And, as Columbia's provost, Jonathan Cole, also hypothesized, we might expect them to pay some price academically for their dedication to their music: "Suppose that you admit four music prodigies into the first year class, each of whom spends scores of hours practicing his or her instrument. These students did wonderfully well in high school, with very high SAT scores and terrific grades while studying the violin, piano, viola, and oboe. Now they are admitted to an Ivy School and Julliard. They decide to go to the Ivy School because they want a liberal arts education as well as to continue their work as a musician. . . . [Because of their music] they have little time to study in their courses, although they get a lot out of them. Their grades, which had always been very high, suffer. They underperform."[16]

But in fact the transference of the athletic model of admissions and academic achievement to the musicians turns out to be illusory. We were able to "tag" students with major commitments to orchestral music and to glee clubs in the '95 entering cohort at two of the Ivy universities, and a consistent picture emerges (see Table 9.1):[17]

- There were fewer musicians in these two organizations than there were recruited athletes; on average, about 40 students in the '95 entering cohort participated in the orchestra or the glee club.
- The academic qualifications of the orchestral musicians and the singers exceeded those of their classmates on admission (with aver-

TABLE 9.1

Comparison Groups: Musicians, by Gender,
1995 Entering Cohort, Princeton and Yale Only

	Orchestra	Glee Club	All Musicians
Number of Musicians			
Male	9	12	21
Female	10	12	21
Musicians as a Percent of All Students			
Male	1%	2%	3%
Female	2%	2%	3%
Admissions Advantage for Musicians (Percentage Points)			
Male			
Female			
SAT Scores, by Musician Status			
Male			
Musicians	1414	1411	1414
Other students	1377	1377	1376
Female			
Musicians	1409	1416	1410
Other students	1355	1354	1354
Percentile Rank in Class, by Musician Status			
Male			
Musicians	56	61	59
Other students	48	48	47
Female			
Musicians	64	66	64
Other students	51	51	51
Underperformance of Musicians Relative to Students at Large **(Rank in Class Percentile Points)**			
Male	2.6	5.3	4.2
Female	5.1	2.9	4.3

Source: Expanded College and Beyond database.

Notes: Regression coefficents shown in **bold** are significant at the .05 level. The positive point estimates in the underperformance columns indicate *over*performance, instead of *under*performance.

age SAT scores of over 1400 for both men and women in both kinds of musical groups).

- Once on campus, musicians had decidedly above-average grades (men ranking in the 59th percentile and women in the 64th percentile).

- Neither group of musicians shows any evidence of academic under-performance; rather, both exhibit a modest, statistically nonsignificant, amount of *over*performance.

In short, these two groups of musically engaged students with specialized talents and interests managed to find the time they needed for their demanding extracurricular pursuits without sacrificing academic objectives. It may be that they had already demonstrated, in high school, the discipline needed to do both, and it may also be that, having had what Provost Cole calls "a Julliard option," they knowingly opted for a setting in which they knew they would be expected to perform well in the classroom as well as in the orchestra or glee club. (The corresponding "Julliard option" for athletes in most sports, and especially the High Profile sports, would be a big-time Division I program requiring a level of talent too high for most of these athletes, and this could be one reason why selection, and especially self-selection, works differently for recruited athletes than it does for musicians.) In any case, these results are generally consistent with a major finding in *The Game of Life*, namely that a broadly defined group of students who were actively engaged in time-intensive extracurricular activities did very well in the classroom and consistently *overperformed* academically.[18]

Legacies

Legacies (generally children or siblings of alumni) constitute a second group of students sometimes singled out for comparison with recruited athletes, presumably because they, too, receive some degree of special consideration in the admissions process. Examination of data for the Ivy League schools reveals some surprises (Table 9.2):

- Legacies were roughly comparable in numbers to recruited athletes (with male and female legacies accounting for, respectively, 11 and 13 percent of the male and female matriculants, as compared with 16 and 11 percent, respectively, for recruited male and female athletes).
- Legacies also enjoyed a statistically significant admissions advantage, but a much smaller one than recruited athletes (26 and 28 percentage points, respectively, for male and female legacies versus 51 and 56 points, respectively, for recruited male and female athletes).
- At the same time, legacies had slightly higher average SAT scores than other students, a finding that seems paradoxical in light of the presence of an admissions advantage but is in fact explainable in terms of the academic strength of the legacy pool and the fact that preference is given to legacies with high SAT scores; athletes have much lower average SAT scores than both legacies and other students.

TABLE 9.2
Comparison Groups: Legacies, by Conference and Gender,
1995 Entering Cohort

	Ivy League Universities	*UAA Universities*	*NESCAC Colleges*	*Coed Liberal Arts Colleges (Other)*	*Women's Colleges*
Number of Legacies					
Male	79	158			
Female	89	162			
Legacies as a Percent of All Students					
Male	11%	28%			
Female	13%	26%			
Admissions Advantage for Legacies (Percentage Points)					
Male	26		29	18	
Female	28		24	15	14
SAT Scores, by Legacy Status					
Male					
Legacy students	1359	1238			
Other students	1354	1239			
Female					
Legacy students	1338	1191			
Other students	1333	1213			
Percentile Rank in Class by Legacy Status					
Male					
Legacy students	48	44			
Other students	47	49			
Female					
Legacy students	54	48			
Other students	51	53			
Underperformance of Legacies Relative to Students at Large (Rank in Class Percentile Points)					
Male	−2.6	**−6.6**			
Female	−1.5	−3.2			

Source: Expanded College and Beyond database.

Note: Regression coefficents shown in **bold** are significant at the .05 level.

- Legacies do fine in terms of grade point average (ranking, on average, slightly above other students), and they demonstrate only slight (and generally nonsignificant) underperformance.

In short, there is little evidence of a "legacy divide." These students, with strong historical ties to the colleges and universities that were important to their parents and siblings, are given some preference in admissions, but only in the top part of the SAT distribution; then, once admitted, they achieve very much the same outcomes as their classmates. (The practice of giving the benefit of the doubt to legacies in the top part of the SAT distribution, but not in the bottom part, bears an interesting similarity to one proposal for reform in athletics that has been suggested by the Middlebury Ad Hoc Committee. The committee proposed that coaches be allowed to "tip" athletes, as they do at present, but that they be able to "tip" only those ranked academically in the top half of prospective students. We return to this idea in Part C of this book.)

Underrepresented Minority Students

This comparison group evokes by far the strongest feelings and the most contentious debate. We devoted an entire section of *The Game of Life* to a discussion of similarities and differences in academic outcomes between athletes and African American students (because there are considerably more data for the latter sub-group in the '89 cohort than for Hispanics or Native Americans). The larger numbers of Hispanic and Native American students present in the '95 entering cohort permits us to include these sub-groups as well as African Americans in our "minorities" category. In brief, and focusing on the Ivy League schools for ease of exposition and consistency, we find (looking at Tables 9.3 and 9.4):

- The numbers of underrepresented minority students and recruited athletes in an entering class were very comparable; on average, there were roughly 200 of each at an Ivy League university, combining men and women, or about 14 percent of the class.[19]
- The admissions advantage enjoyed by recruited athletes in the Ivies (51 percentage points for men and 56 points for women) was almost twice the admissions advantage enjoyed by minority students (26 percentage points for men and 31 for women). Recruited athletes, men and women alike, were admitted at higher rates than minority candidates at every SAT level (see Appendix Table 9.2, which also includes comparable data for other groups of schools).[20]
- The SAT scores of male minority students were, on average, 41 points higher than the SATs of recruited High Profile athletes but 26 points lower than the SATs of Lower Profile male athletes; the SATs of female minority students were 44 points lower than the SATs of recruited women athletes.
- Male minority students had an average rank-in-class that was higher than the average rank-in-class of the High Profile male athletes and

slightly lower than the average for the men playing Lower Profile sports. Minority men were in the 27th percentile, whereas High Profile athletes were in the 19th percentile, and men in the Lower Profile sports were in the 29th percentile. Female recruited athletes fared better than female minority students; the recruited women ath-

TABLE 9.3
Comparison Groups: Underrepresented Minorities,
by Conference and Gender, 1995 Entering Cohort

	Ivy League Universities	UAA Universities	NESCAC Colleges	Coed Liberal Arts Colleges (Other)	Women's Colleges
Number of Underrepresented Minorities					
Male	89	45	25	23	
Female	113	58	32	25	54
Underrepresented Minorities as a Percent of All Students					
Male	12%	7%	8%	10%	
Female	16%	11%	11%	9%	10%
Admissions Advantage for Underrepresented Minorities (Percentage Points)					
Male	26		41	27	
Female	31		46	30	17
SAT Scores by Minority Status					
Male					
Minority students	1240	1160	1089	1118	
Other students	1358	1269	1242	1261	
Female					
Minority students	1205	1124	1070	1098	1146
Other students	1342	1228	1234	1242	1261
Percentile Rank in Class by Minority Students					
Male					
Minority students	27	29	27	26	
Other students	50	49	45	46	
Female					
Minority students	32	38	36	34	33
Other students	56	54	58	57	51
Underperformance of Underrepresented Minorities Relative to Students at Large (Rank in Class Percentile Points)					
Male	**−11.7**	**−8.0**	**−10.4**	**−10.3**	
Female	**−14.6**	**−8.4**	**−11.7**	**−9.7**	**−6.2**

Source: Expanded College and Beyond database.

Note: Regression coefficents shown in **bold** are significant at the .05 level.

TABLE 9.4
Comparison Groups: Recruited Athletes, by Conference
and Gender, 1995 Entering Cohort

	Ivy League Universities	UAA Universities	NESCAC Colleges	Coed Liberal Arts Colleges (Other)	Women's Colleges
Number of Recruited Athletes					
Male	112	43	62	66	
Female	77	26	45	43	
Recruited Athletes as a Percent of All Students					
Male	16%	7%	24%	26%	
Female	11%	5%	17%	15%	
Admissions Advantage for Recruited Athletes (Percentage Points)					
Male	51		37	26	
Female	56		36	20	23
SAT Scores, by Recruit Status					
Male					
Recruited High Profile athletes	1199	1242	1116	1114	
Recruited Lower Profile athletes	1266	1228	1194	1210	
Students at large	1364	1248	1256	1233	
Female					
Recruited athletes	1249	1190	1158	1194	
Students at large	1328	1203	1226	1201	
Percentile Rank in Class, by Recruit Status					
Male					
Recruited High Profile athletes	19	47	23	30	
Recruited Lower Profile athletes	29	51	37	42	
Students at large	51	47	49	46	
Female					
Recruited athletes	39	49	46	54	
Students at large	54	53	58	56	
Underperformance of Recruited Atheletes Relative to Students at Large (Rank in Class Percentile Points)					
High Profile athletes	**−19.0**	−6.9	**−20.4**	**−10.3**	
Lower Profile athletes	**−15.7**	2.9	**−11.4**	**−8.4**	
Female athletes	**−12.9**	−2.3	**−11.1**	−2.0	

Source: Expanded College and Beyond database.

Note: Regression coefficents shown in **bold** are significant at the .05 level.

letes ranked in the 39th percentile, whereas the women minority students ranked in the 32nd percentile.[21]

- Holding constant SAT scores and fields of study, male athletes, both those in the High Profile sports and those in the Lower Profile sports, underperformed academically to a greater degree than did male minority students (–19.0 and –15.7 percentile points, respectively, for the two groups of athletes, versus –11.7 points for the male minority students); recruited female athletes showed slightly less underperformance than female minority students (–12.9 and –14.6 percentile points, respectively).

Using the same criteria related to academic credentials and academic performance invoked in our earlier discussion of the athletic divide, we conclude that there is also an academically driven "racial divide" on these campuses. In addition, we know that minority students, like athletes, are more likely to major in some fields than in others (although the "bunching" of minority students in, for example, the social sciences is far less pronounced than is the bunching of recruited athletes, and minority students are much more likely to major in the sciences and engineering than are recruited athletes). Moreover, minority students, like athletes, tend to spend considerable time with one another and to form, in some instances, a distinct sub-group on campus—although, as demonstrated in *The Shape of the River*, there is also considerably more interaction across racial lines than many people imagine there is.[22]

In our view, pronounced academic "divides" of any kind are worrying— even though we join others in celebrating differences in backgrounds, outlooks, and views of the world that have the potential to enrich the learning environment for everyone. For reasons already stated, we view academic underperformance as a serious problem for both the students involved and the colleges or universities that they attend. In *The Shape of the River*, Bowen and Bok discuss the underperformance of African American students in great detail and describe the pervasive nature of underperformance as their single "most troubling" finding.[23]

Since the publication of *The Game of Life*, new research by Douglas Massey and his colleagues has demonstrated far more powerfully than any prior work the extent to which underperformance by minority students is due to "stereotype threat." Initially proposed by the Stanford psychologist Claude Steele, the theory of stereotype threat holds (according to Massey and his colleagues): "Members of certain minority groups are prone to under-perform academically because of an unconscious fear of living up to negative group stereotypes. If the fear is strong enough, it interferes with performance. . . . The stereotype of black intellectual inferiority is deeply imbedded in American culture and black students are keenly aware of prevailing negative valuations of their mental abilities. Every time that a black student is called upon to perform academically, therefore, he or she is at risk of confirming a deeply-rooted negative stereotype."[24] Massey and his colleagues have constructed social scales that measure various facets of stereotype threat; they then use these scales to predict grade performance. Their principal conclusion is that the "inclusion [in regressions predicting grade point average] of measures relative to stereotype threat eliminates entirely the black-white and Latino-white grade point gap."[25] There are many other aspects to the analysis, including a demonstration that the academic performance of minority students improves when they are part of a more diverse class that does not consist overwhelmingly of white students.[26] For present purposes, however, it is the strong relationship between stereotype threat and underperformance that is most relevant.

Athletes are presumably also susceptible to "stereotype threat," especially on close-knit college campuses where faculty may know what at least some of their students do outside of the classroom. The Amherst and Williams reports provide ample reason to believe that stereotyping can be real and that it may well take a toll academically. Unfortunately, we have no way of assessing just how important stereotype threat is in the case of athletes (especially as contrasted with selection effects growing out of the recruitment/admissions process and with "culture" effects associated with being members of athletic teams). Intuitively, however, we would expect stereotype threat to be appreciably less consequential for athletes than for African American students because (a) they do not have the same deeply ingrained history of having suffered for generations from racial discrimination and stereotyping; (b) in many instances athletes may be less readily identified by instructors than minority students, who are always visible by dint of skin color (the place kicker may escape being perceived as a football player); and (c) recruited athletes, especially men in the Lower Profile sports and women athletes, are more likely than minority students to have attended strong secondary schools and to have come from affluent backgrounds that can bolster self-confidence and offer some protection against intimidation due to stereotyping.

Whatever the underlying causes, we believe it is important for institutions to do all in their power to reduce "academic divides" of every kind and, in particular, to address academic underperformance. The need for colleges and universities to be more proactive in this regard is a major theme of *The Shape of the River,* and there is some evidence that progress is being made. In thinking about how to view the comparison between the academic outcomes achieved by recruited athletes and those of minority students, it is helpful to consider the rather different trends that apply in the two cases. Comparing the '76 and '95 entering cohorts, we find that the academic credentials and the academic performance of minority students have improved, whereas those of the athletes (and especially the High Profile athletes) have moved in the other direction (Table 9.5). A snapshot of the divergent changes is provided in Figure 9.2, which shows (for the four Ivies in the original College and Beyond database) declines in average rank-in-class and increasing underperformance for

TABLE 9.5

Comparison Groups: Athletes and Minorities, over Time,
1976 and 1995 Entering Cohorts, Ivy League Universities
and Coed Liberal Arts Colleges from *The Game of Life*

	High Profile Male Athletes	Lower Profile Male Athletes	Minority Men	Female Athletes	Minority Women
Ivy League Universities					
SAT Scores					
1976	1150	1263	1101	1253	1072
1995	1211	1302	1234	1300	1220
Change	+61	+39	+133	+47	+148
Percentile Rank in Class					
1976	31	46	26	51	23
1995	20	38	27	45	33
Change	–11	–8	+1	–6	+10
Underperformance Relative to Students at Large					
(Rank in Class Percentile Points)					
1976	**–12.0**	**–5.7**	**–9.0**	**–3.7**	**–17.3**
1995	**–17.0**	**–8.5**	**–8.5**	**–8.4**	**–12.7**
Change	–5.0	–2.8	+0.5	–4.7	+4.7
***Coed Liberal Arts Colleges from* The Game of Life**					
SAT Scores					
1976	1129	1187	978	1219	1056
1995	1143	1225	1102	1201	1090
Change	+14	+38	+124	–18	+34
Percentile Rank in Class					
1976	37	42	18	50	22
1995	31	41	27	51	38
Change	–6	–1	+9	+1	+16
Underperformance Relative to Students at Large					
(Rank in Class Percentile Points)					
1976	**–7.2**	**–6.2**	**–10.7**	**–3.1**	**–18.7**
1995	**–11.8**	**–7.6**	**–7.2**	**–4.7**	**–8.1**
Change	–4.6	–1.4	+3.5	–1.6	+10.6

Source: Expanded College and Beyond database.

Note: Regression coefficents shown in **bold** are significant at the .05 level.

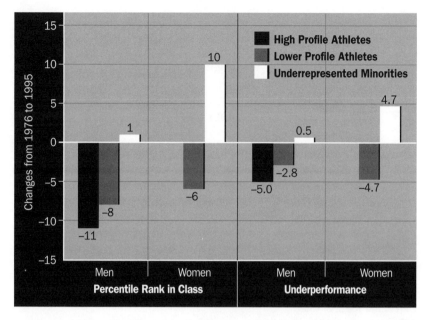

Figure 9.2. Comparison Groups: Athletes and Underrepresented Minority
Students, Changes in Percentile Rank in Class and Underperformance from
1976 to 1995, Ivy League Universities
    Source: Expanded College and Beyond database.

athletes at the same time that minority students, both men and women,
have shown at least modest improvement in both respects.

In any event, there is a far more consequential frame of reference—
namely, values and missions. We need to ask directly how the recruitment
of athletes and the recruitment of minority students fit within the missions of the colleges and universities that they attend, and how they relate to institutional and societal values. One astute reader of *The Game of
Life,* the demographer Marta Tienda (who is also a faculty mentor to
some Princeton athletes), recently observed: "Initially I thought there was
a contradiction between the arguments in the *Shape of the River* and the
Game of Life [a greater willingness to accept some degree of underperformance among minorities than among athletes]—but as I have
thought about this more, I don't believe there is. It is, ultimately, a question of social priorities, values, and social justice."[27]

Professor Tienda, in our view, is exactly right in thinking about
the issue this way. The arguments in favor of recruiting minority students are entirely different from those in favor of recruiting goalies (or
volleyball spikers). The two groups occupy, we would suggest, entirely

different places in a mission-driven hierarchy of values and purposes. Stubborn problems of academic underperformance notwithstanding, the active recruitment of highly qualified minority students is justified on two grounds.

First, as many have argued eloquently, a racially diverse student body enhances the education of all students, especially as colleges and universities seek to prepare students to live and work in an increasingly multiracial, multi-national world. Lee C. Bollinger, formerly president of the University of Michigan and now president of Columbia, writes: "Diversity is not an optional appendage to a first-rate liberal arts education—it is as much at the core as Shakespeare." According to the testimony of the overwhelming majority of the graduates of the colleges in the original College and Beyond database, the presence of a diverse student body has enabled students of all races to have a richer, more valuable educational experience that has served them well in later life.[28]

Second, essentially every selective college and university has sought to enroll larger numbers of minority students in order to contribute, however modestly, to the closing of the racially defined gaps in access to opportunity and power that are such a striking legacy of what Glenn C. Loury has called this nation's "unlovely racial history."[29] The notable success achieved by so many minority graduates of these academically selective colleges and universities, not only professionally but in providing leadership in civic and community affairs, speaks for itself. As Provost Cole has put it: "[The admission of minority students] can serve an extremely important societal purpose with a set of profound social consequences—as important a purpose as I can think of."[30]

These are the reasons, rooted in values, why the case for accepting risks of academic underperformance among minority students, even as we work to encourage improved academic outcomes and eliminate underperformance, seems to us compelling in a way that is entirely different from the way one might seek to justify the recruitment of a soccer player. It is, finally, educational considerations, and considerations of racial justice, that connect the enhancement of opportunities for those left behind for too long to the core missions of colleges and universities chartered to serve the public good.

In this chapter we have shown that the widening athletic divide has grown markedly over the past decades not just because of developments within athletics, but also because of trends within higher education itself—especially increasing stratification (the greater concentrations of talent and resources), the recruitment and advancement of faculty members who are highly focused on their own fields of study, the greater emphasis placed on independent work and other interactive modes of learning rather than on passive attendance at lectures, and admissions philosophies that emphasize special talents and achievements. These trends are likely to continue to influence the size and shape of the athletic divide.

Many colleges and universities are devoting increased attention to the improvement of undergraduate education and residential life, which is all to the good. But not even vigorous efforts to encourage interactions of all kinds, and more "learning from each other," are likely to diminish to any appreciable extent the division on many campuses between conflicting athletic and academic cultures. More fundamentally, it is hard to imagine factors that would—or should—lessen the drive for academic excellence that lies behind so many of the trends within the academy that widen the academic-athletic divide.

Efforts to identify other "divides" indicate that only the recruitment of minority students poses issues at all comparable to the issues posed by the recruitment of athletes. To be sure, there are numerous pockets of specialized talents and interests, but there is no evidence that musicians (to stay with that example) fail to take full advantage of the academic offerings available to them. On the contrary, they do well academically as well as on the concert stage or in the orchestra pit. Legacies admitted by these schools, contrary to what many suppose, are well prepared academically and are strong academic achievers when they matriculate.

Minority students, on the other hand, continue to enter college with lower test scores than their classmates and to underperform academically. However, in contrast to the trend we see for recruited athletes, the gaps for minority students appear to be diminishing rather than increasing. "Stereotype vulnerability" can hurt the academic performance of both minority students and athletes, but this deep-seated problem is almost certainly more pronounced among minority students, who live with histories of racial discrimination. The final and most important point is that the reasons for encouraging the matriculation of minority students are, in our view, far more consonant with the educational missions of these institutions than are the reasons for recruiting athletes—and much more in line with the stated purposes these tax-favored institutions are chartered to serve.

In short, we are driven back, as we always should be, to values and missions.

The Higher Ground: A Reform Agenda

CHAPTER 10

Retaking the High Ground

Douglas Bennet, president of Wesleyan University, began an interview with the editor of his alumni magazine by declaring: "The NESCAC [New England Small College Athletic Conference] presidents all feel that we have a mission: to go back to the high ground in admissions and to compete with each other with teams composed as our student bodies are composed."[1] In our view, this is exactly the right stance for colleges and universities that are clear about their educational values and are troubled by the widening academic-athletic divide. In our view, the "costs" of the divide—which we spell out in the main part of this chapter—have become so substantial that inaction is hard to justify.

ASSESSING THE BENEFITS
OF INTERCOLLEGIATE COMPETITION

There are, to be sure, arguments in favor of paying special attention to intercollegiate athletics that deserve careful consideration and a proper weighting in discussions of reform agendas. They include, from the standpoint of the players, the argument that students should be able to participate in an activity that is, for many, enormously rewarding. "Games" are, first and foremost, simply a source of pleasure and satisfaction. They are also a way of introducing some balance into a student's life. There are health benefits, both psychic and physical ("a sound mind in a sound body"). Competing on intercollegiate teams can also be an important learning experience. As countless athletes have testified, by competing one learns "life lessons": teamwork, discipline, resilience, perseverance, how to "play by the rules" and accept outcomes one may not like. A. Bartlett Giamatti, former president of Yale, once said: "Athletics teaches lessons valuable to the individual by stretching the human spirit in ways that nothing else can."[2] Athletics has often been said to teach "character," although it is notoriously hard to define, let alone measure, that much-prized but elusive attribute. Of course it is also possible to learn from sports, as from other activities, some wrong lessons: a "win-at-all-costs" attitude, lack of respect for one's opponents, and an arrogance that can lead to insufferable behavior.

Participation in varsity sports is also said to prepare young people for leadership roles in later life (according to the Duke of Wellington, "the battle of Waterloo was won on the playing fields of Eton"). In some spheres, this certainly appears to be the case, although again it is hard to sort out all the influences at work. In our earlier study we examined empirically both attitudes toward leadership and actual manifestations of leadership on the part of athletes and their classmates from the 1951 and 1976 entering cohorts at many of these schools. The conclusions we came to were these:

> Athletes were more likely than other students to rate themselves highly as leaders before college began and were also more likely to say, after college, that leadership had played an important role in their lives; yet, surprisingly, neither this greater inclination to provide leadership, nor this stronger expression of its importance, is associated with evidence of having actually provided more leadership. Athletes and their classmates seem about on a par in this regard. Athletes were no more likely than other students to become CEOs, to earn top salaries in professional fields like law and medicine (where earnings may serve as a proxy for leadership), or to be leaders in most civic activities.[3]

Difficult as it is to quantify many of these benefits to the participants, and important as it is not to exaggerate them, they are real. In a recent speech, former Secretary of State George Shultz described vividly the lessons learned from football in "the days when 11 guys on the field played 11 other guys on the field." However, Shultz lamented that, today, "it's one organization versus another organization."[4] Realizing the benefits of sports does not require the kinds of high-intensity athletics programs that have evolved over the past three or four decades. In fact, the most compelling reasons for investing in college sports are undercut, not strengthened, by building teams that are cut off from much of campus life and in significant ways are at odds with the primary educational missions of these institutions. The most basic lessons that sports teach can be learned without compromising academic values.[5]

A rather different argument in favor of strong intercollegiate programs is that they "build campus spirit and community." This benefit was without question given considerable weight by the presidents of the University Athletic Association (UAA) universities when they formed their association. The building of "campus spirit and community" can be lost, however, or at least diminished, when teams are composed of players who have less in common with their classmates than once was the case. In commenting on life in one of Princeton's residential colleges, the college's former master, Professor Charles Berry, reports that the segregation of High Profile athletes from other students had the effect of reducing the interest of others in varsity sports: "They [the non-athletes] were not involved. Their friends were not involved, and there was no reason for them to be interested. I would bet that if you traced, at Princeton, student attendance rates at home football games, you would find a very substantial decline from nineteen-fifty to nineteen-ninety. Part of that may be due to television and the rise of pro football—the Ivy League is also not the Big Ten—but I think much of it is also that the non-athlete student body no longer identifies with the high profile athletes. The two groups are different. They have different interests."[6]

Whatever the reasons, including the simple fact that other students have their own compelling interests and are frequently pressed for time, members of High Profile teams no longer play the role they once played at the center of campus life. Still, however complicated the feelings about athletics may be, successful intercollegiate programs can be helpful in generating goodwill among both alumni and residents of surrounding communities. Success in winning national championships can definitely benefit a college or university through favorable publicity and national visibility. It is much less clear, however, that enhanced external visibility associated with athletics contributes significantly either to fundraising or to student recruitment. Recent econometric research fails to find any correlation of consequence between "winning and giving," and a survey of college-bound high school seniors (by a group that does market research and strategic planning for non-profits) concluded that "intercollegiate athletics have little influence on college choice—intramural and recreational opportunities matter more."[7]

We believe that sound programs of intercollegiate athletics can confer important benefits on both the participants and their institutions. We are skeptical, however, that the most important of these benefits would be sacrificed if determined efforts were made to "reclaim the high ground." Moreover, the value of any "extra" benefits associated with an intensive intercollegiate program needs to be weighed against the very real costs of the attendant "athletic divide"—which seem to us to be both substantial and on the rise. In the language of another well-known aphorism: "the game may not be worth the candle."[8]

THE GROWING "COSTS" OF THE ACADEMIC-ATHLETIC DIVIDE

We put the word *costs* in quotation marks because we are not suggesting that the financial resources required to support intercollegiate teams are the most worrying aspects of the widening athletic divide. The dollar costs are real, and we say more about them later, but it is the other "costs," those that cannot be captured on an income statement or a balance sheet of the conventional kind, that are the most fundamental.

Missions, Messages, and Truth-Telling

At the highest level of abstraction, there is a nest of issues that have to do with mission, the primacy of educational values, and maintaining a right balance or "proportion" among the various aspects of a student's college experience. Never one to mince words, Robert Hutchins wrote in 1938: "Of all the crimes committed by athleticism [by which he meant the professionalization/commercialization of college sports] . . . , the most heinous is the confusion of the country about the primary purpose of higher education."[9] Still earlier, in a 1929 Carnegie Foundation report, Howard Savage listed first among the causes of the defects of American college athletics "a negligent attitude toward the educational opportunity for which the college exists."[10]

In 1980, President Giamatti of Yale extolled the virtues of "amateur" athletics in a beautifully crafted speech that is replete with references to the classics, to British schoolboy traditions, and to Cardinal Newman. Giamatti stressed the importance of the Platonic idea of "proportion": "We must remember that it is our obligation to consider our students as students above all else, and to treat them in an evenhanded fashion, . . . so that their time to develop as thinking and feeling human beings is not deformed by the demands of athletic pursuits. . . . There must be at Yale, in philosophy and in actuality, *proportion* [our emphasis] in how the institution shapes itself and in how it encourages and sanctions a student's behavior. Athletics is essential, but not primary. It contributes to the point, but is not the point itself."[11] Then, near the end of the speech, he said: "I believe there is a lack of proportion, an imbalance, in the way the programs in athletics in the Ivy Group have been allowed to grow. . . . If the Ivy Group wants to be more than a set of financial aid policies and a concatenation of schedules, then I think it must return to its first principles. Else, as a group and as individual institutions, we will lose precisely what is liberating and fulfilling in our kind of college athletics and we will gain nothing save the scorn of those who wonder why we act in a fashion so inconsistent with our ideals and principles."[12] The recent (2001) statements by the NESCAC presidents reaffirming their belief in their founding principles, including "representativeness," are similar in spirit.

A related set of concerns has to do with the "signaling effects" off campus (and on) of the policies and practices of academically selective colleges and universities. Yale's Nobel Prize–winning economist James Tobin spoke for many others when he asked directly: "What message do we convey to schools and towns when the Yale emissaries who do visit them are interested only in star athletes?"[13] For at least two years in a row, *U.S. News & World Report,* in its annual issue on "America's Best Colleges," featured advice on how to use athletics as a "hook" to get into the college of one's choice. In 2001 they quoted Richard Nesbitt, Williams College admissions director, as saying, "There's no question that there's an advantage for a very limited number of impact athletes," and then going on to mention that Williams fills approximately 72 athletic slots each year. In the fall of 2002, the *U.S. News* guide included the following advice: "Admissions officers will be much more impressed by your athletic ability if they hear about it from a coach on their own campus. Athletes can begin trying to attract the notice of college coaches as early as freshman year by joining traveling teams, playing in tournaments, and attending sports camps hosted by colleges."[14]

All of the selective colleges and universities participating in this study are known and respected for their leadership roles in higher education. Given their stature, it is especially problematic when these institutions, by their actions, tell parents, prospective students, secondary schools, and the public at large that they assign a disproportionate degree of importance to athletic achievement. Responsibility for sports craziness at younger and younger ages (including premature specialization) has deep societal roots, but these prestigious colleges and universities would be in a stronger position to help counter such trends if recruited athletes enjoyed less of an admissions advantage.[15]

On the power of signals sent by leading colleges and universities:

In commenting on an early draft of our manuscript, Professor John Emerson at Middlebury urged: "Do not underestimate the degree of influence and power that the top universities and colleges have on the schools, on high school (and younger!) students, and on families. Students in high school and junior high school specialize in one sport at a very intense level, go to the summer camps, etc. because they are convinced that is what will win them admission to selective colleges. They, their counselors, and their families see accomplished athletes being admitted to the best colleges 'over the heads' of other students who are clearly stronger academically. Not surprisingly they are responding to the realities defined by the actions of admissions offices at selective colleges. My evidence here is admittedly anecdotal. But I have a son who taught for two years at Choate–Rosemary Hall after attending Deerfield Academy and then graduating from Middlebury

College in computer science. One of my colleagues on our committee has a brother who is a college counselor at a private high school. A second colleague on the committee has a close friend who is a faculty member at a private school. Each of us has had detailed conversations with the relevant representatives of the secondary schools. To say the least, these conversations have been eye-openers. . . . The actions of selective college admissions offices speak clearly to these professionals!"

Signals are also communicated from one sector to another within higher education. A main finding of *The Game of Life* was that there is an "influence-by-emulation" phenomenon that spreads practices and policies from one set of schools to another. For example, when Division I schools began to recruit more aggressively in the so-called minor sports, the Ivies felt pressure to do the same. Facilities widely available in Division I and the Ivy League (turf fields, for example) have become the standard at other levels of play, including Division III. Intensification of women's athletics programs at coed colleges has spread, almost by contagion, to women's colleges. Both the Ivy League and NESCAC have an opportunity to influence the paths that other non-scholarship schools follow, and they need to recognize the spill-over effects of their policies.

There is, finally, another cost of the athletic divide that fits under the broad rubric of "missions, messages, and principles." It concerns the reputations of institutions and conferences for truth-telling. The headmaster of Kingswood-Oxford school, Lee Levison, writes: "Over the past four years I have been troubled by apparent shifts in the role of sport in society and the impact of such changes on Kingswood-Oxford. It seems to me that there is a growing gap between the rhetoric and reality associated with athletics—at all levels."[16] There are, regrettably, numerous examples at the college level of differences between what schools say about their athletics programs and what really goes on. For example, videos and other pronouncements about the openness of intercollegiate athletics programs to all comers are contradicted by the heavy preference given to recruited athletes when rosters are formed. Aspiring walk-ons, who are unaware either of how things really work or of the level of skill now required to play college sports, are often disappointed, sometimes severely so. One college president was sufficiently alarmed by this disjuncture between expectations and realities that he said bluntly, in a closed meeting, "We are going to change either what we say or what we do."

We have also noted occasional instances in which schools portray academic outcomes on their campuses in ways that differ, sometimes markedly, from the actual situation, as revealed by data. For example, claims that athletes do just as well academically as other students are frequently untrue. We mention no names, since data for individual schools are confidential and we have no intention of embarrassing individuals or institutions in any case; moreover, we recognize that the explanation for such contradictions may rest primarily on lack of knowledge of what is really happening. But it is still troubling to see such discrepancies. More generally, it is discouraging, to say the least, to see the clear disconnect that exists today between the stated principles of groups such as the Ivy League and NESCAC and the realities that they have come to accept. It is time either to change practices or to revise high-sounding statements of principle.

Truth-telling is important, especially for institutions that pride themselves, as colleges and universities should, on inculcating respect for evidence and for their own unequivocal commitments to honest rendering of facts and to faithful reporting. There is something unsettling about reading stories describing the "purity" of athletics at the non-scholarship schools when so many of their leaders are well aware of the compromises that are being made in fielding teams. There is enough cynicism today about the capacity of institutions (whether they be corporations, churches, colleges and universities, governmental entities, or foundations) to be what they claim to be that we certainly do not need additional instances of misreporting, however innocent the intentions.[17]

On the importance of institutional truth-telling:

One faculty commentator on our manuscript put it this way: "The issues here are not so much misrepresentations as they are 'thinking that we know the truth when we don't and cannot without hard-nosed empirical evidence.' We are institutions of truth-seeking and higher learning—we *must* speak the truth and get the account exactly right, just as we try hard to do in our scholarship and teaching. Colleges and universities must practice what we preach about such important, complex, and 'loaded' issues or we will damage ourselves in the long run."

Opportunity Costs

Beneath the intangible but highly significant "costs" associated with these large questions of principle and reputation lie more tangible concerns. In the case of the selective colleges and universities that have many more qualified applicants than they have places, the most obvious concern is the opportunity cost associated with admitting Smith rather than Jones. In many settings, students of exceptionally high quality who are eager to take advantage of the special educational opportunities a particular college has to offer (including many who excelled in high school sports) are turned away because places have been claimed by recruited athletes who are focused so heavily on the success of their teams that they have neither the time nor the inclination to participate fully in the educational life of the institution.

This critically important trade-off can be overlooked all too easily—by coaches, among others—when athletes offer what are, by national standards, more than passable credentials. Time and again, coaches have told us that their players, although admittedly not "shooting out the lights" academically, are doing "OK." "What's wrong with that?" one coach asked. To be sure, the athletes in question have generally graduated, enjoyed their college experience, and learned from their professors and fellow students, and they will continue to benefit from the "credential" represented by the degree earned. But in institutions that have responsibility for rationing access to highly prized educational opportunities, doing "OK" should not be the standard.[18]

We have no way of knowing which specific candidates would have been enrolled had fewer recruited athletes been given places in the class, but we do know that at almost all of these selective institutions the quality of the "admit" list declines very little, if at all, as final selections are made. Selective institutions such as the ones in this study are well known for asserting that they reject at least as many qualified applicants as they accept, and Figures 3.2a–3.2d, which show how many high-scoring applicants with SATs of 1300 and higher were rejected in selecting members of the 1999 entering cohort, confirm this assertion. At these schools the competition for admission by applicants is intense, and the accomplishments of the "students at large," detailed in earlier chapters, are a reasonable proxy for the opportunity costs associated with admitting significant numbers of recruited athletes.[19] *Each recruited athlete who attends one of these schools has taken a spot away from another student who was, in all likelihood, more academically qualified—and probably more committed to taking full advantage of the educational resources available at these schools.*[20]

Caroline Hoxby's research adds an important quantitative dimension to this story, showing that the students rejected in favor of recruited athletes are missing out on an ever more valuable experience. She finds that the "geographic integration" of the higher education marketplace, whereby students are sorted among schools more efficiently, and the corresponding increase in the concentration of the ablest students at the most selective schools, have caused the difference in per-student subsidies across institutions to widen dramatically in both private and public colleges. (The *per-student subsidy* is the amount of resources a college provides to a student over and above the net tuition that the student pays.) Hoxby has found that "nearly all of the widening [between the amount of the subsidy offered by the highest-subsidy and lowest-subsidy schools] has occurred because the upper tail has become more right-skewed." That is, those schools that had the highest per-student subsidies have increased their subsidies the most. "Among both public and private colleges, the ratio of the [per-student subsidy at the] 75th percentile to the median [per-student subsidy] has more than doubled [between 1976 and 1991]."[21] In short, the "value" of the spot occupied by the recruited athlete has increased markedly at the schools in this study.

President Lawrence Bacow of Tufts, an economist who was previously chancellor at MIT, found the evidence on underperformance by athletes to be the most striking feature of this analysis, and he related these findings to the question of how colleges should allocate the resources available to them. In his words: "We have several scarce resources to allocate here. One is spots in the entering class, another is financial resources [discussed later], and there is also the time of the students when they are on our campuses." The fact that recruited athletes are doing less well than they are predicted to do is "alarming," in his view, because it says that the colleges are not using the time available from the students as well as they should be using it. That is, the "value added" is less than it should be.[22]

One very different form of opportunity cost created by the present-day athletic divide centers on access to opportunities to play intercollegiate sports in college. Are the right policies in place to govern who gets to participate? One consequence of the current mode of recruitment and the attendant early forming of teams (often, on paper at least, before school even starts) is that there is relatively little opportunity—less every year, it would seem—for non-recruited students to play varsity sports. It can certainly be argued that regularly chosen students who played sports in high school and would like to continue competing (while also doing many other things on campus) should have some real opportunity to benefit from intercollegiate athletics programs. The fact that these students are not already fully "trained up" when they enter college (or are less fully trained up than their highly recruited and more athletically focused classmates) should not deprive them of an opportunity to play at the intercollegiate level.[23] It seems to us more than mildly ironic that these opportunities—often paid for in substantial measure by tuition payments made by all students—are, in the words of the Middlebury Ad Hoc Committee, "the exclusive privilege of those pre-selected by coaches through the recruiting process."[24] This reality raises serious questions of both fairness and the role of athletics in campus life. In our view, providing broader access to participation in college sports by students in general would be healthy all around. In the words of one president, "Let's give college sports back to the students!"

Dollar Costs

Institutional expenditures are, of course, the usual measure of the "costs" of any activity, and the dollar outlays devoted to intercollegiate sports are considerable at these institutions. The Ivies and the colleges and universities that compete in Division III have always understood that varsity athletics needs to have a claim on general funds; the idea that big-time sports can "pay for themselves" (and perhaps for other sports as well) has never held sway at these institutions. Unfortunately, the publicly available data are not reliable enough to permit the presentation of a detailed picture of either expenditures or revenues. Still, there is enough information available to allow us to conclude that in 2000–01 the direct costs of intercollegiate athletics programs were in the range of $10 million per institution in the Ivies, $2.5 million in the UAA universities, $2 million in the NESCAC colleges, and $1.5 million in the other coed liberal arts colleges in the study.[25]

There are some revenue offsets, especially in the Ivies, but it is even more difficult to quantify these than it is to obtain reliable estimates of expenditures. In the UAA universities, the NESCAC colleges, and the other liberal arts colleges, total revenues attributed to athletics average well under $200,000 per school and consist mainly of sports-related contributions of one kind or another. In the Ivies, our sense is that "earned income" (defined in the traditional sense of ticket sales to the public, guarantees for appearances, radio and television receipts, sponsorships, and advertising) is in the general range of $200,000 to perhaps $1 million. The bulk of the "revenues" reported by the Ivies consist of contributions from alumni/ae and others, often raised by "friends" groups, as well as modest amounts of endowment income and, in the case of some institutions, "activity fees" paid by students. (The practice of using "friends" groups to raise substantial sums of money for athletics raises other issues, including those of influence, if not control, and thus can entail costs of another kind.)

Whatever the appropriate revenue offsets, we know that the direct expenditures reported on the Equity in Athletics Disclosure Act (EADA) forms substantially underestimate the true costs of varsity sports programs as now constituted. Reported expenditures generally fail to capture two major components of cost at every institution: shared administrative and infrastructure costs of various kinds and capital costs. Careful studies at

Williams (based on work by Gordon Winston, an economist and former provost who has pioneered the development of "global accounting") led, first, to the allocation of over $400,000 of central institutional costs to the athletics program—a share of admissions office expenses and so on—thereby raising the total outlays from current accounts by about 25 percent. Far more significant is the attribution of capital costs. Building-by-building estimates of the replacement cost of athletic facilities, combined with very conservative assumptions about depreciation and the opportunity cost of capital, led to an estimate of $2.7 million of capital costs per year. Athletics is a capital-intensive activity, and it is not surprising that at a college with facilities as extensive as those at Williams, capital costs would dominate annual operating costs. In the Ivies, it would hardly be surprising if a similar mode of analysis were to result in annual capital costs of, say, $10 million.[26] It is revealing to note that in explaining the rationale for its decision to terminate its men's and women's swimming and diving programs (a decision that was subsequently rescinded), Dartmouth put considerable weight on the large "investment" in facilities, maintenance, and program costs that would be needed to make these teams more competitive—which it estimated to be in the $20 to $25 million range.[27]

Differences in dollar costs between the groups of schools in this study are driven more powerfully by "level of play" (Division I versus Division III, for example) than by anything else. The Ivies have chosen to spend *much* more on coaching, recruiting, and facilities than the Division III institutions, presumably as a consequence of their decision to compete at the Division I level. A second factor is how programs are conducted within Division III. The UAA universities spend roughly twice as much *per sport* as do the NESCAC colleges or the other liberal arts colleges (for example, an average of $112,000 on women's soccer as compared with $65,000 in a NESCAC college). Roughly half of this difference (say, $30,000) is associated with the higher travel costs incurred by the UAA schools because of the geographic spread of the Association's members. The rest of the difference is due to higher expenditures on coaching and some modest outlays on recruiting. A final factor affecting total expenditures is, of course, the number of sports an institution (or a conference) elects to sponsor. The considerable scale of the typical NESCAC program raises its costs, and the UAA universities have saved money by sponsoring fewer teams.[28]

It is clear that, for historical and other reasons, the colleges and universities in this study spend far more money on intercollegiate teams than they do on any other extracurricular activity. How much is spent, as we have indicated, depends on a wide variety of policy choices. We do not have data on trends in expenditures on college sports, but we have a sense (based in part on comparisons with data collected earlier for *The Game of*

Life) that costs have been rising more rapidly in the past few years in the coed liberal arts colleges than in the universities. Of course expenditures in this sector are rising from a lower base, and it may be that these colleges, which sponsor competition in a wide range of sports, are feeling increasing pressure to move toward the coaching models (head coaches focused on a single sport, year-round) and associated practices common elsewhere; NESCAC is itself engaged in a careful study of costs, both across schools and over time, that should permit much clearer conclusions to be drawn.

None of the schools in this study is likely to base policy decisions concerning athletics primarily on financial considerations, nor should they. But neither can they simply ignore the question of how many scarce resources should be spent on teams that are more and more heavily populated by recruited athletes, especially at a time when adverse trends in financial markets, among other factors, have caused financial constraints to become more pressing. Dartmouth originally announced that in order to offset losses on its endowment, it would terminate its men's and women's swimming and diving teams; this decision was reversed only after parents and alumni/ae pledged to cover the costs out of new funds. Oberlin has said explicitly that it will cut its athletic budget as well as seek economies in many other areas. The unusually favorable financial climate of the 1990s may well have allowed a number of the schools in this study to be more sanguine about expenditures on athletics than they can afford to be today.[29]

Campus Ethos

In tallying the costs of the athletic divide, broader effects on both academic programs and campus ethos also have to be taken into account. The Williams Ad Hoc Committee report provides the clearest indication of how the bunching of athletes in certain fields and courses, combined with the attitudes that many bring to the classroom, can have serious spillover effects on other students and on faculty members. The "dumbing down" of classroom expectations, referred to by one faculty member at Williams, is plainly worrying, as is the evidence in the Amherst report, limited as it is, of disproportionate numbers of disciplinary infractions among athletes in the High Profile sports.[30] It is not surprising that the strongest negative views of the effects of recruited athletes on the academic experience are held by faculty members teaching the courses most heavily subscribed by athletes. It is also noteworthy that negative views about the effects of today's athletic programs are expressed more strongly by students near the end of their college careers, who have seen the cumulative effects of the "athletic culture" on the academic ambience of their school, than by students just starting out. These kinds of "costs" can be consequential in colleges that are both relatively small and enroll large numbers of students who are highly motivated to achieve academically. They may not exist, or may be barely noticeable, in larger places and in settings where academic expectations are more modest.

College sports, once heralded as a means of unifying the campus and building school spirit, have become much less important in this regard as athletes and other students have come to see less and less of each other, as attendance by students at large at athletic events has declined (in part because these students are less likely to feel a bond with players than students of other generations did with their classmates who were star athletes), and as academic pursuits, including greater emphasis on independent work, and other extracurricular activities have become more compelling claimants on time and attention.[31] The ironic twist on this turn of events is that, in some settings at least, athletics programs not only fail to tie elements of a campus community together; they actually are a *divisive* force. As an Amherst undergraduate writes: "Athletic recruiting seems to have divided the Fairest College more than post-tenure review or financial aid policy ever could."[32] The Williams Ad Hoc Committee report includes this telling sentence: "The claim that athletics unifies the student body collides with evidence that varsity athletics is resented by many of our top students."[33] This kind of cost is difficult to quantify, but it cannot be ignored.

A Clear Trajectory

Any number of college and university presidents and other commentators have spoken of "drift," of institutions and conferences at all levels of play moving, at first almost imperceptibly, farther and farther away from their own first principles. The most recent Knight Foundation Commission report cites evidence of "the widening chasm between higher education's ideals and big-time college sports."[34] In our previous study, which traced developments through the time of the 1989 entering cohort, the evidence was clear-cut: the divide between the athletic enterprise and the core educational mission of selective colleges and universities had steadily widened since Meyerson, representing the Ivy League presidents, wrote his memo on this subject in the late 1970s (see Chapter 7).

The new research reported here, which includes data for the members of the '95 entering cohort at a larger number of institutions, only underscores the earlier conclusion. The divide has continued to widen: there is not a single indicator pointing in the reverse direction. Our major concern is that if vigorous actions are not taken to heed the clear directional signals and change course, college sports will become less and less relevant to the majority of regular students at these institutions and more and more at variance with their educational missions. The urgency of taking action stems both from the seriousness of the issues evident today and from the fact that, left to their own devices, the forces that have brought us to this point will lead to even more serious problems in the future. There is no self-correcting mechanism on which anyone dare rely.

GUIDING PRINCIPLES

In turning now to the central question of what we believe should be done, we begin by reiterating once again an absolutely key assumption—*conviction* might be a better word—that intercollegiate athletics has been, can be, and should be a powerfully positive part of college life. In the language of the Original 1954 Ivy Agreement: "Under proper conditions intercollegiate competition in organized athletics offers desirable development and recreation for players and a healthy focus of collegiate loyalty."[35] This is a splendidly succinct statement of beliefs shared by many of those whom we consulted.

The important qualifying phrase, "under proper conditions," plainly requires explication. In our view, conducting intercollegiate programs under proper conditions means adhering to certain core principles, which we believe should drive proposals for reform. These principles are not new, and the quotation marks in the summary presented in the box indicate language adopted by one group of institutions or another over many years.[36]

Core principles to guide athletics programs:

1. "The program in intercollegiate athletics is to be kept in harmony with the essential educational purposes of the institution."[37]
2. "Players shall be truly representative of the student body."[38]
3. "Equal opportunities shall be provided for men and women."[39]
4. "Student athletes shall be measured against the same standards as other students in admissions, financial aid, and academic programs."[40]
5. Athletes, like other students, shall have opportunities to participate in a wide variety of activities (including more than a single sport) and shall be fully participating members of their campus communities, not isolated from others or a "class apart."[41]

---

6. Students in general (not just recruited athletes) shall have reasonable opportunities to compete on intercollegiate teams; "we should encourage non-recruited athletes to earn places on our teams."[42]

7. Athletes should have a reasonable chance to enjoy competitive success, playing against opponents that share common educational and athletic philosophies.

8. A reasonable degree of competitive balance should be sought: "Each member school ought not merely to tolerate, but to value a balance of competitive success within the Group. Although schools may differ in those sports in which they excel, a reasonable competitive balance among institutions over time over all sports should be sought."[43]

THE NEED FOR A NUANCED PERSPECTIVE: ON "WINNING" AND THE "PURSUIT OF EXCELLENCE IN ALL THINGS"

Many of those with whom we have spoken in the course of the research presented here would embrace this set of principles wholeheartedly—indeed, some may well have drafted one or another version of them! Yet it is evident from our findings that, the best intentions notwithstanding, there has been considerable slippage in adhering to these principles—within the Ivies, within the NESCAC colleges, within some of the selective liberal arts colleges, and in High Profile sports more generally. (Even in the UAA universities, which have done so well in adhering to principles like those listed in the box, there are signs of at least modest stress in football.) Having examined the national trends within athletics, and within higher education, that have been so important in producing present-day disjunctions between principles and realities, we present in the next three chapters specific proposals for returning to "the high ground." But there is a final preparatory task. Taking more than token steps toward reform will require presidents and trustees to consider carefully two questions that are highly sensitive and demand a nuanced perspective: (1) what face should be put on "winning," and (2) how should intercollegiate programs be viewed from the standpoint of institutional injunctions to pursue "excellence in all things"?

Winning

The history of reform efforts is replete with situations in which measures of one kind or another (for example, efforts to reduce recruiting) failed because it was thought that they would endanger "competitive equity" within the league or conference—that they would jeopardize a school's chances of winning. Winning is important, and one of the authors of this study (Bowen) remembers well when his young son objected to a lecture on the pure pleasure of competing by saying: "But Dad, the fun of playing is in the winning!" Chris Thomforde, today the president of St. Olaf's College in Northfield, Minnesota, and much earlier the center on the highly successful Princeton basketball teams of the late 1960s, reacted just as strongly when someone downplayed the importance of playing to win: "If they don't keep score, I don't want to play; if they keep score, I want to win."[44] Such views are in no way inconsistent with the case for eliminating the academic-athletic divide or for seeking to achieve some degree of competitive balance.

Giamatti articulated the tension between wanting to win and continuing to respect other values in the same speech to Yale alumni/ae that included his "package of reforms" that did not go anywhere (see discussion at the start of the next chapter). He described the "ambivalence" about how to merge winning and education this way: "Does one place the highest value on winning or does one subordinate victory to the larger values of an educational institution? We think we have chosen the latter idea, but we are nervous, nervous because we do not want to lose at anything."[45] After discussing Yale's recent won-lost records, Giamatti went on to ask:

> Why do I bring up won-lost records in assessing the health of varsity athletics? Because I want there to be no doubt about what I believe. I think winning is important. Winning has a joy and discrete purity to it that cannot be replaced by anything else. Winning is important to any man's or woman's sense of satisfaction and well-being. Winning is not everything but it is something powerful, indeed beautiful, in itself, something as necessary to the strong spirit as striving is necessary to the healthy character. Let all of us without bashfulness assert what the Greeks would find it absurd to suppress. Having said that, and meaning it, I repeat what I said above: our commitment to excellence, of aspiration and achievement, is based on the basic presupposition that athletics plays a *properly proportioned role* within our educational philosophy and program.[46]

It is our sense, based on conversations with a number of athletic directors and coaches, that the entirely healthy desire—nay, the need—to win (at least some of the time) has become too all-consuming in many quarters. One NESCAC coach complained:

> Today, athletic departments are organized from top to bottom to produce winning teams. In the past, physical education administrators understood the calculus of athletics: for every win there is also a loss. The modern emphasis on winning has not changed this. . . . Physical education administra-

tors had the wisdom to understand that important lessons should be learned and good education should be gained from losses as well as wins. A school often had some strong sports, but any school that had too much more than a .500 winning percentage in its overall athletics program was considered greedy, selfish, and worst of all immature.[47]

Finding the right balance, ensuring that activities are properly "proportioned," should be the goal. In reflecting on the history of the formation of the UAA, Rasmussen comments often on concerns for competitive balance, and he states a large objective very well: "When the ball goes up, the pitch is thrown, the whistle blows, or the gun sounds, the outcome should be in doubt."[48] But, he also argues, the search for "perfect balance" can be overdone: "The level playing field is a myth. The fact that institutions may benefit from advantages inherent in the diversity of their recruiting pool, location, size, or other factors is not itself inherently unfair. It simply reflects reality."[49] Surely we can acknowledge and accept this reality and still achieve a higher degree of competitive balance than is sometimes found today.

In considering measures that would lessen present-day pressures widening the athletic divide and permit a return to "high ground," we have to seek the right context (defined by policies, priorities, and working assumptions) in which competition can occur and teams can expect to win. The hardest thing may be to acknowledge that the good of the whole is not served when teams representing one or two schools in a conference (a Princeton or a Williams) are too dominant for too long. No one wants athletes at such schools to do anything but try their hardest to win every time they compete. But some of the "rules of engagement" may need to be re-examined to discourage the wrong forms of competition (for example, recruiting ever more specialized athletes) and to encourage situations in which the outcomes of contests are, in Rasmussen's nice phrase, "always in doubt." It is the schools with the most dominant athletic programs that are in the best position to lead efforts to pursue a serious reform agenda. One objective should be to form orbits of competition that do not result in particular schools' being either perennial winners or perennial losers across the board (see Chapter 13).

Excellence in All Things

The issue of how we think about "winning" often gets joined to an equally important, and equally emotional, issue—whether colleges and universities should aspire to "excellence in all things." Tom Gerety, president of Amherst, told us that in discussions of athletics he is often challenged with the argument that winning teams are an important sign of institutional excellence, as is participating in national championships. President Gerety's own response is that "excellence always requires choices: what's important and what's not, what's central and what's peripheral." Striving for excellence in all aspects of institutional life inevitably entails trade-offs; that is, seeking greater athletic success can result in lowered academic performance (as our study shows). Gerety's view is that excellence in liberal learning is what the NESCAC colleges are all about. He says that an overemphasis on winning teams, while it may fit some people's definition of excellence, is not in the long run consistent with the more central intellectual ambitions of colleges like his. Colin Campbell, who conducted the interview with Gerety, adds that in his view "encouraging and helping students to play as well as they can, and safely, along with promoting good sportsmanship, are the critical components of an excellent athletics program."

In the Ivies and in the NESCAC colleges, the idea of pursuing "excellence in all things" has become more closely tied in recent years to winning national championships. The part of Giamatti's speech to the Yale alumni/ae that provoked the most vigorous reaction was the part in which he questioned whether postseason competition should be seen as "the natural or even necessary consequence of victory." Giamatti argued that "the Ivy championship must be the goal of our students," and he then added: "I am frankly not impressed with the argument that says: . . . why can't we test ourselves against the best?" Among the many letters to the editor of the *Yale Alumni Magazine* provoked by this statement, one of the strongest responses came from Bryan C. Short, class of 1964, who wrote: "What an institution like Yale stands for is bigger than the Ivy League and not to be hemmed in by paternalistic caution. . . . Let Yale not retreat into a carefully defended ideal of a better, more elegant league; let her compete openly in the real and sweaty world as the champion she is. Yale has not world enough and time to protect the coy virginity of her competitive spirit."[50]

We return to the question of national championships, and how they should be viewed, in subsequent chapters. The broader point is that academically selective colleges and universities do not, and cannot, pursue "excellence in all things" without losing their focus and endangering their most fundamental educational purposes. As Gerety said, this mantra fails to recognize the inevitable trade-offs that must be made—the educational values that have to be compromised to meet certain kinds of external competition—and the obvious need to "stick to our knitting." Moreover, as several commentators have pointed out, these colleges and universities do not pursue the same kind of "national excellence" in other extracurricular activities (or make equivalent investments in them) that some advocate in the case of athletics. A number of the institutions in this study compete against the best in the world when it comes to faculty recruitment, scholarship, and education at the graduate and undergraduate levels. But these are the activities in which they are meant to be pre-eminent, and it does not follow that they should be equally committed to compete "against the best" in activities that are peripheral to their main mission. There is no escaping the need to decide what is paramount—and, as Giamatti put it, what "contributes to the point, but is not the point itself."[51]

———————

It is our conviction that there are sensible ways of moving from broad principles to policies that fully respect drives to excel that no one wants to quash. There are practical steps that can be taken to retake the "high ground" in athletics, and we believe that considerable support can be mustered for thoughtful proposals. It is the task of the next three chapters to deliver on these large claims.

Reform at the Institutional and Conference Levels: Recruiting, Admissions, and Coaching

REFORM AGENDAS need to be pursued at both local and national levels. The more we talk with a variety of people interested in doing something about the athletic divide, the clearer it becomes that a number of institutions (Carleton and Macalester are good examples) cannot expect to make progress by working primarily at the local or the conference level, whereas others (such as the Ivies and the New England Small College Athletic Conference [NESCAC] colleges) can accomplish a great deal by working within their own groups. The problem faced by places like Carleton and Macalester is that they are in a conference that has many members with interests that diverge from theirs in fundamental respects—and they are located in a geographic area where there are not that many like-minded institutions. In such situations there is little that can be done within the conference, and national rules are crucial since they set the framework for determining season length, number of contests, the nature of postseason play, and so on.[1] The schools in the Ivy League, on the other hand, are far better able to address fundamental questions such as athletic recruitment and admissions criteria within their own group; it is unlikely that any national organization will ever be effective in addressing issues of this kind, which vary so much from one institutional setting to another. Ideally, reforms at the conference and national levels will be reinforcing, and we favor working in concert at both levels.

In this chapter we begin at the conference level by discussing at considerable length how the recruitment and admissions processes might be altered in those settings where demonstrable problems of academic underperformance exist, issues of opportunity cost cannot be wished away, and there is a fundamental disjunction between stated principles and present-day realities. We then consider what might be done to tie coaches and coaching more directly to the educational missions of their institutions. In Chapter 12 we consider issues of program intensity and scale (including postseason competition and the special case of football), along with campus culture. Then in Chapter 13 we turn to the national level and consider proposals for a new division within the National Collegiate Athletic Association (NCAA) or a new organization outside it, dedicated explicitly to developing "common boundaries" for athletics programs that would be more consistent with educational goals. In Chapter 14 we emphasize the need for collective action and for leadership by school presidents and trustees. Both are needed to overcome the strong forces that continue to widen the academic-athletic divide and the vested interests that are highly resistant to any change in direction—especially any fundamental change. The book concludes with a summary of principal findings and policy recommendations.

PURSUING A HOLISTIC STRATEGY

Separating out different aspects of intercollegiate programs is clearly necessary from an expositional standpoint, but it is both artificial and potentially misleading. We are persuaded that reform measures need to be thought about as packages, and that a holistic approach is essential.

The pieces of this complex puzzle are closely connected. It is easy to understand the temptation to concentrate one's energies on a particular idea for reform, most commonly either limiting the numbers of recruited athletes or raising the threshold academic standard applied in admissions. As one president put it, "It's necessary to start somewhere." This is true enough, but there is considerable evidence to suggest that just "tweaking" the system will not accomplish very much.[2] Wherever one starts, it is important to have in mind a broad framework that is derived from educational values and core principles. Also required is a clear understanding of the interlocking nature of the elements in play—an acute awareness of how closely intertwined are the factors that have led to the "creeping intensification" of college sports and the academic-athletic divide.

In considering reductions in the number of recruited athletes, for example, it is necessary to consider as well the characteristics of those who remain on the recruit list. Will the staff in the admissions office be satisfied as long as this smaller number of top recruits remains over some test score threshold, or will they scrutinize carefully the academic interests and priorities of those recruits who appear on the (shortened) coach's list? When the Ivies sought to raise the academic standards for recruited athletes in the High Profile sports and invented the Academic Index (AI) to do this, those involved in advocating this approach (including one of the authors of this study) failed to see that there could still be a problem—indeed a deeper one—of academic underperformance among recruits who are admitted consistent with the constraints imposed by the AI. In another domain, selection of coaches by these schools is both a consequence of other program decisions (extent of the commitment to recruit top athletes, active pursuit of national championships, ability to focus on a specialized aspect of coaching) and a determinant of the kinds of students who will be recruited and of the degree to which the coaching staff will recognize the importance of a student's academic obligations.

In short, trying to fix the problem one piece at a time is unlikely to be effective. In assessing the failure of Giamatti's 1980 proposals for reform in the Ivy League (which dealt with recruiting, postseason competition, season length, and coaching assignments), James Litvack, who was the executive director of the Council of Ivy Presidents at the time, writes: "The beauty of Giamatti's proposals was in the way they were derived from a consistent view of what a liberal education meant. . . . The proposals were a package that had to be treated together. . . . With all the other proposals that were being considered at the time and with specific subcommittees [of the Ivy Group Policy Committee] dealing with the proposals for change . . . the proposals [were] separated and often evaluated in terms of effects on competitive equity or athletic department costs. *Separated from each other and in an environment somewhat removed from the view of education that had generated them, they had no chance to survive*" (our emphasis).[3]

More recently, President Michael McPherson of Macalester has observed: "It is vitally important to think about reform in a holistic way. It's so tempting to think that there is some one knob you can turn or clever new rule you can put in place, but there really has to be a set of mutually supportive changes to come up with something workable."[4] We agree.

LIMITING RECRUITMENT

A central empirical finding of this study (Chapters 5 and 6) is that the problems associated with the academic outcomes of athletes relate overwhelmingly—and most dramatically—to the *recruited* athletes who were on the coaches' lists (as contrasted with the other students playing varsity sports). Thus one obvious component of a reform agenda is doing something about recruiting as it is practiced today. The NCAA already regulates recruiting in numerous ways at both Division I and Division III levels of play, and both NESCAC and the Ivy League have imposed further restrictions of their own (prohibiting off-campus recruiting by coaches, in the case of NESCAC).[5] Further limitations of various kinds could be considered, and recruiting budgets in the Ivies (which, it should be recalled, now exceed $600,000 per year) could be reduced. Apart from dollar savings, whatever can be done to reduce the increasingly heavy recruiting burden on coaches would give them more opportunity to coach and to participate in campus life.

We are skeptical, however, about the wisdom of sweeping legislative prohibitions, in part because circumstances vary so much. Especially in the less selective Division III colleges, coaches serve their institutions by representing them in off-campus gatherings of many kinds and by encouraging students in general to apply and enroll. New rules could be difficult to design and, if elaborate, difficult to administer and enforce; athletics is, in our view, already over-regulated in many respects. In any case, we believe that recruitment practices per se are much less central to the core issues before us than are other aspects of the recruitment/ admissions nexus.

REDUCING THE NUMBER OF RECRUITED ATHLETES

One of the most popular approaches to reform is to limit the overall number of recruited athletes a school is permitted to matriculate—often in a particular sport such as football, but also sometimes in all varsity sports. This direct way of controlling the number of recruits on campus has obvious appeal, and both the Ivies and the NESCAC colleges have recently moved in this direction. Reducing the "weight" of recruited athletes on a campus could certainly affect campus culture. Representatives of the University Athletic Association (UAA) strongly believe that the relatively small number of recruited athletes in their schools (something like 6 percent, on average) considerably lessens the risk that an athletic culture will dominate or that athletes in classes will affect academic expectations of faculty or the performance of other students. Smaller numbers are just less noticeable and less consequential.

There is also a great deal to be said for creating room on squads for students with athletic ability who want the opportunity to compete, but who were admitted based on other criteria ("regular students," as it were). As Professor Michael MacDonald at Williams has emphasized (in personal correspondence), the philosophical argument about the benefits of broad participation in athletics" makes little sense if the students enjoying these benefits are only (or mainly) those specifically recruited for the purpose of playing varsity sports. In the words of another faculty commentator: "We want to have an athletic program for the students rather than having students for the athletic program."

The Middlebury Ad Hoc Committee report is emphatic on this basic point: "Since its inception in 1971 NESCAC has prided itself in welcoming 'walk-ons' to its teams. We should make every effort to ensure that, in our pursuit of stronger intercollegiate teams, *we do not make playing an intercollegiate sport the exclusive privilege of those pre-selected by coaches through the recruiting process. If we justify intercollegiate athletic programs by their educational benefits with respect to qualities like leadership and self-discipline, then we should make sure that these benefits are available to the students we admit to our colleges* [our emphasis]. In other words, access to intercollegiate athletic programs by interested students should be a part of our ideal."[6] The report goes on to recommend explicitly: "The admission of recruited ath-

letes should be curtailed so that other student-athletes have ample opportunities to participate in intercollegiate sports."[7]

There are, then, strong arguments—having to do with both educational objectives and principles of fair access to opportunities to play
sports—in favor of reducing the numbers of recruited athletes. But focusing on numbers alone, in our view, is inadequate. Why do we say this?
First, to make a real difference, reductions in numbers would have to be
substantial—and there would always be a tendency to compromise and
adopt what can be seen as token reductions. Second, and even more important, there is a serious risk that reductions in the numbers of recruits
would mean that the remaining spots would be assigned to recruits chosen primarily on the basis of their dedication to their sport and their ability to be "impact players." Progress in moving toward the important goal
of "representativeness" could be slowed rather than accelerated by
admitting smaller numbers of recruited athletes chosen on the basis of
"athletics-first" criteria. In commenting on the recent decision by the Ivy
League presidents to reduce the annual intake of football recruits from
35 to 30, John Emerson of Middlebury College asked: "What will be the
characteristics of the five players who won't be recruited, that is, *which* five
[his emphasis]? The five who are least 'with the academic program?' Not
likely."[8]

ADJUSTING ADMISSIONS CRITERIA

There is no substitute for addressing directly the way athletes are evaluated in the admissions process. Perhaps *the* key finding of this study is the
way in which "selection, selection, selection" affects academic outcomes
(Chapter 6). To be sure, selection interacts with "campus culture"; the
two reinforce each other. But the evidence of disappointing academic
performance, even among recruited athletes who do not play at all or
who play for only a year or two, as well as among the four-year players
(compared with students at large and with walk-ons who have similar playing histories), is hard to push aside. Other students with athletic ability
who were not on the coaches' lists when admitted clearly fare much better academically.

Academic Preparation

Part of the problem is straightforward: some part of disappointing academic performance by recruited athletes is rooted directly in their academic preparation and academic credentials. The Ivy League's Academic

Index (which requires that all recruited athletes, especially in the High Profile sports, be above a stipulated threshold and, in addition, that the full set of High Profile recruits have academic credentials that are, overall, within one standard deviation of the school-wide average) is one practical way of making sure that some objective standards are met across the League.[9] Experience with the AI demonstrates that it can—and did— stop the erosion of average test scores (combined with rank-in-class) that was taking place before its adoption.[10]

Some interest has been expressed within NESCAC in adopting a version of the AI, and others have suggested that the Ivies consider raising both the threshold and the AI itself.[11] Whatever specific approach is taken, raising the admission standards for athletes would have the obvious advantage of reducing the substantial degree of "admissions advantage" currently enjoyed by athletes on the coaches' lists. The Middlebury Ad Hoc Committee report points out that it is one thing to have a policy that endorses giving some weight to athletic contributions, as one factor among many, in making admissions decisions; it is quite another to allow the weight of athletic contributions to become dominant: "Even if we accept this premise [that some weight is appropriate] . . . no interpretation would seem to justify the great extent to which we presently weigh athletic talent."[12]

A specific proposal to address this concern is put forward by the Middlebury Ad Hoc Committee. They recommend: "Influence by coaches and the athletics department on admissions decisions should be limited to student applicants who rank relatively high among those students who are admitted, as measured by broad academic criteria. We recommend that athletic recruiting—that is, giving special consideration to potential intercollegiate athletes in admissions—be limited to recruits who would have placed academically in the top half of a college's entering class from the previous year."[13] The Middlebury report continues: "If our admissions offices are to continue giving strong preference to rated athletes who are clearly above average in their athletic talents, we believe that they should focus on those student-athletes who are above average in their academic potential as well." Judging by the distribution of SAT scores— which are one, but only one, measure of academic potential—this proposal might be tantamount to giving roughly the same degree of preference in admissions to athletes that is now given to legacies, who as a group generally rank in the top half of the admissions pool.

We applaud the spirit of this approach. But, much as there is to be said for raising the formal academic standards that recruited athletes have to meet to be admitted, we would add (and we are confident that the members of the Middlebury Ad Hoc Committee would agree) that such actions would not be sufficient, in and of themselves, to solve the problem

of disappointing academic outcomes. The findings in Chapter 6 con-
clusively demonstrate that academic underperformance by recruited
athletes is by no means confined to those in the bottom part of the SAT
distribution. In fact, underperformance is, if anything, slightly *more* pronounced in the broad middle of the SAT range (1250–1400 in the Ivy
League universities and 1150–1300 in the NESCAC colleges). Only at the
highest SAT level (1400+ in the Ivies) does underperformance cease to
be a significant problem for recruited athletes—and in the Ivies only
about 5 percent of recruited High Profile athletes and 10 to 12 percent
of female athletes and men playing the Lower Profile sports meet this
academic standard.

Judging Student Interests, Priorities, and Habits of Mind

Thus there is a deeper problem than the one revealed by focusing just on
the academic credentials of admitted athletes. The persistent, and growing, evidence of academic underperformance among students who pass
"the AI test," including recruits who pass this test easily, tells us that focusing on readily measurable credentials of applicants is insufficient. The
"spread" of underperformance—across teams, across groups of students
classified by the extent to which they actually played on varsity teams, *and
across SAT ranges*—speaks for itself. The introduction of the AI standard
has definitely had positive effects, and we are certainly not opposed to
employing, or even strengthening, such measures. But in our judgment
too much reliance ought not to be placed on meeting formulaic standards of any kind. There is no escaping the evidence that *the interests and
priorities of students when they are admitted,* not just their previous academic
records, are tremendously important.

John Servos, a history professor at Amherst who was an active participant on the special committee that reviewed the athletics situation there,
believes that "admissions could do a better job of assessing a student's
work ethic [and academic interests] along with his or her athletic
prowess." This is a tricky business because admissions staff members are
reluctant to second-guess coaches in deciding which athletes can make a
special contribution to a team searching for talent, but we think there is
much to be said for asking coaches to provide much longer lists of potential athletes and then relying on the admissions staff to decide which
members of the larger pool are most likely to thrive academically at the
school in question. We were told over and over that this is the way the
process works at the UAA schools, and the academic outcomes of their
athletes certainly suggest that they are doing something right. In short, it
seems to us important that rank-ordered coaches' lists be assigned less

priority in the admissions process. The fact that an athlete's academic credentials are over some threshold level—even a high threshold—should not be the determining factor. (This is why "pre-screening" of candidates by coaches and admissions liaisons is no solution to the problem of underperformance.)

Back in the 1960s there was an extensive discussion at Yale, involving both Yale's president, Kingman Brewster, and a faculty committee led by Professor James Tobin, that focused on precisely this set of questions. In responding to the request of a new senior admissions officer for "guidelines," Brewster drafted a memorandum, and his observations seem, if anything, more relevant today than they were then, when admission was much less competitive. He wrote: "Who will make the best use of Yale's resources? This, at bottom, should determine who deserves the privilege of Yale College for four years." He went on to suggest: "The motivation to stretch one's capacity seems to me to have a special value." A key question is "How do you discern the most important quality: 'a sharp and inquiring mind coupled with a capacity and desire to use it?'" Finally, in discussing how one measures such attributes, he suggested that the "relationship between graded performance and tested potential may be a clue." Brewster was pointing clearly to the importance of judging those interests, priorities, and habits of mind that would, at least to some extent, guard against academic underperformance.[14]

Brewster drafted his memorandum following his receipt of a report from a faculty committee chaired by Tobin (called the Admissions Policy Advisory Board). The board concurred with an earlier recommendation that "Yale should seek and admit undergraduate students with the interest and ability to profit from the university environment of the college." It then went on to describe quite precisely how extracurricular activities, including athletics, should be viewed in the admissions process: "One principle is clear. Extracurricular activity of candidates for admission is important only as it tells us something about their qualities of mind and character. We should *not* count extracurricular activity in a candidate's favor simply because it foreshadows success in similar extracurricular activity at Yale. The central business of the university is the mutual pursuit of knowledge by students and teachers. It is not to produce newspapers, singing groups, or athletic teams." The board next expressed confidence that students admitted on the basis of appropriate criteria "will also have the diverse talents and interests needed to man the variety of extracurricular enterprises which add so much to the liveliness and excitement of Yale life," and then turned directly to athletics, where it had this to say:

Athletics is certainly one realm in which [high school students] may display qualities of leadership, cooperation, loyalty, purpose, perseverance, and integrity. We certainly should consider any light which athletic experience can shed on these important dimensions of character. But let it be perfectly clear that it is evidence of these qualities we are seeking, *not* evidence that the candidate will be a star performer in major intercollegiate varsity sports. The relevant evidence can be provided just as well by fencing as by football, just as well by [students] light in weight and short in stature as by the physically well-endowed, just as well by leaders in weak inter-school or intramural competition as by all-state stars, just as well by those whose Yale athletics will be only inter-college competition as by those who will play in the Bowl.[15]

These ideas continue to resonate. In the spring of 2002 a writer for the *Harvard Crimson* drew a similar distinction in insisting that "sporting experiences should be valued, mere sporting ability should not."[16]

There is an even broader issue to ponder. It is our impression that the admissions process, like college sports, has become increasingly "professionalized" and is sometimes thought (rightly or wrongly) to have reached the stage of being at least quasi-scientific. The increases in the number of applicants and the close scrutiny of the admissions process by outside observers combine to put pressure on the system to be more transparent. In and of itself, this is fine as long as those who make admissions decisions are allowed—indeed, are expected—to exercise their own best judgment and not be imprisoned by allegedly "objective" criteria. In a similar vein, a number of people with whom we have spoken have asked if faculty today play as much of a role in admissions as would be desirable. The Amherst Special Committee, in particular, discussed this question at some length in its report, and the faculty at Amherst now formally approve admissions decisions—an act that, while mainly symbolic, is not without value.[17] There is much to be said for re-emphasizing the importance of the admissions process and the need to be sure that it is closely aligned with the institution's educational values.

Monitoring Performance and Fixing Accountability

A recurring theme of this study is that evidence matters. In that spirit, we make a suggestion that seems obvious both in retrospect and in light of the findings presented in this study. Monitoring outcomes is essential, and *the focus should be on students' performance after they have been admitted, not just on their test scores and other incoming credentials.*[18] This is the approach that the UAA has followed from its earliest days. The executive director reviews the grade point averages (GPAs) of all teams and calls to the attention of the presidents any discrepancies with school-wide norms. The process is no more complicated than that. It is impossible to say how much credit should be given to the monitoring process as compared with all the other elements at work within the UAA, but there is no denying that recruited athletes at UAA universities have done much better academically, relative to both their peers and their own incoming credentials, than have recruited athletes at many of the other schools in the study.

In a recently released addendum to their original report, the Ad Hoc Committee on the Future of Athletics at Middlebury stated:

> *By their graduation, student athletes should achieve academically at levels that are not different from those of their peers who are not athletes* [their emphasis]. This goal implies that we need to better understand academic underachievement and find effective ways to address it.

> We believe that NESCAC colleges should be accountable to each other and to their own constituencies for the academic outcomes of their intercollegiate athletes. . . . *Middlebury College and the NESCAC should develop plans for gathering the data needed to monitor our progress toward the ideals and academic goals that we have identified* [their emphasis]. . . . We recommend that such data, including data on the college GPAs of both recruited and non-recruited athletes, be gathered and reported each year.[19]

A related proposal involves an even more direct linking of careful monitoring to the fixing of accountability. What would be the possibility of holding admissions deans and athletic directors (coaches, really) jointly responsible for reducing underperformance substantially, if not eliminating it altogether? Some system of incentive-based rewards and penalties might be concocted, but perhaps it would be sufficient, at least initially, simply to announce such an initiative and indicate that the right person in the institution (presumably the provost or a senior dean, in most cases) would oversee this approach. Since underperformance is, we believe, rooted in a combination of selection and culture, it would make sense to assign responsibility for fixing the problem to a blend of those doing the selecting and those working with recruited athletes on a day-to-day basis.

In sum, recruited athletes should perform academically at more or less the same level as their classmates. Achieving such a goal requires *both* raising initial standards for admission and paying serious attention, on a continuing basis, to how well those admitted perform in relation to their incoming academic credentials. If it appears that disappointing performance is the fault of some other party (say a faculty member who stereotypes athletes and penalizes them), that claim should be examined carefully. Stereotypes often have their roots in some perceived reality, and improving standards and performance is probably the best way of dealing, over time, with any unfairness of this kind.

Rethinking Attrition among Recruited Athletes

Finding ways to ensure that varsity athletes are far more "representative" of their classes (as almost every statement of principles says that they should be) would have another important advantage: although it would not necessarily reduce attrition among recruited athletes, it would remove the concern about allocating spaces in a class to students who will end up leaving their teams. The problem at present, as the 1994 Princeton report notes, is that "almost two students must be enrolled for each one who will remain with the program."[20] The question many properly ask is "How can we justify allocating highly coveted spots to students who are admitted because of their expected contribution to athletics, whom we would not have admitted otherwise, who then drop out of their programs (with some number creating disciplinary problems, and few distinguishing themselves as students in other ways)?" The answer, at present, is "It is difficult to justify this policy, especially when there are so many other outstanding candidates for admission who want to come to the school because they value the educational opportunities that it offers."

Surely the solution to this problem is not to attempt to reduce attrition by focusing recruiting and admissions advantages ever more narrowly on those prospective athletes who are so dedicated to their coaches and teams that the odds of their dropping out are very low; rather, it would be much better to admit prospective athletes who are highly desirable candidates in any event. Then, if some of these students were to decide that they are less interested in athletics than in other activities, it would be fine; the college or university would still be glad to have them. Attrition from teams would no longer be a major concern, as it should not be in schools that want students to feel free to follow new paths.

Lower Yields Must Be Anticipated—and May Even Be a Good Thing

The proposals just outlined, including particularly weakening the bond between the rank-ordered lists of preferred athletic admits prepared by coaches and ultimate admissions decisions, would be certain to lower the percentage of recruited athletes offered places in a class who elected to matriculate ("yields"). We showed in Chapter 3 that yields for recruited athletes, especially for athletes in the High Profile sports in the Ivies, have risen so dramatically that they are now nearly 100 percent in many cases. Early Action and Early Decision programs are partly responsible, but with or without such programs, what often happens is that coaches recommend for admission only candidates whom they are confident will come to their school. In effect, a deal is made whereby coaches agree to press for the admission of a highly sought-after athlete in exchange for a promise by the athlete that, if admitted, he or she will sign on with the school and commit to the athletic program.

If admissions offices chose from a much larger number of potential athletes, and attached much more weight to non-athletic considerations such as the likelihood that a candidate would take full advantage of the school's educational resources, coaches could not expect as many recruits to commit to the school in advance of what would be a much more uncertain admissions outcome. Prospective athletes would need to weigh their other options (which they would be allowed to do under this approach), and yields would fall. This is the situation today in most UAA universities and many liberal arts colleges. Unfortunately, getting as high a yield as possible has become a major status marker for colleges and universities—even though what matters, of course, is not how many candidates reject an offer of admission but the quality of those who ultimately comprise the entering class. Yield per se counts for little, if anything, difficult as it seems to be for many to grasp this central point.[21]

In fact, a case can be made for the superficially perverse proposition that, at highly selective institutions at least, a lower yield confers advantages. The reason is that lower yields imply more self-selection on the part of the students who matriculate. We believe that the athletes at the University of Chicago do well academically in no small measure because an effective *double selection process* has been at work. First, both the coaches themselves and the admissions office have attached a great deal of weight to the expected "fit" between a student's interests and the character/curriculum of the university when deciding whom to recruit and whom to admit (see Chapters 2 and 3). Second, those students who have been admitted have made a selection of their own after considering this question: "Do I really want to go to the University of Chicago, knowing what kind of academic as well as athletic program it offers, or do I want to go somewhere else—perhaps to a school with a more intensive athletic program that is also somewhat less demanding in terms of core course requirements?" Complicating factors at many schools are Early Decision programs and implicit requirements that recruited athletes commit to one school if they are to "deserve" a place on the coach's list. But both of these sources of pressure are driven by the desire on the part of coaches and schools to "force" early commitments. It is this syndrome that we are arguing against. It is better for students to have made a carefully considered decision as to where they really want to go. More time is a friend of thoughtful decision-making.

To recapitulate, we believe that the twin problems of "representativeness" and academic underperformance can be addressed through the recruitment/admissions process by a *combination* of five actions: (1) reduce the time, energy, and resources devoted to recruiting (though this seems to us the least important of the five points listed here); (2) reduce the number of recruited athletes in an entering class; (3) raise academic standards at admission, thereby curtailing the "admissions advantage" that recruited athletes enjoy; (4) place less emphasis, in choosing among candidates for admission, on coaches' rank-ordered lists and more emphasis on assessments by the admissions office of the interests, priorities, and motivations of individual candidates, as these intangibles are expected to affect students' commitments to take full advantage of the educational opportunities offered by the college or university; and (5) monitor academic performance in college and expect admissions offices and athletic departments to be jointly accountable for reducing underperformance, if not eliminating it altogether.

The Need to Accept Lower Skill Levels

Taken together, this set of mutually reinforcing proposals would, without question, reduce skill levels. More "regular students" would earn places on varsity squads. There would be fewer recruited athletes focused primarily on their teams. There would be less "raw talent" in a class, and any set of colleges or universities serious about adopting reform measures of the kinds proposed here would have to accept this reality. But intercollegiate athletics need not be any less "competitive." Players would be expected to play just as hard as they do now, and to play to win. Varsity teams would continue to be composed of highly accomplished athletes, even though they would usually weigh less, not run quite as fast, and have less powerful serves. At the same time, the athletes on these teams would need to yield nothing to the more talented athletes recruited by big-time programs in their zeal, drive, energy level, discipline, or understanding of the game or of the lessons to be learned through competing: indeed, they might actually value good sportsmanship more highly. They might still be able to test themselves against other athletes in postseason competition (consistent with NCAA and conference policies), but they would have to define competitive success more in the context of intra-league competition—as, for example, the original Ivy League statement of principles and the NESCAC statement of principles assumed would be the case. Except in highly unusual situations, academically selective schools that followed the recruitment and admissions policies advocated in this study could not expect to be as dominant at the national level as some of these schools have been in recent years.[22]

Are there candidates of the kind we have been describing who would be interested in attending these schools? Newly available data obtained by linking Educational Testing Service files to the institutional records for the 1995 entering cohorts of the schools in this study provide a most encouraging answer to this key question. *Large numbers of students currently attending these same schools, though not recruited athletes and accepted for reasons apart from their athletic accomplishments, were four-year athletes in high school and in many cases were captains of their teams or award winners.* For example, among students who were not recruited athletes in the Ivy League, 21 percent of men and 19 percent of women played one or more varsity sports for four years in high school, and almost 30 percent of both men and women in the Ivies were either captains or received an award in a varsity sport. The numbers are similar for the NESCAC colleges and the UAA universities and only slightly lower for the other coed liberal arts colleges and the women's colleges in our study. Even more interesting is the finding that in both the Ivy League and NESCAC, the higher scoring students—those with SAT scores of 1350 and above—were slightly more likely (by one or two percentage points) to have participated in high school varsity sports than those with SAT scores below 1350. Academic and athletic accomplishments go together, at least within this select population.[23]

Moreover, we showed in Chapter 3 that the national pool of secondary school students interested in attending the colleges and universities represented in this study included many other candidates who excelled in both academics and athletics. Among the '95 cohort of high school high scorers—here defined as those with SATs above 1200—21 percent of the men and 19 percent of the women intending to apply to universities in the Ivy League had played at least one sport for all four years of high school. Of those intending to apply to NESCAC colleges, 22 percent of the men and 19 percent of the women had played for four years. Thus there certainly appears to be a sizable pool of academically motivated students who were also serious athletes in high school.[24]

Encouraging as these data on academically high-achieving high school athletes are, it must be re-emphasized that athletes of the kind we are describing would be unlikely to have the raw talent, and thus to enjoy the competitive success outside their own conference or outside the orbit of other schools with teams composed of players chosen on the basis of similar criteria, that many schools in this study enjoy today. In some situations, individuals and teams might continue to compete, and even compete well, in regional or national competitions. But it would be naïve to expect that these schools would record anything approaching the number of national championships in either Division I or Division III that they currently claim.

COACHING

Coaches who are charged with taking carefully recruited athletes who are already highly skilled and highly focused when they arrive on campus to still higher levels of performance in college could hardly be expected to welcome the reductions in skill levels that would inevitably accompany the changes in recruitment and admissions strategies proposed here. Many (most?) of the more specialized of these coaches, and those with the clearest Division I aspirations, would presumably seek coaching opportunities elsewhere. In turn, schools that elected to admit larger numbers of academically oriented students who also wanted to compete for places on intercollegiate teams (but who did not arrive on campus already assured of a spot) might well feel the need to hire at least some coaches with different talents and interests than those currently serving. One principle is clear: *the criteria for selecting coaches need to be derived from the criteria used to admit students, not the other way around.*

Several people with whom we spoke suggested that college sports have become too coach-centered. In reflecting on what he had learned from the intensive study of athletics at Williams carried out by the committee that he chaired, Professor MacDonald kept emphasizing "the extent to which the coaches drive the enterprise." He added: "The professional development and personal satisfaction of the coaches are major drivers." MacDonald compares the highly developed athletics program for undergraduates at a college like Williams to the graduate programs at most research universities. Students are recruited because of their talent and interest in a specific area, in which they are expected to specialize while at the school. Working with such students is akin to supervising the Ph.D. dissertation of a talented graduate student, MacDonald suggests, and can be very satisfying for the coaches.

What is needed, a number of commentators have suggested (and we agree), is the return to a model in which coaches are less focused on the recruitment and further training of specialized athletes and more interested in the broadly educational aspects of coaching. As one experienced athletic director put it, coaches today are too much like "jet pilots" who have to focus on their immediate responsibilities and cannot really be expected to have a more general perspective. This is not a healthy state of affairs. Coaches need to understand and identify with the educational mission of the college or university of which they are a part—as many do. Their ability to internalize these educational values will, of course, depend on who they are as individuals, on their backgrounds, on how they are expected to spend their time, and on how they are evaluated and rewarded. Admonition alone, whether it comes from an athletic director or from a president or dean, will not do the job—which is to integrate the coaching staff more fully into the educational life of the institution. How coaches think about their duties—and their priorities—can make an enormous difference. One coach may advise his or her students to schedule courses that involve no conflicts with practices and games (whether or not these are the courses that interest the student the most); another coach may tailor practice expectations around the courses that make the most educational sense for the student. There is a world of difference between these mindsets.

Unfortunately, we have been unable to find systematic data on the educational backgrounds of coaches and how they may have changed over time. There is much speculation, however, that fewer and fewer coaches come from backgrounds in broad-based programs that emphasized learning to coach and to teach. Coaches may also be less likely now than in earlier days to have been students themselves at the kinds of colleges and universities represented in this study (again, data are lacking). Those who did go to a Wesleyan or a Columbia are more likely to appreciate the "cultures" of these institutions, and the academic pressures on students who attend them, than are coaches who as students were themselves at schools that had big-time athletics programs.

Stephen Lewis has suggested that liberal arts colleges that are interested in recruiting coaches with more breadth may need to consider "growing our own." He asks: "Should we have for coaches what we have for academic faculty: seminars, workshops, faculty development programs that spread across institutions on how to be a coach at a first rate liberal arts college or university?"[25] Perhaps the new national organization, or "Division," that Lewis suggests creating (see Chapter 13) could be helpful in this regard.

Assignments and the allocation of time obviously matter. As reported in Chapter 8, a number of coaches who still have responsibility for teaching phys-ed at places like the University of Chicago and MIT report that they value the opportunity to get to know, and to work with, a wide range of undergraduates. Richard Rasmussen favors the adoption of institutional policies that would encourage cooperation between coaches and that would support opportunities for participation in multiple sports. Of course the practicality of such proposals would depend on how much time and energy coaches would be expected to devote to recruiting—and on whether workshops or some other set of educational opportunities could be made available to provide the necessary training. In his 1980 speech, Giamatti presumably annoyed a number of his listeners, and perhaps especially some coaches, when he said: "I believe it must be widely acknowledged . . . that recruiting is not coaching, and that the present practice of recruitment of students who are athletes cannot encroach upon the time and effort that must be devoted to working with the students who are here, working with them and teaching them in one form or the other."[26] Later in the talk Giamatti decried recruiting practices that "force more and more coaching to become hustling in the hustings." He concluded: "I believe it is demeaning to the profession of coaching when one has to spend so much time traveling and wooing off-campus."[27]

Reward structures are important. Rasmussen proposed that institutions "hire, evaluate, and reward coaches more on the basis of educationally based norms and criteria and less on competitively based standards."[28] Professor Servos called our attention to changes in employment arrangements at Amherst, where a system of relatively short-term contracts has gradually supplanted a tenure-track model for coaches. He suggested that the new system may have had "adverse unintended consequences" by adding to the pressure to have a winning season. It seems unlikely that a return to the old system is "in the cards," given present-day conceptions of undergraduate education, and we do not believe that a tenure-track system is the answer in any case. The justification for tenure systems is the protection of academic freedom in the intellectual give-and-take of a campus community, not job security, and we do not believe that any staff members other than regular faculty, who are responsible for guiding the institution's academic program, should be given tenure. President William Adams of Colby believes that we should resist the increasingly professionalized Division I coaching model, "not by returning to the faculty model, but by insisting that coaches are not essentially different from other employees who support in close and critical ways the academic mission of the college." He adds: "We also need to do a better job of acquainting coaches with the role of athletics in our institutions, and of being careful in the hiring process to identify people who understand and want to support our particular view of the limited role of athletics."[29] We believe that college and university presidents and other administrative officers could do more than many do at present to encourage coaches to feel that they are consequential parts of the educational mission of these institutions.

Most basic, of course, is the value system that drives hiring decisions, the setting of incentives, and assessments of performance (and, in turn, one would hope, the behavior of coaches). Reducing the focus on earning points for Sears Cup calculations would help. The success coaches have in helping their players improve and achieve up to their potential as athletes is surely important. (All one-time athletes can remember coaches who were both better and worse in this regard.) Survey instruments and student exit interviews are used by many athletic directors in assessing the performance of coaches, and they too can be helpful, depending on how well designed they are to elicit the information that should be most relevant in making judgments.[30] One important "metric" might be the academic success of the students on various teams, measured in terms both of the absolute results they achieve in the classroom and the laboratory and of whether they underperform.

As difficult as it may be, it is essential to avoid placing excessive emphasis on won-lost records, especially over short periods. Ways need to be

found to assure coaches that decisions concerning extensions of contracts and salaries will in fact be made fairly, and will be consistent with
lofty rhetoric about educational values that can so easily be pushed aside
when individuals are actually being judged. On the academic side of colleges and universities, elaborate policies and procedures are designed to
ensure consistency (as best one can) between stated criteria and the reality of decision-making. Are there examples of analogous procedures
for evaluating coaches that involve the participation of faculty or staff
from outside athletics? Is there a possibility of inventing new models? In
the course of this research, several coaches remarked to us that it would
be so much easier for them to embrace the line of argument being
developed—with which, in principle, a number were sympathetic—if they
did not think that occupying "high ground" would cost them their jobs.

The students who play sports and the coaches who work with them are
the two most important components of college athletics programs. They
are, as it were, the key inputs. Aligning recruitment and admissions of students, and the selection and evaluation of coaches (and athletic directors), with the educational missions of these colleges and universities is
of first importance. As one commentator put it, "If you get the right
people participating, in the right spirit, pursuing the right objectives, all
sorts of good things *can* follow." We write "can," and italicize the word, because there are also elements of program definition that enter the equation, including the scale of the enterprise, its level of intensity, how schedules are managed, the kinds of postseason competition that are (or are
not) permitted, and the role assigned to club sports. "Program definition,"
thought of as encompassing all of these elements, will of course strongly
influence the students who will want to play sports at these schools and the
coaches who will want to coach them. In turn, the experiences that the
athletes have, and the satisfaction that coaches take from their work,
depend on these same things. In short, program definition can either
reinforce or interfere with the educational values that recruitment, admissions, and coach-selection processes are intended to serve. It is these
"program" elements, seen from the perspective of the individual institution and the conference, that are the subject of the next chapter.

CHAPTER 12

Reform at the Institutional and Conference Levels: The Athletic Program

WE TURN NOW to a consideration of the athletic programs themselves. The elements that define a school's athletic program include such factors as the intensity of the program (how it affects the lives of varsity athletes in terms of season length, off-season activities, scheduling, and post-season play); the overall scale of the athletic enterprise (including the special case of football); and the role of club sports.

SEASON LENGTH AND THE OFF-SEASON

The amount of time a college student is expected to devote to his or her sport is one way of defining program intensity. It is difficult to measure in any precise way the combined effects of longer seasons, more contests during the season, more postseason play, and greater off-season practice and preparation. But there is no doubt about the direction of movement—at both Division I and Division III levels. In an article titled "The Non-traditional Season: Turning Point or Full Speed Ahead?" Robert Malekoff observes: "As has been the case historically, we in Division III continue to follow the lead of Division I in that we subscribe to the theory that more is better."[1]

This long-term trend has been a source of concern for decades. Nearly 100 years ago, in 1906, faculty representatives in what was then called the Intercollegiate Conference (now the Big Ten) ruled that the football season must end before Thanksgiving and include no more than five games.[2] Today limits of every kind are legislated in incredible detail by the National Collegiate Athletic Association (NCAA). In 1987, the length of the "playing season" (which includes "traditional" and "non-traditional" segments—see definitions in the box) was limited to 21 weeks in Division III, as compared with 26 weeks in Division I.[3] The intent was to reduce the pressure on students to devote an inordinate amount of time to varsity sports, but by the fall of 1998 it was obvious that students were spending more, not less, time on athletics. In some ways, the 21-week limitation had been turned on its head: some schools that had previously declined to compete in the non-traditional segment of the playing season now felt that they had to fill the entire 21 weeks in order to be competitive. There was a general feeling that the maximum was becoming the standard—as it so often does. There followed a prolonged three-year debate over what to do that in many ways split Division III right down the middle philosophically. (We will say more on this in the next chapter, which deals expressly with reforms at the national level.) The outcome was the adoption in 2001 of Proposal 50, which placed more explicit limits on competition in the non-traditional segment but did not call for a total prohibition, as some had advocated.[4]

Some definitions:

The *playing season* is the period of time between the date of an institution's first officially recognized practice session and the date of the last practice session or competition, whichever occurs later. The *traditional segment* is the portion of the playing season that concludes with the NCAA championship. The *non-traditional segment* is the remaining portion of the playing season. (It would precede the traditional segment in the case of spring sports like baseball and follow it in the case of fall sports like soccer.) The *off-season* is the time outside of the playing season.

Within the "envelope" of opportunities to compete defined by the NCAA, additional limits may be imposed—and often are imposed—at the conference level. In the main, the schools included in this study operate under conference rules that mandate shorter seasons; also, additional restrictions are sometimes imposed on what is permissible in the "non-traditional" season and in the off-season. (See Appendix Table 12.1 for a tabular presentation of data we have assembled on conference rules governing season length and activities during various parts of the year.) For example, the Ivy League permits 12 "practice opportunities," two "competition dates," and "conditioning under a coach's supervision" during the non-traditional season. The New England Small College Athletic Conference (NESCAC) permits no organized team activity (competition or practice) outside of the traditional season. The Minnesota Intercollegiate Athletic Conference (MIAC) allows no competition and only seven practices during the non-traditional segment. The University Athletic Association (UAA), the Centennial Conference, the New England Men's and Women's Athletic Conference (NEWMAC), and the North Coast Athletic Conference (NCAC) all follow Division III regulations by limiting non-traditional segments to five weeks and between three and five competition "dates."

We do not know enough to make detailed, sport-specific recommendations concerning season length and related restrictions—which in any case would have to be tailored to local circumstances, including facts of geography, climate, and history. But we do suggest the following principles:

- Seasons should be shorter. An acceptable maximum, at least for Division III, would be 16 weeks (including pre-season practice and the traditional segment).
- More control should be exerted over what transpires in the non-traditional segment. We suggest that all outside competition in the "non-traditional" segments of seasons be prohibited, if there is a need for such segments to exist at all.
- It is fine for students to continue, during the "off-season," to work out on their own, to maintain fitness, and to hone their skills (as they have been accustomed to doing before coming to college, and just as serious musicians do). But determined efforts should be made to ensure that "voluntary" activities are truly voluntary.[5]
- There is much to be said for requiring definite "time-off" periods, when athletes are not permitted to attend mandatory or captain's practices or any activity supervised by their coach. The Ivy League presidents have recently instituted a "seven-week-off" policy of precisely this kind, and reactions from some coaches are the best indication of why such a policy is needed. A women's lacrosse coach at Cornell is reported to believe that "this rule will inhibit her team's ability to build chemistry and cohesiveness over the course of the off season, which in turn may negatively impact its ability to repeat last year's Final Four appearance."[6] It is important to note how rapidly students in some sports find ways around policies of this kind. We have been told that students have already asked their athletic directors to approve their participation in "club" versions of their sports during these periods. The experience of conferences with "time-off" periods already in place justifies concerns about compliance. The NESCAC Presidents' Council recently felt obliged to reiterate the conference's prohibition of organized athletic activity outside of the traditional season after a serious violation of the rule at a member school.
- Careful attention also has to be paid to myriad scheduling issues, which can be a source of great tension on campus (for coaches, faculty, and students alike). The Athletics Review Committee at Swarthmore, in considering a wide range of issues concerning intercollegiate athletics, "quickly came to the view that [their] most urgent priority was to contribute directly to the scheduling debate." Then, after extensive consultations, the faculty debated and adopted "a set of [eight] guidelines designed to alleviate the scheduling conflicts

faced by student-athletes and to resolve unavoidable ones in a transparent and effective manner."

These guidelines, which flatly prohibit missing a class, lab, or seminar for practice, nonetheless leave many questions open (as they must); the most they can hope to accomplish, as the preceding language suggests, is to "alleviate" conflicts. In the late afternoons, in particular, colloquia and similar activities will continue to compete for athletes' time and attention. There is no complete solution to this problem.[7]

The issues surrounding season length, "voluntary/mandatory" activities in the off-season, and how complete a commitment a student must make to a single sport are clearly important in their own right. They are also important in that they influence the ability of students to play more than one sport at the varsity level. The number of "cross-over" athletes, as they are sometimes called, in turn has implications for recruitment and admissions, in that the fewer cross-over athletes there are, the greater the pressure to set aside more places for athletes "tagged" by a coach to play a particular sport. The debate at Swarthmore over football, to which we turn later in this chapter, illustrates this point very clearly.[8]

POSTSEASON PLAY, NATIONAL CHAMPIONSHIPS, AND NATIONAL RANKINGS

What we have called the growing allure of national championships is one of the main forces causing the athletic divide to widen (as we showed in Chapter 8). Success at the national level has been called "intoxicating" and "standard setting." National aspirations without question drive incentive structures for coaches that are problematic, and they also put pressure on schools in terms of admissions, scheduling, provision of facilities, support services, and, indeed, every aspect of the athletic enterprise. The allure of national championships feeds, in Giamatti's words, "[hunger] for that next event, that sequel, that bigger-league look and feel, that I think violates the essence of what we believe the role of organized athletics in our institutions ought to be."[9] It is important to prevent participation in national championships from becoming the dominant, perhaps even the sole, objective of major parts of a school's intercollegiate athletics program. Economist Alan Krueger favors confronting directly what he refers to as "the national championship obsession," since it generates so much of the demand for coaches to recruit specialist athletes who can compete on a national level.

Ruling out all postseason competition would be a direct and forceful action, and there is much to be said for it. (There is, of course, precedent in the unwillingness of the Ivy League and of NESCAC to allow football teams to compete after the end of the regular season.) The idea that individual athletes have a real choice as to whether to extend their seasons is an illusion. The potential problems are illustrated well by John Emerson's account of an experience with one of his students at Middlebury:

> I teach in the mathematics department, and our department has a one-semester senior thesis requirement for its majors. I recall directing the thesis of a good and motivated student who was also a star athlete. The student's team reached post-season competition, and so the demands of the sport competed with the expectations of the thesis program. For this student and others on the team, the athletic season went on through the reading and examination period. Participation in post-season play won out, and the student completed a thesis that was just minimally acceptable. My own disappointment in the result was likely exceeded by the student's disappointment and conflicting emotions. What should (and would) have been a happy and positive culminating academic experience became much less than that. I fear that the impact of NESCAC's abandoning its prohibition of post-season play too often has consequences like those illustrated; but such consequences are rarely seen and understood by more than a few individuals, and they are certainly not visible "externally."[10]

The seemingly endless debates within NESCAC as to what to do about national championships (see Chapter 7) are a vivid reminder of how difficult it is to make and uphold distinctions and to adopt and enforce conference-wide rules. (Is it fair that individual runners can go to national championships but that track teams made up of many of the same runners cannot? What about relay teams? And on and on.) We are persuaded by the NESCAC experience that there is no substitute for clear conference-wide agreements that have real bite. Bowing to arguments favoring "institutional autonomy" and wanting to be permissive can lead to pressures that are too difficult for the group as a whole to withstand. In an effort to address this problem, the NESCAC presidents voted to allow only one of its members to compete in each sport's national championship; this decision was controversial, however, and has yet to be put into effect.

Why not simply rule out all postseason competitions at the national level? Psychologist Starkey Duncan at the University of Chicago believes that championships are important because they are about "possibilities": "People like the idea that they might possibly get to a national championship, even if there is only a 2 percent chance of their doing so." It is, as someone else put it, "human nature to want to test yourself against the best . . . to see how far you can go." In principle, there is certainly an argument to be made for allowing postseason competition under carefully controlled arrangements that, among other things, protect against exam conflicts (no easy task, given the variety of schedules that are in place).

There would, in any event, have to be controls and constraints. Taken literally, the slogan "test yourself against the best" would imply engaging competitors who are committed to sports above all else, and this would certainly imply widening the athletic divide, no matter what other measures were in place. Presumably any plan for allowing postseason competition would still need to include provisions for "limiting the field" in some appropriate way. Otherwise, the pressure to succeed at the highest level of athletic competition would mandate so much training and focus on sports that it seems highly unlikely that athletes who define success in this way could hope to take full advantage of their educational opportunities.

The key question, we have come to believe, is how national (or regional) postseason championships are structured: who is eligible to compete, on what terms, and on the basis of what schedule? This question, in particular, can be answered only by addressing the issue of "orbits of competition" at the national level, which is an important topic in the next chapter. Only if some sensible nationally determined structure can be found will it be possible to retain a focus on conference-wide or regional results as the proper yardstick of competitive success, meanwhile allowing the outstanding athlete or the unusually successful team to go forward and compete outside the conference on reasonable terms. Framing a sensible set of postseason opportunities is a challenging task, and only time will tell whether the desired result can be achieved. If the right limits cannot be put in place, we would join President William Adams of Colby in arguing: "The philosophical benefits of national championships do not trump the bigger issue of conflicts with educational mission."

It is easier for us to conclude unequivocally that nationwide rankings of *entire sports programs* are a bad thing. We applaud the wisdom of a number of conferences that have resisted temptations to adopt conference-wide versions of the Sears Cup. None of the conferences in this study follow such a practice, and we were interested to learn of the experience of the UAA in debating this issue: "Shortly after its founding the members of the UAA considered establishing a 'Presidents Cup' which would be awarded annually to the institution earning the most points as determined by its collective finishes across all championships sponsored by the UAA. The proposal was approved by the Athletic Administrators Committee and Delegates Committee but unanimously rejected by the Presidents Council. As one president put it, 'We have student-athletes who compete against each other, and we have teams that compete against each other, but we do not compete against each other as institutions.'"[11]

This same logic applies, in our view, to the existence of the Sears Cup on the national level. It serves mainly to fuel the forces widening the athletic divide, and it would be better if it were eliminated.

SCALE OF THE PROGRAM

The emphasis placed on intercollegiate sports obviously depends not only on the characteristics of individual teams and individual athletes, but also on the numbers of teams and participants—in short, on the overall scale of the enterprise. Colleges and universities tend to make decisions about the scale of their athletics programs on an incremental basis. They start from a given point and then generally add teams (especially women's teams in recent years); much less frequently, and with much gnashing of teeth, they sometimes eliminate teams. The result can be "drift" to a larger and larger programmatic scale relative to the size of the student body. As we discuss later in the chapter, we believe that strong club sports programs can do much to ease the problems associated with supporting a great many varsity programs. But our focus here is on the problems of scale associated with sponsoring large numbers of full-fledged intercollegiate teams.

One enormous advantage that the UAA enjoyed when it was formed in the late 1980s was a clean slate: its members could decide, de novo as it were, what program scale made sense in their setting, taking into account admissions considerations, patterns of play, and the dollar costs of travel. The result was an Association decision to "sponsor" 22 varsity sports. Entering classes at these universities average over 1,100 students, and recruited athletes account for roughly 6 percent of the incoming class (athletes in general, including walk-ons, account for about 9 percent).[12] A number of the UAA representatives with whom we spoke credited this relatively small scale with their success in avoiding a number of the problems evident in the Ivy League and in NESCAC, including inordinate pressure on admission slots and the complications of an "athletic culture."

The NESCAC colleges, in contrast, field an average of 27 teams, and recruited athletes make up about 20 percent of the student body. (All athletes, including walk-ons, make up about 38 percent.) In the Ivies the average is 31 teams, with recruited athletes making up about 14 percent of the student body and all athletes about 22 percent. The figures for teams and athletes in the other coed liberal arts colleges in our study (including Macalester and Swarthmore, which we discuss at length later) approach those in the NESCAC colleges but are not quite as large. The commitments to varsity athletics at the women's colleges tend to be more modest.

Adams wonders if NESCAC's scale is viable under today's conditions:

I am coming to worry more and more about the sheer magnitude of the athletic programs at the Ivies and in NESCAC, even if we all agree that recruiting practices and standards must change. The growth we have seen over the past 10–15 years has been fueled by both programmatic and competitive factors. Programmatically, we have been concerned to broaden opportunities for athletic participation, in keeping with our general philosophy regarding the place of athletics in a liberal education. That effort has been accelerated both by competitive admission factors—how can we attract students we desire if we don't have what they want; we have to offer what Middlebury offers if we hope to keep up with them in admission—and by Title IX pressures, which have provided still other reasons for the number of programs to grow. Is this scope of program viable within the more general national context of specialization and professionalization? I am not sure it is. For both educational and financial reasons, we do not want failing programs. And so admission deans . . . feel pressure from across the spectrum to ensure at least some form of success. Whether or not the fundamental measures of "success" can be defined locally in such a way as to offset the current competitive pressures of servicing 30 or more programs is a hugely important question.[13]

Our reading of the history of NESCAC is that its member colleges have long valued extensive participation in athletics, following the philosophy articulated by John Sawyer at the founding of the conference, and so have had large numbers of teams (mostly men's teams) for a very long time. Then two things happened more or less simultaneously. First, men's athletics in NESCAC, as elsewhere, became much more intense and much more specialized, with stepped-up recruiting, greater admissions advantages for athletes, pressures for participation in national championships, and so on. Second, coeducation, the women's movement, and Title IX all combined to lead these colleges to upgrade women's sports so that they would be on a par with men's sports; in practice, this meant adding women's teams, and recruited women athletes, to the pre-existing base of men's teams.[14] The result? A *very* large overall scale, in relation to the sizes of these colleges.

Scale has been an especially vexing problem for Swarthmore, which belongs to the Centennial Conference, because it has the smallest enrollment of any school in this study—354 matriculants in the 1995 entering cohort (as compared, for example, with 544 at Colby)—and yet Swarthmore supported 24 varsity teams prior to the recent review of its program. In December 1999, its Board of Managers appointed a special Athletics Review Committee (including trustees as well as administrators, faculty, and students) in response, in their words, "(a) to dissatisfaction expressed by students and coaches over the lack of competitiveness of our intercollegiate program and (b) to concerns expressed by the faculty advisory group to admissions and the dean of admissions over pressures being placed on the College admissions process by the needs of the athletic program."[15] The committee "repeatedly heard reports from coaches and students about the demoralizing effects of lack of competitiveness," which many traced to a combination of limited recruiting in most sports, a relatively small number of full-time coaches, and inadequate facilities. At the same time, the faculty were concerned that 17 percent of an entering class was already composed of slotted athletes, with pressures mounting to admit more athletes.[16]

A point of comparison from long ago, contributed by Clark Kerr, the distinguished president-emeritus of the University of California:

"Swarthmore College, which I entered in the fall of 1928, was the greatest transformational experience of my life. It was so beautiful—even more now, because of the inspired care of the Scott Arboretum. It was small, so I could participate in all those activities I had missed in high school without being very good at any of them—sports (soccer, basketball, track), the weekly newspaper (Jim Michener was editor my freshman year), the yearbook, debating (I was captain of the team), student government (I was president of men's student government), and much else. I was trying to follow the Aydelotte ideal of the all-around student."[17]

A number of the Ivies, in spite of their much larger enrollments (averaging nearly 1,500 matriculants per class) have also worried about the overall scale of intercollegiate athletics programs—especially when there were severe budgetary pressures. They, too, have had a history, since the late 1960s, of adding teams (often in the wake of decisions by member schools to become coeducational) that is very similar to the history of the NESCAC colleges. The Princeton Trustee Committee report of 1994 keeps coming back to the question of scale: there are so many teams to support, there is a relatively small student body, there are other interests to respect, and so on. The 1994 report also notes that freshmen teams were given up in part to conserve resources (dollars and spaces in the class), at a time when all of the Ivies were adding women's teams.[18]

If a Colby, a Swarthmore, or one of the Ivies were to want to reduce their programmatic scale somewhat by cutting back on the number of varsity teams, how could they do it? Much depends on a school's compliance with Title IX. Most schools with football programs fail to meet the "substantial proportionality" test, and we do not think that any across-the-board reduction in men's and women's teams would be possible at such schools without altering football programs in some substantial way. In the early part of 1992, Brown University attempted to address budget problems by cutting the financial support given to its women's gymnastics and volleyball teams, as well as to its men's golf and water polo teams—seeking, as it were, a proportionate scaling down of the University's commitment to men's and women's sports. Women athletes filed suit (*Cohen v. Brown University*), arguing that women were already underrepresented in athletics at Brown and that cutting their teams violated Title IX. The district court ruled in favor of the female athletes, the U.S. Court of Appeals for the First Circuit upheld that decision, the U.S. Supreme Court declined to hear Brown's appeal, and Brown agreed to a settlement in June 1998.[19]

Especially in light of *Cohen v. Brown University*, it seems highly unlikely that any school not comfortably in compliance with Title IX would risk legal action, or just bad publicity, by starting down the path Brown attempted to follow.[20] More favorably situated schools have a wider range of options. Just as this book was going to press, Dartmouth announced that, for budgetary reasons, it was eliminating its men's and women's swimming programs. In announcing this "difficult decision" (which was subsequently reversed), Dartmouth referenced the same problems of scale and the need to support large numbers of other sports that figured so prominently in Swarthmore's review of its athletic program (discussed later). In the questions and answers accompanying the announcement of its decision, Dartmouth explicitly rejected any connection between the elimination of these programs and Title IX: "Dartmouth is one of the most gender-equitable athletic programs in the country, among the top five of the 324 Division I institutions in terms of 'substantial proportionality.'"[21]

Swarthmore, on the other hand, sought to address the serious problem of scale on its campus in the most direct way: by eliminating its football program entirely (and also wrestling and women's badminton). Nor has Swarthmore been alone in considering whether it should compete in football. Macalester is another small liberal arts college (with an entering enrollment in 1995 of 437, as compared with 354 at Swarthmore) that recently gave serious consideration to dropping the sport. It decided to continue playing, but in a different competitive context. These two carefully considered (and hotly debated) decisions bring us directly to "the special case of football." Considered together, these two recent case studies provide a window through which to examine the factors to be considered by schools concerned about their football programs.[22]

THE SPECIAL CASE OF FOOTBALL

What is so special about football? William M. Chace, president of Emory, regards football as "problematic": "It is vastly more expensive [than other sports], it requires many more people, it has a much stronger culture surrounding the sport, and it is much more likely to cause injury." He added that it does not surprise him that football players are often involved in disciplinary cases, considering the conflicting messages they receive about when to use violence and when not to use it. To this list we would add that football is a highly visible and extensively covered college sport, with strong historical traditions and often intense alumni loyalties; that specialization has probably gone further in football than in any other sport; that physical size and strength are especially important at some positions; and that football is pre-eminent among "contact sports." At the same time, we also suspect that interest in football at the secondary school level has not increased at anything like the same pace as interest in women's sports generally, in other team sports such as basketball and soccer, and in individual "Olympic" sports, such as tennis and swimming, that are promoted nationally much more actively than they were in earlier days.[23]

Macalester's internal review of its athletics program focused exclusively on football. In explaining the need for the review, President Michael McPherson echoed many of the themes just noted:

> As things stand, our football program is not in satisfactory shape. Obviously our conference won-lost record is disappointing.[24] A larger concern is that the imbalance we face in squad numbers and player weight in the Minnesota Intercollegiate Athletic Conference (MIAC) may put our players at serious risk of injury. . . .
>
> Football, more than most sports, is a game of numbers. Macalester and Carleton have among the lowest enrollments among co-ed colleges in the MIAC. . . . The average football squad size in the MIAC is over 75, and some schools dress more than a hundred players for football. This year Macalester's squad size is listed at 38, the lowest in a number of years. Only four students whom the coaches identified as strong football prospects entered Macalester this fall. . . . It is extremely hard in football to succeed against teams that have half again as many or more players as we have. Given the high level of specialization in modern college football, just one or two injuries can leave us without a player who can fill a particular position. And having players playing out of position or playing too many minutes increases the risk of serious injury.[25]

Discussions on individual campuses rarely focus on the academic performance of athletes, in part because it is very awkward to seem to "put down" fine people who are by any normal standard good students and are presumably trying hard and doing well in their own spheres of interest. In addition, there is an understandable desire to protect the privacy of students even when using "averaged" student records, especially on a small campus, and to resist tendencies toward stereotyping that, as we have seen, are all too prevalent. For these reasons, both official statements and student newspapers generally refer only obliquely, if at all, to academic qualifications and academic outcomes. Faculty, on the other hand, are likely to be especially concerned about such matters, and the data we compiled for this study document the extent to which football is "special" in terms of disappointing academic outcomes:

- Football players enter with appreciably lower SAT scores than almost all other athletes.[26] In the Ivy League the average football player scored 81 points lower than other male athletes and 144 points below the average male student at large, while in NESCAC the gaps were 90 points and 136 points, respectively.
- Football players are more likely to "bunch" in certain fields of study (especially the social sciences) than other athletes and students at large. Almost 60 percent of football players in NESCAC majored in the social sciences, as did over 40 percent of football players in the Ivies and in coed liberal arts colleges outside of NESCAC.
- As a group, football players perform much less well academically than other athletes and students at large—both absolutely and in relation to their predicted performance. Indeed, in each group of schools, playing football is associated with underperformance of at least nine rank-in-class points in addition to the underperformance associated with being a recruited athlete; no other sport shows such consistently high underperformance (Appendix Table 6.1a).[27]

Program reviews are naturally provoked when there is a combination of worries about admission slots, losing records, risks of injury, and below-average academic performance.[28] In thinking about what options exist, there are three basic questions to ask: (1) Should the college play the sport at all? (2) If so, against which teams should it compete? (3) Under what rules and regulations?

To Keep Football?: The Macalester and Swarthmore Cases

In his first letter to his campus community, President McPherson of Macalester raised this question directly: "We either have to find a workable way to put our football team in a more reasonable competitive position, or we have to decide to forego competition in football in favor of other

ways of advancing our goals in athletics. . . . We therefore need to see if
there is indeed a strategy, consistent with our values and the demands on
our resources, which will allow us to succeed at football. I want to make
my own view clear: If we cannot identify a clear, workable strategy that
we have confidence in—and we have not to this point discovered such a
strategy—then we should drop football. We should not allow ourselves
simply to muddle through and hope for the best."[29] McPherson also candidly acknowledged, from the first, that there would be a real downside to
any decision to end the football program: "I well recognize that there
would be real drawbacks to eliminating football. No doubt, some alumni
and supporters of the college would be upset and might withdraw support.
Some folks, including some prospective students, would interpret an announcement that we were dropping football as demonstrating a lack of
commitment to athletics. There is also a risk that the local press would
read the story that way. We would also in the future lose some fine students
who would be drawn to Mac by the opportunity to play football. I am
acutely aware that such a decision would also come as a bitter disappointment to the current members of Macalester's team."[30]

These concerns were certainly understood by Swarthmore as well as
Macalester, and it is instructive to ask why these two leading colleges came
to such different decisions. First, Swarthmore was under much greater
pressure than Macalester to "save" student places committed to football
so that they could be used for other purposes. In fact, like many other
coed liberal arts colleges, Macalester would like to increase the ratio of
male to female students, and a viable football program can help in this
regard. Swarthmore, in contrast, is smaller than Macalester, more selective, and has an appreciably higher ratio of male to female students.[31]

At the time of Swarthmore's review, the school's twelve men's intercollegiate teams had 99 "slotted athletes" on their rosters and 66 athletes
not admitted through slotting (excluding seniors); of the 99 slotted athletes, 38, or nearly 40 percent, were on the football team.[32] This is obviously a substantial share of a modest total, and it is far from obvious that
there was any approach other than dropping football that would have
given Swarthmore any real relief from the pressing problem presented by
the scale of its varsity program seen in relation both to its enrollment and
to the needs of other men's teams for admissions slots. Here again, the
situation at Macalester was different in an important respect: whereas
other men's teams at Swarthmore had real difficulty being competitive,
the men's teams at Macalester, other than the football team, tended to be
respectable competitively. The aggregate won-lost percentage for men's
teams at Swarthmore, other than football, was 30 percent, as compared
with 60 percent at Macalester.[33] Thus the other men's teams at Macalester

had far less need for the admissions slots assigned to football than did the other men's teams at Swarthmore.[34]

In one other respect, however, the case for dropping football must have seemed weaker at Swarthmore than at Macalester. Whereas Macalester undertook its review following a series of extremely disappointing football seasons, Swarthmore began its review just at the time that a three-year effort to reinvigorate the football program appeared to be having some success—at least as judged by won-lost records. At the end of the 1997 season, Swarthmore had not won a football game in two years. A new coach was hired, and a decision was made to rebuild. The first year under the new coach was again winless, but team statistics improved. The second year (the 1999 season) saw Swarthmore win its first game in four seasons, crushing a winless Oberlin team 42–6. The third year of the new regime (the 2000 season) saw the team end with a 4–5 record.[35] Still, the fundamental problem of scale remained: the number of spaces in each entering class was severely limited, the football team claimed nearly half of all the slots allocated to athletics, and Swarthmore had great difficulty fielding competitive teams in other men's sports.

There are important lessons to be learned from the processes followed at the two schools (discussed at the end of Chapter 14). Here it is sufficient to note the following.

First, the decision to drop football at Swarthmore was highly contentious and even led to the rare spectacle of a recorded vote (21 to 8 in favor of eliminating football) at the climactic December 2000 meeting of the Board of Managers, rather than the usual agreement by consensus, and then to a second meeting of the Board in early January where the Board decided, based on a "sense of the meeting," to let the earlier decision stand. There were campus protests, much debate, and a sense on the part of some football players that they had been betrayed.[36] Subsequently, a number of football players transferred so that they could play in other programs, and the campus began to tire of this issue. ("Fatigue" set in, according to one report.)

Second, an important substantive outcome at Swarthmore was the decision to target the upper end of the approved 10–15 percent range of places in the entering class reserved for slotted athletes (for the entering class enrolled in the fall of 2001, the actual percentage was 15.8, and it has been said that the upper end of the range was reached again for the class entering in the fall of 2002). The Athletics Review Committee, in its final report, recommended that "the college continue to target the upper end of this range during the present period of revitalization." Also, Swarthmore has moved aggressively to add an associate director for intercollegiate athletics, hire five new full-time coaches, and make substantial facilities improvements.[37] One faculty member commented wryly, "It's Christmas time in athletics." There is also said to be some faculty dissatisfaction with the small net reduction in admission slots for athletes. Prior to the elimination of football, roughly 17 percent of places in the class were reserved for athletes, and, as we have noted, the new percentage is around 15 percent. Tensions present prior to the review persist. Some clearly believe that the college has over-reacted, has over-committed itself to athletics—perhaps to demonstrate to those critical of the decision to eliminate football that it is not "anti-athletic."

Third, no one knows how the effort to strengthen other sports will work out, since the competitive stakes keep being raised externally as a result of all the forces we have documented in this study. As the final report of the Athletics Review Committee put it: "It is critical to recognize that the priorities of competitor schools represent a powerful constraint on what the athletics program can achieve, in terms of competitiveness, with any given amount of admissions or other resources. . . . The college operates within an athletic culture that is increasingly remote from the 'amateur but excellent' ethos articulated by President Courtney Smith in the 1960s." The Athletics Review Committee then went on to urge the college to work with "other like-minded competitor schools to explore the scope for coordinated reductions in recruiting requirements and other resource demands of the intercollegiate program."[38] These last observations connect directly to one of the reasons that Macalester came to a different decision about football than the one reached, albeit painfully, at Swarthmore.

Finding Suitable Opponents

A principal reason that Macalester decided to retain its football program was that it saw a new way to schedule its games. (Another reason, mentioned by several people, was the "can-do" attitude of many of the supporters of football, who did not just sit back and object to the idea of eliminating the sport, but asked: "What do we need to do to make this work?") In looking back over Macalester's experiences in the MIAC, McPherson observed: "It is hard to see how we could achieve real competitive balance in a conference that allows schools to have teams with more than a hundred players and that at this point lacks any mechanism for enforcing the NCAA rules against awarding aid on the basis of athletic promise." Then, looking ahead, he saw this alternative:

> I have concluded that we should focus our energies on building an exciting and challenging independent football schedule for Macalester. A number of liberal arts colleges and small universities in our region have expressed

tremendous enthusiasm for scheduling Macalester. These include Lawrence University, Colorado, Grinnell, and Beloit Colleges, and the University of Chicago. At the same time, the presidents at several of our traditional rivals in the MIAC have expressed interest in continuing to play us as independents. These include Carleton College, Hamline University, and St. Olaf College. Taken together with several non-conference schools in the Twin Cities whom we have often scheduled in the past, I feel sure that over the next year or two we can build a terrific independent schedule. We'll be playing schools that are similar to us, with programs that match up well with ours. I also expect that alumni in cities like Denver and Chicago will be excited to know we are playing football in their neighborhood. [McPherson added that Macalester would remain in MIAC for all sports other than football.][39]

Looking even further ahead, McPherson shares the hope of many others: that there may be new competitive options generated by reform efforts at the national level (see the next chapter). Meanwhile, Macalester will be charting a new path for itself as a football independent, but it faces uncertainties because of the same concerns about national trends expressed at Swarthmore. Although no one can be sure that Macalester's new experiment will work, there seem to be enough reasons for optimism to justify going ahead—including the fact that Macalester's football team finished 5–5 in 2002, their best finish since 1986. Of course if the effort does not succeed, Macalester will then be positioned to justify the more drastic step of dropping football. Although it expressed similar sentiments and long-run hopes for a new competitive environment, Swarthmore could not identify any practical steps it could take in the near term to insulate its football program from the rigors of competition in the Centennial Conference, where squad sizes average 85.

The chair of Swarthmore's Athletics Review Committee, Jennie Keith (also the provost of the college), reported her finding: "In the short term, at least, a shift in our context of competition (to independence or a different conference) is not a realistic solution. The trend within Division III is away from independence [in large part because of incentives created by rules of qualification for national championships, we would add]. It would be very difficult for the College to create schedules for independent competition year by year. Forming a new conference would be a long-term effort and, even if successful, would pose severe challenges in terms of the travel time needed for our athletes to compete with the other schools who might join us, most of which are in the Midwest."[40] This perceived scheduling reality was obviously a factor in Swarthmore's decision to drop football altogether. Geography and the nearby availability of congenial competitors make a great deal of difference. NESCAC, the Ivies, and the UAA universities all benefit from being able to work on common problems within a framework of largely shared assumptions, values, and academic characteristics.

Rules and Regulations

Large squad size is without question one of the singular problems presented by football. Squad size, in turn, is directly related to "the rules of the game," as former Notre Dame coach Ara Parseghian emphasized in an interview. Squads could be smaller in the days of one-platoon football. Schools seeking to deal with problems of scale, caused in no small measure by the need to field large football squads, might well consider whether there are conference-wide modifications in rules that would help. According to published Equity in Athletics Disclosure Act (EADA) data, average football squad sizes today are 103 in the Ivy League schools, 71 in the UAA universities, 80 in the NESCAC colleges, and 56 at the coed liberal arts colleges in our study. They are 85 in the Centennial Conference and 84 in MIAC.[41] The Division I average nationwide is 104, and the Division III average is 83.

Irv Cross, former NFL player and now athletic director at Macalester, estimates that 50 is a reasonable squad size. This would allow 2 players for every position (22 offensive, 22 defensive, and 2 kickers) plus a few specialty players. According to Cross, most conferences limit travel squads to about 50 to 60 in order to contain costs. Thus there does not appear to be a question of being able to play a single game with this number of players; there is, however, the problem of injuries over the course of the season. Doug Weiss, the long-time college trainer at Swarthmore, stipulated 60 as the squad size required for safe practice, based on his 40 years of experience with football as well as his professional research.[42] At a roundtable discussion on college sports reform sponsored recently by The Andrew W. Mellon Foundation, the consensus seemed to be that squad sizes in the mid-60s might be workable.

An alternative way of addressing the problem of scale is to limit not squad size but the number of football recruits, as both the Ivies and some of the NESCAC colleges do at present. This approach strikes more directly at the concern over the allocation of places in the entering class and has the advantage of allowing walk-ons to participate. There are, however, two disadvantages of focusing solely on recruits. One is that it can be hard to define who is a recruit and therefore hard to monitor compliance.[43] A second is that large squad size can be a substantial competitive advantage, giving a team greater flexibility in substituting for injured or fatigued players. These considerations lead us to favor limiting *both* squad size and the number of recruits. It will be interesting to see if the recent Ivy League decision to reduce the average number of football recruits in the entering class from 35 to 30 is the end of the process of cutting back or is only one step along a path toward further reductions. Some have spoken in favor of 25 or even 20 as an appropriate target.

Still another approach, one that could be complementary rather than competitive with either of the two just discussed, is to change the substitution rules to give coaches less incentive to lobby for large squads. The one-platoon idea, which keeps surfacing but never seems to be taken seriously, is one variant. Another would be to devise limits on substitutions (compare soccer) so that a coach would teach and plan for games on the basis of a different set of assumptions as to the number of players that would be used. (Cross, who is an advocate of this approach, notes that Parseghian, his former coach at Northwestern, was a master at just this kind of management of talent. Cross adds that having to learn more than one position can be very instructive and can add to a player's enjoyment of the sport. He also believes that the worries that such an approach would lead to more injuries are overstated and not supported by evidence.)

We believe that the "structured incentive" idea has merit. In sports such as soccer, coaches limit squad size because substitution rules make a large squad unnecessary. Those who do not make the varsity squad can join junior varsity teams or club teams, if such exist, or pursue other activities, within or without athletics. There is certainly no obligation to include on the varsity football squad every student who wishes to suit up; the notion of limiting the number of students who can be accommodated in an activity is commonplace. If there were to be interest in pursuing the idea of changing the substitution rules in football, experienced coaches and athletic directors would have to take the lead in formulating new rules, perhaps in conjunction with national norms that might be part of a new set of understandings above the conference level. Several athletic directors with whom we have spoken are highly skeptical that conference-wide rule changes have any possibility of working, given the need to train officials, the issue of what would happen when schools played outside their conference, and so on. Radical proposals of this kind would, we believe, be conceivable only in the context of a new national structure that was embraced by a fairly large number of schools.

CLUB SPORTS

Club sports—which are usually defined in terms of their informal mode of organization, with students themselves providing the leadership, arranging practices, and even, in some instances, coaching each other—represent another dimension of athletics programs. Investing in club sports is a natural complement to the need to place limits (either conference-wide or by individual schools) on the number of sports that will be officially sponsored and heavily supported by the institution.

Club sports appear to be thriving at many of the schools in this study. At Wesleyan, John Biddiscombe estimates that they provide opportunities for approximately 200 students to compete each year. The club sports program at New York University is particularly well developed. According to Director of Athletics, Intramurals and Recreation Christopher Bledsoe, the university's 27 club teams attract approximately 1,000 students. All of these teams have paid coaches and are fully funded by the athletic department—unusual characteristics in a club program. The large-scale and generous funding of its club sports program may be due in part to the fact that New York University supports ten men's and eight women's varsity sports; many traditional sports, such as baseball, softball, and lacrosse, are available as club sports only. To a great extent, the school's club team offerings serve as a complement to the varsity sport offerings.

At Princeton, the club sports program is even larger and more diverse than the program at New York University. Princeton has between 1,100 and 1,200 students (out of a total undergraduate population that is significantly smaller than NYU's) participating in 34 club sports. The sports are administered by an associate director of athletics and a council of student representatives from the various club sports. Unlike the situation at New York University, Princeton's club sports generally do not have paid coaches. This is in part because the athletic department budget for club sports is only $35,000 (a little over $1,000 per team). But it also reflects Princeton's philosophy of student-driven and student-led club sports.

Bryn Mawr also has student representatives leading its club sports teams. Indeed, although a few club teams have existed for some time, in 2002 the Bryn Mawr Athletic Department began to offer substantial administrative support. The rationale, as Amy Campbell explains, is that with guidance and support, club sports offer the best educational experience when students provide the leadership and are accountable for the organization and outcomes. Currently there are club teams in six sports, and the number of teams is expected to grow rapidly. For Bryn Mawr, the development of the club sports program represents a major threshold: interest in athletics has increased to the point where different levels of play and interest in sports beyond the 12 sports offered at the varsity level have made it desirable to provide administrative support.

There is widespread agreement that club sports, at their best, offer splendid educational opportunities. Students learn leadership skills, are given responsibility for managing budgets and setting schedules, must cope with sometimes difficult teammates, and can have fun in a setting for which they themselves have major responsibility. Malekoff notes: "Some participants in club sports love to compete as much as their peers playing on intercollegiate teams, but they do not want their schedule and experience dictated by a full-time coach."[44]

Things are far from perfect in the realm of club sports, however. As one commentator put it: "For all the club sports programs that are well conceived and organized, . . . at least as many suffer from poor student management, a lack of institutional oversight, and general disorganization."[45] Widespread evidence suggests that it is a mistake to treat club sports like all other student-led organizations. The most significant issues concern: (1) safety and health, (2) legal liabilities of institutions, and (3) behavior problems. There is no shortage of accounts of improperly planned trips, sometimes in unsafe vehicles; failure to arrange in advance for a medical trainer to be present for a contest; and rowdy behavior. (Such stories about rugby teams, in particular, abound.)

In our view, careful consideration should be given to increasing investments in club sports. These should include clearly fixing responsibility for them, ideally through a mechanism that involves both the athletics department and a dean's office; insisting on proper oversight; making reasonable budgetary support available; providing access to adequate facilities at reasonable times; and showing appreciation for the contribution club sports can make to campus life.[46] At a time when colleges and universities are striving to meet student needs within a context of rather static resources, a well-staffed and well-supported club sports program can be a great asset; it can yield a high return on a relatively modest investment. In addition to providing opportunities for purely recreational participation in sports, club sports teams can offer competitive opportunities for students at a less intense level than varsity sports, and in some situations they offer opportunities for emerging or prospective varsity sports to demonstrate that they have "grassroots" support.

In short, club sports need to be understood as an important component, and not "the poor cousin," of an integrated athletics program that offers opportunities that span the range from varsity to intramural competition. In the words of one experienced athletic director: "The student-centered aspect of club sports is of tremendous value, . . . [especially at a time when] the intensity of competition in varsity athletics has made college sports much more coach-centered, and not always for the good."[47]

THE ATHLETIC/CAMPUS CULTURE

The evident existence of an academic-athletic divide on many campuses leads to a last set of reform proposals, specific to individual institutions, in a slightly different area than we have discussed at length before: finding ways to integrate athletics more closely into the fabric of a school, and especially into its academic core. The conclusion of Swarthmore's Athletics Review Committee was that scheduling conflicts are a main source of the problem on their campus, and the Committee hopes that the new guidelines that have been developed will ease this source of friction. On other campuses, efforts are being made to encourage coaches to participate more actively on faculty-staff committees and otherwise to be more engaged with non-sports pursuits.

The 1994 Princeton Trustee Committee report is notable for concentrating most of its recommendations in this area. The report emphasizes the importance of "effective integration of athletes and athletics into the broad Princeton educational experience." Recommendations include:

> Under the leadership of the Dean of Student Life, foster more productive collaborations between members of the Department of Athletics and those in other parts of the university; support continuing efforts by residential colleges to incorporate coaches into the life of the College; with the assistance of the Faculty Advisory Committee on Athletics, develop and monitor initiatives that will enhance connections between the Department of Athletics and academic programs; provide more effective advising for athletes; under the leadership of the Director of Athletics, make clear to all coaches their responsibility to advance the broad educational mission of Princeton.[48]

There was follow-up on these recommendations, and by all accounts these measures have helped—but only to a limited extent. There is, as one person put it, only so much anyone can do. The findings reported in this study on the academic outcomes of the '95 entering cohort in the Ivies speak for themselves. (Princeton is not an outlier.)

Taylor Reveley, who chaired the Trustee Committee on Student Life, Health, and Athletics at Princeton that was responsible for preparation of the 1994 report, is now skeptical about the ability of such measures to bring about fundamental change, and he also questions how many resources the university can justify devoting to such efforts. Charles Berry, the former master of Rockefeller College at Princeton, whom we cited earlier, has come to a similar conclusion. Having tried hard to bring athletes and other students together at his residential college (with very limited success—see Chapter 8), and having thought about other ways of encouraging the right kinds of interactions, he too now believes that there is no substitute for going to the core of the problem: the motivations, interests, and other characteristics of recruited athletes.[49]

We are certainly not opposed to efforts to harmonize cultures; they are all to the good and, within reason, should be promoted. Such steps should not, however, be allowed to serve as palliatives—as excuses for overlooking the deeper sources of the academic-athletic divide.

———————

Thinking "holistically" about the numerous recommendations contained in the previous two chapters reinforces our sense of their interlocking nature. We conclude:

- *If* recruitment and admissions philosophies are revised in line with at least some of the suggestions made here, with a consequent change in motivations and priorities as well as academic qualifications of athletes (and recognizing that there will be a reduction in skill levels);
- *If* these changes, in turn, affect the kinds of coaches who continue to want to be at these institutions and the ways that coaches are selected and evaluated;
- *If* ways are also found to reduce the length of seasons, the intensity of practice and training in the off-season, and the relative degree of emphasis placed on winning national championships;
- *If* the scale of the overall athletic enterprise, including the resources devoted to football, can be kept within manageable limits (by thinking carefully about the number of varsity sports that can be supported, as well as, in football, considering limits on squad sizes and the rules of substitution in addition to limits on the number of recruits);
- *If* the emphasis given to club sports can be increased; and, finally,
- *If* efforts of many kinds can serve to re-integrate athletics more closely into the mainstream campus culture,
- *Then* these many elements of a structured package of reform proposals can reinforce each other.

There will surely be feedback or second-order effects. The more academically oriented students with athletic talents and interests who would be admitted under these proposals—and who would want to compete, and to compete ferociously, but under the new kinds of banners that could now be flown—would not opt for the self-segregation so often noted now. In the language of the Original Ivy Agreement, they would be "truly representative" of their student bodies. There should then be much less stereotyping and no sense on the part of athletes that they were "outcasts." At the same time, the most high-powered, highly focused high school athletes would not only be less likely to be recruited by these schools; they would also be less likely to want to come. Self-selection of athletics programs by students would be an important part of the dynamic that could, eventually, recalibrate the entire enterprise. Self-selection of schools by coaches who share the educational philosophy outlined here would be important as well. Selection (and self-selection) of students and of coaches are sure to affect "culture," just as culture, in turn, influences selection.

These kinds of reforms, which can be pursued at the level of the individual school and the individual conference, can succeed only if they are placed within a thoughtfully conceived national structure. As we argue in the next chapter, this structure should have as one of its primary objectives the creation of "orbits of competition" that bring together schools that share common educational and athletic philosophies.

CHAPTER 13

Reform at the National Level

CHANGES IN POLICY at the level of the school and the conference are essential, but these institutions do not live in a vacuum. Context is critical: at the most basic level, reform-minded schools must have suitable competitors—institutions that share their philosophies, admissions practices, playing/practice rules, and educational priorities. Needed is an overall structure that reinforces, rather than undermines, their efforts. Such a structure is especially important for liberal arts colleges like Carleton and Macalester (and Bryn Mawr, Haverford, and Swarthmore) that play within conferences that include a wide variety of schools with a wide variety of athletic philosophies. Historic conference alignments may not work well in all settings, and a new grouping of like-minded schools (a "Division X") might be able to facilitate a healthier climate for athletic competition. Nor are schools that already compete in conferences that include a number of like-minded schools immune from the effects of permissive national structures. No matter how serious an entire conference may be about reform, it is unlikely that its members will succeed in upholding their values if they have to operate within a larger framework that does not embrace them. The intensified athletic pressures within the Ivy League and the New England Small College Athletic Conference (NESCAC) illustrate how even schools that play in "tight" conferences with well-articulated philosophies can stray from their principles when immersed in a larger competitive environment that pulls them away from their core beliefs. For all of these reasons, it will not suffice to rely on reforms within conferences, tempting as it may be to avoid confronting difficult issues at the national level.

FAULT LINES IN DIVISION III AND THE IDEA
OF A NEW DIVISION ("DIVISION X")

How might national structures be modified to support efforts to "reclaim the game"? There are ideas worth exploring within Division I (to which we turn at the end of this chapter), but we begin with Division III because that is where both the issues and the opportunities are clearest.

Debates in Division III do not center on statements of intent. The Division III schools in this study seem generally satisfied with the current statement of the division's philosophy (see addendum to the introduction), which begins as follows: "Colleges and universities in Division III place highest priority on the overall quality of the educational experience and on the successful completion of all students' academic programs. They seek to establish and maintain an environment in which a student-athlete's athletics activities are conducted as an integral part of the student-athlete's educational experience." The pressing questions are more prosaic. They have to do with how this sweeping statement can be translated into operating principles and practices that will lead to a narrowing rather than to a widening of the athletic divide.

Institutional Diversity within Division III and Its Implications

A root problem is that the Division III tent is all-encompassing: the 424 institutions that live under it (at this writing) are a highly diverse lot. Eighty percent of these schools are private institutions, and 20 percent are public. Their individual characteristics vary widely. For example, the first 10 schools listed alphabetically under the letter *C* in the NCAA's Division III membership directory (shown in Table 13.1) range from the California Institute of Technology, which is highly selective and known around the world for the excellence of its graduate programs, to Calvin College in Michigan, an undergraduate institution that accepts almost all of its applicants. Several schools have religious affiliations, and one, California State University–Hayward, is part of the publicly funded California state university system. Readers will also recognize the names of two very different schools from this study on the list—Carleton College and Carnegie Mellon University. At all 42 Division III institutions listed under the letter *C*, undergraduate enrollments range from 529 to 11,997. No graduate students are enrolled at 12, while 10 enroll more than 1,000 graduate students; 8 are doctoral/research universities.[1]

Differences in missions and in circumstances (especially differences in admissions, in curricula, and in the extent to which undergraduate colleges are enrollment-driven) inevitably lead to differences in priorities, and there is now a Joint Subcommittee on the Future of Division III that is looking into Division III membership requirements, student eligibility requirements, how the prohibition of athletic scholarships is regulated, national championship formats, and playing and practice seasons.[2] As already noted, a parallel, but less formal, set of discussions has been stimulated by the former president of Carleton, Stephen R. Lewis.[3] Others have also spoken out in favor of exploring new organizational mechanisms (often noting that, in the words of one president, "the cur-

TABLE 13.1
Characteristics of the First 10 Division III Schools Listed under the Letter C

School Name	State	Undergraduate Enrollment	Graduate Enrollment	Carnegie Classification*	Acceptance Rate
Cabrini College	Pennsylvania	1,635	461	Master's Colleges and Universities II	86
California Institute of Technology	California	942	1,116	Doctoral/Research Universities—Extensive	15
California Lutheran University	California	1,823	1,000	Master's Colleges and Universities I	83
California State University—Hayward	California	9,528	2,597	Master's Colleges and Universities I	89
Calvin College	Michigan	4,117	37	Baccalaureate Colleges—General	98
Capital University	Ohio	2,611	406	Master's Colleges and Universities II	79
Carleton College	Minnesota	1,922	0	Baccalaureate Colleges—Liberal Arts	37
Carnegie Mellon University	Pennsylvania	5,194	3,278	Doctoral/Research Universities—Extensive	31
Carroll College (Wisconsin)	Wisconsin	2,480	241	Baccalaureate Colleges—General	85
Carthage College	Wisconsin	2,042	85	Master's Colleges and Universities II	88

Source: NCAA Database of Active NCAA Member Institutions, available at the NCAA's Web site (http://www.ncaa.org).
* Carnegie Foundation for the Advancement of Teaching, *The Carnegie Classification of Institutions of Higher Education*, 2000 edition, second revision, 2002, electronic data file.

rent division tries to span too many interests"), and the numerous conversations that Lewis has had with other college presidents have led him to conclude that "a large number of institutions believe that we need to undertake some major reforms."[4] Our research confirms the existence of an appetite for actions at the national level that would reduce some of the "intensification" pressures felt today by many Division III schools. There is clear sentiment in favor of defining "new boundaries" that would be tighter in numerous respects and of creating "new orbits of competition."

It is conceivable that the Joint Subcommittee on the Future of Division III will gain division-wide support for a set of proposals that will counter the more worrying trends in college sports (thus obviating the need for a new division). But it seems to us unlikely that a "one-size-fits-all" approach is going to work when the underlying institutional population is so diverse. For example, the opportunity cost of aggressively recruiting athletes (denying admission to better-qualified candidates) is substantial in the highly selective schools and nonexistent in others; in fact, many Division III colleges use athletic recruitment to bolster their enrollment. Thus we suspect that sweeping agreements will prove elusive. There is recent evidence. The protracted and rather inconclusive nature of the debates over the length of playing seasons and how the non-traditional season should be viewed, with all the attendant differences of opinions and compromises, reveal how hard it is to marshal the across-the-board political support needed to reduce the "creeping intensification" of athletics at the Division III level. Moreover, it is far from easy to find enough college and university presidents who are willing to withstand the backlash from coaches and players on their campuses who want to keep doing what they have been accustomed to do for so long.[5]

Still, the basic questions remain: Why is any new set of organizational arrangements needed? Why can't we just rely on individual conferences to adopt more restrictive rules than apply to Division III in general (as some do now)? The answers are straightforward: Schools need to find "suitable opponents" outside their conferences as well as within them. And the availability of suitable opponents depends on the willingness of a reasonably large number of schools to follow a common set of rules. Conferences will feel that they can be more restrictive if the members of other conferences (with whom they are likely to compete at the regional or national level) are behaving consistently. As Robert Malekoff has pointed out, it is difficult to resist the "keeping up with the Joneses" line of argument. In short, the individual conference, although very important, is not "big enough" to establish the tighter common boundaries that many believe are needed.

Goals and Principles That Might Govern a New Division

Broadly speaking, in creating a new division the goal would be the establishment of an organizational structure that would do more than Division III does today to encourage the alignment of academic and athletic values. Principal objectives would include re-emphasizing the educational values that college sports are intended to foster and ensuring that:

- Athletes are truly representative of their student bodies (with academic outcomes similar to those achieved by other students);
- Opportunities to participate in intercollegiate athletics are widely available to both men and women and not limited to "recruits";
- Athletes are integrated into campus life and participate in a wide range of activities;
- There are extensive opportunities for vigorous competition, structured so as to avoid a preoccupation with national rankings and national championships;
- Bureaucratic regulation is kept to an absolute minimum.[6]

We are persuaded that membership in any new division should depend on *self-selection;* it should be based on whether a particular school does or does not want to play within the parameters of a somewhat more restrictive, more educationally oriented organizational structure. We do not favor starting out by assuming that only schools of a certain size, or only schools with a certain academic profile, should be affiliated—an approach that would strike many as reflecting the worst kinds of "elitism." Rather, the test should be agreement with the broad purposes of the division and the specific means chosen to achieve them. It is critical that schools making the choice to join any such new organization be genuinely committed to the set of values the organization embraces.

What kinds of principles and policies might define the new entity? What would the members be expected to agree to when they signed on? It would be presumptuous to offer detailed prescriptions, but perhaps it will help clarify our intentions if we offer a list of basic propositions, all in the spirit of providing "thought-starters that might deserve consideration."

1. Increase emphasis on participation opportunities. It may be desirable to raise the minimum number of sports that member institutions must sponsor and to encourage walk-ons to compete for places on teams. The present requirement that schools in Division III must sponsor at least five men's and five women's teams could be reviewed with an objective of broader participation in mind. Consideration could also be given to adjusting the minimum sponsorship requirement so as to avoid requiring schools with very small enrollments to sponsor more sports than made sense in their settings. It is anomalous that Division III, which emphasizes participation, has lower sponsorship requirements than Division I; raising the minimum requirement would ensure that all schools in the new division were prepared to invest in broad-based programs. Of course the educational case for broad participation assumes that the opportunities made available are not reserved for recruited athletes pre-selected by coaches. (The discussion of recruitment and admission in Chapter 11 is directly relevant here.)

2. *Tighten rules on athletic eligibility.* "Red-shirting"—the practice of allowing an athlete to gain an extra year of eligibility by practicing but not playing a sport—should be eliminated, and means should be found to make sure that a school's interest in utilizing a student's athletic talents does not affect the student's course schedule or timely graduation. Eligibility might also be tightened in other ways to discourage the enrollment of athletes who are not serious students, and to require timely progress toward degree completion. However, we do not envision anything like the detailed regulation of eligibility criteria that is a hallmark of Division I. The proper location of responsibility for setting and enforcing academic standards is the individual institution and conference.

3. *Strengthen the prohibition on athletically related student aid.* This will require defining the prohibition more precisely and establishing more effective monitoring practices. At present there is considerable suspicion that "merit aid" is being used to provide what are de facto athletic scholarships. Any such behavior clearly contradicts the most central tenet of the Division III philosophy—that college athletes should not be rewarded financially for their athletic ability—and ways need to be found to ensure that the no-athletic-aid philosophy is connected to practice.[7] Athletes should not receive preferential packaging (more grant money relative to loans and work-study funds) in a need-based aid framework; they should be treated in the same way as other students who are similarly situated.

A National Collegiate Athletic Association (NCAA) Division III Financial Aid Audit Task Force is already at work. It is collecting data, wrestling with conceptual issues such as preferential packaging, and also addressing more technical questions such as how much variation between the aid given to athletes and that given to other students should be considered acceptable.[8] The goal is to have a set of legislative proposals to present to the 2004 NCAA conference. It will be instructive to see how successful this broadly constituted task force is in reaching clear agreement as to what course of action is best.

4. *Tighten restrictions on the number of coaches and integrate them more fully into educational programs.* Limits should be placed on the number of

unpaid as well as paid coaches. The objective would be not only to control costs and ensure some measure of competitive equity, but also to discourage athletic departments from devoting excessive amounts of time to recruiting. Simple regulations on recruiting are necessary, though excessive detail should be avoided. A useful byproduct might be to encourage the hiring of coaches who would expect to participate broadly in campus life. Efforts should be made to prepare coaches for such larger roles, through workshops and other means, at local, conference, and national levels.

5. Address issues of playing and practice seasons. We favor shorter seasons, fewer contests, no supervised athletic activities in the non-traditional seasons, and explicit prohibition of informal (student-led) practices in the off-season. All out-of-season activities should be strictly voluntary. Common dates for the beginning and end of the fall, winter, and spring seasons should be agreed upon (with the understanding that some flexibility is necessary because of differing academic calendars). There should also be limits on the number of contests played during the regular season and the time that can be devoted to practice, as well as requirements for "time off" from supervised athletic activities.

6. Place limits on squad size, at least for traveling squads, especially in football. This is another area in which collective actions are needed to avoid situations in which individual institutions or conferences feel pressured to ratchet up what they do; the objectives are to control the number of places in a class that are required to field teams and to discourage competitive imbalances.

7. Rationalize postseason play and regional/national championships. A new set of regional and/or national championships could be organized for the members of this new group of institutions, thereby avoiding some of the competitive mismatches that occur when a single competition includes institutions that adhere to very different athletic philosophies. Such an approach would reduce the pressure that is present today when schools feel that they must "bend more" in recruiting and admissions to compete successfully against the wide variety of athletics programs in Division III. This could be one of the most important functions performed by a new grouping of schools. As we said in the previous chapter, the willingness of conferences to allow postseason play should depend on whether such competitions can be structured to maximize the fun of playing and the satisfactions to be gained from competitive success without engendering the excessive pressures with regard to recruiting, admissions, coaching, and scheduling that are so much in evidence. Postseason play should be scheduled to fit within overall season-length constraints that make sense to the division members. For example, postseason play might be allowed to continue for no more than two weeks beyond the end of the regular season. In addition, it is essential that whatever plan is put into place be structured to avoid conflicts with exam schedules and other end-of-the-year academic obligations.

Careful thought would also have to be given to policies governing access to championships. There is a three-part tension that grows out of wanting to limit the number of spots in postseason competition (in part to prevent the competition from going on too long), wanting to emphasize the inclusion of conference champions (to keep the primary focus on success at the conference level), and wanting to make room for deserving independents and some number of at-large entrants (so that everything does not depend on conference alignments and outcomes). We have no magic formula to propose, but we do think that participation in postseason championships should be seen as a "rare opportunity" and not as the normal, expected thing. We also believe that there is room for creative thinking that might generate new ideas. For instance, one could imagine giving some degree of preference to teams (among those over a high threshold of competitive success) that had not reached the postseason level for some number of years.[9] An even more radical idea would be to condition eligibility on the meeting of certain academic standards by the team *as a whole* (or on "bonus points" given in the selection process to teams that had done exceptionally well academically as well as athletically).[10]

8. Establish greater flexibility in conference alignments—and allow "football-only" conferences. Experience teaches us that schools need access to an array of potential opponents who will play by roughly equivalent "rules." Historically determined conference alignments may not produce ideal sets of potential opponents in every sport, as the recent experiences of Macalester in the Minnesota Intercollegiate Athletic Conference and of Swarthmore (and Bryn Mawr and Haverford) in the Centennial Conference indicate. Some new orbits of competition may need to be formed, or at least encouraged, and the appropriate "orbits" are likely to differ sport by sport and from one region of the country to another. Football is clearly a special case, and schools like Macalester would like to play some of the Ohio colleges such as Denison and Wooster in football rather than the "football-heavy" schools in their own conference; in other sports, staying with the local conference and adhering to more geographically based schedules may work fine. The cost of travel and concerns about time away from class must of course affect thinking about schedules and opponents. The general principle we advocate is flexibility.

Easing restrictive conference alignments and allowing schools to find suitable opponents on a sport-by-sport basis should reduce the risk that a school will end up as a perennial doormat. This is important because, as Ted O'Neill at the University of Chicago explained to us, what really drives up the intensity level of college sports, even at a place like the University of Chicago, is "the fear of humiliation." It remains to be seen how the right degree of flexibility can be achieved. Various suggestions have been made, including arrangements that would allow sub-groups of neighboring schools to shift alignments over time depending on won-lost records, so that schools could move from one sub-group to another if results indicated that such movement would contribute to competitive balance. The University Athletic Association (UAA) has had considerable success with tournament and "festival" models whereby, in sports that lend themselves to this format, teams can come together for, say, a weekend of competition against a variety of opponents. Tournaments can also bring together similar schools from across conferences, as occurs in the Seven Sisters Tournaments, in which five of the "Seven Sister" schools—Bryn Mawr, Mount Holyoke, Smith, Vassar, and Wellesley—compete along with allied schools such as Haverford, Swarthmore, and St. Joseph College.

Deciding Whether to Compete Inside or Outside the NCAA

A next question to ponder is whether a new grouping of schools, of the kind we have been describing, could (or should) be created within the NCAA or outside it. The ongoing work of the NCAA's Joint Subcommittee on the Future of Division III presumes that any needed changes, including the possibility of a split of Division III into two or more pieces, could be accomplished within the structure of the NCAA. There are several reasons to proceed in this way.

- It would be far less disruptive and far less complicated to split the existing Division III and yet keep the resulting sub-groups within the NCAA than it would be to create an entirely new organization. The Division III staff works hard on behalf of member institutions, and there is much to be said for continuing to take advantage of their experience.
- For symbolic as well as other reasons, many athletics programs would surely prefer to remain within the NCAA.
- Division III programs receive financial support from the NCAA, and attempting to set up a new structure, including new national or regional championships, outside the NCAA would require new resources. The NCAA's budget of expenses for 2002–03 shows $13.43 million, or 3.18 percent of its total expenses, allocated to Division III.

These moneys primarily cover the costs of national championships, including the provision of some travel and per diem money to participants. Division III schools receive additional association-wide benefits, such as catastrophic insurance and other student-athlete and membership services.[11]

• There would also be an advantage for the NCAA at large in having any new sub-group established within the Association. The NCAA could have a "reputational" problem, of at least modest dimensions, if a number of leading colleges—and conceivably a few well-known universities—were to leave the Association. The NCAA works hard to promote an image of concern for the student and for educational values, and that image would not be helped if it were to lose some number of academically selective institutions that expressly stated their interest in "reclaiming the game."

There is another argument that can be made for continuing to work within the NCAA—namely, that institutions with strong educational programs and commitments to supporting athletics within the context of their educational missions have an opportunity (even, some might say, an obligation) to work to reform the NCAA itself. It is hard, however, to find evidence to substantiate a belief that this hope represents anything more than naïveté in today's highly commercialized world of big-time sports. In conducting his study of athletics sponsored by the American Council on Education, George Hanford had "hoped that perhaps the Ivy League would be the leader in the athletic procession, serving as a model of academic priorities and athletic proprieties."[12] On the contrary, as Mark Bernstein points out, the Division IA schools increasingly came to resent the influence that the "sanctimonious Ivy League" tried to exert (which was one reason for pushing the Ivies into Division IAA in 1981). Bernstein also discusses various moments in Ivy history when the Ivies contemplated leaving the NCAA. He quotes Jeffrey Kabaservis as writing, in his history of Yale's role in the formation of the Ivy League: "The Ivies continued to delude themselves that they could exert a beneficial influence on the NCAA, and that the organization was forever teetering on the brink of redemption."[13]

There are also arguments in favor of making a clean break and creating a new structure outside the NCAA. Some advocates of a new structure believe that staying within the NCAA will inevitably involve being caught up in the regulatory machinery and bureaucracy of a large and complex organization that is dedicated primarily to purposes that reform-minded members do not support. One experienced observer (speaking on condition of anonymity) put it this way: "It may be better to create a new culture, and invite like-minded institutions to join it, than to attempt to change the culture of the NCAA."[14]

At the end of the day, the question of how a new structure should be established, and under whose auspices, may depend on extremely practical matters, such as the willingness of the NCAA and its Division III members to accommodate the needs of a set of institutions that want to march to the beat of a somewhat different drummer.

DIVISION I ISSUES: POSSIBLE FURTHER REALIGNMENTS?

The Ivies (and other schools outside this study, such as those in the IAA Patriot League) face different issues as a result of their membership in Division I. At the most practical level, scheduling is affected by present NCAA rules that place strong limits on the number of contests that Division I schools can play against Division III schools.[15] These rules and requirements make it extremely difficult for an Ivy League school such as Columbia or a Patriot League school like Lafayette, for example, to play a substantial part of its schedule in any sport against Division III schools in its region. The need to play Division I schedules in all sports puts tremendous pressure on schools in terms of recruiting and admissions.

It is far from clear to us that the Ivies (or the members of the Patriot League, for that matter) should try to compete within Division I indefinitely. Jonathan Cole, provost at Columbia, has suggested that although athletic skill levels in the Ivies continue to rise on an absolute basis, they are falling relative to skill levels in the big-time programs.[16] Moreover, Division I programs are increasing, not reducing, their commitments to athletic scholarships outside football,[17] which will make it harder and harder for schools like Columbia to attract the small number of students who are both fine athletes and exceptional students. At the same time, academic standards at the highly selective schools in the Ivies will continue to rise. Thus the academic-athletic divide should be expected to continue to widen because of pressures from both the athletic and the academic sides. Recent efforts within the Ivies to reduce the number of recruited athletes and institute "time-out" periods could, if continued and augmented by other measures, sharpen even more the contrast between Ivy programs and those of most of the rest of Division I.

There is also a fundamental issue of principle. The Ivies have to ask themselves if they can, in good conscience, continue to operate indefinitely under the Division I philosophy statement, which so blatantly contradicts their own statement of principles.[18] It is by no means clear that the Ivies or a number of other Division IAA schools will be comfortable in the long run in Division I—especially if teams in all sports have to compete at this level. It is hard to know what the NCAA divisional landscape will look like in 25 years.

There are also longer-run questions to be asked from the perspective of a Division I member such as Northwestern that bear upon this subject. It is not hard to imagine that a Big Ten school such as Northwestern might want to avoid some of the costs and other consequences of competing at the Division I level in all sports. From Northwestern's perspective, it might make sense, say, to play more soccer games against regional Division III schools such as Macalester and the University of Chicago. Northwestern would presumably have to adopt "Division III rules" in such sports—including especially the rule prohibiting athletic scholarships—for the idea to have any currency. Even so, one experienced person with whom we consulted warned that Division III schools would resist such a "mixed structure" (with a school such as Northwestern playing at Division I and Division III levels in different sports) because the Division I school would be too dominant in the Division III sports. The explanation given was that the superior facilities and infrastructure of a Northwestern would give it a tremendous advantage in all sports.[19]

Another approach might be more realistic than the mixed divisional model.[20] The continuing worries about the ever-escalating costs of competing at the Division I national level in every sport (baseball is a good example) could stimulate, at some point in the future, a discussion within Division I of a further sub-division along the lines of the football split between Divisions IA and IAA. Some Division I schools might remain purely Division I in all sports, as today everyone has to (except in football), while some schools might opt for, say, a Division I^x model in some number of Lower Profile sports. This hypothetical Division I^x model might entail no athletic scholarships; competition on a regional rather than a national level, with regional rather than national championships; and so on. Regional consortia might emerge. The cost savings could be considerable, and a lower-keyed approach to competition in certain sports might also be appealing to some schools on other grounds.[21]

What we are really talking about here is a "loosening up" of constrictions within Division I as well as within Division III. Individual schools would have more options. If a Division I^x model were to evolve over time, it might also make it easier for some schools such as Rutgers to find a niche that would be more appropriate than Division I appears to be for them.[22] Introducing more fluidity into the NCAA structure could have many advantages.

The pursuit of reform at the national level is complicated enormously by the wide range of institutions that have to try to find common ground. When institutional characteristics and institutional missions differ markedly, it is inevitably hard to agree on new directions. This is a major reason why we believe that careful consideration should be given to sub-dividing what is now Division III (and, ideally, finding new names for the divisions) into at least two parts, with self-selection to determine which schools go where. Also, some further sub-division of Division IA may make a great deal of sense. The natural tendency to "punt" on such questions is understandable, as is the companion tendency to excuse inaction by saying that individual conferences can make decisions about issues such as season length, coaching, and postseason competition for themselves. The problem is that many of the Division III colleges and universities seeking to narrow the academic-athletic divide belong to conferences in which many of the other members are pleased with the status quo, are undisturbed by the trends documented in this study, and in some cases are actively seeking to ratchet up the athletic enterprise. Moreover, colleges and universities compete outside their conferences (both in the regular season and in the postseason) and thus need a framework in which shared philosophies and common rules prevail.

The most sensible competitive framework may well vary from sport to sport—in Division I as well as in Division III—and this is another strong argument for rethinking present organizational arrangements and loosening up divisional structures. There is, without doubt, genuine interest at many schools in exploring new options. Presidents of colleges and universities, executive directors of conferences, and the leadership of the NCAA need to respond affirmatively and creatively to these expressions of interest in finding a new direction. It would be short-sighted in the extreme simply to "circle the wagons."

CHAPTER 14

Achieving Change

IN THINKING BACK over the history of efforts to reform intercollegiate athletics, John R. Thelin has come to this sobering conclusion: "The historical legacy is that whereas changing the curriculum has been compared to 'moving a graveyard,' reforming college sports is like excavating a minefield."[1] No one can read Thelin's depressing account of the failure to alter trajectories through clear articulations of principle without feeling the exhaustion that has generally accompanied reform movements—and has almost always persisted after them.

WHY REFORM HAS BEEN SO DIFFICULT TO ACHIEVE

In Division IA a major barrier has been the financial benefits perceived to be associated with big-time programs. The country's most elite athletics programs, at public and private universities, generate substantial revenues, primarily due to successes in postseason competition at the highest levels (reaching the Final Four in basketball and winning bowl games in football). Thus a school like Notre Dame would need to weigh carefully the economic consequences of any decision to alter the course of its athletic program. Notre Dame is, of course, an outlier. In point of fact, the great majority of Division I schools (public and private) end up subsidizing their athletic programs heavily out of unrestricted funds. But this is a reality that tends to be forgotten when television revenues are distributed and dreams of "winning big" are kindled anew each year.[2] In any event, the "commercialization" of athletics at the highest levels of competition is by now so complete that probing questions about real financial impacts are most unwelcome, even though people do not like to admit this.[3]

Yet it would be a mistake, in our view, to be pessimistic about the possibilities of achieving real reform *within the academically selective set of institutions included in this study*. The national studies that Thelin recounts were all focused on big-time programs, and the financial barriers to reform at that level are far higher than they are at the non-scholarship schools we are studying. The most important difference is that *in the two settings dollar signs point in opposite directions*.

In the Ivies and the Division III colleges, intercollegiate athletics programs are understood by everyone to be major cost centers (quite apart from the large capital expenditures that they entail), and the possibilities of changing direction in athletics should be enhanced by the evident budgetary trade-offs. As noted earlier, and as documented in *The Game of Life*, these schools spend far more money on varsity sports than they do on any other extracurricular activity.[4] At a time when financial pressures on many of these institutions are again severe, in part as a result of the dramatic change in the performance of financial markets, the prospect of reallocating funds to purposes such as providing financial aid for needy students, supporting the library, and filling faculty vacancies should be especially compelling.[5]

This is not to say, however, that reform can be easily accomplished. Other barriers exist, and they explain in large measure why even in these settings it has been so hard to resist trends that many deplore. A short list of these barriers would include (1) lack of information as to the seriousness of the problem—specifically, the extent to which the academic-athletic divide has been widening; (2) practical difficulties of schools' acting in concert; (3) the need to mobilize leadership among various constituencies; (4) fear of negative reactions from coaches, players, alumni, and influential trustees; and (5) competing institutional priorities combined with the power of inertia.[6] This study will, we hope, fill a large part of the information gap that has been a significant impediment to concerted action. The rest of this chapter discusses ways to overcome the other barriers.

THE NEED TO ACT IN CONCERT

On one proposition, at least, everyone seems to agree: collective action is required if significant reform is to occur. The Knight Foundation Commission's recent report contains an entire section titled "The Need to Act Together," which invokes the language of the arms race that has become a staple of these discussions to explain why "unilateral disarmament" will not work.[7] Paul Hardin, whose tenure as president of Southern Methodist University ended abruptly after he brought to light corruption in the athletic department, offered this stark observation: "One or two presidents acting alone can affect a local situation but perhaps lose their jobs."[8] Thelin, in his history of reform movements, emphasized the same theme: "Abuses in college sports tend to defy solutions by a single institution because they are, by nature, an interinstitutional venture. Only when like-minded institutions act in concert, whether in conferences or in associations, is essential reform likely to take place."[9]

As easy as it is, in principle, to agree on the need for collective action, it can be excruciatingly difficult to decide, collectively, what in fact should be done. The long tradition of institutional autonomy conflicts directly with the need for common policies, and of course differences in institutional self-interest abound.[10] The long debate within NESCAC over postseason competition (see Chapter 7) is an excellent illustration of the problem. Recently President William Adams at Colby, in discussing this "dangerously contentious issue," has suggested that "for the sake of unity on other matters and the general stability of the conference, we have had to become much too permissive, in my view, on this issue."[11]

The long history of debate within the Ivy League over every possible aspect of an athletics reform agenda is equally revealing. It is very hard for institutions to avoid arriving at what might be called "lowest-common-denominator" outcomes. The understandable, and proper, desire to be collegial can be a serious impediment to achieving a significant change in direction. The Ivy League's efforts to address the issues raised by Martin Meyerson and Bart Giamatti in the late 1970s and early 1980s vividly illustrate how hard it can be to maintain momentum and come to agreements that really address the fundamental issues. The search for consensus can easily lead to proposals to which no one will object too strongly. A real commitment to work together, registered and constantly reinforced by college and university presidents acting in concert with their trustees, is essential—and even then care has to be taken to avoid too much of a tendency to "blend and reconcile."[12]

THE IMPORTANCE OF LEADERSHIP

There is no point in debating whether presidents of colleges and universities or their trustees are more important in the development and prosecution of a reform agenda. Both are essential, and they have complementary roles to play. First, it is a president's responsibility to provide overall direction and leadership for his or her institution, and this certainly includes responsibility for articulating a proper place for athletics within it. Insisting on the right relationship between college sports and educational values is preeminently the job of the president. Obvious as it may seem to many, reasserting presidential control of athletics is essential. Presidents also have to be prepared to withstand internal criticism by athletic administrators, coaches, and players, who will of course resist any efforts to curtail their activities and constrain their programs.[13]

Trustees, in turn, need to understand and support the president's efforts (presuming that they agree with the direction being proposed), but they cannot be expected to be the change agents.[14] There is ample evidence, however, that trustees have the power to obstruct, and a key role for the president and the trustee leadership is to involve the board as a whole in early-stage discussions of matters about which many are passionate. It is particularly important to avoid ending up in situations in which a small number of trustees, strongly committed to this or that athletic program, dominate board discussions and decision-making. It can be tempting to "defer to the expert" (or to the board member who is most passionate and claims to be the expert), but this can be a sure path to inaction. A major collective responsibility of trustees is to take the long view and to think hard about institutional/educational priorities. The steady widening of the athletic divide that has occurred at most of the schools in this study should be reason enough for trustees to encourage forthright discussion of this subject, which can too easily be pushed aside. Looking ahead, we wonder if there is more that can be done by trustees of like-minded institutions working together. Collaborations at the trustee level could reduce the risk that any one president, or any one board, would feel singularly exposed to charges of being anti-athletics. Trustees can also be particularly effective in mobilizing strong and sensible alumni/ae leadership.

Although college and university presidents need to be active proponents of aligning athletics and academics within their own institutions (and more broadly within higher education), realism is needed in understanding what presidents can and cannot do. The main thing that they can and must do is set directions. Then, in organizing follow-through, the presidents have to rely on loyal and committed colleagues, including provosts, deans, and other senior administrators. Presidents will differ both in their detailed knowledge of this complex terrain and in their interest in it. Thus presidents interested in shaping the future of varsity sports on their campuses will need help, not obstruction, from many quarters. The attitudes of other administrators can affect the tone and character of the debate in major ways. One worry expressed by a faculty member (who asked not to be quoted) is that development officers are an increasing problem in that they may be close to donors interested in athletics and may easily subvert reform efforts unless—and this is an important responsibility of the president—there is a clear and consistent articulation of the overall direction of the institution. Directors of alumni offices can find themselves in similarly delicate roles.

Athletic directors are in especially critical and often difficult positions. They feel responsibilities to their coaches, to players, and perhaps to alumni/ae especially concerned about athletics. Thus even those most strongly committed to educational values and to the institutions that they serve, including many who are well aware of the problems posed by the athletic divide, can be quite conflicted. Their expertise and understand-

ing of the issues will be critically important to the success of any effort to
achieve reform, but their role needs to be specified clearly and understood all around. It is not, after all, the job of the athletic director to substitute his or her view of institutional priorities for that of the president
and trustees. Rather, athletic directors need to contribute their own perspectives and those of their coaches, and then to support the overall mission of the institution as the president and the trustees define it. En-
trenched athletic directors who are either out of sympathy with broader
institutional goals or just do not understand the trends leading to a
widening of the athletic divide can undermine reform efforts. Presidents
have to be prepared to recruit new leadership for the athletics program
in such situations. The tendency to be collegial can be overdone, and
seeking paths that will appeal to everyone within the institution can lead
to what someone referred to as "nibbling around the reform agenda,
without really addressing it."

One other group of great potential importance is the faculty. We have
been impressed by the high quality of several internal reports released recently that either were drafted by faculty members at the schools in our
study, or took advantage of their analytical contributions. Particularly
noteworthy are the reports of the faculty committees at Middlebury and
Williams and the trustee-led committee at Amherst. Also, faculty members at Swarthmore have expressed strong interest in the effects of athletics programs on the composition of their college's student body and
on its academic program.[15] These are just a few examples of faculty interest that have come to our attention, and we expect that systematic efforts to engage faculty in thinking through these issues would be productive. Several of the faculty with whom we spoke have commented on
their sense of "isolation," and efforts to encourage conversations among
faculty across institutions, especially in settings such as NESCAC, might
be valuable. One problem for faculty in individual institutions is that
they may not have enough data to feel confident about the validity of what
they believe they are observing; they may also wonder if their college is
peculiar in one respect or another. Getting together can be an effective
way of addressing both concerns.

It is also worth asking whether tougher financial constraints will lead
to more faculty involvement in issues of this kind. Writing in the early
1970s, at another time when severe economic pressures were being felt,
George Hanford raised this question very directly:

If the general economic crunch in higher education continues as expected
and if rising net costs compel athletic departments supporting big-time programs to seek general support as predicted, that support will have to come
from the already limited funds available to higher education. Such a move
will put the sports enterprise into direct competition with academic depart-

ments for the dollars available. At that point faculty attention will most certainly be reengaged, not only at first at institutions supporting big-time sports programs but subsequently by faculties at other colleges and universities whose interest would be aroused by the controversy.[16]

The long period of economic expansion and relative prosperity that characterized both the economy in general and higher education in the 1990s may have dulled concerns about budgetary trade-offs—which may now be felt more keenly once again.

THE VALUE OF A GOOD PROCESS

How a review process is handled will determine in no small measure whether differences of opinion within an institution and across institutions will be productive (in leading to fuller understanding of issues and a more sophisticated sense of the consequences of pursuing a particular line of inquiry) or counter-productive (preventing any resolution of questions that need to be resolved). In working at either the conference level or the national level, there is an especially great danger that the process will be fragmented and that ideas will be "committeed to death." The fate of the reform efforts within the Ivies in the late 1970s and early 1980s is a case in point. Once a package of proposals that needed to be considered together was divided up among different groups (admissions officers, athletic directors, and so on), the holistic nature of the effort was lost, lowest-common-denominator decision-making prevailed, and very little happened.[17]

Among recent efforts to bring about reform, we regard the work of the NESCAC presidents as particularly promising. This group of presidents appears committed to retaining control over the process, and they have already adopted a formula for reducing the number of recruited athletes.[18] Similarly, the Ivy League presidents seem committed to following their recent decision to reduce the annual intake of football recruits with consideration of further reductions in recruiting, perhaps extending beyond football. At the same time, there are many unanswered questions. In the case of the Ivies, some individuals close to the process were disappointed that the presidents "split the difference" with the athletic directors over the size of the reduction in the number of football recruits: the presidents had initially proposed moving from the present number of 35 to 25, and the final decision was 30. It also remains to be seen how successful the NESCAC presidents will be in retaining their capacity to look at all of the interrelated facets of the "divide" at the same time.

President Michael McPherson at Macalester has provided schools interested in considering the future of football programs with a model process. He was forthright in making clear at the outset what the outcome of the process at his school might be (the elimination of football), so that there could be no surprises. He also articulated the reasons why he felt the program had to be reviewed and the criteria he would invoke in recommending a course of action to the college's trustees. Provision was made for extensive consultation so that everyone who had a viewpoint or something to contribute would be heard. At the same time, McPherson made it clear that he would make his own decision, and that the decision-making process was not to be regarded as "democratic." He established a timetable that was not too long and that was related to recruiting and admissions schedules. Finally, he invested a great deal of his own time in analyzing Macalester's options. Then, when he made a decision (to keep football, but with a number of important changes), he explained why he had come out where he had and what would have to happen for the result to be a success.

The processes followed earlier by Princeton in deciding to eliminate wrestling and by Swarthmore in deciding to eliminate football cannot be given such high marks. Princeton's preparation and communication were poor. That university did not make plans to offer the wrestlers who were already on campus an alternative athletic experience, nor did it persuasively explain why it was doing what it was doing. It also took important constituents by surprise.[19] Swarthmore was not clear in announcing in its review that the fate of the football program was a key question, very much on the table. Also, the Swarthmore review occurred right after a highly publicized effort had been made to strengthen the football program—with some early indications of success. Finally, the initial timetable of the Swarthmore review did not mesh well with recruitment and admissions schedules; when this timing problem was recognized, the timetable was moved up, but the result was a sense on the part of some that the process had been rushed and that inadequate efforts had been made to communicate disappointing news to key trustees in a timely way.

Both the Princeton and the Swarthmore experiences had after-effects. The 1994 Princeton Trustee Committee report, which was prepared right after the wrestling decision, "pulled its punches" (in the words of one trustee), largely because the entire wrestling experience had caused so much resentment. The report overlooked academic problems, in part because of the lack of data, but also because "people just didn't feel that they could 'bite the bullet' again in the immediate aftermath of the wrestling fiasco."[20] As noted in Chapter 12, there was an analogous concern at Swarthmore that, following the decision to drop football, the college not be perceived as anti-athletic. The result was a series of decisions to support other facets of athletics at Swarthmore that some faculty clearly regard as excessive and as over-reactions to criticisms of the football decision. Problems with process clearly have consequences. But they can also be learning experiences. President McPherson of Macalester is quick to credit his counterpart at Swarthmore, President Alfred Bloom, for having given him good advice as to how to handle his own situation, in the light of the (earlier) Swarthmore experience.

To be sure, it is no easy matter to find approaches that permit wide consultation, which is surely needed and very important, but that avoid excessive desires to compromise key choices and culminate in outcomes that will enjoy a strong base of support. One model that can work is for a president to identify a strong individual who will understand the president's goals and see that they are kept in mind all through whatever process is deemed necessary. But for this model to work, the right person must be available to take the lead. Such a person might be given a title like "Special Assistant to the President." A similar model can be tried at the conference level, with a senior person who is outside athletics but familiar with the issues chosen to represent the group of presidents in working with the various parties who need to be involved.

Executive directors of conferences or leagues can conceivably play such a role, but they are often conflicted by a sense of obligation (and close personal relationships) to the athletic directors to whom they are, in some measure, responsible. Also, individuals who agree to serve as executive directors of conferences will often end up in such positions in part because they have a commitment to athletics that may be too singleminded. But this is certainly not true in all settings. In any event, it is critical to find the right person to lead the pursuit of a vigorous reform agenda as a top priority—and for everyone to know that this person is acting with the strong support of the president (or a group of presidents).

One "fact of life" that has to be recognized by anyone interested in altering the course of intercollegiate athletics is that strong voices will be raised in opposition to any proposed change of consequence. This is a certainty. So many of us enjoy sports precisely because they evoke passions. The vehement reactions engendered by the debate over wrestling at Princeton and by the decision at Swarthmore to drop football are instructive. However thorough the work done in arriving at conclusions, however extensive the review of data and viewpoints, those who do not like the outcome will not like the process. At the trustee level, one particular source of difficulty is that leading trustees may well have been star athletes in earlier days and may have difficulty recognizing that circumstances have changed dramatically.

On-campus discussions are also certain to be contentious and highly charged, in part because students who were recruited under one set of understandings will naturally feel aggrieved if any changes in the program are proposed. There have been strong initial reactions on some

NESCAC and Ivy League campuses to decisions by the presidents of these two sets of schools to limit out-of-season activities. At both Colby and Cornell, for example, athletes have complained vociferously that their personal commitments to their sports are not being respected.[21] Such reactions have to be anticipated, especially when a campus population includes large numbers of recruited athletes who have brought with them from high school expectations of ever more intensive athletic competition.

Much will depend on how carefully those responsible for decision-making explain their reasons for coming to new conclusions.[22] In the long run, sound decisions will be their own best justification. One of the striking findings from the survey data reported in *The Game of Life* is that alumni/ae in general, including the most generous donors, are far more interested in the educational quality of their colleges and universities than they are in intercollegiate athletics. Moreover, the respondents to that survey (which had a very high response rate) were, if anything, more in favor of reducing the emphasis on intercollegiate athletics than in favor of increasing it.[23] Necessary as it is to anticipate controversy, there is no reason to be immobilized by worries about the consequences of making educationally sound decisions.

The single most effective opponent of efforts to "reclaim the game" is inertia. Presidents of colleges and universities have far too much to do; they do not normally seek out issues that they know will be divisive and engender passionate debate, and it is therefore very tempting just to look the other way. There are, to our way of thinking, four compelling reasons why the pull of inertia should be overcome.

First, we are not dealing with a static situation. The academic-athletic divide has been steadily widening, and there is no reason to believe that the underlying forces at work will dissipate on their own. Failure to act now will lead only to even more serious divisions, and even greater problems, in the future.

Second, the present disjuncture between lofty statements of educational mission and the realities of today's academic-athletic divide challenges both the primacy of educational values and the very integrity of outstanding institutions—institutions that are committed to truth-telling and to leading through their actions and not just through their words.

Third, the institutions in this study have a responsibility for the stewardship of the resources entrusted to them. The students they select are highly privileged: they are given access to extraordinary educational opportunities and receive degrees that provide further benefits. The ever more intense competition for admission to these schools is one indication of the value that they are thought to confer on their students. There is, then, an obligation on the part of the colleges and universities that bestow such gifts to be sure that they give them to those individuals who are most deserving—who will make the most of their educational opportunities and then use what they have learned in the service of society. It seems to us difficult in the extreme to reconcile acceptance of systematic underperformance by recruited athletes with the satisfaction of this obligation.

Finally, what is at stake in this debate is access to *athletic* as well as academic opportunities. There is much to be said for the rallying cry "Let's give athletics back to the students!" College sports need to be restored to their rightful place in campus life. This requires making sure that there are opportunities for regular students, who have come to highly selective colleges for the right reasons, to play competitively—to learn the lessons that sports can teach and to have fun in the process. This is what it means to "reclaim the game."

KEY FINDINGS

1. Athletes, and recruited athletes in particular, comprise a much larger percentage of the student body at small liberal arts colleges than at research universities. At the colleges in the New England Small College Athletic Conference (NESCAC), 43 percent of male students and 32 percent of female students were athletes. Recruited athletes alone made up 24 percent of the male student body and 17 percent of the female population. Relative to schools in Division IA, the percentages of the student body who are recruited athletes are high at all the schools in this study; at the Ivies, 25 percent of men and 19 percent of women were athletes, and more than half of those athletes were recruited.

2. Recruited athletes—defined as those applicants included on a coach's list—enjoy a significant admissions advantage over other applicants. This advantage was most pronounced in the Ivy League, where recruits were four times more likely to be admitted than similarly situated applicants who were not on a coach's list, but it was present and substantial in each group of schools for which we have data.

3. Recruited athletes arrive on campus with substantially lower SAT scores than both their fellow athletes and other students. Recruited High Profile athletes (men playing football, basketball, and hockey) had SAT scores more than 100 points below those of students at large at the Ivy League universities, the NESCAC colleges, and other coed liberal arts colleges. Though not as pronounced, there are also SAT gaps between students at large and recruited male Lower Profile athletes and female athletes.

4. Athletes tend to be concentrated in social science and business fields of study, to spend large amounts of time together even outside of the formal demands of membership on a team, to limit extracurricular activity to their sport, and to live with other athletes—evidence that points to the existence of a separate athletic "culture."

5. Recruited athletes earn far lower grades than both their fellow athletes who were walk-ons and other students. At the Ivy League uni-

versities, 81 percent of recruited High Profile athletes were in the bottom third of the class, as were 64 percent of recruited Lower Profile male athletes and 45 percent of recruited female athletes. A similar pattern was present at the NESCAC colleges.

6. Recruited athletes earn far lower grades than what might be expected on the basis of their incoming academic credentials and demographic characteristics. This striking "underperformance" phenomenon appears to be related directly to the criteria used in recruiting and admitting these athletes—and not to time commitments, differences in race or socioeconomic status, field of study, or the intensity of the athletic experience. Recruited athletes underperform even in seasons or in years when they are not participating in athletics.

7. Other groups with heavy time commitments, such as musicians, do not demonstrate any underperformance. Nor, for the most part, do legacies. In fact, these groups tend to achieve impressive academic results, and musicians, in particular, tend to outperform their classmates.

8. Although students from underrepresented minority groups also receive an advantage in the admissions process and exhibit underperformance, this group has shown steady improvement in both their entering academic credentials and their academic outcomes over the past quarter century—a period when the academic performance of athletes has declined steadily. Moreover, there are, in our view, compelling reasons for giving underrepresented minority students an admissions advantage, related directly to the educational missions of colleges and universities and the needs of the country, that do not pertain to athletes.

9. Self-generated and mutually reinforcing pressures in both the athletic and academic areas (at the pre-collegiate, collegiate, and post-collegiate levels) have led to increased specialization and intensity in athletics, a growing concentration of academic talent at the most elite schools, and therefore a widening academic-athletic divide. The academic credentials and performance of students at large have improved dramatically at the same time that recruited athletes have become increasingly focused on their sports (often at the expense of academics). These trends continue unabated.

10. The University Athletic Association (UAA) has largely avoided the problems associated with the recruitment of college athletes. Of the

schools in our study, only the UAA schools have recruited athletes who look like their peers in terms of entering academic credentials and subsequent performance. This may be the result of less formalized recruitment processes, more careful monitoring of academic performance, the relatively limited size of the athletics programs on these campuses, the absence of intense traditional rivalries, and the strong presidential control of the athletic enterprise.

RECOMMENDATIONS FOR REFORM

1. The problems relating to recruitment, admissions, and academic performance must be addressed. Major ideas to pursue at the conference and institutional levels include reducing the number of recruited athletes, adjusting admissions criteria to raise standards for the academic preparation of recruited athletes, paying more attention in admissions to recruited athletes' academic interests and motivations, monitoring academic performance of recruited athletes, and holding both admissions offices and athletics departments accountable for underperformance.

2. Efforts should be made to encourage athletic participation by students admitted on the basis of qualifications other than having been on a coach's list—the students we refer to as "walk-ons." Recruiting large numbers of athletes not only claims places in the entering class; it also results in greatly diminished opportunities for other athletically interested (and talented) students to play on intercollegiate teams.

3. Coaches should share the goals of the institution, including those related to the place of athletics within it. Hiring and evaluation of coaches should be based on their overall performance as teachers and campus citizens rather than primarily on their won-lost records.

4. The time commitment required to participate in varsity athletics should be reduced. This includes shortening playing and practice seasons, eliminating class and exam conflicts, restricting activities outside of the traditional season, and requiring "time-off" periods.

5. The competitive goals of the athletics program should be focused on success during the regular season at the local and regional levels. In keeping with these goals, access to national championships should be a "rare opportunity," and regional or conference championships should be emphasized.

6. No athletic scholarships should be given, and monitoring systems should be established to ensure that merit aid and preferential packages of need-based aid are not provided on the basis of athletic ability.

7. Football presents unique problems of scale, underperformance, and culture. Some schools may need to consider dropping football. Others will need to find appropriate opponents, and football-only conferences have promise. Limiting squad size may also be desirable.

8. Competition should be between institutions of similar character, but there should be "flexibility within structure" to allow for orbits of competition that might vary by sport to encourage competitive balance. Some realignments within conferences and within the National Collegiate Athletic Association (NCAA) itself seem necessary.

9. A new national organizational structure may need to be created, within the NCAA if possible. We favor admission by self-selection. Thus, we propose that any institution be granted membership in this organization so long as its leadership agrees to adhere to principles such as: (a) athletes should be truly representative of their student bodies (with academic outcomes similar to those achieved by other students), (b) opportunities to participate in intercollegiate athletics should be widely available to both men and women and not limited to "recruits," (c) athletes should be integrated into campus life and participate in a wide range of activities, (d) there should be extensive opportunities for vigorous competition structured so as to avoid a preoccupation with national rankings and national championships, and (e) bureaucratic regulation at the national level should be kept to an absolute minimum.

IMPLEMENTING REFORMS

1. Accomplishing real change will require a holistic approach. History teaches us that piecemeal reforms run the risk of being subverted and are likely to prove ineffective.

2. Because intercollegiate athletics is a competitive enterprise, collaboration is essential to the success of any reform agenda. "Going it alone" will almost surely lead to nothing but losing records and demoralization. Institutions and conferences must work together under strong presidential leadership.

3. Although leadership is essential at the presidential level, it is also crucial for trustees, alumni, faculty, and athletic administrators to be proactive in pursuing new directions.

4. Process is important as well; the best plans for reform can be undone by poor timing, insensitivity to the quite natural reactions of coaches and athletes, exclusion of affected parties from the decision-making process, and failure to present compelling arguments.

5. Difficult decisions need to be made about the rationing of academic and athletic opportunities, the scale and financial cost of athletics programs, and the role of athletics in the educational experience. However, the trends documented in this study make clear that these decisions will become ever more difficult. Now is the time to "reclaim the game."

Chapter 1   Introduction

1. Gordon Witkin and Jodi Schneider, "College Sports," *U.S. News & World Report,* March 18, 2002, pp. 48–50. We briefly describe the structure of the National Collegiate Athletic Association (NCAA) and the differences between Divisions IA, IAA, and III in the addendum to this introduction. *U.S News* is now considering a separate set of rankings for Division III institutions—having started with Division I.

2. The *New York Times* ran an editorial at the time of the 2002 basketball championships calling attention to the graduation rates of the men's and women's teams that made the Final Four. (One, the Oklahoma men's team, had a zero percent graduation rate.) "College Hoops and Academics," *New York Times,* March 29, 2002, p. A28. In a memorable juxtaposition, Chevrolet named the coach of the Oklahoma team its "coach of the year" in a between-games program extolling the contributions Chevy has made over the years to college scholarship funds. The irony may have been lost on most viewers, but not, we presume, on all of them.

3. Knight Foundation Commission on Intercollegiate Athletics, *A Call to Action: Reconnecting College Sports and Higher Education* (Miami, Fla.: John S. and James L. Knight Foundation, 2001).

4. See, for example, Robin Lester's splendid history of football at the University of Chicago, *Stagg's University: The Rise, Decline, and Fall of Big-Time Football at Chicago,* Illini Books edition (Urbana: University of Illinois Press, 1999), which is really a history of football from its earliest days to the outbreak of World War II.

5. The Ivy League published an excellent account of the early successes of women's sports in their setting. See Paula D. Welch, *Silver Era, Golden Moments: A Celebration of Ivy League Women's Athletics* (Lanham, Md.: Madison Books, 1999). Similarly, the publications of the University Athletic Association (UAA) highlight the achievements of the many remarkable students in their Association who excel not only in athletics but in all aspects of campus life. See, for example, University Athletic Association (UAA), *UAA: University Athletic Association: Where Theory Meets Practice,* at the UAA Web site (http://www.uaa.rochester.edu/), accessed January 2, 2002.

6. Amy Campbell, "Division III Intercollegiate Athletics" (paper commissioned by The Andrew W. Mellon Foundation for this study, April 2002), p. 1.

7. James L. Shulman and William G. Bowen, *The Game of Life: College Sports and Educational Values* (Princeton, N.J.: Princeton University Press, 2001). Edward B. Fiske observed: "Everyone knows that universities that compete in the National Collegiate Athletic Association's Division I sustain their big-time programs by awarding athletic scholarships to students who may or may not have much interest in academics. Not so well known is the significant role that athletic ability plays

in access to elite colleges in Division III—where athletic scholarships are banned, but coaches can offer something even more valuable over the long run: access to a top-rated college." See "Gaining Admission: Athletes Win Preference," *New York Times, Education Life Supplement,* January 7, 2001, pp. 22–23, 40–41; quote on p. 22. Similarly, John Hoberman observed: "That these unhappy developments can be observed at schools with relatively small sports programs, such as Yale, Duke, Smith, Swarthmore and Wesleyan, makes this report all the more sobering." See "Mind Games," *Wall Street Journal,* February 16, 2001, p. W12. And Louis Menand wrote: "It's true, as you would expect, that the S.A.T. scores of the typical football or basketball player at a big-time sports school like Michigan or North Carolina are much lower than his classmates', but the S.A.T. scores of the typical varsity tennis player at a coed liberal-arts college are also much lower—a hundred and forty-three points lower—than his classmates'." See "Sporting Chances: The Cost of College Athletics," *New Yorker,* January 22, 2001, pp. 84–88.

8. When the results reported in *The Game of Life* were published, the presidents of the participating colleges and universities, and especially the presidents of the New England Small College Athletic Conference (NESCAC) colleges and the Ivy League universities, wanted to know more. Although the book dispelled a number of myths and answered some important questions, it raised many others. To their great credit, the presidents did not ignore the findings or try to "wish them away." Instead, in meetings and phone conversations they asked us if, in a follow-up study, we could update the data, include more schools, probe more deeply into what was causing the athletic divide (and especially the phenomenon of underperformance), and make our own suggestions as to reform measures.

9. George Hanford, author of a 1974 study of intercollegiate athletics sponsored by the American Council on Education, deserves credit for encouraging systematic research in this area and calling attention to what Hanford then called "scholarly inattention." Hanford was cited by John R. Thelin in *Games Colleges Play: Scandal and Reform in Intercollegiate Athletics* (Baltimore: Johns Hopkins University Press, 1996 [1994], p. 172). Thelin went on to observe that "organized intercollegiate athletics has tended to resist systematic analysis. . . . This siege mentality has perpetuated the erroneous stereotype that those who have studied the condition and character of college sports were by definition a lunatic fringe intent on abolishing varsity sports" (p. 198).

10. The full set of 33 colleges and universities included in this study is also listed in Appendix Table 1.1, with the sizes of their entering classes. Capsule descriptions of the conferences and their histories are presented in the addendum to this introduction, along with a brief description of the NCAA divisions within which they compete. We are very much aware that these colleges and universities are by no means representative of all colleges and universities outside the Division IA structure. They were not chosen with that aim in mind. Rather, they were chosen to reflect the characteristics of important parts of the academically selective sector of higher education on which this study focuses. All told, the records of nearly 30,000 students are included in the 1995 cohort that now forms part of an expanded College and Beyond (C&B) database. The original C&B database used in *The Game of Life* included only four of the eleven NESCAC schools and only four of the eight Ivies, and it was conceivable that these schools were "out-

liers." The previous study included only four coed liberal arts colleges outside NESCAC, and to broaden the geographic coverage of these colleges we added Carleton, Macalester, and Pomona. We also decided to look much more closely at the experiences of the members of the UAA, which consists of eight urban research universities that have developed an alternative model of play at the Division III level; thus, we collected detailed data for Carnegie Mellon, Emory, the University of Chicago, and Washington University. Finally, we updated the data for the four women's colleges included in the original study (Barnard, Bryn Mawr, Smith, and Wellesley). Data for Barnard are not, however, included in the findings presented here. Barnard competes with Columbia in the Ivy League and thus differs from the other women's colleges included, all of which compete in Division III. Cornell is also a special case in that we included only athletes and other students from two schools (Arts and Sciences and Engineering), in order to achieve comparability with the other Ivies. This approach works well when we are comparing athletes with other students at Cornell in these same schools (and measuring underperformance), but it does not allow us to present a full picture of the characteristics of all athletes at Cornell, since many are enrolled in other schools.

11. In a review published in *University Business,* one of the most persistent and caustic critics of big-time sports, Murray Sperber complained, "After a couple of hundred pages of their radical critique of intercollegiate athletics, including charts and detailed tables, the authors present their blueprint for reform—and fall flat. . . . After painstakingly constructing a beautiful bomb, they, in the final analysis, refuse to light the fuse." See "The Sports Authorities," *University Business,* online edition, April 2001. Quotations not otherwise identified in this paragraph, and elsewhere in the book, are from interviews conducted by the authors of this study.

12. Percentages calculated from data provided by the University of Michigan Athletics Department and Office of Budget and Planning; the U.S. Department of Education, Office of Postsecondary Education, *IPEDS College Opportunities Online,* available at http://ope.ed.gov/athletics/; and Chronicle of Higher Education, *Chronicle of Higher Education: Facts & Figures: Gender Equity in College Sports,* available at http://chronicle.com/stats/genderequity/. Private universities such as Northwestern, Duke, and Stanford are intermediate cases, and in this regard can be more like the Ivies than like Ohio State or the University of California. There is great variation among the Division IA universities in the number of sports they sponsor.

13. In the 1989 entering cohort, academic underperformance among male athletes in both High Profile sports (football, basketball, and ice hockey) and Lower Profile sports was as pronounced at the Division IA private universities as it was at the Ivies and the coed liberal arts colleges. Women athletes at the Division IA private universities also underperformed academically, but not as markedly as the men. See Shulman and Bowen, especially figures 3.4 and 7.4.

14. This occurs through a process of "emulation" and "contagion" that we described in our earlier study. See Shulman and Bowen, especially pp. 284–87.

15. See, for example, Murray Sperber, "The NCAA's Last Chance to Reform College Sports," *Chronicle of Higher Education,* April 19, 2002, p. B12.

16. For example, Sack and Staurowsky set up their study by contrasting "The Big Ten and the Little Three," suggesting that a Little Three contest is an idyllic

example of how college sports should be organized. (Allen L. Sack and Ellen J. Staurowsky, *College Athletes for Hire: The Evolution and Legacy of the NCAA's Amateur Myth* [Westport, Conn.: Praeger, 1998], pp. 1–3.) This is accurate if the problems of the Little Three programs are viewed in comparison with those of big-time programs. But it is not the case if they are seen on their own terms—as we argue in this book.

17. The earlier Bowen-Bok study of affirmative action identified underperformance as a serious issue for minority students enrolled in academically selective colleges and universities. William G. Bowen and Derek Bok, *The Shape of the River: Long-Term Consequences of Considering Race in College and University Admissions* (Princeton, N.J.: Princeton University Press, 1998), pp. 72–90. In Chapter 9 we explicitly contrast the academic results achieved by minority students, recruited athletes, other students actively committed to extracurricular activities (musicians, in particular), and legacies. Outcomes differ across these groups, and recruited athletes and minorities are seen to have the most serious problems of underperformance. There are, however, major differences in the reasons why colleges and universities recruit athletes and minority students. As we argue in Chapter 9, the appropriate policy responses in these two situations ultimately depend on educational missions and values.

18. One important part of assessing the relative academic performance of athletes (and other groups of students) is recognizing the confounding effects of grade inflation. When the vast majority of grades given are "bunched" around a few top grades (A, A-minus, B-plus, and B), a student may earn what appears to be a perfectly "respectable" GPA and yet be doing far worse than his or her peers. As one coach proudly told us, her students were doing fine in school—in her words, "they may not be earning B-pluses, but their grades are solid"—but she may not have realized that at many schools even a B-plus (to which her players apparently did not even aspire) can be lower than the average grade.

19. We agree with Hutchins that there is little to be said for exhorting individuals to act counter to their own inclinations. When urged to speak out more forcefully in favor of "good behavior," Hutchins said that in his experience "all attempts to teach character directly . . . degenerate into vague exhortations to be good which leave the bored listener with a desire to commit outrages which would otherwise never have occurred to him." Robert Maynard Hutchins, *No Friendly Voice* (Chicago: University of Chicago Press, 1936), p. 93. To be sure, we have no evidence on this important question (and evidence in such a realm is hard to find), but our intuition is the same as the intuition that guided Hutchins.

20. Bowen and Bok; Shulman and Bowen. Our previous studies contained much longitudinal data on outcomes after college—pursuit of graduate degrees, choice of careers, amounts of money earned, leadership activities, and evidence of continuing loyalty to the school—for classes that entered college in the 1950s, the mid-1970s, and the late 1980s. Obviously there is nothing yet to be known about the post-college lives of those who began college in the mid-1990s.

21. We have chosen to separate male athletes into those playing the High Profile and Lower Profile sports to highlight the important differences between the two groups. Although our decision to include only football, basketball, and ice hockey among the High Profile sports is surely open to debate, our data show

that this grouping is empirically justified (that is, there are systematic differences between the High Profile and Lower Profile sports in almost every variable that we measure). Finally, as we explain in the preface to *The Game of Life,* we prefer the term *High Profile sports* to the more often-used *revenue sports* because at most of the schools in this study football, basketball, and hockey do not generate much revenue. See Shulman and Bowen, p. xxxi.

Addendum   Principal Conferences and Associations

1. There is a further distinction to be drawn, for football programs only, between Division IA and Division IAA. The truly big-time programs are all in Division IA.

2. This revenue stream consists mainly of receipts generated by Division I national championships and related activities. Extensive information about the NCAA, including discussions of its history, organization, and finances, is available at the NCAA's Web site (http://www.ncaa.org). The NCAA published a 75th anniversary history in 1981: Jack Falla, *NCAA: The Voice of College Sports: A Diamond Anniversary History, 1906–1981,* 1st ed. (Mission, Kan.: National Collegiate Athletic Association, 1981). Additional history of the NCAA can be found in Walter Byers and Charles H. Hammer, *Unsportsmanlike Conduct: Exploiting College Athletes* (Ann Arbor: University of Michigan Press, 1995) (Byers was executive director of the NCAA from 1951 through 1987); Sack and Staurowsky; and Arthur A. Fleisher, Brian L. Goff, and Robert D. Tollison, *The National Collegiate Athletic Association: A Study in Cartel Behavior* (Chicago: University of Chicago Press, 1992).

3. Division II of the NCAA is composed of 290 institutions that share many of the athletic values of Division I institutions—offering athletic scholarships, for example, and seeking to serve both the campus community and the general public with their athletics programs—but that spend less on athletics and emphasize regional competition more than their Division I counterparts.

4. Excerpted from National Collegiate Athletic Association (NCAA), *2001–02 NCAA Division I Manual,* Section 20.9. The full statement of Division I propositions (including references to academic standards and gender equity) is included in Addendum Table 1.

5. Excerpted from NCAA, *2001–02 NCAA Division III Manual,* Section 20.11. The full statement of Division III propositions is also included in Addendum Table 2, along with its preamble.

6. See "What's the Difference between Divisions I, II and III?" at the NCAA Web site.

7. In his discussion of the history of events leading up to the founding of the Ivy League, Bernstein provides a long account of Harold Stassen's tenure at the University of Pennsylvania, including the introduction of televised football games by Penn, raging controversies with the NCAA over the control of televised sports events, and eventually Stassen's departure. Mark F. Bernstein, *Football: The Ivy League Origins of an American Obsession* (Philadelphia: University of Pennsylvania Press, 2001), pp. 193–205.

8. Council of Ivy Group Presidents, *The Ivy Manual 2001–2002* (Princeton, N.J.: Princeton University Press, revised August 2001), p. 1. We refer to the re-

vised form of the original 1954 agreement as the "Revised Agreement," as contrasted with the "Original Agreement," which is published as an appendix in the manual. The third important document is the "1979 Statement of Principles," which is also included in the *Ivy Manual,* and which we refer to simply as the "Statement of Principles."

9. *Ivy Manual,* p. 2.

10. Ibid.

11. Ibid.

12. Ibid.

13. The Division I membership requirements include "financial aid minimums," which require members to provide either a certain number of grants in men's and women's sports or a minimum total dollar outlay for grants (figure 20–1 of the *2001–02 Division I Manual* provides a useful summary of all "general requirements"). The Ivies are, however, exempted from this requirement. Section 20.9.1.2.7 provides that "member institutions that do not award any athletically related financial aid in any sport as of January 11, 1991, shall be exempted from the minimum requirements." Most Patriot League schools may also be exempted under this provision. Others may meet the test because of the way they package need-based aid: giving athletes all grants. Such aid is "countable" for NCAA purposes.

14. There are three principal sources for the history of NESCAC: Lee M. Levison, "Origins of the New England Small College Athletic Conference" (unpublished paper based on work done at Trinity College in 1981); Karin Vélez, "The New England Small College Athletic Conference, 1971–1997: A Retrospective" (unpublished report submitted to the NESCAC presidents on August 9, 1997); and Daniel Dexter Covell, "To Keep a Proper Perspective on the Role of Athletics: An Examination of the Perceived Role of Intercollegiate Athletics in the New England Small College Athletic Conference" (Ph.D. dissertation, University of Massachusetts at Amherst, September 1999). Vélez was given full access to NESCAC files and records, and her excellent report is based largely on these primary source documents. Covell's dissertation includes extensive references to both general studies of sports in America and publications in NESCAC campus publications that would be difficult for many people to find, as well as an extensive literature review (Chapter 2). The primary purpose of Covell's dissertation, however, was to "explore the specific perceptions of, attitudes toward, and the proper role of intercollegiate athletics at NESCAC member schools" (p. 23). Data for his research were collected using an elaborate survey instrument. Covell's most general finding was that "the greatest perceptual differences overall . . . were registered between faculty and student-athletes. Faculty were considerably more skeptical of the values to be gained from the time and effort expended on intercollegiate athletics, while student-athletes consider these same expenditures to be not only valuable, but on an equal plane with those made in the academic realm" (p. vi).

15. This memo, written in October 1968, is cited in Levison, p. 7. John Sawyer, president of Williams College, is quoted to much the same effect (p. 8).

16. Levison, p. 8.

17. Memorandum of May 25, 1969, cited in Levison, p. 9.

18. Memorandum of July 26, 1968, cited in Levison, p. 6.

19. Levison, p. 7.

20. Memorandum written in 1967 and cited in Vélez, p. 3.

21. Reproduced in Vélez, p. 5. The full text of the 1971 Agreement is an appendix to that paper.

22. Vélez, pp. 6–7.

23. Richard Rasmussen, "The Role of Intercollegiate Athletics in the Academy— A Case Study of the Formation of the University Athletic Association" (Ed.D. dissertation, University of Rochester, 1997), pp. 47ff. This excellent study of the history of the UAA, written by its executive secretary, who was also involved in its founding, provides detailed institutional profiles of all nine members, plus MIT, which participated in the discussions leading up to the establishment of the Association but decided not to join (figure 5, p. 48). Our account of the evolution of the UAA owes much to Rasmussen's study, as well as to subsequent discussions with him and with representatives of 8 of the 9 member universities. Rasumussen also provided us with many background documents, including the extensive materials provided at the key meeting in Rochester in October 1985, when many of the most important decisions about the UAA were debated. See also University Athletic Association (UAA), *Background Information, 2001–2002,* which is available at the UAA's Web site.

24. See UAA, *Background Information,* pp. 5–6.

25. Rasmussen (1997), p. 91. The reason for the number "ten" is that MIT was in these conversations at the time this statement was made. John Schael, director of athletics at Washington University, also emphasized that "the UAA was created from the top. The presidents were the people who made it happen, not the ADs, not deans, and so on. Thus, everyone knew from the beginning that the new organization had the sustaining support that it was going to require."

26. See Richard Rasmussen (1997), pp. 51ff, for capsule histories of each of the UAA universities that describe in some detail the playing arrangements prior to the establishment of the UAA. The University of Chicago, for example, competed primarily with a group of small liberal arts colleges with which it had some academic ties and with members of the Associated Colleges of the Midwest. As the undergraduate college at Chicago grew during the 1970s, differences in size, academic standards, and philosophy made this competitive association less than a comfortable fit (pp. 72ff).

27. Rasmussen (1997), pp. 104–05. Starkey Duncan, a professor of psychology at the University of Chicago, worked hard on his campus to convince the faculty that the UAA was a good idea. He succeeded, in part because the faculty at Chicago much preferred the institutional associations that the UAA permitted to those that they had had before in the Midwest Collegiate Athletic Conference, which consisted mostly of smaller liberal arts colleges that had very different academic standards.

28. Rasmussen (1997), p. 89.

29. Ibid., pp. 51ff.

30. Ibid., pp. 114, 117.

31. Ibid., p. 122.

32. Ibid., p. 2.

33. UAA, *Background Information*, pp. 1–2.

34. Rasmussen (1997), p. 51. To cite just one example of the specific decisions made by these schools: In 1946, Arthur Compton, then chancellor of Washington University, "set a new direction for his institution and others when he declared that the one-time charter member of the Missouri Valley Conference would no longer offer athletic scholarships but would redirect the emphasis of its programs by embracing a truly amateur approach to intercollegiate athletics." Rasmussen (1997), p. 50.

35. As cited in Rasmussen (1997), p. 2.

36. M. Elizabeth Tidball, et al., *Taking Women Seriously: Lessons and Legacies for Educating the Majority* (Phoenix, Ariz.: Oryx Press, 1999), p. 6.

37. Gertrud Pfister, "Her Story in Sport: Towards the Emancipation of Women?" (paper presented at the World Conference on Women and Sport, Montréal, May 2002), p. 9.

38. Pfister, p. 9.

39. Shulman and Bowen, p. 120.

40. See Shulman and Bowen, pp. 120–21, for a discussion of the Association for Intercollegiate Athletics for Women (AIAW).

41. Leotus Morrison (first president of the AIAW), presentation to Mary Baldwin College's Parents' Council, March 15, 2002.

42. For an analysis of the interaction between the NCAA and the AIAW that led to the AIAW's collapse, see Ying Wu, "The Demise of the AIAW and Women's Control of Intercollegiate Athletics for Women: The Sex-Separate Policy in the Reality of the NCAA, Cold War, and Title IX" (Ph.D. dissertation, Pennsylvania State University, December 1997).

Chapter 2   Recruitment of College Athletes

1. Quoted in Craig Lambert, "The Professionalization of Ivy League Sports," *Harvard Magazine* 100 (September–October 1997): 36–49, 96–98; quote on p. 38.

2. Robert Malekoff, "Division III Athletics: Issues and Challenges" (paper commissioned by The Andrew W. Mellon Foundation for this study, May 2002), p. 9.

3. Quotations are from Lester, pp. 45, 47, 49.

4. Lester, pp. 50, 109–10. Stagg also recruited by promising prospective players participation in baseball tours to Japan.

5. Stephen Rodrick, "Big Man Temporarily On Campus," *New York Times Magazine*, November 25, 2001, pp. 56, 58–59; quote on p. 59.

6. Francis and James Killpatrick, in the sixth edition of their student-athlete's guide to college sports, write: "Over the past few years, the official NCAA policy manual has tripled in size. Whereas it used to weigh about the same as a fair-sized city's telephone book, now it's like a large city's white and yellow pages combined. Its hundreds of pages might well have been written by a team of corporate lawyers. The rules are extremely complicated and confusing. But they are the rules—and they apply to you [the typical high school athlete who wants to play college sports] just a surely as they do to the 40-point-a-game scorer being courted by every Division I school in the country." *The Winning Edge: The Student-Athlete's Guide to College Sports,* 6th ed. (Alexandria, Va.: Octameron Associates, 1999), p. 17.

7. The recruiting guides are available at the NCAA's Web site.

8. There is a considerable literature on recruiting that offers advice to coaches, students, and parents on how to recruit or be recruited, including how to comply with the myriad rules in effect. For coaches, see Stephen J. Brennan, ed., *Inside Recruiting: The Master Guide to Successful College Athletic Recruiting*, vol. 3 (Omaha, Neb.: Peak Performance Publishing, 2000); Lynn R. Fielitz, "Using the Internet for Athletic Recruiting," *Journal of Physical Education, Recreation, and Dance* 71(2) (February 2000): 13–15. For students, see Rodney J. McKissic, *How to Play the Sports Recruiting Game and Get an Athletic Scholarship: The Handbook and Guide to Success for the African-American High School Student Athlete* (Phoenix, Ariz.: Amber Books, 1998); Killpatrick.

9. Bernstein, p. 217.

10. Lambert, p. 36.

11. Ibid., pp. 39–40.

12. NCAA (2001a), Article 13, "Recruiting."

13. This is the estimate given, for example, by the women's soccer coach at Harvard, Tim Wheaton (Lambert, p. 38).

14. A. Bartlett Giamatti, "Yale and Athletics," in *The University and the Public Interest* (New York: Atheneum, 1981), pp. 77–104 (adapted from a speech delivered to the Association of Yale Alumni, April 1980); quotes on pp. 90, 99.

15. Andy Katz, "Why Wait? Recruits Choosing Colleges Early," ESPN.com, July 18, 2001, updated July 22, 2001; Andy Katz, "Unofficial Visits Are Becoming Way to Go," ESPN, August 17, 2001. Interviews confirmed Katz's accounts.

16. Taylor Bell, "A Junior to the NBA?: Nation's Top 100 Seniors," *Chicago Sun-Times*, August 19, 2001, p. 119.

17. Emily Kimball, "For Athletes, Brown U.'s Recruiting Requirements Jump-Start College Admission Process," *Brown Daily Herald*, September 13, 2000, online edition.

18. In the Dartmouth student paper, Athletic Director Dick Jaeger is reported as having observed "a trend in recent years for coaches to encourage athletes to apply under the Early Decision plan because it allows admissions to focus in on athletes who really want to attend Dartmouth." The same article reports that in 1999 around 90 percent of the Men's Cross Country recruits who applied Early Decision were accepted. Abigail Johnson, "Dartmouth Coaches Face Own Early Decisions," *The Dartmouth*, November 22, 2000, online edition.

19. Tufts Men's Lacrosse Coach John Daly recently described his ideal recruit as follows: "In the lacrosse program, we recruit to find athletes who are lacrosse junkies and who want to work and improve themselves." Ethan Austin, "Under a New Ruling, Athletes Must Now Wait until Season," *Tufts Daily*, October 31, 2002, online edition.

20. Lambert, pp. 38–39. This comment is a good illustration of the growing role that technology plays in the recruitment process. This is true at Division III schools as well as in the Ivies. Malekoff (2002) has pointed out that "thanks to videotape and recruiting camps, college coaches can better evaluate virtually all potential recruits. In addition, scouting services—once available in only men's basketball and football—exist for all sports" (p. 6). One online recruiting service, topjock.net, recently sent a mass e-mail (subject line: "College Recruiting For The

High School Student Athlete Made EASY!!") promising that "the Athlete can build a Professional Profile with STATISTICS, VIDEO, and PICTURES FAST!!"

21. Lambert, p. 37.

22. Quoted in Lambert, p. 43, in a box titled "Team Global."

23. Brennan, ed., pp. 1–9.

24. See addendum to Chapter 1. To make sure that athletes would "be representative of the student body," recruitment was forbidden on and off campus, financial aid was to be unrelated to athletic participation, and information about student financial aid and scholarship awards was to be shared among NESCAC presidents (see Levison; Vélez).

25. John Biddiscombe, "Comments and Perspectives on Division III Athletics" (paper commissioned by The Andrew W. Mellon Foundation for this study, May 2002), p. 6.

26. Amherst Faculty Committee on Admission and Financial Aid, *Admission to Amherst: A Report to the Faculty and Administration* (September 1999).

27. Ibid., p. 14.

28. Ibid., pp. 14–15.

29. Middlebury Ad Hoc Committee on the Future of Athletics, *Report of the Ad Hoc Committee on the Future of Athletics,* May 9, 2002, p. 13.

30. Campbell, p. 2.

31. Richard Rasmussen, "Perspectives on Trends and Issues in Division III Athletics" (paper commissioned by The Andrew W. Mellon Foundation for this study, May 2002), p. 8.

32. Reifert's comments were repeated almost verbatim by Starkey Duncan, a professor of psychology at the University of Chicago, who has a long-standing interest in the athletics program. In commenting on recruitment, he said that "coaches simply have to focus on 'fit' with the academic values and the curriculum at Chicago. If they don't, they will get bad results." As Duncan explained, the Chicago curriculum is broadly demanding, and all students have to take serious science and philosophy courses as well as work in the social sciences. In his words: "They have to be generalists and to have broad interests. They can't be narrow or parochial."

Chapter 3   The Admissions Advantage

1. Recruitment of athletes and support of a visible, successful athletics program can also be positive forces in building an image of a healthy student environment that can, in turn, be valuable in meeting other admission goals. As we saw in the addendum to the introduction, this was a major consideration in the formation of the UAA.

2. Jane Gross, "Different Lives, One Goal: Finding the Key to College," *New York Times,* May 5, 2002, online edition. Although it may appear from this quotation that Washington University rejects more students than Harvard, this is not, in fact, the case. The number of "places" does not equate with the number of students admitted. All institutions admit more students than they have places available with the expectation that some admitted students will choose not to attend. The yield (the percentage of admitted students who do attend) varies widely

across institutions, and because it has such a high yield, Harvard's admissions rate (11 percent) is actually much lower than Washington University's (30 percent). (See Appendix Table 9.1 for the admissions rates of the schools in this study.)

3. Awarded annually by the National Association of Collegiate Directors of Athletics (NACDA), the Sears Directors' Cup goes to one school each in NCAA Divisions I, II, and III and the National Association of Intercollegiate Athletics (NAIA). Schools win by achieving competitive success in a broad selection of men's and women's sports throughout the year.

4. Readers interested primarily in the data and not in descriptions of admissions processes and their tensions can turn directly to the second part of the chapter.

5. Karla Kingsley, "Ivy League Reconsiders Role of Athletics in Admissions," *The Dartmouth,* May 2, 2002, online edition.

6. For example, one dean of admissions who prides himself on requiring that every prospective athlete fill out all the forms carefully and submit all the recommendations required for an application to be complete told us that "at some places, athletes clearly don't fill out the forms themselves and don't have to submit recommendations." A representative of one NESCAC college bemoaned what he called the pernicious "surrender" of the authority of the admissions office to the coach. An admission dean at an Ivy League school voiced suspicion that one school in the League had promised admit slots to outstanding hockey players even before the start of the school year.

7. For example, athletes recruited by Harvard in designated sports are required to have higher SAT scores and high school grades than athletes recruited by Ivy schools that in general admit students with somewhat lower average test scores and grades. The "AI," as it is commonly called, was adopted by the Ivy presidents in the early 1980s because of a shared desire not to allow the academic credentials of athletes to "drift" too low or to deviate too much from the credentials of their fellow students. We evaluate the experience with this approach to maintaining standards later in the book. See Shulman and Bowen, pp. 13–14, 46, for a fuller discussion. The AI floor, originally designed for the men's High Profile sports, now applies to all sports. Jeff Orleans, executive director of the Ivy Group, reports: "The standard deviation requirements are not applied rigorously outside the High Profile sports, but from time to time these numbers are also reviewed, and if a sport had all of its players at the AI threshold, questions would be raised and something would be done."

8. Bernstein, p. 229.

9. Gross (2002).

10. The discussion of this subject in Shulman and Bowen (pp. 282–84) contains a long quotation from a former dean of admissions and financial aid at Hotchkiss describing how the emphasis on "hooks" and the enrollment of "spiky" students evolved. (This quote also appears in Chapter 9.)

11. Amy Potter, "Ivy Presidents Announce Recruitment Changes," *Daily Pennsylvanian,* August 29, 2002, online edition. Two other changes—a shift from six full-time and six part-time football coaches to seven full-time and three part-time coaches and the institution of a seven-week "rest period" that is free from required and supervised athletic activity—were announced at the same time.

12. Conferences and schools that participate in the National Letter of Intent Program, which is administered by the Collegiate Commissioners Association, agree to observe a common "signing" date for potential athletes, when students accept a school's offer of admission and athletic-related financial aid in return for a commitment to remain on the team for which they were recruited for at least a year. The program was started in 1964 in an effort to scale back recruitment excesses, and once a student has signed a letter of intent with one school, other participating schools may no longer attempt to recruit that student. All Division I institutions except for the Ivy League universities and the military service academies participate in the National Letter of Intent Program, and, according to NCAA Division I regulations (Article 13.10.1), all schools must respect the National Letter of Intent date as the earliest possible time to sign admissions and financial aid agreements. For more information on the National Letter of Intent Program, see http://www.national-letter.org/.

13. Jeff Durso-Finley, former associate director of admission and liaison to the athletics department at Brown University, has been quoted as saying that at Brown they "usually matriculate a good three quarters of those students [admitted athletic recruits], if not [a] higher [percentage]" (Kimball). Similar comments have been made by representatives of other Ivy schools.

14. There is confusion about the relationship between yields and the displacement of students who really want to attend a particular school. It is sometimes argued that accepting applicants who are "shopping around" for offers of admission but may not be serious about attending a specific college to which they apply (which implies a lower yield) displaces other applicants who are deeply committed to the school in question. But of course the applicant who "really wants to come" can be displaced from the next year's class only by someone who in fact matriculates. It is the number of places in the class that is fixed, not the number of offers of admission (which can be adjusted depending on the yield). What matters finally is the quality of the group of students who actually enroll, not the yield experienced in enrolling them.

15. See Figure 1.1 and Appendix Table 1.1.

16. See Appendix Table 9.1 for the admit rates of the Ivy League and NESCAC institutions, as well as the other schools discussed in the book.

17. Amherst Faculty Committee, pp. 15–17.

18. This paragraph is based on an excellent article by Welch Suggs, "Tipping the Athletic Scale: Williams Struggles with Athletics and Admissions," *Chronicle of Higher Education*, March 8, 2002, online edition. Recently the NESCAC presidents, as a group, have decided to rebalance the role of athletics in their programs, and we comment on the progress they have made in Chapter 7 and, more generally, in Part C.

19. Mike Jensen, "Swarthmore Dropping Football Creates a Firestorm," *Philadelphia Inquirer*, December 10, 2000, online edition; Lane Hartill, "Some Schools Make a Tough Call: Drop Football," *Christian Science Monitor*, February 6, 2001, p. 14; David L. Marcus, "Student Athletes, R.I.P.? Swarthmore College Cans Its Football Program," *U.S. News & World Report*, December 18, 2000, p. 57.

20. Michael McPherson, "The Future of Macalester Football: Statement by President Michael McPherson," November 27, 2001.

21. Despite (or perhaps because of) the efforts to bring the athletics and admissions departments together, some coaches have more success than others in getting their recruits admitted. Smith notes that this is largely a result of some coaches being more selective than others in compiling their lists. Regardless of their sport, most highly rated athletes benefit by being protected from "need cuts": the admissions office sets aside its need-conscious admissions policy when considering recruited athletes.

22. Christopher Avery, Andrew Fairbanks, and Richard Zeckhauser, *The Early Admissions Game: Joining the Elite* (Cambridge, Mass.: Harvard University Press, 2003), pp. 161–62. Emphasis in original.

23. Thanks to the cooperation of the schools involved, we were able to obtain complete admissions files, plus lists of athletes on the coaches' lists and complete SAT scores, for four Ivies (Columbia, Penn, Princeton, and Yale), nine NESCAC colleges (Amherst, Bowdoin, Colby, Connecticut, Hamilton, Middlebury, Trinity, Tufts, and Wesleyan), seven other coed colleges (Carleton, Denison, Kenyon, Macalester, Oberlin, Pomona, and Swarthmore), and two women's colleges (Smith and Wellesley). Because of the timing of data collection, the other four Ivies and the UAA universities were not asked to provide admissions files. Readers of *The Game of Life* may recall that a limitation of that study is that we had complete admissions files for only one university.

24. Kimball.

25. The SAT data for the '99 applicant pool are recentered and therefore cannot be compared directly with the SATs for the 1995 entering cohort shown in the next chapter (which are not recentered). Because SAT scores are optional in the Bates admissions process, Bates is excluded from analyses involving SAT scores, including the admissions analysis here and the underperformance regressions shown in Chapter 6. Bowdoin applicants also have the option of not submitting standardized test scores. However, because we have SAT data for about 94 percent of Bowdoin's '95 cohort and about 80 percent of the '99 applicant pool, we include Bowdoin in our calculations.

26. There is also a "No SAT" category, but again recruited athletes do not appear in it more frequently than other applicants (generally 5 to 10 percent of all applicants have no SATs).

27. More specifically, we use separate logistic regressions for men and women at each school that control for SAT scores, minority status, legacy status (where available), and recruit status to predict the probability of admission. A logistic regression is used rather than an ordinary least squares (OLS) regression because admissions decisions are categorical (yes or no). But because the coefficients of a logistic regression are more difficult to interpret than those produced by an OLS regression, we present the results as an "adjusted admissions advantage." We use the coefficients from the logistic regression for each school to estimate the average probability of admission across all applicants to the school as if all applicants were athletic recruits and the average probability of admission across all applicants as if all applicants were not recruits, regardless of the actual recruit status of each applicant. The difference between these two averages is the adjusted admissions advantage (of recruits over other students) for the school; averaging this value for all schools in a group (the Ivy League, NESCAC, etc.) gives us the adjusted ad-

missions advantage for the group. The result of this complicated procedure can thus be thought of as the "average advantage" (over all SAT ranges, ethnicities, etc.) that recruited athletes enjoy over students at large in admission probability. It is not, as some might misconstrue it to be, the "advantage at the average" SAT score.

28. In every case, the adjusted admissions advantage is *greater* than the simple difference between admit rates for recruited athletes and all other candidates mentioned at the start of the section. The reason, of course, is that the adjusted admissions advantage takes account of the positive relationship between SAT scores and admit rates, and recruited athletes tend to have lower scores than other applicants.

29. The overall admissions probability for recruited athletes in NESCAC equals the 30 percent base probability plus the 33 or 34 percentage points of admissions advantage, or 63 to 64 percent in total—compared with 30 percent for other candidates. Outside NESCAC, the base admissions probability is on the order of 50 percent, to which we need to add the admissions advantage of 25 points or so to get an overall admissions probability of roughly 75 percent for the recruited athletes.

30. The strength of this relationship can be shown most clearly by comparing overall acceptance rates with "odds ratios" favoring athletes over other candidates in the admissions process. At schools with higher acceptance rates, the odds ratios favoring athletes are generally lower than at schools with low overall acceptance rates. (For a general discussion of odds ratios, see Bowen and Bok, especially pp. 340–44.)

31. One limited piece of evidence consistent with this interpretation is the ratio of the number of athletes on the coaches' lists to the number of teams supported. The ratio is hard to interpret for male athletes because of the role played by football (in terms of both squad size and the relative importance of recruitment), but for female athletes the pattern is clear: there are more listed athletes per team in the other coed liberal arts colleges than there are in either the Ivies or the NESCAC colleges.

32. Carleton, Colby, Hamilton, Kenyon, Middlebury, Swarthmore, and Trinity.

33. See Shulman and Bowen, figures 2.3 and 6.2 and the accompanying discussion.

34. James Fallows, "The Early-Decision Racket," *Atlantic Monthly,* September 2001, pp. 37–52; quote on p. 37.

35. For a thorough analysis of the pros and cons of the desirability of offering Early Decision (and Early Action) programs, see Avery, Fairbanks, and Zeckhauser. In December 2001 Richard Levin, president of Yale University, sparked a continuing debate by arguing that Early Decision programs have harmful effects on secondary education and are not in the interest of most students. Karen W. Arenson, "Yale President Wants to End Early Decisions for Admissions," *New York Times,* December 13, 2001, p. D1.

36. Avery, Fairbanks, and Zeckhauser, pp. 60–62. Later the authors provide other examples, including some at Division III schools in our study, that demonstrate the extent to which an Early Decision program can be seen as a "must" in the recruiting process (pp. 117–18). They also examine the strong interaction be-

tween athletic recruiting and Early Decision programs from the perspective of a secondary school that they study in detail (pp. 121–22).

37. In April of 2002, the University of North Carolina at Chapel Hill announced that it would abandon its Early Decision admissions policy beginning next year. An article about that announcement cites concerns about putting too much pressure on high school students to speed their decision-making about college and favoring wealthier applicants (who have more access to help in completing forms early and who have less need to shop around for financial aid packages). See Christopher Flores, "U. of North Carolina at Chapel Hill Abandons Early-Decision Admissions," *Chronicle of Higher Education,* April 25, 2002, online edition. Most recently, Stanford and Yale have both announced that they are going to end their Early Decision programs and that they will replace them with "Early Action" programs that will allow students to obtain an early response from the school but will not commit the students to attend. Jeffrey R. Young, "Yale Drops Early Decision, but Defies Admissions-Counseling Association's Guidelines," *Chronicle of Higher Education,* November 7, 2002, online edition; Jeffrey R. Young, "Stanford U. Revises Early-Admissions Policy, Adopts a Nonbinding Plan Similar to Yale's," *Chronicle of Higher Education,* November 8, 2002, online edition.

38. According to the Middlebury Ad Hoc Committee (2002a), Middlebury offered admission for the class of 2006 to 138 students "for whom athletic talent figured significantly in the admissions decision" and expects to "matriculate about 110 of these students" (p. 11)—for a yield of 80 percent. These broader results are based on examination of the 1999 admission files of those schools that were able to identify matriculants as well as admits. The actual yields for recruited athletes versus other students were as follows: in the two Ivy League schools for which we have data, 85 percent for the recruited male athletes and 83 percent for the female recruits, versus 65 percent for all other men and 63 percent for all other women; in five NESCAC colleges, 60 percent for the recruited male athletes and 49 percent for the female recruits, versus 35 percent for all other men and 32 percent for all other women. The yields did not vary systematically by SAT interval.

39. Much of the basic research for this section was done by our colleague Cara Nakamura, who transformed the High Test-Takers database described below into a useful instrument for our purposes. The Educational Testing Service (ETS) also provided key data.

40. The High Test-Takers database was originally created by Stephanie Bell-Rose at The Andrew W. Mellon Foundation to analyze the characteristics of African American students who had high SAT scores. With the assistance of the Urban Institute (which worked with Ms. Bell-Rose on her study) and ETS, we have adapted the data for our purposes. In addition to reporting the test scores of the test-takers and the colleges or universities to which they say they are likely to apply, the Student Descriptive Questionnaire administered by ETS asks all test-takers if they played high school sports and, if so, for how many years (along with many other questions). In Chapter 11 we present similar data on high school athletic participation for the non-recruit students *who actually attended* the schools in the study.

41. The College Admissions Project is a 1999–2000 "survey of more than 3,000 applicants from more than 400 prestigious high schools, both private and public, across the United States" (Avery, Fairbanks, and Zeckhauser, p. 9). It is described

as follows at the College Admissions Project Web site (http://www.nber.org/ ~hoxby/collegeadmissions/methodology.html): "Participating counselors were instructed to select 10 students at random from the top portion of their senior classes—generally the top 10% of the class at public schools and the top 20% of the class at private schools." Data from this survey are used extensively in the Avery, Fairbanks, and Zeckhauser study of Early Decision programs referred to earlier. We are indebted to Caroline Hoxby for running special tabulations that yielded the data on high athletic achievement.

42. Middlebury Ad Hoc Committee (2002a), p. 13.

43. Gross (2002).

44. Louis Menand, in his early review of *The Game of Life* in the *New Yorker,* explicitly highlighted this comparison. He wrote: "Many articles and books have been written to explain why admissions policies that take race into account are pernicious and ought to be abandoned. The University of California is now required by law not to use race as a criterion in admissions. That black Americans have historically been denied access to higher education is indisputable. That affirmative-action policies at élite colleges and universities have increased the number of black Americans in the higher-status professions is established by Bowen and Bok's book. By 1992, of the seven hundred black students who had entered selective colleges under affirmative-action criteria sixteen years earlier, seventy were doctors, roughly sixty were lawyers, a hundred and twenty-five were business executives, and more than three hundred had become civic leaders. How many crusaders against affirmative action in college admissions will now speak out against the preferential treatment of athletes?" Menand, p. 88.

Chapter 4 Athletes in College: Academic Credentials, Athletic Participation, and Campus Culture

1. Unfortunately we have too little data on recruited athletes in the women's colleges in the study to permit us to include statistically reliable estimates of numbers and percentages in many of the figures in this chapter. But we are confident, qualitatively, that recruiting (although increasing in importance) still affects smaller numbers of athletes in these schools than at most of the other liberal arts colleges in the study.

2. See David L. Marcus, "What Are Your Chances of Getting in through the Coach's Door?" *U.S. News & World Report,* September 17, 2001, p. 94. Marcus offers this advice: "If you think you've got the talent to make a college team, you should be showcasing your skills at summer camps that draw college scouts; golfers and tennis players should be getting in some tournament play. Ask your high school coach to contact college coaches on your behalf, and follow up with a letter and video highlights of your play."

3. Some commentators have asked if coaches deliberately leave off their lists athletes whom they want badly but are confident will be admitted anyway (saving their stated preferences for the more problematic admits). While this is certainly conceivable, admissions officers are likely to monitor such behavior carefully, and at least one assured us categorically that he would "kill" any coach he caught employing such a stratagem. Also, admission to the schools in this study is so com-

petitive that coaches would generally be reluctant to gamble on a highly desired athlete being admitted absent the coach's endorsement. Recall the discussion in Chapter 3 of the inclination of admissions deans to favor non-athletes over athletes after they have addressed the needs of coaches by admitting some number of recruits. For these reasons, we are doubtful that there are many athletes highly desired by coaches who are admitted without having been on a coach's list.

4. Welch Suggs, "Left Behind," *Chronicle of Higher Education,* November 30, 2001, pp. A35–A37.

5. Mary Lord, "Athletics for All: Harvard Tops the Scoreboard with a Sporting Smorgasbord to Foster Sound Bodies and Minds," *U.S. News & World Report,* March 18, 2002, pp. 68–69; quote on p. 69.

6. Malekoff (2002), pp. 5–6.

7. Biddiscombe adds: "Today, one-sport college coaches have more time to recruit, and they know how crucial this work is to their success." Technology has also played an important role. Thanks to videotape and recruiting camps, college coaches can better evaluate virtually all potential recruits. In addition, scouting services—once available in only men's basketball and football—exist for all sports. For all of these reasons, the level of collegiate play has dramatically improved, further limiting opportunities for walk-ons as we are reminded by the following comment on the evolution of lacrosse at Wesleyan: "The improvement of college teams has made it very difficult for novice athletes to compete for a position. . . . In watching a recent Wesleyan men's lacrosse game with four men's lacrosse alumni from the 1974 team, all of whom learned the game in college, their comments were that the ability of the players today would have made it impossible for them to have played on the current team. All of Wesleyan's current players have played the game prior to Wesleyan and many have played extensively before entering secondary school." Biddiscombe, p. 3.

One former professor/coach laments that his grandson, a talented soccer player, decided to give up the sport because "Princeton and other schools had a set-up that unless you are recruited in a sport you basically can't be a walk-on and must join the JV squad, which starts practices weeks later." Tristram Coffin (Denison University tennis and soccer coach), letter to Bowen, December 12, 2001. A Williams official relates the story of an All-Minnesota high school hockey goalie who chose to attend Williams over Princeton, believing that this choice would allow him to play college hockey. He arrived on campus only to learn that the coach had recruited not one, but *two,* All-American goalies from other secondary schools and had little interest in him. Especially on teams where squad sizes are limited, only athletes previously identified as truly exceptional are welcome. Coaches often are hesitant to devote time and resources to someone who may be a less proven or less dedicated player. At an extreme end of the spectrum, some even voice outright hostility. A now-retired Washington University (St. Louis) Division III volleyball coach who ran a highly successful program describes her feelings about walk-ons: "What about walk-ons? In the fall, I have a walk-on tryout, open to the entire campus. It's at 7 A.M. Why? Because I don't really want them to come. I just tell it like it is. I don't really want to take a walk-on." Teri Clemens, "Closing the Deal in Division III," in Brennan, ed., pp. 17–27; quote on p. 25.

8. If we were to add data on additional measures of pre-collegiate academic accomplishment, the picture presented in this section would be essentially the same. We recognize that SAT scores are only one predictor of college performance, and in Chapter 6 we investigate the effects of including a number of other variables such as high school grades, SAT II scores, and intention to apply for Advanced Placement credit. We focus on the test score parameter here in order to simplify the exposition.

9. We suspect that the lower SAT scores of walk-ons in the High Profile sports outside the Ivies and NESCAC may be the result of our failure to tag all football recruits in the colleges—or, as suggested in Chapter 3, of a tendency on the part of admissions officers to give football players in general a break because of the difficulty in enrolling enough of them.

10. Gaps in average SAT scores by sport and conference are at least a partial indicator of the opportunity cost of the admissions advantage given to particular groups of recruited athletes (since presumably their places could have been given to other candidates whose academic qualifications were not very different from those of the students at large who were admitted). At these highly selective schools, the pools of top candidates are so deep that it would easily be possible to admit more students at large without any appreciable fall-off in academic qualifications. In making comparisons of this kind, it is also important to recognize that the reported gaps may even understate the true differences in performance on standardized tests. We have been told that some High Profile athletes take the SAT as many as eight times in order to achieve a score above a school's threshold.

11. This comparison is based on the recentered scale and 2001 percentiles.

12. See the reference in the previous chapter to the study at Williams College that showed the small number of football recruits who had high ratings on both academic and athletic scales.

13. The availability of coaching at JV levels varies appreciably, and opportunities for walk-ons are much greater where coaching (and other) resources exist below the varsity level.

14. These data are available for the Ivies only for Dartmouth, Harvard, and Penn, and for the NESCAC colleges only for Bowdoin, Middlebury, Wesleyan, and Williams. We do not have data on level of play for the UAA universities or for enough Division III colleges to examine these relationships for those groups. Athletes are counted as having played varsity if they ever played at the varsity level, JV if they ever played at the JV level, and freshmen if they ever played at the freshman level. A single athlete may thus be counted in all three categories.

15. We identified starters from published football programs (for randomly selected mid-season games) for the five years for which the cohort was eligible. If in any of the five years a student was listed in the starting offensive or defensive line-up, that student is marked as a "starter."

16. An article in the *Barnard Bulletin* describes one such student, Christy Thornton, who quit the Barnard-Columbia basketball team prior to her sophomore year after discovering "that her passion for sports could not compete with her ever-growing passion for 'theater, politics, and the whammy of all commitments, the *Barnard Bulletin*.'" As the article makes clear, Thornton did not take

this decision lightly. "She'd been playing basketball her entire life, and had applied only to schools that could accommodate her Division I aspirations. She explained that people from her small town were proud to send an athlete off to a Division I school, and not a liberal arts women's college." The *Bulletin* described her activities after leaving the team: "When she is not at the *Bulletin* office meticulously putting together the next issue, she spends her time and energy on theater, advocacy for the homeless, and community gardening." Anjali George, "The Trials and Tribulations of an Ex-College Athlete: What Happens When the Game Is Over?" *Barnard Bulletin*, February 21, 2001, pp. 12–13.

17. These data are presented for the Ivies where we can most reliably identify which sport an athlete was recruited to play.

18. We were not able to calculate an admissions advantage for the UAA universities because we do not have applicant data.

19. Quoted in Lambert, p. 40.

20. Malekoff, p. 4.

21. Quoted in Lambert, p. 42.

22. The time series numbers are calculated for Columbia, Princeton, Penn, and Yale only. Given the high degree of overlap between cross country, indoor track, and outdoor track, these sports are counted as one in all tabulations of multi-sport participation.

23. These comparisons are based on data for Denison, Hamilton, Kenyon, Oberlin, Swarthmore, Wesleyan, and Williams.

24. Malekoff, pp. 2–3. The value placed on single-sport coaching in Division III schools is evident in a description of Smith College athletics that the Friends of Smith Athletics (FOSA) posted at their Web site: "There is much to be excited about as athletics at Smith continues to grow and excel. We are expanding the coaching staff, allowing more coaches to focus on a single sport." Friends of Smith Athletics, *About FOSA*, available at http://www.smith.edu/athletics/friends/fosa_aboutfosa.html, accessed January 13, 2003.

25. Biddiscombe, p. 1.

26. Rasmussen (2002), p. 5.

27. This point was made clearly in the lengthy examination of the Swarthmore athletics program and the discussion of the forces that were causing Swarthmore to have problems fielding competitive teams. See Min Lee, Sonia Scherr, and Nathan Ashby-Kuhlman, "Finding the Right Balance: Making Athletics and Academics Work Together," *Swarthmore Phoenix*, April 27, 2000, online edition.

28. "[Athletic recruitment] draws people from places and backgrounds and parts of the country where excellence and achievement is much more identified with athletic prowess than with academic prowess," says Dean of Harvard College Harry Lewis. William M. Rasmussen and Rahul Rohatgi, "Ivy League Debates Recruiting Reduction," *Harvard Crimson*, May 15, 2002, online edition. Reporting on a recent NCAA convention, Robert Lipsyte describes the plan of the president of Utah State University, Kermit L. Hall, to increase diversity on his campus by adding a women's basketball team. See "Backtalk: Lesson No. 1: Mixed Messages Part of Curriculum," *New York Times*, January 20, 2002, Section 8, p. 11.

29. "Underrepresented minorities" are defined here in the conventional way as African American, Hispanic, and Native American students.

30. The report by a faculty committee at Middlebury presents new data that support this conclusion. At Middlebury, "in a recent year, 89 percent of our athletes classified themselves as Caucasian, whereas 74 percent of other students classified themselves as Caucasian." Middlebury Ad Hoc Committee (2002a), p. 7.

31. "Black women don't row. Or play soccer or lacrosse. Or compete in equestrian sports," writes reporter Welch Suggs (2001c), p. A35. It may be that some coaches, valuing experience over potential, are defining their recruiting pools too narrowly.

32. We are not able to identify aid recipients at Carnegie Mellon University, Connecticut College, or Wellesley College.

33. These findings are consistent with those from *The Game of Life* (pp. 50–52, 137), which used parental education and private secondary school attendance as proxies for socioeconomic status. The Middlebury faculty committee found that "approximately 26 percent of athletes (compared with 21 percent for non-athletes) are from families with incomes over $200,000." Their report continues: "Together, these findings [this one and the finding reported earlier on racial diversity] suggest that athletes tend to reduce somewhat the socio-economic diversity of Middlebury's student body, and they have contributed little to our recent important gains for ethnic diversity." Middlebury Ad Hoc Committee (2002a), pp. 7–8.

34. The broad range of institutional benefits associated with having an intercollegiate athletics program is a still larger subject, which we discuss at the start of Chapter 10 (alongside the "costs" of such programs).

35. Amherst Special Committee on the Place of Athletics, *The Place of Athletics at Amherst College: A Question of Balance,* May 2002, p. 30. Similarly: "When asked to rank the factors that cause groups of students at Amherst to bond together socially, the student leaders all placed membership on an athletic team at the top of their lists" (p. 31).

36. Williams Ad Hoc Faculty Committee on Athletics, *Report on Varsity Athletics,* May 2002, p. 9. Later, in its concluding section, the report says this about campus culture: "Williams has produced an environment in which *non-athletes* [our emphasis] are a sub-culture, with all that implies of limited social possibilities" (p. 20). This carefully prepared report contains a wealth of data based on surveys of faculty and students at Williams.

37. Charles Berry, letter to Bowen, February 28, 2001. Thomas Wright, vice-president and secretary at Princeton, has pointed out that the construction of major new athletic facilities at Princeton has also widened the athletic divide. Varsity athletes who used to use Dillon Gymnasium, at the center of the campus and the location for many club sports and intramural programs, now practice and compete at Jadwin Gymasium and the DeNunzio Pool, which are located in an area of their own, next to the football stadium.

38. The precise average for athletics is 19.26 according to the Richards and Aries study and 19.30 according to Cantor and Prentice. The averages for these other activities are 6.78 and 6.79, respectively, in Richards and Aries and 8.56 and 8.10 in Cantor and Prentice. See Shaunette Richards and Elizabeth Aries, "The Division III Student-Athlete: Academic Performance, Campus Involvement, and Growth," *Journal of College Student Development* 40(3) (May–June 1999): 211–18; Nancy E. Can-

tor and Deborah A. Prentice, "The Life of the Modern-Day Student-Athlete: Opportunities Won and Lost," paper presented at the Princeton Conference on High Education, Princeton, N.J., March 21–23, 1996. The Cantor-Prentice article relies on data from two Ivies (Columbia and Princeton) and one NESCAC school (Amherst). The Richards-Aries article relies on data from Amherst. In a study commissioned by the NCAA, athletes in 42 Division I institutions were found to spend between four and ten hours more each week on their main sport than non-athletes spent on their main extracurricular activity. See Center for the Study of Athletics, *Report No. 1: Summary Results from the 1987–88 National Study of Intercollegiate Athletes* (Palo Alto, Calif.: American Institutes for Research, 1988).

39. Cantor and Prentice, p. 15 and table 7.

40. Amherst Special Committee, p. 32.

41. Williams Ad Hoc Committee, p. 7.

42. Amherst Special Committee, p. 31.

43. Richards and Aries report a rating of 3.25 (on a scale of 1 to 5, with 1 indicating much easier to meet others and 5 indicating much more difficult) for athletes on this measure as compared to 2.47 for other students (p. 214). Cantor and Prentice, in table 6, compare athletes to members of performing arts groups, separately comparing men and women, and report similar findings. The athletes' average ratings were 3.38 and 3.43 for men and women, respectively, the performing arts groups' 2.57 and 2.62.

44. Amherst Faculty Committee, p. 23. The following satirical piece by Suzanne Feigelson, published in the *Amherst Student* (December 2, 1998, online edition) under the title "A Recruit's Confessions," provides an insider's sense of the implications for "culture" of recruiting at a small college:

> We've heard over and over again how athletics are no different from any other social club on campus, in spite of the fact that only athletes are recruited. But recruiting makes all the difference.
>
> Let's imagine I was recruited for Women's Chorus—well, not exactly recruited—but strongly encouraged to sing for Amherst. Let's say the director of Women's Chorus called me and said what a terrific school Amherst is, and what a great chorus it has. She said she knew I love to sing, and told me that at other colleges I'd probably have to spend a lot of time in the junior chorus before I could sing in the performance choir. Finally, she said that if I applied to Amherst, she would mention my name to the admissions office, and if I got in, she would guarantee me a full-time spot in the soprano section of the chorus.
>
> I know these choral director guarantees don't always come through; after all, how could the admissions office take orders from them? So it is safe for me to assume it was the overall strength of my application that got me admitted—not the mere plug from the choral director. But what I found out in the early months of my Amherst experience tells me this plug went a long way.
>
> At pre-frosh weekend I attended a meeting for students "interested in Women's Chorus." I met a great group of girls from diverse backgrounds. . . . We found that each of us had received a similar phone call, encouraging us to apply, or in some cases, to matriculate. The director had promised one girl a part in the second soprano section, guaranteed another girl a seat among the first altos and assured another girl that she would have the opportunity to sing as a second alto.

Yes, imagine I had a great time on pre-frosh weekend, and a few of us decided to room together freshman year. I figured this would make me feel secure in the beginning of college.

I made it to sophomore year, loving my Amherst experience so far. Women's Chorus took up most of my time outside of classes, and since I was recruited, I felt it was my obligation to stick with it. But I liked to sing, so this was fine. All of the recruited singers formed bonds stronger than I could have imagined—like a sorority. We ate together in Valentine, and partied on the weekends.

Suppose one day I found myself talking to a girl who auditioned for Women's Chorus and was rejected, and I felt terrible for her. She told me she sang a lot in high school—not like the solos my friends and I performed—but she enjoyed it anyway. She decided to go to Amherst partly because she thought it would be easier to sing here than at a larger school.

She told me she was having trouble finding extracurricular activities because everything seemed so closed off. All the writers for the newspaper were also recruited, so it was impossible for her to get a byline. The Amherst Feminist Alliance also didn't have any openings: all the members were specialists in the art of feminism, hand-picked from their high schools. She said she also wanted to work at the Hungry Newt, but all the cookie-bakers had been lured to Amherst precisely for their baking skills, leaving no room for amateurs. The manager of the Hungry Newt suggested she participate in intramural cookie-baking.

Of course, it worked out beautifully for me. I came to college knowing I liked to sing, and I expect to sing for the rest of my experience here. And at times, I am glad Amherst carved out my niche at college for me. I don't feel lost, and don't have to fill my time with random activities I didn't do in high school. Amherst does a really good job of telling people what they're good at and encouraging them to continue doing it.

45. After what was described as a "near-brawl" during a tennis match between Princeton and the University of Pennsylvania, Princeton's senior co-captain wryly observed: "Fortunately, no one was hurt." See Anne Hong, "M. Tennis Defeats Penn in Near-Brawl, W. Tennis Drops Match to Quakers," *The Daily Princetonian*, April 2, 2002, online edition.

46. Williams Ad Hoc Committee, p. 8. See also Princeton Trustee Committee on Student Life, Health and Athletics, *Report on Princeton Athletics*, November 30, 1994, which states: "The Committee also received information that appears to indicate that recruited athletes are disproportionately represented among those receiving non-academic disciplinary penalties" (p. 15). In a similar vein, the recent Amherst Special Committee report tells us: "Available evidence suggests that athletes—particularly male athletes—and, within that group, especially, high-profile-team members—are responsible for more than their per capita share of disciplinary violations." Amherst Special Committee, p. 33. There is also some evidence that dorm damage is greater where male athletes tend to congregate.

47. Williams Ad Hoc Committee, pp. 18–19.

48. Amherst Special Committee, p. 27.

49. Williams Ad Hoc Committee, pp. 15–16.

50. Still, it is obviously worrying when 42 percent of the academic faculty at Williams believe that varsity athletics detracts from the educational mission of the college; this view is held by over half (52 percent) of the faculty in the social sci-

ences, where many of the male athletes concentrate. Williams Ad Hoc Committee, pp. 11–12.

51. Richards and Aries.

Chapter 5   Academic Outcomes

1. There is a considerable body of literature that compares academic results
for athletes with results for other students, but almost all of these studies are
confined to individual schools or statewide systems. The results obtained in many
cases are either mixed or hard to interpret, often because the authors are forced
to work with limited information and aggregate data, thereby losing the ability to
make key distinctions (such as whether athletes were or were not recruited). We
are very fortunate to have comparable data for 33 schools, and to have enough
detail to permit us to disaggregate results by sport as well as by school and conference. Other studies include Kenneth A. Kline, "The Relationship between Academic Achievement and Athletic Participation of Female and Male Athletes at the
NCAA Division III Level (Women, Men)," Ph.D. dissertation, University of Connecticut, 1997, which examines Connecticut College; John Robst and Jack Keil,
"The Relationship between Athletic Participation and Academic Performance:
Evidence from NCAA Division III," *Applied Economics* 32 (5) (April 2000): 547–58,
which looks at Binghamton University undergraduates from 1990–91 through
1995–96; Michael T. Maloney and Robert E. McCormick, "An Examination of the
Role that Intercollegiate Athletic Participation Plays in Academic Achievement:
Athletes' Feats in the Classroom," *Journal of Human Resources* 28 (Summer 1993):
555–70, which studies Clemson University student records for 1985–89.

2. Middlebury Ad Hoc Committee (2002a), p. 11.

3. Lester, pp. 138, 161.

4. Jeff Glasser, "King of the Hill," *U.S. News & World Report,* March 18, 2002,
pp. 52–60, quote on p. 56. Cooper is also quoted as saying: "I think a school like
Ohio State, if you let a kid in, there ought to be a curriculum to keep him there."

5. Later we compare fields of study elected by recruited athletes with fields of
study elected by walk-ons; as we saw in previous chapters, the overwhelming majority of athletes playing the High Profile men's sports are recruited.

6. History is included in the humanities and psychology in the social sciences.
These clusters of departments do not capture all students, which is hardly surprising given the differences among schools in the curricular options available
to students. Some major in "other fields" (often interdisciplinary or pre-
professional) or are missing a major (in some cases because they left school before
declaring a major). So the totals of the three clusters shown here do not equal
100 percent; but such large majorities of students (usually around 90 percent)
fall in one of these three clusters that the general picture is clear.

7. Shulman and Bowen, pp. 74–78. This pattern was *not* evident in the 1951
entering cohort (though it was present in the '76 cohort and, even more strongly,
in the '89 cohort). The trend is clearly toward more concentration of male athletes in the social sciences.

8. We say "appears to be" because we have fewer data for the recruited High
Profile athletes in the UAA. One of the four UAA universities in the study

(Emory) does not play two of the three High Profile sports (football and ice hockey) and has too few basketball players in a single cohort to permit meaningful comparisons; a second UAA university, Chicago, does not have the same kinds of lists of recruited athletes that we find elsewhere. We do have complete and comparable data for Washington University and Carnegie Mellon, and it is the data for these two universities that are reported in Figure 5.1a. In an effort to see if these data limitations are distorting the general picture presented here, we made alternative calculations for all athletes in High Profile sports, which allowed us to add data for the University of Chicago. The general pattern is exactly the same. Also, the UAA data for athletes in Lower Profile men's sports and women's sports fit this same pattern.

9. For a general analysis of factors affecting choice of major by men and women in different sets of schools, see Sarah E. Turner and William G. Bowen, "Choice of Major: The Changing (Unchanging) Gender Gap," *Industrial and Labor Relations Review* 52 (2) (January 1999): 289–313. Turner and Bowen found significant differences between men and women in how they "convert" various degrees of proficiency in earning high SAT scores, especially high math SATs, into specific majors in the sciences and social sciences. One major factor driving these differences appears to be the much stronger interest of women in psychology and the life sciences and the much stronger interest of men in economics and the physical sciences.

10. The UAA is the single exception to this generalization, and the limitations of the data for High Profile athletes in these schools (see note 8) caution against reading too much into this single figure.

11. We do not present similar data for women walk-ons because the recruited women athletes do not differ significantly in their choice of major from women students at large. That is true of women walk-ons as well.

12. Williams Ad Hoc Committee (2002a), pp. 13–14.

13. Shulman and Bowen, especially Chapters 3 and 4. The Astin survey, which is the source of the data on attitudes and interests among members of the '89 cohort, is not available for the '95 cohort and so cannot be used here; and since we could not tag "recruits" in the '89 cohort, we cannot compare the attitudes and interests of recruits and walk-ons even in the '89 cohort.

14. Since most colleges do not require their students to select majors until at least their second year, these group dynamics have ample opportunity to take effect.

15. Williams Ad Hoc Committee (2002a), pp. 15–16.

16. "Faculty in these heavily enrolled fields have less time to spend with individual students, are not able to provide as many detailed comments on papers, and in general may not be able to devote as much attention to their students as they might wish. The parent of one athlete known personally to us was distressed by the lack of attention his son's senior paper had received. But then he noted that this was true for all the students majoring in political science at the school in question." Shulman and Bowen, p. 77.

17. National Collegiate Athletic Association (NCAA), *NCAA 2002 Graduation-Rates Report,* available at http://www.ncaa.org/grad_rates, accessed September 26, 2002. Graduation rates improved from those reported the previous year, when

only 40 percent of men's basketball players who entered Division I schools in the 1994–95 academic year graduated in six years. See Welch Suggs, "Male Basketball Players' Graduation Rates Fall Again," *Chronicle of Higher Education,* September 10, 2001, online edition. The report issued by the Knight Foundation Commission in 2001 discusses graduation rates extensively and suggests that "by 2007, teams that do not graduate at least 50 percent of their players should not be eligible for conference championships or for postseason play" (p. 26). According to the *Chronicle of Higher Education,* applying this criterion in the 2000–01 academic year would have excluded 28 of the 50 football teams that played in Division IA bowl games, as well as 33 of the 65 men's basketball teams and 13 of the 64 women's basketball teams that participated in the NCAA Division I March Madness championship tournament. Suggs (2001b).

18. Myles Brand, "Academics First: Reforming Intercollegiate Athletics," address delivered to the National Press Club, January 23, 2001, *Vital Speeches of the Day* 67 (12) (April 1, 2001): 367–71; quote on p. 370.

19. Hutchins, p. 23. Today a part of the problem in Division IA may in fact be that institutions devoted to athletic development at the pre-professional level in some sports are neither numerous nor inexpensive. Big-time college basketball and football often serve purposes that the minor league system fulfills in baseball.

20. Shulman and Bowen, Scorecard 3.1, p. 317. There is a single exception for the men: intercollegiate athletes at the Division IA private universities in the '89 cohort graduated at a slightly lower rate than students at large. Women athletes also graduated at consistently higher rates than women students at large (figure 7.1, p. 142).

21. Closer inspection of the data for the High Profile athletes in the '95 cohort demonstrates that the tendency for graduation rates to be below the norm for all students is especially pronounced among male basketball players at most (but not all) of the Ivies.

22. The figures given here are five-year graduation rates rather than the six-year graduation rates reported in *The Game of Life* and published by the NCAA. The '95 cohort entered too recently to allow six-year graduation rates to be calculated, so we went back and redid the '89 data (as well as the data for the '51 and '76 cohorts) to put them on the same five-year basis. The '89 data are for all High Profile athletes, not just those who were recruited, since we could not tag recruits prior to the collection of the '95 data. But since such a high proportion (around 90 percent) of the High Profile athletes were recruited, this discontinuity is of minor importance. We reclassified the '95 data to permit a calculation of graduation rates for all High Profile athletes in that cohort, and there is a change of only 1 percentage point in the result (the graduation rate improves to 87 percent from 86 percent).

23. In the case of the male Lower Profile sports, what was once an 11- to 12-point advantage has disappeared; female athletes in the Ivy League continue to graduate at higher rates than their peers, but the size of their advantage has declined from 12 percentage points in the '76 cohort to 2 points in the '95 cohort. The historical data for the Ivies are based on figures for the four Ivy League schools that participated in the original *Game of Life* study (Columbia, Princeton, the University of Pennsylvania, and Yale), but the results for these four schools

are so similar to the results for all eight Ivies in the '95 data that there is no reason to question the "representativeness" of the four schools in the original study.

24. For a general discussion of the "spreading" or "contagion" phenomenon, see Shulman and Bowen, pp. 284–87.

25. Amherst Faculty Committee, p. 24.

26. Middlebury Ad Hoc Committee (2002a) presents data for that particular college that are consistent in all respects with the data for NESCAC described here. Readers interested in the specific facts for an identifiable college should consult this well-done report, as well as the reports for Amherst and Williams cited frequently in this study.

27. The 1989 data for the women's colleges are presented (along with the data for female athletes at the other schools) in Shulman and Bowen, Scorecard 7.1). In the '95 cohort, the largest gap in average rank-in-class was 9 points at one of the women's colleges: the typical athlete was in the 42nd percentile, whereas the typical student at large was in the 51st percentile. A gap of 5 points was found at one of the other two women's colleges; in the third, female athletes were, on average, in the 53rd percentile, whereas the mean for students at large was the 49th percentile.

28. Henry Rosovsky and Matthew Hartley, *Evaluation and the Academy: Are We Doing the Right Thing?* (Cambridge, Mass.: American Academy of Arts and Sciences, 2002), pp. 2–3. Rosovsky and Hartley document the fact that grade inflation has occurred (pp. 4–7), noting that it has been "especially noticeable in the Ivy League," and they also cite a Consortium on Financing Higher Education (COFHE) study by C. Anthony Broh in rejecting the argument that grade inflation "merely reflected a more academically talented student body." Recently the Harvard faculty voted to modify its grading scale and limit the number of students allowed to graduate with honors to 60 percent of the class. Anemona Hartocollis, "Harvard Faculty Votes to Put the Excellence Back in the A," *New York Times,* May 22, 2002, p. A20.

29. Amherst Special Committee, p. 25. See also Bates College Office of Institutional Planning and Analysis, "Memorandum on the *Game of Life* at Bates and NESCAC Follow-up Study," December 10, 2001, for an example of the argument that differences in actual grades are small and not all that important.

30. Using the detailed GPA data made available to us, we calculated that in the 1995 entering cohort at the Ivies, 23 percent of all students had a cumulative GPA of at least A-minus, 57 percent had an average of at least B-plus, and 20 percent had an average of B-minus or lower. In the '95 cohort at the NESCAC colleges, 13 percent of students had an average of A-minus or higher, 49 percent had a B-plus or higher, and 25 percent were in the B-minus or lower range. The grade distributions for the '95 cohort at the UAA universities, the other coed colleges, and the women's colleges are more like the distribution for students in NESCAC than for those in the Ivy League.

31. We calculated these rank-in-class measures from the actual cumulative GPAs on the transcripts of individual students. Since the percentile scale runs from 1 to 100, the average rank-in-class for the largest group (students at large) is bound to be somewhere around the 50th percentile. However, the average for all *men* is often below the 50th percentile, and the average for all *women* is often

above it, because the women in these colleges generally earn higher grades than the men. In the case of both men and women, the absolute value of the average rank-in-class of students at large is affected by the number of athletes and the grades they earn. Other things equal, the more athletes there are in the class and the lower their grades, the higher the average rank-in-class of the students at large.

32. Again, we are unable to present a panel for the women's colleges because we could not distinguish recruited athletes from walk-ons at more than two of them.

33. These last comparisons illustrate why it is so important to have appropriate benchmarks. On its face, an average percentile rank-in-class of 46 might look just fine—until one recognizes that the female students at large in NESCAC had an average percentile rank-in-class of 58 (not 50, as one might assume). In fact, the gap between the recruited female athletes and the students at large in NESCAC is nearly as large as the gap in the Ivy League (12 versus 15 points in rank-in-class), because the typical female student in NESCAC does better academically, relative to her classmates, than does the typical female student in the Ivy League. It is the differences between the heights of the bars that matter.

34. Amherst Special Committee, p. 24. Professor Geoffrey Woglom at Amherst did considerable additional research on other cohorts of students at Amherst and replicated a number of the findings reported for NESCAC in our own work.

35. The fact that we have data for only four of the eight UAA universities is entirely a reflection of our slowness in realizing the importance of the UAA for this analysis. Every UAA university that we asked to cooperate was glad to do so, and we have no doubt that the other four would also have contributed their records had we approached them in a timely way.

36. The UAA presidents and the UAA executive secretary have sought from the beginning of the Association to monitor academic *performance* so that they could be sure that athletes were meeting the regular academic standards of the universities—that is, that they were "representative" of their classes in this important respect. In contrast, the Council of Ivy Presidents has focused on admission standards.

37. Internal studies within UAA universities are consistent with the findings reported here. For example, Professor Starkey Duncan at the University of Chicago told us that he had done some statistical work at Chicago comparing GPA distributions for athletes with GPA distributions for other students and had found them to be essentially identical.

38. Williams Ad Hoc Committee, p. 16.

39. In discussing these results with representatives of one UAA university, we were interested to see that they were surprised by the difference in outcomes between football players and other students on their campus. They surmised that perhaps they had been so pleased by the extremely good overall results for athletes in general that they had just overlooked this pattern—another example of the dangers of overaggregation.

40. To correct rigorously for these problems, it would be necessary to have access to far more detailed data both on grading distributions within courses (some faculty may be easier graders than others) and on how smart the students are who

take a particular course. The second problem is somewhat analogous to ranking sports teams by adjusting for strength of schedule. In the next chapter we introduce some controls for the division within which a student concentrated (since we do know the typical grades given in a division and thus are aware, for example, that grades in science and engineering tend to be somewhat lower than grades in the social sciences). But this is only a very partial correction for the underlying problem, in part because, as just noted, individual departments (never mind divisions) may be "bifurcated," with, for example, the math track in economics being much more challenging than the less analytical track. Athletes in economics, one professor surmised, are much less likely to take the math track than are other students.

41. Williams Ad Hoc Committee, p. 17. A vice president at another college said in an interview that the faculty at this school are disturbed by "their [the athletes'] tendency to register in large classes and sit in the back row and do nothing."

42. Williams Ad Hoc Committee, p. 17.

43. We had hoped to be able to compare these patterns of high academic achievement in the Ivies with comparable figures for the UAA universities, but lack of data prevent meaningful comparisons. The limited data that exist suggest, once again, that the UAA athletes are more successful than their Ivy peers in earning honors, but these data are not definitive. (One complicating factor is that UAA institutions such as Carnegie Mellon University have different academic emphases and thus somewhat different forms of academic recognition.)

44. Suggs (2002b). In a similar fashion, a former football player at Notre Dame, John Osmar, recalls sitting beside former nose tackle (and later pro football player) Mike Oriard (now an academic and an author) in freshman chemistry: "I can vouch for his academic strength. He aced those weekly quizzes. . . . The college experience was enhanced for all of us who had friends for whom football was not No. 1." John Osmar, "College Football As It Used to Be," letter to the editor, *New York Times,* January 6, 2002, Section 8, p. 7.

45. Rasmussen and Rohatgi.

Chapter 6   Academic Underperformance

1. See Shulman and Bowen, especially Chapters 3 and 7 as well as pp. 262 and 270–71.

2. The Amherst Special Committee report points out: "The term 'underperformance' thus refers, not to a simple differential between all athletes and all non-athletes, but rather to a difference *between athletes and otherwise identically situated non-athletes*" (p. 24). Additional research done by the Office of Institutional Research at Amherst, and by Professor Geoffrey Woglom using even more recent data, found results quite similar to those reported here.

3. Williams Ad Hoc Committee, pp. 9–10, 15–16.

4. Shulman and Bowen, pp. 270–71.

5. The distances on both sides of the point estimates of the degree of underperformance are 1.96 standard deviations from the mean and thus define a 95 percent confidence interval around the point estimate. Showing these intervals helps us know how confident we can be that the finding of underperformance is real,

and not a statistical artifact. There is less than a 5 percent chance that the actual point falls outside the 95 percent confidence interval surrounding the estimate. The use of 95 percent confidence intervals is discussed at greater length in the introduction. (In NESCAC, Bates is excluded from all underperformance analysis because we have SAT scores for less than half of the 1995 entering cohort.)

6. In the High Profile sports (really football), recruited athletes at UAA schools underperform by 6.9 percentile points, a point estimate that is nearly statistically significant (left side of Figure 6.1c). It is not surprising that football seems different from other sports even within the UAA (see the discussion of the "special case of football" in Chapter 12).

7. In our own regressions used to estimate underperformance, the variable for SAT scores is a relentlessly significant predictor of rank-in-class. Other studies include Cameron Fincher, "Is the SAT Worth Its Salt? An Evaluation of the Use of the Scholastic Aptitude Test in the University System of Georgia over a Thirteen-Year Period," *Review of Educational Research* 44 (3) (Summer 1974): 293–305; Susan F. Ford and Sandy Campos, *Summary of Validity Data from the Admissions Testing Program Validity Study Service* (Princeton, N.J.: College Board, 1977); and L. Ramist, C. Lewis, and L. McCamley-Jenkins, *Student Group Differences in Predicting College Grades: Sex, Language, and Ethnic Groups,* College Board Report No. 93-1, ETS RR-94-27 (New York: College Board, 1994).

8. Data on SAT II scores and self-reported intention to apply for AP credit were provided by the Educational Testing Service.

9. We do not have high school class rank for students at Bowdoin, Wesleyan, or Williams.

10. We have data on SAT II scores for five Ivy League schools (Columbia, Dartmouth, Pennsylvania, Princeton, and Yale) and five NESCAC schools (Colby, Hamilton, Middlebury, Wesleyan, and Williams). For these schools we compared the regression results with and without a control for the student's highest SAT II score.

11. We also performed the analysis using standardized GPA, and again the findings are essentially the same. Standardized GPA is a conversion of GPA such that the average GPA is set equal to 0 and the standard deviation is set equal to 1 for each school. This has the benefit of correcting for differences between schools without the possibly distorting effect of percentile rankings.

12. Williams Ad Hoc Committee, p. 17.

13. Because we are testing whether being a recruited athlete is actually only a proxy for receiving need-based financial aid, this analysis is not limited to recruited athletes; however, recruited athletes and walk-ons are treated separately.

14. We had to exclude Carnegie Mellon University and Connecticut College from this analysis because we do not have data on financial aid for these schools.

15. These effects are additive, so the underperformance of athletes on aid is the sum of the two main effects and the interaction effect. Thus recruited female athletes on aid at the Ivies underperform by –7.4 (for being on aid) plus –11.9 (for being recruited athletes) plus +5.3 (interaction effect), for a net of –14.0 percentile points.

16. More specifically, for the Ivies the categories are "low" = combined SAT scores below 1250; "mid-level" = scores between 1250 and 1400; and "high" =

scores above 1400. For the NESCAC colleges the categories are combined SAT scores below 1150, between 1150 and 1300, and above 1300.

17. It is worth reiterating that the question in not whether those athletes with lower SAT scores earn lower grades than other athletes (which would be expected), but whether those athletes with lower SAT scores perform less well *relative to their credentials* than other athletes.

18. It is important to note that all these speculations refer to sport-to-sport differences, not team-to-team differences. It is almost surely the case that there is significant variation from team to team in underperformance. An individual coach's demands and expectations and the tone set by the team captain all must be expected to affect how seriously athletes on the team take their academic responsibilities.

19. We also analyzed the interaction effects between recruitment and individual sports in order to ascertain whether there were certain sports in which being recruited was particularly costly in terms of academic performance. This analysis did not yield any clear patterns, except that in almost every case the recruit-sport interaction variables were not significant. Thus, as we concluded earlier, it does not appear that the underperformance of recruited athletes is driven by recruits in a few sports.

20. Amherst Special Committee, p. 26.

21. Shulman and Bowen, pp. 69–70. We recognize, however, that this comparison is qualified by both the high degree of inflexibility in terms of scheduling and the consistency of the time commitment required of athletes.

22. We do not have year-by-year grades for Columbia, so it is excluded from this analysis.

23. Relatively few recruited athletes chose not to play in their freshman year, so we do not present the estimates for freshman year performance for those (few) athletes not playing in their freshman year.

24. For example, Dalibor E. Snyder, a Harvard undergraduate, was recently quoted as saying: "When tennis demands the most time from me, I am more productive in my academic life because it forces me to manage my time more efficiently and effectively." Rasmussen and Rohatgi.

25. We have grades for individual terms for Brown University, Cornell University, Dartmouth College, and Yale University. The analysis is limited to those students who were enrolled for both the spring and fall terms of their sophomore year.

26. These data are available for Dartmouth College, Harvard University, and Princeton University in the Ivy League and for Bowdoin College, Middlebury College, Wesleyan University, and Williams College in NESCAC.

27. We were able to identify starters in football for Brown University, Dartmouth College, Princeton University, the University of Pennsylvania, and Yale University.

28. We performed this analysis for men only because the female athletes show no significant bunching in certain majors (see Chapter 5).

29. Amherst Special Committee, p. 28. The Williams Ad Hoc Committee report also notes that "almost half of varsity athletes claim to experience discrimination 'sometimes' or 'often' from faculty in class" (p. 9). At Princeton there has also been considerable discussion of the effects of faculty attitudes, and Dean

Nancy Malkiel believes that there is likely "some truth to the point," though again the magnitude of such effects is debatable.

30. Shulman and Bowen, figure 6.5: "Intellectual Self-Confidence and SAT Scores." Claude M. Steele, who has written extensively on stereotype threat, describes it as "the social-psychological threat that arises when one is in a situation or doing something for which a negative stereotype about one's group applies . . . it is a situational threat—a threat in the air—that, in general form, can affect the members of any group about whom a negative stereotype exists (e.g., skateboarders, older adults, White men, gang members)." "A Threat in the Air: How Stereotypes Shape Intellectual Identity and Performance," *American Psychologist* (June 1997): 613–29. See Chapter 9 for a further discussion of stereotype threat, including references to more recent studies by Douglas Massey and others. One commentator has also suggested that whatever stigma effects are present will be offset at least in part by the presence of some "halo" effects as well.

31. Middlebury Ad Hoc Committee (2002a), p. 12.

32. Correlation is measured on a scale from −1 to +1, where a correlation coefficient of −1 implies perfect negative correlation, a coefficient of +1 implies perfect positive correlation, and a coefficient of zero implies no correlation.

Chapter 7　Orbits of Competition: The Role of the Conference

1. James Litvack, "Ivy League Reform Efforts" (paper commissioned by The Andrew W. Mellon Foundation for this study, May 2002), p. 5.

2. December 1978 memo from Ivy League presidents, cited in Litvack, p. 6. The Policy Committee monitors Ivy Group policies and programs to ensure that they conform to the Ivy Agreement. The 12-member committee is composed of one representative of each of the Ivy presidents (generally a senior university officer), one athletic director, one admissions officer, one director of financial aid, and one senior associate athletic director.

3. Included in the *Ivy Manual 2001–2002*, p. 4. The bracketed material after principle 7 indicates when the present wording was adopted later.

4. This was the observation of Susan Anderson, a member of the Mellon Foundation's staff, in a report on the history of the Academic Index that she based on a perusal of the Ivy League files. Anderson, "A Review of the History of the Academic Index" (report prepared for The Andrew W. Mellon Foundation, August 12, 1997), p. 1.

5. Both memos are cited in Litvack, pp. 5, 6–7. It was concerns of this kind, which could not be documented at the time, that later led Bowen to propose the creation of the College and Beyond database and the writing of *The Game of Life*.

6. Bernstein, pp. 243 ff, 254.

7. In his description of the movement of the Ivy League from Division IA to Division IAA in football, Bernstein notes, "The Ivies had been dodging this bullet since the NCAA created Division IAA in 1978. The issue was money. Major college teams, which were battling the NCAA over television revenues and eligibility rules, resented the influence exerted by smaller schools, particularly the sanctimonious Ivy League. Henceforward, in order to remain in Division IA, a football team would have to draw an average of at least seventeen thousand fans

to home games over the preceding four years or play those games in a stadium that could seat at least thirty thousand people at once. As Ivy Cassandras had warned all along, the NCAA now defined bigtime football not in terms of a college's commitment to athletics, but in terms of spectators and revenue." In the Fall of 1981, at a special meeting of the NCAA in St. Louis, the delegates voted to institute criteria that expelled the 8 Ivy League teams and 29 others to second tier Division IAA. Bernstein, pp. 247–48.

8. The Eastern College Athletic Conference (ECAC) was founded in 1938 by 58 member institutions as a coordinating office for regional championships. It has since grown to a membership of 315 Eastern colleges and universities from Divisions I, II, and III of the NCAA and now sponsors 111 championships in 35 men's and women's sports. While technically a conference, the ECAC is perhaps best described as a regional version of the NCAA. See the ECAC Web site (www.ecac.org).

9. See Litvack, pp. 11–12. The Ivies had added a 10th football game in 1980 to increase revenues. There are still 10 games on the football schedule.

10. Council of Ivy Group Presidents. Statement, June 20, 2002.

11. Quoted in Vélez, p. 8.

12. See the extensive survey results obtained by Covell (1999), along with the many volunteered comments that he quotes and the reactions to the compromise on postseason competition cited later. See also Ethan Austin, "Captain's Practice Rule Ain't All It's Cracked Up to Be," *Tufts Daily*, November 7, 2002, online edition, an editorial on NESCAC's prohibition of out-of-season practices. Austin writes that "the fact of the matter is that this rule hasn't stopped any team from holding practices. I've talked with numerous athletes and coaches, from various sports, all of whom admit that teams are practicing together." Austin cites the competitive disadvantage faced by teams that cannot practice while "every other team in the nation has been practicing for months. Legally." Then he asks, "Is it in the spirit of the NESCAC to tell athletes they can't practice the sport that they're supposed to put their hearts and souls into?"

13. Levison, pp. 15–16; also quoted in Vélez, p. 10. The rest of this account is based on Vélez.

14. Vélez, p. 14. The account presented here draws mainly on two sources: Vélez, pp. 14–21, and Covell (1999), pp. 2–23. Other issues have included how to handle the impact of Title IX, how to achieve "competitive balance," and specific issues such as the regulation of foreign travel in the summer. See Vélez.

15. An equally important argument was that NESCAC colleges could expect to have a reasonable chance of success in Division III competition, whereas they could never have hoped to compete with Division I schools. The fact that the NCAA supported the costs (or at least some of the costs) of participating in NCAA championships was yet another consideration, as was the growing difficulty of finding alternative ways of concluding seasons. (The ECAC regional championships, which were also being affected by the ever-increasing pulling power of the NCAA events, were less and less attractive options.)

16. The coach of Amherst's women's tennis team was quoted by Covell (1999) as saying: "As a coach, I don't stress the NCAA's, but with the way this team has come so close, it was hard (in 1999) for the kids to think about anything else. The kids probably would have hung themselves if they didn't get to go" (p. 4).

17. Cited in Vélez, p. 20.

18. NESCAC Presidents' statement of 1998, cited in Covell (1999), p. 18.

19. Brian Katten, sports information director at Wesleyan, certainly represented this point of view: "I don't think there is an SID [sports information director] among us who does not feel the intended NESCAC restriction on postseason play is a farce. A quick look at the ten sports during the Fall and Winter (1998–99 academic year) that have postseason tournaments show 54 NESCAC teams qualifying thus far. That would be only ten under this ridiculous new proposal, meaning 44 teams staying home. Last year (1997–98), it was 77 teams in 17 sports. Only 17 go and 60 stay home. Really worthwhile." Cited by Covell (1999), p. 22.

20. "NESCAC Presidents Decision on Post-season Participation: Teams Permitted to Accept NCAA At-large Bids for 2001–02," news release, September 28, 2001. There is a related issue concerning conflicts between the scheduling of national championships and course examinations. Currently NESCAC allows individual schools to request (or not to request) waivers, a policy that was at the bottom of the 1995 controversy at Williams over whether the women's lacrosse team (and other teams) could compete that year. The question of whether there should be a binding conference-wide policy or local autonomy is tied directly to the broader issue of how much authority the conference should have over its members. For a good discussion of this issue, see Vélez, pp. 34–36.

21. Vélez, p. 22.

22. Edwards's report is reproduced in Vélez, and the quotations in the text are from pp. 5 and 9. Vélez discusses the use of the African proverb on p. 43 of her own report. Certainly the kind of success enjoyed in athletics by Williams spurs other members of the conference to recruit more aggressively, build better facilities, and so on. Vélez quotes a May 1997 article in the *Wesleyan Argus Magazine* as noting "with frustration" that "Williams, a school almost half Wesleyan's size which prides itself on athletics and whose winning percentage is consistently in the 70s, was awarded the Sears Cup last year as the top Division III sports program in the nation. *Not in NESCAC. In the country*" (p. 44; emphasis in original).

23. A limitation of 75 was adopted in 1997 and went into effect in September 2001. New England Small College Athletic Association, *NESCAC Manual: Agreement and Official Interpretations,* revised (n.p.: NESCAC, September 25, 2002), p. 20.

24. Vélez, p. 28.

25. Data are taken from Figures 5.1a, 5.3a, 5.4a, and 6.1b. The recruited male athletes in the Lower Profile sports and the recruited women athletes in the NESCAC colleges also differ significantly from their classmates in these respects, even though the gaps are largest among the men in the High Profile sports.

26. President Edwards of Bowdoin recognized this point clearly in his report on football when he noted that the issues of "judgment" that he was raising about football might seem "quixotic in an age in which NESCAC is widely viewed as a clearing in the jungle of egregious greed and corruption in sport" (p. 2).

27. Text of statement, dated October 1, 2001, as provided by William D. Adams, president of Colby and the chair of the NESCAC Presidents' Conference Committee at the time the statement was prepared.

28. NESCAC (2002), pp. 18–19.

29. See the description of the founding of the UAA in the addendum to the introduction.

30. Rasmussen (1997), p. 127. Brandeis and New York University each participated in 20 sports out of the 22 sponsored by the UAA, and at the other extreme, Johns Hopkins participated in just 11. For a summary by school, see Rasmussen (1997), figure 8, p. 130.

31. At the key planning meeting in Rochester, Rasmussen presented detailed projections based on carefully crafted models of competition that, in turn, had imbedded within them strategies for minimizing costs (such as having men's and women's teams travel together and having men's and women's festivals held at the same place and the same time). Everyone recognized that, in Rasmussen's words, "the level of funding required to support team travel among [the geographically dispersed] UAA institutions represented a substantial increase in funding over levels provided for purely regional competition. . . . Estimates provided by Mr. Rasmussen during the initial meetings at Rochester suggested that the increase in costs could range on the high end from $240,000 to $326,000 over current levels. . . . This generally represented an increase of 10 percent to 20 percent in funding for athletics among these institutions. Because the concept of the UAA was an initiative of chief executive officers and senior academic administrators, these increases were evaluated more in the context of the overall operating budgets of the institutions rather than in the context of their athletics budgets. As one chief executive commented when asked about the financial commitment during a campus press conference to announce the formation of the UAA, the increase amounted to less than two hundredths of a percent of the overall operating budget of the institution. . . . The expected returns to the institutions would come in the form of direct benefits to the participants, improvements in the quality of student life on campus, an enhancement of institutional identity through association with the other members, greater institutional visibility, and recruitment of new students." Rasmussen (1997), pp. 125–26. Similarly, the director of athletics at Brandeis (Jeff Cohen) told us that moving from prior (regional) arrangements to compete in the UAA raised expenses roughly $300,000 a year. Cohen related a story in which one faculty member cornered him and asked, "How can you justify spending the millions of dollars you do to travel all over the country with your athletes?" To which Cohen responded: "If only you knew what we actually spend." The fact that all of the UAA universities are in urban centers with major metropolitan airports close at hand has been important in keeping travel costs under control and was one of the criteria that the UAA had in mind in considering potential candidates for membership.

32. We were unable to obtain data on travel costs in the Ivies (which are reported on worksheets that the Ivy League preferred to keep confidential), but it may be as revealing to make another kind of comparison: with *recruiting* costs, which are reported on publicly available Equity in Athletics Disclosure Act (EADA) forms that all coeducational institutions in the NCAA are required to fill out for Title IX compliance purposes. Direct recruiting costs in the UAA average $93,000. In the Ivy League, on the other hand, direct recruiting costs (which do not include salary allocations despite the major amounts of time devoted by

coaches to recruiting) average $616,000—more than the $522,000 of travel costs per UAA school. A summary of these and other cost data, including total expenditures for men's and women's sports and figures for some individual sports, is provided in Appendix Tables 7.1, 7.2a, and 7.2b. The data on travel costs are based on our analysis of the worksheets underlying the EADA forms that were supplied to us by 5 of the 8 UAA members and 10 of the 11 NESCAC colleges. Direct recruiting costs for the Ivies are taken from the public EADA forms.

33. Several coaches told us that their players enjoy traveling to New York and other major cities, the camaraderie engendered by team travel, and getting to know players on other teams. Professor Starkey Duncan at the University of Chicago observed: "Students like the UAA much better than the arrangement they had before. Flying off to New York is much better than busing to Grinnell."

34. Washington University and Emory have been strong competitors more or less across the board, but other individual schools have found niches that work for them: New York University in fencing, Brandeis in track and field, and so on. Moreover, the short history of the UAA reveals that there is a "pendulum effect"; some universities will do poorly for a time but will then resuscitate teams, usually as a result of coaching changes. Detailed records of team championships, players of the year by sport, and team finishes by year in all sports are contained in the UAA "Record Book."

35. In addition to thinking about why some schools have dropped out of the UAA (either partially or entirely), it is useful to consider the reasons why MIT, which was one of the 10 universities that actively discussed forming the UAA, decided not to join but rather to go its own way. In summarizing why MIT eventually decided not to participate, Rasmussen notes that "MIT was . . . the most academically selective of the institutions invited to the UAA meetings. . . . Its athletic program was also the most extensive, not just among this group but among all institutions regardless of division within the NCAA. MIT sponsored intercollegiate athletic competition in thirty-six sports. . . . MIT had its pick of teams when it came to scheduling. . . . Because of its reputation and the nature of the institute, MIT recruited students very successfully on a national basis. Ninety-five percent of its students were from out of state [and many were foreign students]. In short, many of the factors and circumstances that moved other research universities to consider an association like the UAA did not carry the same import for MIT." Rasmussen (1997), p. 85. The leadership of MIT also expressed great concern about the time away from campus that would be required of its student athletes, given the rigor of its academic offerings and the large number of labs. MIT today has tight restrictions on absences from campus and from class, including a policy precluding overnight trips for sports competitions (unless special permission is obtained). A further consideration was that participating in the UAA in some sports but not others would inevitably create a tiered athletics program at MIT, given the large number of sports that it sponsors. MIT also thought that the UAA was putting too much emphasis on athletics by flying students all over the country to play. Finally, MIT differs from almost all other schools in that it has an extensive physical education requirement (as does the University of Chicago); coaches are expected to have degrees in physical education, and all teach physical education

classes. In short, MIT inhabits an entirely different world. Candace Royer, director of athletics at MIT, believes that the conference in which MIT competes today, the New England Women's and Men's Athletic Conference, is a good fit in terms of academic priorities and athletics programs and is very convenient from the standpoint of geography. There is no doubt about MIT's commitment to athletics—it is building a $50 million athletic facility—but the emphasis is on serving graduate and undergraduate students of all kinds, as well as faculty and staff. MIT represents a model of intercollegiate athletics that is entirely different from any of the others described in this study.

Three other universities were invited to join the initial discussions that led to the formation of the UAA. One, Cal Tech, declined outright, in part because of its location on the West Coast and in part because it just was "very different" (like MIT). The other two, Rice and Tulane, indicated interest but declined to attend the initial meetings primarily for what Rasmussen calls "political reasons" related primarily to trustee views. According to Rasmussen, "Administrators from Rice and Tulane indicated strong personal preferences for athletic competition within a Division III context. Their current athletic programs were a financial drain, and they routinely faced conflicts between the academic and athletic interests of the institution. But the sagas of their athletic programs, their alumni interest, ties to boosters in the community and state, and the ethos of bigtime sports in their area of the country formed what for them was an insurmountable hurdle to a change as radical as moving to Division III." Rasmussen (1997), p. 84.

36. The UAA football players have an average GPA that puts them in the 40th percentile of their class; the Ivy League football players rank, on average, in the 21st percentile and the NESCAC players in the 26th percentile (Table 5.4 and Figures 5.5a and 5.5c).

37. Chapter 6, especially Figures 6.1a, 6.1b, 6.1c. There does appear to be a mild tendency toward underperformance among High Profile male athletes in the UAA—nothing like what we see elsewhere, but still worth noting. When we look specifically at football and control for differences in race, field of study, SAT scores, and institutional selectivity (Table 6.5a), we do find significant underperformance.

38. Andrew Schaffer, general counsel at New York University with oversight of athletics, repeated (in an interview) a mantra a number of others have articulated when he said: "If you don't have football, don't get it."

39. UAA (2002a), p. 1.

40. See Appendix Table 8.1 for standings in the Sears Cup competition and Appendix Table 8.2b for a summary of recent results in NCAA Division III championships achieved by various schools in this study. The dominance of NESCAC is clear.

41. William M. Chace, "Athletics and Academic Values Don't Have to Compete at a Research University," *Emory Edge*, February 2002, p. 1.

42. Gordon White, "Colleges Find Advantages in Conferences," *New York Times*, February 24, 1980, p. S10. The theme of the article is the growing role of conferences in defining eligibility for NCAA championships and shares in NCAA revenues. This trend continues today and has led the NCAA to tighten eligibility rules for membership in Division IA.

Chapter 8　The Widening Athletic Divide

1. Amherst Special Committee, p. 30.

2. Williams Ad Hoc Committee, p. 9.

3. Amherst Special Committee, pp. 28–29. The report goes on to say: "According to one faculty member, the hostility toward athletic programs expressed by a 'small, but very vocal, group of Amherst faculty,' has 'created a perception among many students that a group of faculty members is simply biased against athletes.' Is it any wonder, this faculty member mused, that there is a 'great divide' between athletes and non-athletes? 'Groups that feel persecuted tend to become insular, do they not?'" (p. 30).

4. Even within the UAA universities, which have avoided paying the same academic price for their recruitment of athletes as have the NESCAC colleges and the Ivies, we have heard similar refrains about the separation of athletes from other students (compounded, in the case of the UAA, by the heavy travel schedules of the athletes). In the coed liberal arts colleges outside NESCAC, football seems to create a "divide" all its own.

5. Rasmussen (2002), p. 9.

6. Jennifer Jacobson, "Dashing from Classroom to Locker Room: Professionalization of Sports and the Demands on Professors Make the Dual Role Difficult," *Chronicle of Higher Education,* May 3, 2002, p. A39.

7. Malekoff (2002), p. 4.

8. Lambert, p. 40. Lambert quotes Harvard Track and Field Coach Frank Haggerty: "Coaches seem to develop a sense of proprietary right over the student. We really have to guard against it. It's a very natural by-product of recruiting: you worked hard to identify these kids, convinced them to apply to Harvard, then they get in. But once they get here, suppose they want to play another sport or find something more attractive than athletics? For a coach, it's hard not to be frustrated. You don't own them."

9. Shulman and Bowen, especially Scorecards 3.2 and 3.6.

10. To cite just one striking statistic, 50 percent of High Profile athletes in the coed liberal arts colleges now majored in the social sciences, as compared with 29 percent of the students at large; in the 1951 entering cohort, 25 percent of the High Profile athletes at these colleges majored in the social sciences, as compared with 24 percent of the students at large (Scorecard 3.6).

11. Williams Ad Hoc Committee, p. 1.

12. Campbell, p. 3.

13. Biddiscombe, p. 1.

14. Teresa M. Walker, "Justices Consider Dispute over Prep Sports Recruiting," *Associated Press State and Local Wire,* October 8, 2000, Sports News.

15. Kathy Slobogin, "Toddler Athletes a Growing Trend," CNN.com, June 7, 2002, available at http://www.cnn.com/2002/HEALTH/06/06/cov.super. toddlers/index.html.

16. Robin Lester credits the University of Chicago with initiating the "professionalization" of college coaching in America by appointing Amos Alonzo Stagg as "Associate Professor and Director of the Department of Physical Culture and Athletics" with full tenure. Lester, p. 17. Ironically, it is the move away from fac-

ulty status and tenure appointments that is today associated with the further professionalization of coaching.

17. The *Chronicle of Higher Education* article cited earlier profiles a professor of political science at Whittier College (Michael J. McBride) who has coached its women's softball team for most of the past two decades. But the main story line emphasizes how unusual this arrangement has become: "There were once a fair number of people like Mr. McBride coaching in the afternoons, and many a coach taught physical education or other subjects. . . . But now virtually all of the few coaches who still teach in the classroom are at small, liberal arts colleges, with programs in Division III of the NCAA. The professionalization of both jobs (demands for top-notch scholarship from professors and for time-intensive recruiting and preparation for coaches) has made it nearly impossible for professors to coach, or coaches to teach." Jacobson, p. A39.

18. Peter Slovenski, "How You Play the Game," unpublished essay sent to James Shulman and William G. Bowen, February 14, 2002.

19. Larry D. Hensley, "Current Status of Basic Instruction Programs in Physical Education at American Colleges and Universities," *Journal of Physical Education, Recreation and Dance* 71 (9) (Nov.–Dec. 2000): 30–36. Just under 50 percent of the schools in Hensley's study require students to have physical education credit to graduate. Among the schools in this study, physical education is required in 3 out of 8 of the Ivies, 4 out of 8 of the UAA schools, 5 out of 11 of the NESCAC schools, 3 out of 7 of the other coed liberal arts colleges, and 2 out of 3 of the women's colleges. (The figures are based on descriptions found in the schools' catalogs and at their Web sites.)

20. Campbell, p. 9.

21. Malekoff (2002), p. 8.

22. Biddiscombe, p. 6.

23. Malekoff (2002), p. 8. Similar sentiments were expressed, in almost the same language, by a number of other directors of athletics.

24. Rasmussen (2002), p. 7.

25. Biddiscombe observes: "In Division III basketball, some college teams have a head coach, an offensive coach, a person responsible for teaching defense, and another who coordinates scouting" (p. 6).

26. Biddiscombe, p. 6.

27. Rasmussen (2002), p. 8.

28. Malekoff (2002), p. 9. Campbell comments: "As institutions invest more resources and provide auxiliary structures which support athletics, there is a greater expectation of winning. Even in Division III, coaches are dismissed if they are not successful. . . . All one needs to do is to watch the transaction section in the sports section following the football or basketball season to see the dramatic effect winning and losing has on coach employment." Campbell, p. 10. Biddiscome at Wesleyan observes: "The life of a losing coach is not fun. In today's athletic environment, even good coaches who continually lose will not survive." He adds that, therefore, "It is important for college administrators to provide the resources and the tools for coaches to be successful or withstand the pressure to release a competent coach whose teams are losing. . . . The high cost of attracting the most qualified athletes must be recognized." Biddiscombe, p. 7.

The late James Tobin (a Nobel laureate in economics on the Yale faculty) recalled when Bart Giamatti appointed him to the faculty athletics advisory committee in the late 1970s: "I found that the other faculty members were Jocks." Tobin went on (in a personal letter to Bowen, dated Dec. 12, 2001) to report: "When the Director of Athletics told us that he had to fire the lacrosse coach, my questions elicited the information that the coach was an excellent teacher of the game, he just couldn't recruit a winning team. So what, I asked. . . . The trouble is, the AD said, that Cornell and Princeton have national aspirations in lacrosse, and the rest of the league has to keep up."

29. Rasmussen (2002), p. 7.

30. These averages were calculated from the publicly available EADA (Equity in Athletics Disclosure Act) forms for each school for the year 2000–01. We summed the number of FTEs in head coaching and assistant coaching roles for men's and women's teams. In some respects, even these figures understate the true situation. For example, they do not include "stipend/intern" coaches at Princeton (where, according to the university's EADA report, there were 37 in 2000–01 in addition to the 47 full-time-equivalents in the "Head Coach" and "Assistant Coach" columns).

31. Biddiscombe, p. 6.

32. William Holder, "NESCAC Fights the Trend," *Wesleyan,* Spring 2002, p. 18.

33. Malekoff (2002), p. 9.

34. Rasmussen (2002), p. 8.

35. Campbell, p. 12.

36. According to Falla, this competition was held "to determine the national intercollegiate champion" (p. 177).

37. Falla, pp. 177–81; see also National Collegiate Athletic Association (NCAA), "A Brief Chronological History of the National Intercollegiate Championship Series," in *NCAA National Collegiate Championships Records* (Indianapolis, Ind.: NCAA, 2000), pp. 9–12.

38. Quoted in Malekoff (2002), p. 2. The capsule history in this paragraph is based largely on Malekoff's excellent summary of major events.

39. Falla and NCAA (2000).

40. Shulman and Bowen provide a summary of the debate and references to the extensive literature associated with it (chapter 5).

41. Biddiscombe, p. 8.

42. Malekoff (2002), p. 9. It is of course the huge financial success of the NCAA Division I basketball tournament ("March Madness") that provides the financial fuel for all of these activities. The contract negotiated between the NCAA and CBS Sports is "worth a minimum of $6 billion over 11 years." Welch Suggs, "CBS to Pay $6 Billion for TV Rights to NCAA Basketball Championships," *Chronicle of Higher Education,* December 3, 1999, p. A54. Suggs goes on to note: "The NCAA keeps 6 percent of the revenue to finance some of its own costs, including the operation of its assorted championships." The NCAA distribution to the Ivy League amounted to $3,708,302 in 2001–02. In addition to this sum, the Ivies received a portion of the $45,505,840 that went to support Division I championships. Although Division III schools do not participate in the same type of revenue-sharing plan as the Ivies, they do receive NCAA support for championships and

programs, an amount that came to $9,832,397 in 2001–02. The NCAA also covers the premiums for catastrophic injury insurance for schools in all divisions. See National Collegiate Athletic Association (NCAA), "NCAA Revenue Distribution: Total Distribution to Members," available at http://www1.ncaa.org/finance/7-yr_conf_summaries/total_distribution, accessed November 26, 2002; NCAA, *2001 NCAA Membership Report*, April 1, 2002, available at http://www.ncaa.org/library/membership/membership_report/2001; NCAA, "Proposed Budget for Fiscal Year Ended August 31, 2003," July 30, 2002, available at http://www.ncaa.org/financial/2002-03_budget.pdf. We discuss the importance of NCAA financial support for Division III in Chapter 13.

43. Dempsey's speech is mentioned in Welch Suggs, "New NCAA President Calls for Gender Equity, Stronger Commitment to Reform," *Chronicle of Higher Education,* January 13, 2003, online edition.

44. National Association of Collegiate Directors of Athletics (NACDA), "Sears Directors' Cup Final Standings," available at http://nacda.ocsn.com/searsdirectorscup/nacda-searsdirectorscup-previous-scoring.html, updated June 18, 2002. Before the fall 2002 season, Sears terminated its sponsorship of the award and it is now known as the NACDA Directors' Cup. Because this study deals with the years before this change, we refer to the award as the Sears Cup throughout the book.

45. Campbell, p. 11.

46. Witkin and Schneider.

47. New England Small College Athletic Conference (NESCAC), "Statement by the NESCAC Presidents in Declining to Participate in a *U.S. News & World Report* Survey of NCAA Division III Athletic Programs," press release, February 11, 2003, available at http://www.nescac.com/Releases/NESCAC_U.S.News%20Survey%20Statement.htm. In the statement, the NESCAC presidents explain that rankings of athletics programs, such as the one proposed by *U.S. News,* "raise serious concerns for us with regard both to the validity of such rankings and to their effect in influencing our own priorities."

48. "College Sports Gets Network," *New York Times,* June 7, 2002, Sports Desk, p. D2. Allen and Company, which helped back the network now operating as ESPN Classic, is one of the investors in the new network.

49. Biddiscombe, p. 8

50. Campbell, p. 2.

51. Malekoff, p. 11.

52. Biddiscombe, p. 8.

53. Malekoff (2002), p. 10.

54. Letter dated May 31, 2002.

55. Rasmussen (2002), p. 10.

56. Campbell, p. 11.

57. In 1971–72 there were 29,992 women playing college sports (170,384 men); in 2000–01 there were 150,916 women playing on varsity teams (208,866 men). This nearly sixfold increase in women's participation did not occur steadily and was in fact slow in building, in part because of considerable uncertainty as to what Title IX really meant and how it was to be interpreted and enforced. (See discussion in note 62.)

58. The 30th anniversary of the adoption of Title IX has led to an outpouring of opinion pieces and efforts to assess what has been accomplished as well as open issues. See, for example, Welch Suggs, "Title IX at 30," *Chronicle of Higher Education,* June 21, 2002, pp. A38–A42; Billie Jean King, "For All the Good Things It Has Done, Title IX Is Still Plagued by Myths," *New York Times,* June 23, 2002, sports section, p. 7; Sally Jenkins, "Title IX Opponents a Bunch of Sad Sacks," *Washington Post,* June 24, 2002, p. D01; "A Sporting Chance for Girls," editorial, *New York Times,* June 2, 2002, section 4, p. 12; and Ellen Goodman, "No Letup in Myth-Making about Women and Sports," *Boston Globe,* June 20, 2002, p. A15. One reason for the tenor of a number of these pieces is that opponents of the ways in which Title IX has been interpreted continue to ask the U.S. Department of Education to modify how the law is applied. See, for example, Christopher Flores, "Wrestling Coaches Sue Department of Education Over Title IX," *Chronicle of Higher Education,* January 17, 2002, online edition. See also Jodi Schneider, "The Fairness Factor," *U.S. News & World Report* (March 18, 2002): 63–65. The National Women's Law Center, on the other hand, has criticized colleges for failing to provide a "fair share" of athletics resources, including scholarships, to women. National Women's Law Center, "The Battle for Gender Equity in Athletics: Title IX at Thirty," a report of the National Women's Law Center, June 2002. Most recently, as Welch Suggs reports, the Education Department has convened a "Commission on Opportunities in Athletics" to study the effects of Title IX on college sports. Suggs, "Education Department Announces Panel to Review and Strengthen Title IX," *Chronicle of Higher Education,* June 28, 2002, online edition.

59. See the discussions in the addendum to Chapter 1 and in Shulman and Bowen, chapter 5. For an excellent history of the AIAW and its interactions with the NCAA, see Mary Jo Festle, *Playing Nice: Politics and Policies in Women's Sports* (New York: Columbia University Press, 1996); see also Welch. For background on the long history of women and athletics, see Allen Guttmann, *Women's Sports: A History* (New York: Columbia University Press, 1991). For more detail on men's views of the acceptability of women's playing sports, see Donald J. Mrozek, "The 'Amazon' and the American 'Lady,'" in *The New American Sport History: Recent Approaches and Perspectives,* edited by S. W. Pope (Urbana: University of Illinois Press, 1997), pp. 198–214. For accounts of the NCAA takeover, see Festle, Chapter 8; Murray Sperber, "The NCAA as Predator: The Rape of the Association for Intercollegiate Athletics for Women," in *College Sports, Inc.* (New York: Henry Holt), pp. 322–32. See also the account by Merrily Dean Baker in Welch, pp. 60–64.

60. It has not proven easy to close this gap. The gender gap in participation rates is present today (or at least was at the time of the '95 entering cohort) at every set of coed schools in the study, with the size of the gap ranging from a low of 2 percentage points in the UAA to a high of 11 points in NESCAC (Figure 1.2). At the seven coed liberal arts colleges for which we can make the comparison, the female participation rate increased from 19 to 23 percent between the '89 and '95 cohorts, but the male participation rate also increased, from 32 to 35 percent. Data for the '89 cohort are reported in Shulman and Bowen.

61. Rasmussen (1997), p. 21.

62. The relevant history is fairly recent. It was not until 1988, when Congress passed the Civil Rights Restoration Act, that closure was achieved on the key is-

sue of whether Title IX applied to *all* operations of any institution receiving federal funds (including athletics) or only to specific programs that were federally funded. Then, in 1992, the Supreme Court ruled that students can sue educational institutions under Title IX for monetary damages. In 1996 Brown University lost a closely watched case in which it was found to have discriminated against female athletes by dropping their sports (discussed in Chapter 12). In that same year, the Department of Education issued a "policy clarification" affirming its 1979 guidelines and emphasizing what is called the "substantial proportionality" test—which means that achieving a close match between the proportion of athletes who are female and the proportion of undergraduates who are female is a "safe harbor." See Suggs (2002d) for an extended discussion of this history; an even more detailed chronology may be found at the Web site of the University of Iowa Gender Equity in Sports Project (http://bailiwick.lib.uiowa.edu/ge), last updated October 16, 2000. It is true, as the report of the National Women's Law Center emphasizes, that a school can be in compliance by meeting any part of the so-called "three-pronged" test, which includes not just achieving "substantial proportionality" but also demonstrating that it either "has a history and a continuing practice of expanding opportunities for female students" or "is fully and effectively meeting its female students' interests and abilities to participate in sports." However, schools seem reluctant to rely on satisfying either of these other two tests, which are more subjective and less quantitative.

At the smaller Division III colleges, the "substantial proportionality" test of Title IX may have even greater direct effects on the academic-athletic divide than it does at larger (and wealthier) schools in this study. This is the line of argument developed by David Hooks in his dissertation titled "Complying with Title IX: An Examination of the Effects on Three NCAA Division III Colleges in Pennsylvania and the Difficulties the Law's Interpretation Has Created for Small Colleges Attempting to Achieve Gender Equity" (University of Pennsylvania, 1998). Hooks argues that small colleges are often more worried about the threat of lawsuits than larger schools that are better able to defend themselves (p. 218). This is a serious concern, because these schools (which cannot offer athletic scholarships and generally have a much thinner applicant pool than the Ivies or the NESCAC colleges) have difficulty getting sufficient numbers of women to commit to their schools as student athletes. The danger, then, is that to meet the quantitative tests of Title IX schools of this kind with football programs "would have to attempt to recruit an inordinate number of female prospects" (p. 220).

The Education Department's Commission on Opportunities in Athletics has made several recommendations that could alter the tests for meeting Title IX significantly. The commission's proposals include using surveys to determine athletic interest, counting the number of roster spots or the number of recruited athletes instead of the number of actual participating athletes in proportionality calculations, redefining substantial proportionality to include "wiggle room" of 3 to 4 percentage points, and exempting "non-traditional" students (part-time students or students who begin their undergraduate careers several years after finishing high school—most of whom are women) from the measure of total undergraduate students. Welch Suggs, "Smoke Obscures Fire in Title IX Debate as Federal Panel Adjourns," *Chronicle of Higher Education*, February 7, 2003, online edition.

Responding to the publication of the commission's report, *"Open to All": Title IX at Thirty,* Education Secretary Roderick R. Paige said that his department will act only on the 15 recommendations approved unanimously by commission members. These include suggestions that the Department of Education "give equal weight to all three parts of the test governing Title IX compliance and encourage schools to understand that the Department of Education disapproves of cutting teams in order to comply with Title IX." Welch Suggs, "Cheers and Condemnation Greet Report on Gender Equity: Federal Panel Focuses on Protecting Men's Sports, to the Dismay of Women's Advocates," *Chronicle of Higher Education,* March 7, 2003, online edition; U.S. Department of Education, Secretary's Commission on Opportunity in Athletics, *"Open to All": Title IX at Thirty* (Washington, D.C.: Department of Education, 2003), available online at http://www.ed.gov/inits/commissionsboards/athletics; and Roderick Paige, "Statement Regarding Final Report of Commission on Opportunity in Athletics," February 26, 2003, available at http://www.ed.gov/pressreleases/02-2003/02262003a.html.

63. Indeed, a main focus of the report of the Women's Law Center is on the failure of Division I programs to provide women with a "fair share" of athletics scholarships. See Welch Suggs, "Women's Law Group Warns 30 Colleges about Imbalances in Athletic Scholarships," *Chronicle of Higher Education,* June 19, 2002, online edition.

64. The change in coaching patterns is very clear. According to Lena Williams, "When Title IX was enacted, more than 90 percent of women's teams were coached by women. Currently, 45.6 percent of the coaches of women's teams are women.... Of the 534 new [coaching jobs in women's sports] in the last two years, women have been hired in only 107." Williams, "Women Play More, but Coach Less," *New York Times,* May 3, 2000, p. D8. The author is summarizing results obtained by R. Vivian Acosta and Linda Jean Carpenter in the most recent update of their continuing studies of women's sports.

65. Festle documents in extraordinary detail the way in which fear of legal consequences, dating back to the early 1970s, eventually drove the NCAA to "embrace" women's sports and sponsor national championships for women. She writes: "The NCAA's concern centered around avoiding trouble, not doing the right thing. The well-being of female athletes and women's sports appeared to be conspicuously absent from the NCAA's list of priorities." Festle, p. 119.

66. Vélez, p. 14.

67. Donna Lopiano, executive director of the Women's Sports Foundation, is quoted as follows in a story in the *New York Times:* "It's Not Title IX's fault, it's chicken college presidents and athletic directors who won't bite the bullet on the irresponsible spending of their football programs." See Bill Pennington, "More Men's Teams Benched as Colleges Level the Field," *New York Times,* May 9, 2002, pp. A1, D4; quote on p. A1. Pennington then goes on to cite many situations in which men's programs are being cut, often because of concerns about achieving "substantial proportionality." Lopiano's position is supported by (among many others) Emeritus Professor Joseph S. Larson of the University of Massachusetts, who criticized Athletic Director Robert Marcum for proposing the elimination of Lower Profile male teams in order to meet budget requirements rather than moving football into a non-scholarship conference—which, he argues, would have "al-

lowed the campus to maintain all current men's and women's teams." Larson, letters to the editor, *Chronicle of Higher Education,* May 10, 2002, p. B22. John R. Thelin provides a useful historical analysis of the "political economy" of inter-collegiate athletics and concludes that it is unfair to blame Title IX for the budg-etary problems of big-time men's sports in "Good Sports? Historical Perspective on the Political Economy of Intercollegiate Athletics in the Era of Title IX, 1972–1997," *Journal of Higher Education* 71 (4) (July–August 2000): 391–410.

Data collected by the national General Accounting Office speak directly to some of the issues in the debate over the effects of Title IX on the number of men's teams. Between 1981–82 and 1998–99, the number of men's teams in-creased (from 9,113 to 9,149)—rebutting any simple assertion that the addition of women's teams has led to an equivalent reduction in the number of men's teams. U.S. General Accounting Office (U.S. GAO), *Intercollegiate Athletics: Four-Year Colleges' Experiences Adding and Discontinuing Teams: Report to Congressional Re-questers* (GAO-01-297) (Washington, D.C.: The Office), March 2001, pp. 12–13. The number of men's teams has, in fact, increased markedly in sports like soccer and lacrosse at the same time that there has been a decrease in the number of men's teams in some other sports, with wrestling the most extreme case. Between 1981–82 and 1998–99, the number of men's soccer teams increased from 744 to 879, the number of lacrosse teams from 138 to 197; the number of wrestling teams fell from 428 to 257. More generally, the GAO report found that "about 80 per-cent of schools added one or more women's sports teams during the 1992–93 to 1999–2000 period, and more than two-thirds did so without discontinuing any teams." Yet there is, of course, the "other third," and concerns for gender equity were one of three reasons cited most frequently for the elimination of men's teams ("insufficient student interest" and "resources needed for other sports" were the other two main reasons). See U.S. GAO, pp. 13, 14, 19.

The tables in the GAO report also indicate in which women's sports the largest increases in numbers of teams have occurred. The biggest increase has occurred in women's soccer (where the number of teams increased from 80 in 1981–82 to 926 in 1998–99), but recently there has been an upsurge in the number of women's rowing programs, in part because rowing teams can accommodate large numbers of participants. In describing the crew program at UCLA, Jodi Schnei-der notes that "UCLA added varsity women's crew this year not only to provide sporting opportunities but to comply with one of the key requirements of . . . Ti-tle IX [proportionality]." See Schneider, p. 63.

68. Bill Finley with Brandon Lilly, "St. John's Cites Fairness in Cutting 5 Men's Teams," *New York Times,* December 14, 2002, p. D5.

69. For example, the 1994 Gender Equity Assessment carried out by NESCAC explicitly says that "dropping men's sports in order to achieve the goal of equity in our athletic programs is not a method which we support. Not only would such actions be in direct opposition of NESCAC and NCAA Division III philosophies which place a premium on participation, but cutting men's sports in effect limits opportunities for women." Quoted in Vélez, p. 13.

70. Quoted in Pennington (2002a).

71. Jane R. Eisner, "Title IX Levels the Field in Aspects Good and Bad," *Arizona Republic,* January 29, 2001, p. B7. Another commentator (a sports sociologist) ex-

presses a similar thought in the language of her own discipline: "Female athletes have been required to legitimatize themselves as athletes within a value system that says you have to be brutish and willing to do anything to win. Of course women are capable of doing that. So they chase the phantom of legitimacy, and the bar keeps moving. Masculine culture gets hyper-masculinized, and the stakes keep getting higher and higher. Women are constantly in pursuit, and men never turn around to see that women might have something to offer. . . . That dynamic doesn't produce what I would call progress." Ellen Staurowsky, Ithaca College, quoted in *NCAA News,* May 13, 2002, p. 4.

Chapter 9   The Athletic Divide in Context

1. Columbia University, Princeton University, the University of Pennsylvania, and Yale University are the four Ivy League universities included in the original College and Beyond database; however, Columbia is excluded from the average shown for women in Figure 9.1b since it was not coeducational in 1976. The Division III universities include Emory University, Tufts University, and Washington University in St. Louis (even though Tufts is in NESCAC, not the UAA). The coed liberal arts colleges in this study include Denison University, Kenyon College, Oberlin College, Swarthmore College, Wesleyan University, and Williams College. The women's colleges in this study for which we have consistent data are Bryn Mawr College, Smith College, and Wellesley College. The SATs were re-centered after the April 1995 test, and so data for the 1995 entering cohort are unaffected by the recentering and thus comparable with the SATs of earlier cohorts.

2. Caroline M. Hoxby, "The Effects of Geographic Integration and Increasing Competition in the Market for College Education," May 2000 revision of NBER Working Paper No. 6323, appendix table 1, p. 46. For an explanation of the construction of her panel, see Hoxby (2000), p. 21. Reasons for the decline in all SAT scores include the much larger population of students who pursue higher education now than in earlier years, the socioeconomic and ethnic diversity of this population, and the increase in foreign students attending American colleges and universities. The steady decline in average SAT scores led to a recentering of the SAT after the April 1995 test, and SAT scores reported today are, on average, 60 to 80 points higher than they were before recentering. None of the SAT data in this study have had to be adjusted to correct for recentering.

3. This paper by Cook and Frank appears in Charles T. Clotfelter and Michael Rothschild, eds., *Studies of Supply and Demand in Higher Education* (Chicago: University of Chicago Press, 1993), pp. 121–44. See this paper and the references cited therein for an explanation of the term *tournament.* See also their later book *The Winner-Take-All Society: How More and More Americans Compete for Ever Fewer and Bigger Prizes, Encouraging Economic Waste, Income Inequality, and Impoverished Cultural Life* (New York: Free Press, 1995).

4. Cited in Cook and Frank, p. 133. More specifically, this particular comparison is for a student with the following characteristics: "white Protestant male only child, financially dependent on his parents, resident of the Middle Atlantic states, public high school graduate in the top 10 percent of his class, father with college degree, applicant for financial aid, family income is $40,000 in 1987 dollars."

Estimates based on most other combinations of characteristics would show essentially the same pattern.

5. Hoxby (2000). The following quotation is from p. 1.

6. Ibid., p. 10. For a more extensive discussion of the factors that have caused college market integration, see Caroline M. Hoxby, "The Changing Market Structure of U.S. Higher Education," mimeo, Harvard University, 1997.

7. Hoxby (2000), table 1b, p. 10. Hoxby also uses a number of other measures (including a Herfindahl Index of Concentration) to support this same point.

8. Hoxby (2000), appendix table 1, p. 46, and appendix figure 4, p. 52.

9. Ibid., p. 41.

10. Taylor Reveley, letter to Bowen, July 8, 2002.

11. There is no shortage of anecdotes concerning faculty members who lack good command of the English language or are otherwise thought to be unsuitable as undergraduate teachers or advisors—and the presumption is that faculty with less interest in undergraduates will be especially uninterested in undergraduates who assign priority to a non-academic activity such as athletics. It is much more difficult to find reliable evidence as to the actual state of affairs. The faculty surveys conducted by the Higher Education Research Institute at UCLA are one source. Surprisingly (given the concerns frequently expressed), answers to one relevant question fail to suggest that less emphasis is being placed on teaching. In 1989–90, 10.8 percent of respondents at private universities listed "faculty rewarded for good teaching" among the attributes "noted as being very descriptive of the institution"; in 1998–99, the corresponding figure was higher, not lower (14.5 percent). At private four-year colleges, the corresponding figure was 19.2 percent in both years. Alexander W. Astin, William S. Korn, and Eric L. Dey, *The American College Teacher: National Norms for the 1989–90 HERI Faculty Survey* (Los Angeles: Higher Education Research Institute, UCLA, 1990); Linda J. Sax, Alexander W. Astin, William S. Korn, and Shannon K. Gilmartin, *The American College Teacher: National Norms for the 1998–99 HERI Faculty Survey* (Los Angeles: Higher Education Research Institute, UCLA, 1999). Similarly, the authors of a recent study of shifts in faculty time allocations between 1972 and 1992 conclude: "Our findings provide rather compelling evidence refuting the assertions of many critics of higher education that faculty are spending less time engaged in teaching. . . . The greatest proportional increase in teaching time occurred at liberal arts colleges." On the other hand: "Across all institutions, there was a statistically significant decrease in the amount of time faculty spent advising and counseling students." Jeffrey F. Milem, Joseph B. Berger, and Eric L. Dey, "Faculty Time Allocation," *Journal of Higher Education,* 71 (4) (July–August 2000): 454–75; quotes on pp. 466–67.

12. Some have also suggested that the "internationalization" of graduate training and faculty recruitment has led to an increase in the relative number of classroom teachers who were born overseas or are still foreign citizens—the presumption being that these individuals will be less familiar than most American-born faculty with traditional American college activities, including intercollegiate sports, and perhaps less sympathetic to the scheduling complications and other priorities of students who compete on intercollegiate teams. It is certainly true that there has been a steady increase in the share of doctorate recipients who have come here for graduate study from outside the United States. In-

formation from the Survey of Doctorate Recipients (SDR) on the countries of origin of faculty shows that the percentage of full-time science (including social science) and engineering faculty who are foreign-born grew from 11.04 percent in 1973 to 15.5 percent in 1985 to 18.5 percent in 1999. National Science Board, *Science and Engineering Indicators—2002* (Arlington, Va.: National Science Foundation, 2002). Data from the UCLA-HERI surveys of faculty teaching undergraduates do not go back as far as the SDR data, but they show that 19.2 percent of those teaching at private universities and 10.1 percent of those teaching at private four-year colleges were born outside of the United States. These are very close (within two percentage points) to the percentages reported for 1995–96. Jennifer A. Lindholm, Alexander W. Astin, Linda J. Sax, and William S. Korn, *The American College Teacher: National Norms for the 2001–2002 HERI Faculty Survey* (Los Angeles: Higher Education Research Institute, UCLA, 2002); Linda J. Sax, Alexander W. Astin, Marisol Arredondo, and Williams S. Korn, *The American College Teacher: National Norms for the 1995–96 HERI Faculty Survey* (Los Angeles: Higher Education Research Institute, UCLA, 1996).

13. Robin Wilson, "Report Says Undergraduate Education Has Improved in Recent Years," *Chronicle of Higher Education,* March 22, 2002, online edition.

14. Quoted in Shulman and Bowen, p. 283.

15. See Chapter 4.

16. Jonathan Cole, letter to Bowen, July 8, 2002.

17. Note that we are unable to calculate an admissions advantage for the musicians because we cannot identify all promising musicians in the data for all applicants. We elected to focus on orchestral musicians and members of university-sponsored glee clubs because these are well-defined groups of students with highly developed interests in their music. In this regard they are more akin to varsity teams than are some of the other musical groups that are more informal and, in some instances, primarily "social."

18. Shulman and Bowen, pp. 69–70.

19. There is, of course, some overlap between these categories, but, as we showed in Chapter 4, the degree of overlap is modest.

20. We collected 1999 admissions data for two Division IA public universities and found the same pattern: recruited athletes, both men and women, were more likely than minority students to be accepted at all SAT levels.

21. This is one instance in which the overlap between being a minority group member and being a High Profile athlete could lead to misleading results. To guard against this possibility, we reran the tabulations of average rank-in-class excluding all recruited athletes in the Ivies who were from minority groups. As one would expect, this exclusion has the effect of raising the average rank-in-class of the recruited High Profile athletes, but only slightly, from the 19th to the 21st percentile—still well below the average rank-in-class for all male minority students (27th percentile).

22. Bowen and Bok, especially pp. 229–40. For data on major fields of study, see appendix table D3.7, p. 384.

23. Bowen and Bok, especially pp. 76–90.

24. See Douglas S. Massey and Mary J. Fischer, "Stereotype Threat and Academic Performance: New Data from the National Longitudinal Survey of Fresh-

men," University of Pennsylvania mimeo, June 2002. The quotation is from pp. 2–3. The paper contains numerous references to the original work by Steele and others, which included laboratory tests of the power of the hypothesis. Massey has also completed an analysis of the backgrounds and earlier family and educational experiences of students from most of the colleges and universities included in the original College and Beyond database. See Douglas S. Massey, Camille Z. Charles, Garvey F. Lundy, and Mary J. Fischer, *The Source of the River: The Social Origins of Freshmen at America's Selective Colleges and Universities* (Princeton, N.J.: Princeton University Press, 2003). This study is directly relevant to the discussion because it demonstrates, among other things, that peer effects (i.e., the argument that close friends in the same sub-group discourage academic achievement) have less to do with racial differentials in academic achievement than has generally been assumed. See Chapter 1 for a description of and reference to Steele's work.

25. Massey and Fischer, p. 21. Massey and Fischer focus on three stereotypical traits related to academic performance: "intelligence, laziness, and diligence." The authors construct indices—"felt performance burden," "stereotype internalization," and "stereotypical judgment expectation"—from survey responses related to the three stereotypical traits. These indices are then used as independent variables in a regression predicting cumulative GPA. Massey and Fischer, pp. 9–18.

26. Massey and Fischer, p. 20.

27. Marta Tienda, e-mail to Bowen, July 28, 2002.

28. The Bollinger quote is from a talk given at the Macalester College Forum on Higher Education, St. Paul, Minnesota, June 3, 1999, cited in Shulman and Bowen, p. 85. Bowen and Bok report considerable survey evidence indicating that the vast majority of former matriculants at the colleges in the study believe that going to college with a diverse body of fellow students made a valuable contribution to their education and personal development. See chapter 8 of their study.

29. Glenn C. Loury, foreword to *The Shape of the River: Long-Term Consequences of Considering Race in College and University Admissions,* by William G. Bowen and Derek Bok, paperback edition (Princeton, N.J.: Princeton University Press, 2000), p. xxvii. In his recent book, *The Anatomy of Racial Inequality* (Cambridge, Mass.: Harvard University Press, 2002), Loury provides a powerful new analytical apparatus for understanding the "durability" of racial inequality in America. His analysis emphasizes the power of what he calls "racial stigma" and is a strong intellectual foundation for continuing efforts to achieve racial justice.

30. Jonathan Cole, letter to Bowen, July 8, 2002. Bowen and Bok included in their book a great deal of information on the achievements in later life of minority students who attended these selective colleges and universities. The leadership contributions of these students have been especially noteworthy (see chapter 6 of Bowen and Bok).

Chapter 10   Retaking the High Ground

1. Douglas J. Bennet, Nancy Hargrave Meislahn, and John Biddiscombe, "Return to the High Ground," interview by William Holder, *Wesleyan,* Spring 2002, p. 22.

2. Giamatti, p. 82.

3. Shulman and Bowen, p. 265; see also Chapter 9, which is devoted entirely to the subject of leadership. Athletes were more likely than their classmates to be leaders in sports clubs and youth groups (men only), and CEOs who were athletes are more likely than others to be leaders in alumni affairs. As Charles McGrath observed in an article on the effects of Title IX, "Sports, it's true, teach us something about teamwork and about the rewards of focus and sustained effort—but no more, say, than putting on the school play does or getting out the newspaper. Sadly, one of the main lessons sports teach is that the more talented you are as an athlete, the less is expected of you socially or academically, and the more the rules will be bent for you." McGrath, "The Way We Live Now: 9-15-02: A Whole New Ballgame," *New York Times Magazine,* September 15, 2002, p. 21.

4. The quote is from a speech delivered by Shultz at the Ivy Football Association Award Dinner, New York, January 22, 2003.

5. The Williams Ad Hoc Committee report contains a discussion of the benefits of intercollegiate athletics (pp. 3–5) that is similar to the discussion presented here.

6. Charles Berry, letter to Bowen, February 28, 2001. The average per-game attendance at Princeton home football games declined by more than half, from about 32,000 in 1965 to 14,419 in 2001. Scott Oostdyk, "Where Have All the Fans Gone?" *Princeton Alumni Weekly,* December 15, 1982, p. 16, cited in Bernstein, p. 245; National Collegiate Athletic Association (NCAA), *Official NCAA Football Records 2002* (Indianapolis, Ind.: NCAA), 495.

7. See Sarah E. Turner, Lauren A. Meserve, and William G. Bowen, "Winning and Giving: Football Results and Alumni Giving at Selective Private Colleges and Universities," *Social Science Quarterly* 82 (4) (December 2001): 812–26. Also, extensive data on patterns of giving by individuals fail to support the argument that athletes are likely to be especially generous themselves, nor are the truly "big donors" especially interested in intercollegiate athletics; overall, they are more likely to favor placing less emphasis on intercollegiate athletics than they are to favor placing more emphasis there. See Shulman and Bowen, chapter 10. The research relating intercollegiate sports to admissions was carried out by Art & Science Group, LLC, and published under the title "Intercollegiate Athletics Have Little Influence on College Choice—Intramural and Recreational Opportunities Matter More" in *StudentPOLL* 4 (4): 1–12.

8. This expression is thought to have originated at a time when one gambled by candlelight. Thus an unsuccessful evening might be judged not to have been worth [the price of] the candle. See "Not Worth the Candle," *The Phrase Finder 2000,* available at http://phrases.shu.ac.uk/bulletin_board/6/messages/1018.html, accessed December 2, 2002.

9. Hutchins, p. 23.

10. Howard J. Savage, *American College Athletics* (New York: Carnegie Foundation for the Advancement of Teaching, 1929), p. 306.

11. Giamatti, p. 85.

12. Ibid., pp. 98–99.

13. James Tobin, "The Ivy League and Athletics: The President's Views Deserve Support," *Yale Alumni Magazine and Journal* 44 (1) (October 1980): 40–41; quote on p. 41.

14. David L. Marcus, "What Are Your Chances of Getting in Through the Coach's Door?" *U.S. News & World Report* (September 17, 2001): 94; Rachel Hartigan Shea and Justin Ewers, "Work Hard, Stay Sane—and Get In," *U.S. News & World Report*, September 13, 2002, online edition.

15. See Shulman and Bowen, pp. 278–80, for an extended discussion of "sending signals," including quotations from Henry Louis Gates, Jr., on how such signals are read by African Americans, and from a secondary school headmaster (Peter Philip) on messages sent to his set of schools and their constituents. Craig Lambert observes: "The choices we make about the future of intercollegiate sports ripple out far beyond the academy. College sports priorities affect not only professional athletics but, more importantly, the lives of students in secondary schools and even children in grade schools" (p. 36).

16. Lee Levison, "Thoughts on Athletics," letter to James Shulman, 1998, p. 2.

17. This is not a problem rooted solely in athletics, and one of the main themes in the study of Early Decision programs by Avery, Fairbanks, and Zeckhauser is that there is a *huge* difference between what a number of colleges and universities say is the effect on an applicant's chances of applying early and the real effect. Avery, Fairbanks, and Zeckhauser provide compelling evidence of the extent of this dichotomy—which, we hasten to add, may well result mainly from schools' not knowing themselves how much of an advantage they are conferring on applicants to Early Decision programs. Whatever the explanation, the schools' reputation for truth-telling is not helped by evidence of this kind.

18. There is also the question, which is explored extensively in Shulman and Bowen (2001), of whether these opportunity costs extend into later life. That analysis of later life outcomes in *The Game of Life* was based on survey data that are unavailable for the more recent cohorts on which this study focuses. Nor would new survey data help us much here since it takes time—years—to know much about later life outcomes. What can be said is that the data available for members of the '76 entering cohorts indicate that (a) athletes and other students seem about on a par in terms of the leadership they provide in their communities (see discussion in the first part of this chapter) and (b) athletes tend to earn somewhat more money than other students, but primarily (in the case of men) because of the career paths they have elected. Shulman and Bowen, pp. 262–65. However, the characteristics of athletes and of other students have changed markedly over time, as has the external environment. The college athletes from the '51 and '76 cohorts whose activities in later life are traced in *The Game of Life* compiled quite different records in college than their successors in the '95 cohort. It is not appropriate, therefore, to assume that today's recruited athletes, functioning in today's markets, will have career paths that closely resemble the paths followed by the athletes of a quarter century ago.

19. This is not true, however, at the less selective colleges and universities. We saw earlier that the gap in qualifications and accomplishments between recruited athletes and other students is much larger at the most selective institutions than elsewhere. For this reason, the opportunity cost of recruiting athletes looms much larger at small, highly selective colleges like Amherst than it does at large and more heterogeneous universities such as Cornell (or, even more so, at a Michigan or a Penn State).

20. A trustee of a college that recently reduced the number of recruited athletes admitted to the incoming class said that, thanks to this decision, his college was able to enroll 12 more outstanding students, who really wanted to come "for the right reasons," than would have been possible otherwise.

21. Hoxby (2000), p. 37.

22. Comments made at an off-the-record meeting of a group of college presidents and reproduced here with President Bacow's permission.

23. We recognize that many of these schools offer club sports that are populated by regular students, and we discuss these club programs in detail in Chapter 12. Although club sports can offer a great athletic experience, the students playing at this level do not benefit from the same kinds of coaching, training, and financial support that are provided for intercollegiate teams.

24. Middlebury Ad Hoc Committee (2002a), p. 13.

25. The expenditure figures reported on the forms by individual Ivy League universities range from $5 million at one school to $13.5 million at another, with the variation almost surely due to a host of major inconsistencies in accounting and reporting. For a lengthy discussion of the problems of making sense of these data, see Shulman and Bowen, chapter 11. In our earlier research and in the research for the present book, we have had the benefit of detailed data provided by some schools on a confidential basis, and our "ballpark" figures are based both on the published data and on these additional sources of information. One fundamental problem is the treatment of "infrastructure" costs (for maintenance of facilities, computer systems, and the like), which may or may not be attributed to athletics. In its November 25, 2002, announcement of a decision (subsequently rescinded) to discontinue its men's and women's swimming and diving programs, Dartmouth reported that the operating budget of its athletic department is $10.8 million—which suggests that our ballpark estimate of $10 million for the typical Ivy League university is, if anything, on the low side. See Dartmouth College, "Dartmouth Announces Elimination of Varsity Swimming and Diving Programs," press release, November 25, 2002.

26. See Shulman and Bowen, especially pp. 249–51, for a fuller explanation of Winston's work. It was a similar line of thinking that led another economist, Roger Noll, to write: "No university [at the Division IA level] generates a large enough surplus to justify the capital expenditures necessary to field a football team." Noll, "The Business of College Sports and the High Cost of Winning," *Milken Institute Review* (third quarter, 1999): 28.

27. See Dartmouth College.

28. It is tempting—but very dangerous—to calculate costs per participant in different conference settings. The main problem with this approach is that football is such an expensive sport overall, and basketball is an expensive sport per participant. Thus conferences that offer the High Profile sports and a relatively small number of other sports tend to show a considerably higher cost per participant than conferences that sponsor large numbers of sports that are relatively inexpensive per participant. In short, there is an "apples and oranges" problem here that has to be recognized. Shulman and Bowen, chapter 11, contains a detailed discussion of these questions as part of a broader examination of "the financial equation." The data in this paragraph are based on an examination of EADA

worksheets provided by UAA members and almost all of the liberal arts colleges participating in the study.

29. For accounts of the budget situations at Dartmouth and Oberlin, see Martin van der Werf, "Endowment Losses Force Dartmouth to Cut Its Budget," *Chronicle of Higher Education,* August 26, 2002, online edition; John L. Pulley, "Well-Off and Wary: Even Small, Wealthy Private Colleges Like Oberlin Are Feeling the Economic Pinch," *Chronicle of Higher Education,* June 21, 2002, online edition.

30. See Amherst Special Committee, p. 33 . According to the Williams Ad Hoc Committee report, p. 8, disciplinary actions "overwhelmingly involve male students," including male athletes and especially members of two (unspecified) teams.

31. An article in the *New York Times,* in commenting on the Brown-Harvard football game, notes: "It is probably true that interest in football has declined in the Ivy League in the last 20 years or so, since the Ivy League was pushed from I-A and forced to accept a more or less minor league designation of I-AA." Ira Berkow, "College Football; A Button for All Occasions, Including Brown vs. Harvard," *New York Times,* September 28, 2002, pp. D1, D5; quote on p. D5. In an article on scramble bands, the comical marching bands that play at most Ivy League (and some other) football games, Warren St. John characterizes their audience as follows: "Because students at Ivy League schools are largely apathetic toward their football teams, attendance is a hodgepodge of alumni, players' parents and locals, with a few students mixed in." St. John, "And the Band Misbehaved On . . . ," *New York Times,* September 29, 2002, section 9, pp. 1, 7; quote on p. 7. League-wide, attendance dropped from an average of 20,000 per game in the mid-1960s to about 9,400 in the 1990s. Jennifer Wulff, "Playing the Game," *Dartmouth Alumni Magazine,* March 1998, pp. 20–23, cited in Bernstein, p. 264. It is important to remember that attendance may be determined based on ticket sales or an actual head count and that it also may not be uniformly calculated from game to game. So, these are rough averages—but the drastic decline is apparent, nonetheless.

32. Steve Vladeck, "A College Divided: Athletics and Amherst," *The Amherst Student,* December 2, 1998, online edition.

33. Williams Ad Hoc Committee (2002), p. 7.

34. Knight Foundation Commission, p. 4.

35. This language is from the Original Ivy Agreement of 1954 and has been retained in the current version of the Revised Agreement. See Council of Ivy Group Presidents (2001), p. 2. The Princeton Trustee Committee report on athletics offers a more contemporary statement of support for athletics provided that certain conditions are met. It reads: "We believe strongly that competitive athletics has an important continuing role in Princeton's undergraduate program, but only as a fully integrated component of the primary educational programs of the University. To the extent that some student athletes perform below their academic potential or even are disruptive of the educational environment, to the extent that some faculty perceive student athletes as uninterested in the intellectual and cultural life of the institution and consequently fail to extend a full educational effort and opportunity towards them, to the extent that some student athletes are prevented from participating adequately in the full interpersonal life and richness of the University, the institution is failing to achieve its purposes"

(p. 15). The indictment stands. Statements to the effect that intercollegiate athletics is fine "provided that . . ." abound. What has been missing on many campuses is documentation of the failures to meet the stated conditions. But from the evidence we have marshaled and the standard enunciated in the Princeton statement, it appears that "the institution is failing to achieve its purposes."

36. It is useful to note that many of the institutions in this study have accepted these principles and would like to believe that they adhere to them, when in reality they do not. We realize that principles, as important as they are, are not enough, and in the next three chapters we propose specific reform measures.

37. This language is from the NESCAC 1971 Founding Agreement, reproduced in Vélez, p. 5. The full text of the 1971 Agreement is an appendix to Vélez's paper. This wording appears to have been modeled on the Original Ivy Agreement of 1954, which says: "In the total life of the campus, emphasis upon intercollegiate competition must be kepy in harmony with the essential educational purposes of the institution." Council of Ivy Group Presidents (2001), Appendix A, p. 165. In language adopted more recently by the UAA in their initial agreement of February 27, 1986, the Association states that it is "committed to the principle that a program of athletics must be conducted in a manner consistent with the central educational process of its member institutions." Cited in Rasmussen (1997), p. 98.

38. Language from Original 1954 Ivy Agreement, which went on to add these words: "and not composed of a group of specifically recruited athletes." Council of Ivy Group Presidents (2001), appendix A, p. 165. To exclude recruitment altogether is not possible today, and it is unclear how a complete prohibition would even be defined (but recruitment can, of course, be limited and restricted in various ways).

39. UAA principles, as cited in Rasmussen (1997), p. 2; also 1979 Statement of Ivy Principles, as cited in Council of Ivy Group Presidents (2001), p. 4.

40. UAA principles, as cited in Rasmussen (1997), p. 2.

41. "Athletes and athletics should remain important components of the broad Princeton educational experience . . . [and] *they must be fully integrated into it.*" Princeton Trustee Committee, pp. 3–4; our emphasis.

42. The 1979 Statement of Ivy Principles also says explicitly: "Wide participation in intercollegiate athletics should be sought." Council of Ivy Group Presidents (2001), p. 4.

43. Ibid.

44. We are indebted to President Michael McPherson of Macalester for bringing this quotation to our attention. Thomforde is a strong advocate of "reclaiming the game."

45. Giamatti, p. 81.

46. Ibid., p. 92; our emphasis.

47. Slovenski.

48. Rasmussen (1997), p. 124.

49. Ibid., p. 150.

50. Bryan C. Short, letter to the editor, *Yale Alumni Magazine and Journal* 44 (1) (October 1980): 42. In the same issue, Professor Tobin responded: "To characterize the President's proposal [to emphasize Ivy competition and to rethink par-

ticipation in national championships] . . . as one of favoring 'mediocrity' is a thoughtless evasion of the real issues" (p. 41).

51. Giamatti, p. 85. For a further discussion of the "excellence in all things" argument, see Shulman and Bowen, pp. 300–01.

Chapter 11   Reform at the Institutional and Conference Levels: Recruiting, Admissions, and Coaching

1. This is why Stephen Lewis, retired president of Carleton, is a strong advocate of working principally at the national level. His view is that "reform couldn't come at the institutional or conference level, since the national rules on season length, numbers of contests, etc., set the (lowest) common denominator." Lewis, letter to Bowen, August 11, 2002.

2. This was a recurring theme in a roundtable discussion that was held at The Andrew W. Mellon Foundation on September 25–26, 2002. Participants included several of the athletic directors commissioned to write papers for this study, several college presidents and senior academics, and members of the Foundation's staff.

3. Litvack, p. 15.

4. Michael McPherson, letter to Bowen, October 7, 2002.

5. Recruiting regulations for Division I and Division III of the NCAA are laid out in Article 13 of each division's manual and have been discussed here in Chapter 2. These regulations restrict the time during which prospective athletes may be contacted, limit the number and type of contacts, and delineate how recruiting funds may be used and by whom. Several differences between the two divisions are worth noting. While Division I coaches cannot contact a prospect until July 1 after the student's junior year of high school, Division III coaches may contact athletes as soon as his or her junior year is completed. Student-athletes are restricted to five official (expense-paid) visits to Division I schools but there is no limit on the number of unofficial visits in either division. Institutions in Division I may participate in a national letter of intent program, in which a student commits to attend a specific school at the beginning of senior year; Division III schools are prohibited from using these plans. In addition to the NESCAC ban on off-campus recruiting, there are several other conference-specific rules of note. NESCAC schools are not permitted to pay for the transportation of prospects to campus. NESCAC (2002), p. 25. In the Ivy League all expenses of an official visit must be covered by a "friends" group, not by the institution. Council of Ivy Group Presidents (2001), p. 148.

6. Middlebury Ad Hoc Committee (2002a), p. 13. This report cites statistics showing the high percentage of regular students admitted by Middlebury who expressed the hope that they could play an intercollegiate sport.

7. Middlebury Ad Hoc Committee (2002a), p. 16.

8. John Emerson, Letter to Bowen, August 12, 2002. There are two other important issues. One is how "athletic matriculants" are defined. If they are defined as those athletes who would not have been admitted otherwise—thus excluding those who would have been admitted anyway because of strong academic credentials or their legacy or minority status—the stated numbers can be mislead-

ing. "Underperformance," as we have seen, is a problem not only among those with lower test scores. Second, unless numbers are assigned sport by sport (which is difficult because of differences among schools in histories and athletic priorities), competitive imbalances can develop. If school A recruits in lacrosse and school B does not, lacrosse players at school B (and the lacrosse coach) may feel unfairly disadvantaged. We return to this problem later in the chapter; the only way to deal with it, in our view, is through changes in admissions criteria that apply across the board.

9. The Academic Index (AI) is calculated for every student admitted at each Ivy League university. It is an average of three components: the student's scores on the SAT I, a measure of his or her rank-in-class, and the highest of the student's scores on the SAT II (achievement tests) or on the SAT I counted again. The AI is used primarily for screening recruits for the High Profile sports, though there is also some general review of recruits playing other sports. In all cases, admittees are expected to have an AI above the threshold value of 169. Although the concepts are the same, somewhat different methods are used to set AI targets for players in basketball or ice hockey, on the one hand, and in football, on the other. In the case of basketball or ice hockey, a target mean AI for the incoming admissions cohort is obtained by averaging the mean AIs for the four admissions cohorts currently enrolled and then subtracting one standard deviation. In football the focus is on matriculated players, not on admits (but since yields in football are now close to 100 percent, there is no real difference between the two groups). A "band" system is employed. Using existing numbers to illustrate how the system works (based on 30 incoming players in each class or a four-year total of 120), no more than 8 of the 120 can have AIs between the AI threshold of 169 and 2.5 standard deviations below the mean AI for the school; 28 can be between 2.5 and 2 standard deviations below the mean; 52 can be between 2 and 1 standard deviations below the mean; and at least 32 must be above the 1 standard deviation reference point. With "bands" in use, the average SAT score for the entire football team is no longer calculated. We are indebted to Jeffrey Orleans, executive director of the Council of Ivy Presidents, for this explanation of the current system.

10. Shulman and Bowen, p. 46.

11. There are, however, problems with any formulaic approach such as the AI. One is the tendency to "game the system" by admitting some recruits with high AIs to "make the numbers," even though the coach knows that these admits are unlikely to be substantial contributors and may be unlikely to play at all. One way of quantifying this phenomenon is to compare the entering qualifications of starters to those of non-starters. If the non-starters have higher SAT scores, this may be evidence of "gaming the system." Using data from five Ivy League universities for which we know the identities of the football starters, we found that the average combined SAT score for recruited starters was 1185; for recruited non-starters, it was 1227. Gordon Winston at Williams has proposed an ingenious way of discouraging such behavior by introducing the idea of a "play-weighted academic index." Winston, memo to Williams Provost Catherine Hill, January 5, 2002. But the added complexity of such an approach is likely to discourage its adoption.

12. Middlebury Ad Hoc Committee (2002a), p. 14.

13. Ibid., p. 16. The committee left the definition of how one measures "the top half" vaguely specified in order not to "presume reliance solely on either SAT scores or high school grades to define the upper half." John Emerson, letter to Bowen, August 12, 2002.

14. These quotations are taken from the undated draft of a memorandum to the director of the admissions staff at the time, John Muyskens, which was sent to us by Professor Tobin. We believe the document dates from late 1966, since the report of Tobin's Advisory Board, which was issued preceding it, is dated October 31, 1966. Brewster's way of phrasing the most important criteria is more appealing to us than many statements of current-day policies. References to "representativeness" and to valuing "academic promise" and "personal qualities" are fine, but they do not capture the sharp sense Brewster conveyed of the need to look for evidence of a deep commitment to learning and a passion for taking full advantage of the educational opportunities offered by the school in question. Motivation and priorities matter a great deal.

15. Yale University, Admissions Policy Advisory Board, "Second Report and Addendum: Problems in Admitting Artists," October 31, 1966, pp. 7–8 [copy sent to us by Professor Tobin].

16. Nicholas F. Josefowitz, "Ending Athletic Preference," *Harvard Crimson,* April 29, 2002, online edition.

17. Amherst Faculty Committee, pp. 27–32.

18. The need for rigorous monitoring of actual outcomes is illustrated by many examples of the understandable desire of interested parties to "believe" they know what the data show without having really looked at them. The Princeton Trustee Committee report offers one good example: "It [the committee] found particularly noteworthy the Dean of Admissions' estimates that approximately half of our student athletes would have been admitted independently of their athletic abilities. For the others, athletic skills were an 'extra element' that was decisive for each of them in achieving admission. Their athletics 'extra' was of course comparable to the other 'extras'—of musical talent, or overcoming adverse circumstances, or family legacy—that contributed similarly to their other classmates' admissions portfolios" (p. 11). Both of these assertions (pertaining to the number of recruited athletes who would have gotten in on their own and the alleged equivalence of the boost associated with being a recruited athlete to the boost given to those with musical talent or to legacies) are incorrect, as shown by the data for the Ivies in Chapters 3 and 9. (Princeton does not differ from the other Ivies in these respects.) We are not suggesting that there was any intent to deceive—we do not believe that there was. It is just too easy to believe what one would like to believe in the absence of rigorous (and, ideally, independent) analysis of actual outcomes. More recently, the excellent Williams Ad Hoc Committee report is also wrong in this one respect. Recruited athletes at Williams do not do as well academically as students at large with the same incoming credentials.

19. Middlebury Ad Hoc Committee on the Future of Athletics. "Addendum to Report of the Ad Hoc Committee on the Future of Athletics: Elaboration of Recommendation 3," September 6, 2002.

20. Princeton Trustee Committee, p. 5; see also p. 14.

21. An editorial in the *Philadelphia Inquirer* (July 30, 2002, p. A10) rightly decries preoccupations with "rankings in overvalued polls" and the resulting "collective frenzy distorting a key decision for young people." It continues: "A school's desirability is measured by 'selectivity' and 'yield.' Selectivity measures how frequently a college rejects students; yield measures how frequently students accept a college. To rise in these indexes, colleges must attract a large pool of candidates and reject most of them, while being rejected by as few as possible. . . . The competitive pressure also ratchets up the 'early decision' frenzy, which unfairly favors well-to-do applicants. These unholy numbers games ignore the rightful goal: Matching students with the best school to give them the education they want."

An objection to the line of argument that we are presenting here—which also implies less reliance on Early Decision programs—is that lower yields will make the admissions process "less efficient" in the sense that there will be more multiple applications, that it will be harder to manage enrollment numbers, and so on. We find these arguments unpersuasive. Life in the admissions office may be somewhat more complicated, but that cannot be a driving determinant of how to handle the recruitment/admission of athletes. Waiting lists are, of course, one obvious way of managing enrollment in the face of some uncertainty over yields. Moreover, the degree of "statistical uncertainty" should not be exaggerated. Patterns develop, and the probabilities of acceptance/rejection for groups of candidates are neither that hard to estimate nor that subject to sharp fluctuation.

One recurring and, to our way of thinking, particularly foolish objection to reduced reliance on Early Decision programs and a more deliberate process of choice by high school students is the view attributed to one dean of admissions: "The student I worry about is the one who is narrowly turned down by her first choice college in favor of a student with twelve other acceptances who has no intention of attending." Surely this statement makes sense if and only if the total number of offers of admission is fixed. But that is a very strange assumption. Presumably the number that is "fixed" is not the number of admits, but rather that of the projected size of the entering class. Thus, if the admissions pool includes more candidates who are admitted at "twelve places" (which it will if Early Decision is eliminated or restricted), the projected yield will go down and the total number of students who should be admitted to produce a class of given size will go up. It is a logical fallacy to suppose that the student who really wants to go to a given school can be displaced by a student who ends up going elsewhere. A prospective student cannot be displaced by someone who does not matriculate. Of course, it may well make sense, within limits, to give preference to the student who really wants to go to the school, but that is a different point. What matters ultimately is not how many people were offered admission (or what the yield is), but the quality and character of the set of students who matriculate.

22. In his description of the decline of football at the University of Chicago, Lester emphasizes the "drastic decline in material . . . due to the raising of entrance scholarship at the university." The effects on skill levels of changes in academic standards and in the curriculum at the University of Chicago were decisive factors in making it impossible for the Chicago football team to compete in the Big Ten. Lester, pp. 133 ff.

23. At Swarthmore, for example, 43 percent of the members of the Class of 2004 participated in varsity sports in high school. Swarthmore College Athletics Review Committee, "FAQ—Answers to Frequently Asked Questions," available at http://www.swarthmore.edu/news/athletics/faq.html, question 9, accessed September 12, 2002.

24. One reader of the manuscript (McPherson) raised the question of the distribution of these academically strong high school athletes by sport. If we look only at non-recruited students attending the schools in this study with SATs of 1250 or higher, we find that the average number of high school athletes does vary markedly by sport. In general, there are lots of baseball, basketball, soccer, and tennis players, and also a considerable number of athletes involved in track, field hockey, and volleyball. At the other end of the distribution, there are relatively few ice hockey players and not nearly enough football players interested in applying to these schools (especially at the coed liberal arts colleges like Macalester) to field a team. Detailed tabulations of the data we reviewed to draw these conclusions are available on request.

25. Stephen Lewis, letter to Bowen, August 11, 2002.

26. Giamatti, p. 90.

27. Ibid., p. 100.

28. Rasmussen (2002), p. 6.

29. William Adams, letter to Bowen, September 4, 2002.

30. As one example, Irv Cross at Macalester uses a survey of athletes to evaluate his coaches. The survey asks questions about personal qualities (such as whether the coach has "high moral and ethical values," "is concerned about athletes' academic progress," and "places the importance of the athlete above winning"), organizational abilities (such as whether the coach "abides by NCAA rules and regulations," is "effective in scouting opponents," and "communicates well with athletes"), and knowledge of aspects of physical education including conditioning and nutrition (such as whether the coach can "effectively counsel injured athletes" and understands "pre-season conditioning requirements").

Chapter 12   Reform at the Institutional and Conference Levels: The Athletic Program

1. Robert Malekoff, "The Non-traditional Season: Turning Point or Full Speed Ahead?" *The Intercollegiate Athletic Forum* 6 (3) (December 1998): 1–2, 4; quote on p. 2.

2. Lester, pp. 79 ff. This measure and others were called "the 1906 reforms."

3. Summary based on extensive materials supplied by Dutcher, chief of staff for Division III of the NCAA. See also Susan Anderson, "Memorandum to William G. Bowen Regarding Nontraditional Season Deliberations," January 16, 2002.

4. Proposal 50 stated that in the non-traditional segment no class time could be missed due to athletic activities; all practice and competition was to be limited to a maximum of five weeks; and teams that play their traditional seasons in the fall or spring were to be limited to four or five contests against outside opponents. Anderson, p. 6. Malekoff is skeptical that Proposal 50 actually reduced time commitments to any significant extent. Robert Malekoff, letter to Susan Anderson, December 2, 2001.

5. In the words of one athletic director (John Biddiscombe): "I strongly believe that off-season training should be at the discretion of the individual athlete and without peer pressure." Biddiscombe, p. 6. Malekoff echoes this sentiment: "I admire a student who is inclined to spend a significant amount of time voluntarily improving his or her conditioning and skill levels outside of the approved NCAA practice seasons. I don't believe such passion and work ethic should be discouraged unless it unduly minimizes intellectual development, limits athletes from interacting with non-athletes, or means that student-athletes will be less likely to even consider the value of other extracurricular activities. However, when off-season training becomes more mandatory than voluntary—a critical distinction—students may be put in a position where they are an athlete first, a member of the student body second." Malekoff (2002), p. 9.

6. Owen Bochner, "Taking Time out of Year," *Cornell Daily Sun*, September 6, 2002, online edition. The seven weeks (49 days) can be distributed throughout the year as each coach sees fit, but each "off period" must last at least seven consecutive days. Yale's head football coach, Jack Siedlecki, is quoted as saying: "You are taking seven weeks of opportunity away." Jeremy Licht, "Players, Coaches Unhappy with Ivy Changes," *Yale Daily News*, September 4, 2002, online edition. A University of Pennsylvania senior linebacker and captain, Matt Dukes, was also displeased: "I don't know what the presidents were thinking. No one is happy about [the changes] on the football team. This has a huge negative impact on the program. . . . We're struggling to compete with other schools in the country. We already don't have scholarships—we need some leverage." Amy Potter, "Ivy Presidents Announce Recruitment Changes," *Daily Pennsylvanian*, August 29, 2002, online edition. President Shirley Tilghman wrote a particularly fair-minded and compelling response to those protesting the "time-off" rule for the campus newspaper. See Tilghman, "Why a Moratorium for Student-Athletes?" *Daily Princetonian*, December 4, 2002, online edition. Richard Rasmussen (2002, p. 6) recommends relaxing restrictions on the opportunity for casual contact between coaches and athletes outside defined playing seasons, and the idea of moving from more to less regulation is appealing; but the pressures to "push the envelope" are so strong that practical considerations seem to us to require tighter regulation in this area than we would prefer in an ideal world.

7. Swarthmore College Athletics Review Committee, *Final Report,* July 26, 2002, available at http://www.swarthmore.edu/news/athletics/final_report.html. The Williams Ad Hoc Committee report also focused on scheduling issues (pp. 10, 18–19), and it includes this comment: "[Scheduling conflicts are] the outcome of having an athletic program that has outstripped the College's methods of regulation. . . . The College's mechanisms for balancing the conflicting imperatives of successful athletics and academics are insufficient" (pp. 18–19). Rasmussen (2002), pp. 4–5, provides a useful context for considering these issues by calling attention to the major changes in academic calendars that have been an independent source of scheduling conflicts.

8. See Swarthmore College Athletics Review Committee (2000d), question 18, and the later discussion of the Swarthmore debate in this section.

9. Giamatti, p. 99.

10. John Emerson, letter to Bowen, August 12, 2002.

11. Taken from comments by Richard Rasmussen on an early draft of the manuscript, August 2002.

12. Refer back to Figures 1.1 and 4.1.

13. Taken from a comment on an early draft of the manuscript. Nancy Hargrave Meislahn, dean of admissions and financial aid at Wesleyan and formerly an associate dean of admissions at Cornell, commented in an interview in *Wesleyan:* "The number of sports we are attempting to support is a distinctive feature of NESCAC schools. For small schools to be fielding 27 or 29 teams is significant in lots of ways. It's a wonderful demonstration of what we believe, yet it certainly puts pressure on resources within the institutions, including admission." Bennet, Meislahn, and Biddiscombe, p. 22.

14. Of the 11 NESCAC schools, 3 were coeducational from their founding (Bates, Colby, and Tufts), 1 (Middlebury) became coeducational in 1883, and the other 7 became coeducational at various times and in various ways between 1969 and 1975.

15. Swarthmore College Athletics Review Committee (2002d), question 1.

16. The unrelenting external forces creating an "athletic divide" at many selective colleges and universities have clearly made their presence felt at Swarthmore. According to one press release, dated December 4, 2000: "The Athletic Review Committee noted the strain that increased specialization in intercollegiate competition has placed on Swarthmore's athletic program. Fewer student-athletes walk on to teams, and fewer play more than one sport. This pressure is particularly challenging to Swarthmore, which values its small size (approximately 1,400 students) and its rigorous academic program." Available at http://www.swarthmore.edu/Home/News/Media/Releases/00/athletics.html. President Alfred Bloom made essentially the same point in an end-of-the-school-year letter, dated June 1, 2001: "In the rapidly changing world of Division III intercollegiate athletics, to offer our athletes the quality of competitive experience they now seek, we must, across virtually all men's and women's sports, specifically reserve admissions spaces for students with particular talent and interest in each sport. For a college the size of Swarthmore, attempting to support 24 intercollegiate teams in this way comes directly into conflict with the need to accommodate the full range of other talents and interests we seek in each class." Alfred H. Bloom, "Letter to Alumni, Parents, and Friends [of Swarthmore College]" June 1, 2001, available at http://www.swarthmore.edu/Home/News/Media/Sources/abloom2.hmtl. In the succinct language of perceptive Swarthmore students: "The debate is best characterized as a difficult negotiation between the deep-seated intellectual values of Swarthmore and the changing realities of modern collegiate athletics." Lee, Scherr, and Ashby-Kuhlman, p. 2.

17. Clark Kerr, *The Gold and the Blue: A Personal Memoir of the University of California, 1949–1967,* vol. 1 (Berkeley: University of California Press, 2001), pp. 12–13.

18. Princeton Trustee Committee, especially pp. 4–6.

19. The district court issued a preliminary injunction requiring the reinstatement of the gymnastics and volleyball teams in December 1992. Following subsequent decisions at various judicial levels (culminating in the decision by the Supreme Court not to hear Brown's appeal), Brown agreed to a settlement that guaranteed the allocation of more money for four women's sports for three years

and agreed to ensure that the percentage of athletes who are women would be no more than 3.5 percentage points lower than the percentage of women enrolled. Furthermore, the agreement stipulates that if Brown eliminates or downgrades women's teams or improves men's sports without doing the same for women's sports, it will be required to keep its sports participation rate for women within 2.25 percent of the enrollment percentage for women. "Brown to Settle Title IX Suit," *New York Times*, June 24, 1998, p. C3, and Jim Naughton, "Judge Approves Settlement of Brown U.'s Title IX Case," *Chronicle of Higher Education*, July 3, 1998, p. A31.

20. As an alternative, in theory at least, a school could reduce the number of its men's varsity teams without cutting back on women's teams and without touching football. But such decisions are often painful, lead to great controversy, and are subject to reversal. (See the vignette in Shulman and Bowen, pp. xxix–xxxiii, describing the intense controversy set off in 1993 when Princeton decided to end its varsity wrestling program. That controversy sparked the review that culminated in the 1994 Trustee Committee report that is cited at various points in this study.) Moreover, any such actions that excluded football would almost certainly have only a limited impact on the total number of recruited athletes and on the overall scale of the athletics program.

21. Dartmouth College (2002) and the accompanying "Q & A: Swimming and Diving." Dartmouth subsequently reversed this decision, but because funding constraints were altered by the success of parents and alumni/ae in raising private funds, not because of any Title IX considerations.

22. We should also recall that three of the nine original members of the UAA do not play football at all (Brandeis, Emory, and New York University), and two others (Johns Hopkins and Rochester) have elected to compete in football outside the UAA. The lack of a football program is less of an oddity than many may think who have gone to a school where football was a well-established part of campus life. Nearly half (49 percent) of the Division III schools do not play varsity football. Corey Bray, comp., *1982–2001 NCAA Sports Sponsorship and Participation Report* (Indianapolis, Ind.: National Collegiate Athletic Association, 2002).

23. Although the number of high school football participants increased 6 percent from 1980–81 to 2000–01, the number in boys' soccer increased by 149 percent and the number in boys' lacrosse by 395 percent. In the same period, the number of girls' soccer participants increased by 993 percent! "National Federation of State High School Associations Participation Study 1971–2001," in Bray, pp. 175–91.

24. Macalester's conference won-lost record was 0–9 in 2000 and 1–8 in 2001. Minnesota Intercollegiate Athletic Conference (MIAC), *2000 Football Statistics*, available at http://www.miac-online.org/Stats/Archivedstats/footballstats2000.html, accessed March 11, 2003; and *2001 Football Statistics*, http://www.miac-online.org/Stats/football2001/MAC.HTM, accessed March 11, 2003. Macalester also enjoys the dubious distinction of being listed by ESPN as having had one of the ten worst college football teams of all times; the reference is to the 1974–80 period, when Macalester lost 50 games in a row. See ESPN, *Worst College Football Teams of All Time*, September 16, 2002, available at http://espn.go.com/page2/s/list/colfootball/teams/worst.html. Columbia, Oberlin, and Swarthmore, among the schools in our study, also appear on this list of ten.

25. Michael McPherson, "A Statement from the President on Football at Macalester College," memorandum to the Macalester community, September 18, 2001.

26. Male ice hockey and basketball players in the Ivies have still lower scores (Figure 4.4a).

27. Football players rank (on average) in the 21st percentile in the Ivy League, in the 26th percentile in NESCAC, in the 25th percentile in the other coeducational colleges in our study, and in the 40th percentile in the UAA (Table 5.4). Underperformance of recruited High Profile athletes (a category dominated statistically by football players) is pronounced in the Ivies, in the NESCAC colleges, and in the other liberal arts colleges (Figures 6.1a to 6.1d).

28. We do not present outcomes data for individual schools in this study. But we can report that neither Macalester nor Swarthmore is an outlier. Studies carried out by two economics professors at Swarthmore (Thomas Dee and Larry Westphal) came to essentially the same conclusions about academic outcomes that we have reached for a larger number of coed liberal arts colleges outside NESCAC.

29. McPherson (2001a).

30. Ibid.

31. According to data on their 2000–01 EADA forms, Macalester's ratio of males to females is about 7:10; Swarthmore's is about 9:10. Macalester's admission rate is 53 percent, and Swarthmore's is 24 percent. College Board, *College Search,* available at http://www.collegeboard.com, accessed October 25, 2002.

32. Our calculation is based on raw data published in Chart A, Swarthmore College Men's 1999–2000 Intercollegiate Athletic Teams, available at http://www.swarthmore.edu/news/athletics/chart1.html, accessed September 12, 2002. More generally, we know from the data collected during the course of this study (Figure 4.2 and Table 4.3) that very high percentages of football players, and of High Profile athletes overall, are recruited athletes regardless of the conference in which a school plays (generally over 75 percent, nearing 100 percent in some situations). Football players comprise a high percentage of all recruited male athletes (often around 30 percent).

33. These are rough data for the 1999–2000 season calculated from the Centennial Conference Web site (http://www.centennial.org) for Swarthmore and from Macalester's own Web site (http://www.macalester.edu). They are incomplete in that they cover only the main team sports and, in the case of Swarthmore, ignore men's tennis, which has been quite successful. An even more vivid sense of the competitive problem faced by men's sports at Swarthmore is obtained when we note the records of some specific teams: baseball (8–20), basketball (3–21), soccer (4–15), and wrestling (3–10). On the plus side of the ledger were lacrosse (8–6) and swimming (7–4)—two teams, not coincidentally, that, along with football and tennis, received a considerable number of admissions "slots." The situation in women's sports was radically different at both schools, with Swarthmore's women's teams doing very respectably (five of seven for which we have data posting winning records) and Macalester's women's teams struggling (with the notable exceptions of soccer and volleyball).

34. In 2000–01, the academic year before the Macalester community began its debate over its football program, the men's basketball team was 10–13 (8–12 in MIAC), the men's soccer team was 12–4–2 (7–1–2 in MIAC), and the baseball team was 15–23 (10–10 in MIAC).

35. In the 1997 season 10 different members of one of Swarthmore's opponents in the Centennial Conference, Johns Hopkins, scored touchdowns against Swarthmore in a single game, setting a Division III record. The Swarthmore-Oberlin game between two teams with long losing streaks attracted considerable national publicity because one of the two had to end its losing streak. There were stories in the *New York Times, Sports Illustrated,* and other publications about "the game that somebody had to win." See, for example, Chris Broussard, "College Football: One Team Had to Win: It's Swarthmore Routing Oberlin," *New York Times,* September 4, 1999, section 8, p. 9; Jack McCallum, "Streak Buster: After 28 Straight Losses, Swarthmore Finally Won a Ball Game, but that Wasn't What Made the Day Special," *Sports Illustrated,* September 13, 1999, p. 54; Romesh Ratnesar, "A Quaker Beating: When Swarthmore Routed Oberlin in the Season Opener, It Won Much More Than a Game," *Time* (September 20, 1999): p. 8. This summary of Swarthmore's recent football history is based on the excellent account in Brendan Karch, "Football Commitment Perceived Incomplete," *Swarthmore Phoenix,* December 7, 2000, online edition.

36. See Rachael Burstein, "Football Players at Swarthmore Talk about Past Year after Sport Is Cut," *Swarthmore Phoenix,* December 13, 2001, online edition.

37. In its report to the Board of Managers (pp. 1–3), the Athletics Review Committee concluded that "the current intercollegiate program was unsustainable" and that football, wrestling, and women's badminton should be dropped as varsity sports, with the resources saved through these decisions, plus additional resources, used to strengthen the remaining programs. Other sports were allocated more admissions slots. The "number of students enrolled in a class based on special recognition of their interest and talent in athletics [was] to be in a range from 10–15% . . . ; all varsity intercollegiate sports [were to] have full-time coaches . . . and athletics facilities [were to] receive institutional priority." Swarthmore College Athletics Review Committee, *Report to the Board of Managers,* May 5, 2001, available at www.swarthmore.edu/news/athletics/report.html.

38. Swarthmore College Athletics Review Committee (2002b), pp. 3–7.

39. Michael McPherson, "The Future of Macalester Football: Statement by President Michael McPherson," November 27, 2001. We have been told that a number of representatives of MIAC schools were angered by Macalester's decision. One person speculated that they wanted to keep "an easy win" on their schedules so that their records would look better when the NCAA was selecting schools to participate in national championships. Fortunately for Macalester, MIAC rules do not require conference participation in all sports. In an analogous situation, Pomona, which plays in the Southern California Intercollegiate Athletic Conference (SCIAC), also elected to play an independent schedule in football. It was threatened with a boycott of its teams in other sports by SCIAC members, but this threat was removed when President Peter Stanley of Pomona said that he would counter any such move by challenging its legality.

40. Swarthmore College Athletics Review Committee (2002d), question 11.

41. The football squad size for St. John's University was determined from the football team roster posted at St. John's athletics Web site (http://www.gojohnnies.com) because, as an all-male school, St. John's is not required to submit an EADA form.

42. Swarthmore College Athletics Review Committee (2002d), question 15.

43. To give just one example, the Little Three (Amherst, Wesleyan, and Williams) in NESCAC have agreed to limit the number of football "tips" to 14, but minority students and legacies will not count, and it is not entirely clear how the schools will treat the academically superior student who is also judged by the coach to be an excellent athlete. Welch Suggs, "Colleges in New England Cut Back on Admitting Athletes," *Chronicle of Higher Education,* January 11, 2002, p. 48. For these reasons, Emerson at Middlebury prefers the definition of a "recruit" used in this study—a recruit is anyone on a coach's list, whatever the individual's other characteristics. John Emerson, letter to Bowen, August 12, 2002.

44. Malekoff (2002), pp. 6–7.

45. Ibid., p. 7.

46. In the course of their review of the Swarthmore athletics program, that college's Athletics Review Committee spent considerable time working on a handbook for club sports that would address a number of specific and recurring issues. See Swarthmore College Athletics Review Committee (2002b) and Minutes of the Athletics Review Committee meeting of April 26, 2002, available at www. swarthmore.edu/news/athletics/Minutes-Apr%2026,%202002.pdf.

47. Biddiscombe, p. 4.

48. Princeton Trustee Committee, p. 1. These points are elaborated on pp. 15–17.

49. Charles Berry, letter to Bowen, February 28, 2001. Berry quotes an athletically active former Princeton undergraduate of a decade ago as telling him bluntly that attempting to "fix" other aspects of student life (the role of the eating clubs, the nature of the residential colleges, and so on) was too difficult a task to bring off, and also unnecessarily indirect. In this person's words: "Get rid of the athletic admits for football, baseball, and hockey, which is something you *can* do, and you'll get rid of most of the problems."

Chapter 13   Reform at the National Level

1. Information on Division III as a whole taken from National Collegiate Athletic Association (NCAA), *Division III Facts and Figures,* available at http://www1. ncaa.org/membership/governance/division_III/fact_sheet_d3_2, last updated May 8, 2002; enrollment and acceptance rates from College Board (2002b) and in Peterson's, *Peterson's Four-Year Colleges 2003* (Princeton, N.J.: Peterson's, 2002).

2. See National Collegiate Athletic Association (NCAA), "Future of Division III," available at http://www1.ncaa.org/membership/governance/division_III/ d3_future, accessed October 4, 2002, for a description of the joint subcommittee's charge, its timeline, agendas, minutes, and "updates" (including an outline of the issues on which it is focused with lists of policy options). The joint sub-

committee was formed from the two governing groups, the Division III Presidents Council and the Division III Management Council (which includes athletics administrators and faculty athletics representatives). An initial "convention discussion" took place in January 2003, with further discussion and possible legislation to take place at the January 2004 convention.

3. See Welch Suggs, "A Split Decision? The NCAA's Division III Debates Whether to Divide into 2 Groups," *Chronicle of Higher Education,* September 20, 2002, online edition; Stephen R. Lewis, letter to "Colleagues Interested in the Place of Intercollegiate Athletics," March 4, 2002, which was sent with a memorandum to Bowen headed "Further Thoughts on Division IIIA," January 25, 2002.

4. Lewis (2002a). Lewis has often referred to the possibility of creating a "Division IV," and we are reminded of the serious problem of nomenclature that arises whenever reorganizations are proposed. It would be much better if real names could be found for the various groups of schools so that the Division I, . . . III, IV terminology could be avoided altogether.

5. According to Robert Malekoff, in 1987 Division III adopted a 21-week limit on the length of playing seasons in each sport in an effort "(1) to control costs in intercollegiate athletics; (2) to afford student-athletes the opportunity to explore other aspects of college life; and (3) to permit member institutions a means by which to support broad-based athletics programs"—goals that drive at least some of the continuing discussions of the length of the practice and playing season. Although the 21-week limit was shorter than Division I's 26-week playing season limit, it still gave teams enough leeway to practice and compete during the non-traditional segment of the season, which might precede or follow the traditional segment (allowing baseball teams, for example, to practice for several weeks during the fall). The 21-week season did not receive unanimous approval at the time it was adopted; some schools objected that by allowing practice and competition during the non-traditional segment, it was not restrictive enough, and others objected that it limited institutional autonomy. By the time a January 1999 set of straw votes among Division III members indicated a desire to modify the 21-week limit, some conferences within the division were playing to the 21-week limit, others were following the same practice but were considering further limits, and others had adopted season lengths that either reduced or eliminated non-traditional practice/competition time.

In January 2000, Division III members considered, but voted to send back to the Presidents Council, a proposal to prohibit competition (except in golf and tennis) during the non-traditional part of the season. In the spring of 2000, the Division III Management Council recommended that the Presidents Council sponsor legislation to prohibit missed class time and overnight travel for competition during the non-traditional season. The Presidents Council declined to sponsor this legislation both because they wanted to encourage members to sponsor legislation and because they felt that the limit on missed class time might not sufficiently curb activities in the non-traditional season, while the limit on overnight travel would be too regulatory.

At the 2001 convention, Division III members voted on three proposals to modify practice and competition during the non-traditional part of the season and two of these were adopted. The proposal that was rejected would have allowed for a four-week period of limited practice (including practice supervised by team captains) and competition during the non-traditional segment. Proponents felt that this proposal would limit missed classes, would save money, and would still give athletes ample opportunity to practice. Others, including the NCAA Management and Presidents Councils, objected to this proposal because it was not sufficiently tailored to individual sports and because of the possible risks associated with student-supervised practices. One of the two proposals that was adopted applied only to baseball and to softball. It eliminated the option to count the days of baseball and softball tournaments, where multiple games might be played, as one contest, and it set the maximum number of contests per season at 45, with no more than 40 of these occurring during the traditional segment of the season. Finally, in what Donna Ledwin of the New Jersey Athletic Conference called a "solution that addresses the concerns of both the presidents and the student-athletes and accommodates the broad range of approaches to the Division III philosophy," members adopted Proposal 50, which applies to the team sports of baseball, field hockey, lacrosse, soccer, softball, and women's volleyball. Proposal 50 prohibits students on these teams from missing class time due to athletics during the non-traditional segment of the season, and it limits practice and competition in the non-traditional segment to five weeks. Under the revised regulations, teams can continue to compete, as well as to practice, during the non-traditional segment (though, because of the five-week limit on that segment, their overall season length may be reduced). See National Collegiate Athletic Association (NCAA), *NCAA Convention Proceedings,* 1999–2001. Convention proceedings starting with 2001 are available at http://www.ncaa.org. Earlier years can be found in many libraries. For an overview, through 1998, of the Division III debate on the non-traditional season, see Malekoff (1998).

Division III members revisited the issue of limits on the playing and practice seasons at the 2003 NCAA Convention. Once again, the membership failed to reach consensus. As Kay Hawes reported in the *NCAA News,* "by a margin of only 30 institutions [out of more than 400], the membership rejected Proposal No. 41, as amended, which would have standardized playing and practice seasons and provided for a modest reduction in contests in some sports." Hawes, "Division III Convention Actions Speak Louder Than Words in 'Future' Issue," *NCAA News,* January 20, 2003, p. 1.

6. These principles and objectives, as well as the following list of functions to be served by a new grouping, are in harmony with the letter and accompanying materials prepared by President Stephen Lewis. See Lewis (2002a and 2002b).

7. The shakiness of this tenet is evident in a recent article that describes how Swarthmore athletic teams have fared since the school dropped football. A number of coaches have expressed pleasure in their teams' outcomes since they have received more athletic admissions slots than they were allowed when Swarthmore sponsored football. Nevertheless, when asked how Swarthmore might expand its recruiting practices, Athletic Director Bob Williams responded: "We need to remain competitive. And who's to say down the road we won't be awarding aid for athletic merit?" Matthew Fitting, "Taking a Swing at a New Way of Slotting," *Swarthmore Phoenix,* October 3, 2002, online edition.

8. See Kay Hawes, "Financial Aid Audit Takes One Step Back, Two Ahead," *NCAA News,* April 1, 2002, online edition; National Collegiate Athletic Association (NCAA), *Division III Financial Aid Audit Proposal,* available at http://www1.ncaa.org/membership/governance/division_III/docs/financial_aid_audit_task force/financial_aid_task_force, accessed October 7, 2002.

9. We even considered suggesting the limited use of a lottery approach in assigning places to some number of at-large or independent schools that ranked above a competitive threshold; the logic behind this suggestion is that the introduction of a certain random element into the process would be consistent with the thought that postseason competition should be a "rare opportunity" and not something on which a team can count. However, any such approach would no doubt seem unfair to many and inconsistent with the idea that the "best" teams should be the ones included (with *best* defined according to some objective criteria). Similarly, we contemplated recommending that teams not be allowed to compete at the national level more than, say, two or three years in a row, but here, too, there are serious issues of fairness. Why, students would surely ask, should this year's team be excluded because some former team from the same school competed the previous year?

10. We are told that a proposal of this general kind has been under discussion within Division I. There is, of course, the risk that any such approach would create perverse incentives: for example, putting pressure on athletes to take easier courses.

11. NCAA (2002d).

12. Thelin (1996), p. 170.

13. Bernstein, pp. 247–48.

14. One modest advantage of starting over is that the awkward problem of nomenclature within the NCAA structure would be avoided. To some people "Division III" (or "Division IIIA" or "Division X") sounds pejorative. This is not a new concern. Jack Falla's *Diamond Anniversary History* of the NCAA notes that there was considerable discussion of "labeling" when the current divisional structure was established. Some favored using colors to avoid the "one, two, three" implication. Falla, p. 232.

15. As noted earlier, Division I schools must play 100 percent of the minimum number of contests required in a sport against other Division I opponents—and 50 percent of any additional contests. Thus, Lafayette plays in Division I (Division IAA in football within the Patriot League), and its field hockey team scheduled 19 contests for the 2002 season. The minimum number of contests for field hockey is 11. Thus Lafayette field hockey could play a maximum of 4 Division III opponents (50 percent of the "extra" 8 contests). The difficulties of competing across divisional lines are compounded by the NCAA's requirement that Division I schools offer a minimum number of athletic scholarships in a wide variety of sports (with minimum scholarship requirements becoming more stringent). Schools that offer athletic scholarships are generally able to attract the most talented players, which causes a significant ability gap between these schools and the non-scholarship schools of Division III. Recall from the addendum to the introduction that the Ivies are exempt from Division I scholarship requirements because of a grandfather clause.

16. In the sports pages of the *Daily Princetonian* David Baumgarten recently (October 4, 2002) described such a situation in a headline that read, "Tops in Ivies, but Weak Outside, Field Hockey Faces Old Dominion." The article went on to describe Princeton's dilemma: "The field hockey team stands poised to take home the Ivy League crown for the ninth straight year. Out of conference, however, the team has been anything but dominating."

17. Gary T. Brown, "Management Councils Take Mountain-Sized Steps at Denver Session," *NCAA News,* April 5, 2002, online edition; Paul Letlow and Barry Johnson, "I-A Schools Set to Adapt Sports for Rule Changes," *News-Star* (Monroe, La.), April 28, 2002, p. 1A.

18. Recall that the Division I statement of philosophy emphasizes "regional and national excellence and prominence" and maintains that college athletics— particularly "the traditional spectator-oriented, income-producing sports of football and basketball"—serve both "the university or college community . . . and the general public." See the addendum to the introduction. In reflecting on the history of this question, the Princeton Trustee Committee says: "The University could have decided 30 years ago to reduce the number of varsity sports or to lower the levels at which its varsity teams compete. This was not the course adopted. Instead, the University and its Ivy League competitors chose to maintain participation in Division I, providing students with opportunities to excel at this high national level. To accomplish this objective, the University accommodated itself to the forces of change in athletics" (p. 9). It would have been very difficult 30 years ago to anticipate all the "accommodations" that would be required as a result of the changes in intercollegiate sports, especially at the Division I level, that have taken place in the intervening years.

19. We were also told that 15 or 20 years ago the restrictions on who a school could play were much looser. In those days a school like the University of Dayton would play basketball at the Division I level but otherwise play mostly in Division III. Dayton used to win the Division III football championship, which greatly annoyed the "pure" Division III schools. Thus it was the Division III schools, not the Division I schools, that wanted tighter restrictions on "mixed" divisional play. We are indebted to James Delaney, commissioner of the Big Ten, for many helpful comments on various parts of this section.

20. At present Division III schools are allowed to play at the Division I level in one sport, which explains why the Johns Hopkins lacrosse team is allowed to compete for the Division I championship in lacrosse even though Hopkins is a Division III university and was a member of the UAA. But this limited class of exceptions is very different from a more generalized mixed-division model.

21. Such a partial realignment within Division I would no doubt require reconsideration of the distribution of NCAA revenues among Division I schools, but continuing debates over the right distribution of these large sums of money are inevitable in any case.

22. See, for example, the recent op-ed piece by William C. Dowling, a longtime member of Rutgers 1000, or RU1000, "a coalition of Rutgers students, alumni, and faculty [that] have worked to end the sorry reign of 'professionalized' sports at Rutgers." It is titled "The Liberty League: It's Time" (*Daily Targum,* September 10, 2002, online edition), and in it Dowling argues that Rutgers

should move either to Division IAA or to Division III. He suggests that Rutgers might take the lead in forming a new Division IAA non-athletic-scholarship conference that would include other "colonial" state universities such as the University of Delaware, the University of Massachusetts, and the College of William and Mary. Alternatively, he suggests going the Division III route, as New York University, Tufts, and others have done. A CNN Sports Illustrated columnist, Mike Fish, reports on Dowling's efforts and then quotes a number of Rutgers officials and others as remaining strongly in favor of the Division I model. Fish, "Lights Out for Knights? Rutgers Football Facing a Struggle On and Off the Field," CNN Sports Illustrated, September 27, 2002, available at CNNSI.com.

Chapter 14   Achieving Change

1. Thelin (1996), p. viii. In his earlier study, widely regarded as the most systematic history of this subject, Thelin observed: "The recurrence of the same language and motifs in the national studies every two decades or so leaves a perplexing question: if the reform reports were consequential, why have the same problems persisted without solutions over more than a half century? . . . One explanation is that invocation of the same themes and words by each generation of sports reformers has tended to obscure an unfortunate drift. The vocabulary has remained the same, but the expectations have changed almost beyond recognition. . . . An equally durable legacy has been the capacity of athletic departments and their supporters to defer publicly to the rhetoric of reform while simultaneously diluting the intent of the new policies and proposals." Thelin (1996), pp. 197–98.

2. Thus we are certainly not suggesting that big-time athletics programs generally "make money." In very, very few cases is this true, even when the financial equation excludes capital costs. When capital costs are also taken into account, it is doubtful that *any* Division I school earns a dollar return on its athletics program. See Shulman and Bowen, pp. 244–57. From a strictly financial standpoint, most Division I schools would be better off moving to Division III. It is more than a little curious that financial justifications are often used to support programs that are, in fact, financial drains, but it is perceptions, not realities, that are often most important. Of course great public universities, such as the University of Michigan, also need to be sensitive to the role of successful big-time sports programs in building political support for their budgets within the state legislature.

3. Some hope is provided by reports that financial pressures were at least part of the motivation in the creation of a coalition between the Association of Governing Boards, a large organization that represents college and university trustees, and the faculty senates of several Division IA universities intent on scaling back intercollegiate athletics. Bill Pennington, "Unusual Alliance Forming to Rein In College Sports," *New York Times,* January 17, 2003, online edition.

4. Shulman and Bowen, pp. 251–53.

5. Commitments to create new facilities or renovate old ones (both athletic facilities and facilities of many other kinds) can lead to high debt charges that can endanger budget stability, especially if endowments are hurt by the disappointing performance of financial markets. Standard & Poor's released a report in late

November 2002 discussing this issue and other financial and accounting problems. Martin van der Werf, "Many Colleges Could Close or Merge Because of Financial Problems, Standard & Poor's Warns," *Chronicle of Higher Education*, November 27, 2002, online edition.

6. For an elaboration of these barriers to reform, see Shulman and Bowen, pp. 290–94.

7. Knight Foundation Commission, pp. 24–25.

8. Cited in Dan Covell and Carol A. Barr, "The Ties that Bind: Presidential Involvement with the Development of NCAA Division I Initial Eligibility Legislation," *Journal of Higher Education* 72 (4) (July–August 2001): 11–12.

9. Thelin (1996), p. 10.

10. See Middlebury Ad Hoc Committee (2002a), p. 14, for a good discussion of the tension between institutional autonomy and the need for collaborative action.

11. William Adams, letter to Bowen, October 2002.

12. A phrase describing higher education in America that has been attributed to the historian Laurence Veysey by Thelin (1996), p. xx.

13. No one likes criticism or wants to spend time contending with angry groups of people. See the further discussion of this important barrier to reform in the next sub-section, "Orchestrating a Good Process."

14. "It is generally true that whatever attitudes the members of any given board collectively hold about the role of college sports, they are most likely ones that evolved under earlier boards and are being supported by the current administration. In this and other similar regards, *trustees tend not to be agents of change*, yet it will be important . . . to gain the attention of boards of trustees and to develop . . . suggestions for reform in terms that will make sense and appeal to them." George H. Hanford, *An Inquiry into the Need for and Feasibility of a National Study of Intercollegiate Athletics* (Washington, D.C.: American Council on Education, 1974), p. 28.

15. At the national level, the Drake Group has devoted considerable time and energy to discussing and writing about conflicts between educational values and athletics programs. Their emphasis, however, is mainly on issues at the Division I level, whereas we are concerned primarily with the Ivies and with Division III programs. One well-known member of the Drake Group, Allen Sack, a professor at the University of New Haven, is quoted as saying: "Our role is to dig in our heels and take back our classrooms." For a report on the meeting of the Drake Group last March, see Stefan Fatsis, "March Brings Usual Madness: Basketball over Academics," *Wall Street Journal*, March 22, 2002, online edition. The Drake Group Web site (http://www.thedrakegroup.org) includes their "Proposals for Action"; notes from their 1999, 2000, and 2002 meetings; and a copy of their brochure. See also John R. Gerdy, "Facing Up to the Conflict between Athletics and Academics," *Priorities* 16 (Summer 2001): 1–15, and Welch Suggs, "Can Anyone Do Anything about College Sports?" *Chronicle of Higher Education*, February 23, 2001, p. A50.

16. Hanford, p. 34; emphasis in original.

17. It is worth repeating the trenchant post-mortem prepared by James Litvack, who was at the time the executive director of the Council of Ivy Group Presidents. He explains the failure of the Ivy proposals as follows: "The proposals

were a package that had to be treated together. With the recent creation of the Policy Committee, it was clear the proposals had to go to them for analysis and discussion. With all the other proposals that were being considered at the time and with specific subcommittees dealing with proposals for change, it . . . [was] also clear that the proposals would be separated and often evaluated in terms of effects on competitive equity or athletic department costs. The proposals were not designed to address these issues. Separated from each other and in an environment somewhat removed from the view of education that had generated them, they had no chance to survive." Litvack, p. 15.

18. Norman Fainstein (president of Connecticut College and 2002–03 NESCAC chair), "Statement on NESCAC Reforms," sent to authors December 20, 2002.

19. In the words of the Princeton Trustee Committee report: "Unfortunately, once the decision was made it was not effectively communicated. Further, appropriate arrangements were not made beforehand to provide a meaningful intercollegiate, if non-varsity, experience for recruited students already in the program. These shortcomings weakened the institution's capacity to explain adequately what had been done, and why. The Trustees recognize—and regret—the errors in handling this matter and have taken steps to assure ourselves that these will not be repeated in the future" (p. 24).

20. Comments by Thomas H. Wright, secretary of the university and an active participant in the process.

21. A rower at Cornell, Per Ostman, writes (in an article titled "The Death of Sport"): "They are killing me. They are threatening my way of life. 'They' are the members of the Council of Ivy League Presidents, including our own Hunter R. Rawlings III. . . . Its members are trying to kill all Ivy League sports." The writer is referring to the decision to declare an official "time-off" period from organized practice and supervised training. *Cornell Daily Sun*, October 11, 2002, online edition.

22. See Tilghman for a model response.

23. Shulman and Bowen, especially pp. 199–204.

List of Figures

Chapter 9

List of Tables

APPENDIX TABLE 1.1

Colleges and Universities Included in the Expanded College and Beyond
Database, with the Sizes of Their 1995 Entering Cohorts

Ivy League Universities	
Brown University	1,370
Columbia University	1,158
Cornell University*	1,780
Dartmouth College	1,034
Harvard University	1,609
Princeton University	1,208
University of Pennsylvania	2,356
Yale University	1,364
Total	11,879
Average	1,485
UAA Universities	
Carnegie Mellon University	1,209
Emory University	1,203
University of Chicago	976
Washington University in St. Louis	1,184
Total	4,572
Average	1,144
NESCAC Colleges	
Amherst College	409
Bates College	429
Bowdoin College	449
Colby College	544
Connecticut College	451
Hamilton College	488
Middlebury College	580
Trinity College	504
Tufts University	1,158
Wesleyan University	709
Williams College	524
Total	6,245
Average	568
Average excluding Tufts**	509

(continued)

APPENDIX TABLE 1.1 (*Continued*)

Coed Liberal Arts Colleges (Other)	
Carleton College	463
Denison University	700
Kenyon College	438
Macalester College	437
Oberlin College	763
Pomona College	392
Swarthmore College	354
Total	3,547
Average	506
Women's Colleges	
Bryn Mawr College	353
Smith College	631
Wellesley College	584
Total	1,568
Average	523
Total	27,811

Source: Expanded Colledge and Beyond database.

* Cornell University data are limited to the College of Arts and Sciences and the College of Engineering.

** The average excluding Tufts is presented to reflect the average size of the more "typical" NESCAC college.

APPENDIX TABLE 3.1
SAT Distribution for Recruited Athletes and All Other
Applicants, 1999 Applicant Pool, Coed Liberal Arts Colleges
(Other) and Women's Colleges (percent)

	Male Recruited Athletes	*All Other Male Applicants*	*Female Recruited Athletes*	*All Other Female Applicants*
Coed Liberal Arts Colleges (Other)				
No SAT	17	14	14	16
Below 1000	1	2	2	3
1000–1099	6	4	5	6
1100–1199	13	9	14	11
1200–1299	21	16	22	18
1300–1399	24	23	24	23
1400–1499	13	21	16	18
1500–1600	5	11	4	6
Women's Colleges				
No SAT			5	10
Below 1000			4	4
1000–1099			9	7
1100–1199			12	13
1200–1299			36	22
1300–1399			20	23
1400–1499			12	16
1500–1600			3	5

Source: Expanded College and Beyond database.

APPENDIX TABLE 3.2

High School Athletic Participation, by Gender, for High-Scoring Takers
of the SAT (SAT > 1200) Intending to Apply to GOL, Ivy League,
and NESCAC Schools, 1989 and 1995 Test-Takers (percent)

	Percent of Men Playing HS Sports	Percent of Men Playing Four Years	Percent of Women Playing HS Sports	Percent of Women Playing Four Years
1989 Test-Takers Intending to Apply to:				
GOL institutions*	47	13	44	12
Ivy League universities	48	13	46	13
NESCAC colleges	44	13	41	11
1995 Test-Takers Intending to Apply to:				
GOL institutions*	60	20	50	19
Ivy League universities	59	21	51	19
NESCAC colleges	62	22	53	19

Source: Special tabulations from the High Test-Takers database.

* GOL institutions include Amherst College, Barnard College, Bates College, Bowdoin College, Bryn Mawr College, Carleton College, Colby College, Columbia University, Connecticut College, Denison University, Duke University, Emory University, Georgetown University, Hamilton College, Kenyon College, Macalester College, Miami University, Middlebury College, Northwestern University, Oberlin College, Pennsylvania State University, Pomona College, Princeton University, Rice University, Smith College, Stanford University, Swarthmore College, Trinity College, Tufts University, Tulane University, the University of Michigan, the University of North Carolina, the University of Notre Dame, the University of Pennsylvania, Vanderbilt University, Washington University, Wellesley College, Wesleyan University, Williams College, and Yale University.

APPENDIX TABLE 4.1

Percent of Athletes Who Are Recruited, by Conference,
Gender, and Sport, 1995 Entering Cohort

	Ivy League Universities	UAA Universities	NESCAC Colleges	Coed Liberal Arts Colleges (Other)
Men				
Baseball	84	50	62	61
Basketball	82	41	64	61
Crew	27		20	
Cross country	63	59	36	59
Fencing	38			
Football	83	81	72	79
Golf	57		58	67
Ice hockey	89		64	
Lacrosse	73		56	70
Other sports	42		48	
Sailing	15		40	
Soccer	64	50	52	69
Sprint football	9			
Squash	46		38	
Swimming	82	63	54	73
Tennis	58		28	61
Track	56	44	42	59
Wrestling	81		46	
Women				
Basketball	75	69	60	58
Crew	28		16	
Cross country	64	43	37	51
Fencing	38			
Field hockey	64		58	69
Gymnastics	69			
Ice hockey	70		69	
Lacrosse	62		59	64
Other sports	45		45	
Sailing	20		27	
Soccer	59	53	58	45
Softball	63		48	43
Squash	54		33	
Swimming	70	62	52	74
Tennis	72	37	48	49
Track	63	40	51	52
Volleyball	56	73	54	60

Source: Expanded College and Beyond database.

APPENDIX TABLE 4.2

Percent of Athletes and Students at Large Who Receive Need-Based Aid, by Conference, Type of Sport, and Recruit Status, 1995 Entering Cohort

	Ivy League Universities	UAA Universities	NESCAC Colleges	Coed Liberal Arts Colleges (Other)
High Profile Male Athletes				
Students at large	47	42	46	49
Walk-on athletes	40	69	53	70
Recruited athletes	74	64	64	78
Lower Profile Male Athletes				
Students at large	47	42	46	49
Walk-on athletes	43	65	37	44
Recruited athletes	53	38	45	57
Female Athletes				
Students at large	51	47	50	57
Walk-on athletes	41	49	39	50
Recruited athletes	53	60	46	51

Source: Expanded College and Beyond database.

APPENDIX TABLE 5.1

Distribution of Athletes and Students at Large across Fields of Study,
by Conference, Type of Sport, and Recruit Status,
1995 Male Entering Cohort (percent)

	Ivy League Universities	UAA Universities	NESCAC Colleges	Coed Liberal Arts Colleges (Other)
Social Sciences/Business				
Male students at large	33	26/36*	36	34
High Profile recruits	55	35	61	51
High Profile walk-ons	45	50	52	42
Lower Profile recruits	41	45	55	46
Lower Profile walk-ons	35	37	38	42
Sciences				
Male students at large	41	46/38*	24	20
High Profile recruits	18	42	13	19
High Profile walk-ons	36	46	21	26
Lower Profile recruits	27	36	18	26
Lower Profile walk-ons	38	50	28	21
Humanities				
Male students at large	21	7/12*	31	27
High Profile recruits	17	5	20	20
High Profile walk-ons	13	0	20	29
Lower Profile recruits	24	14	28	18
Lower Profile walk-ons	24	12	31	23

Source: Expanded College and Beyond database.

* The first number includes data for Carnegie Mellon University and Washington University only, and the second number also includes Emory University. This is because the data for High Profile athletes in the UAA universities are limited to Carnegie Mellon and Washington, while the data for Lower Profile male athletes in the UAA universities also include Emory.

APPENDIX TABLE 5.2

Five-Year Graduation Rates of Athletes and of Students at Large, by
Conference, Type of Sport, and Recruit Status, 1995 Entering Cohort (percent)

	Ivy League Universities	UAA Universities	NESCAC Colleges	Coed Liberal Arts Colleges (Other)
High Profile Male Athletes				
Students at large	91	79	82	73
Walk-on athletes	96	83	86	76
Recruited athletes	86	88	87	78
Lower Profile Male Athletes				
Students at large	91	79	82	73
Walk-on athletes	92	88	89	83
Recruited athletes	89	82	90	88
Female Athletes				
Students at large	93	83	86	81
Walk-on athletes	95	96	93	90
Recruited athletes	95	89	94	89

Source: Expanded College and Beyond database.

APPENDIX TABLE 5.3
Average Percentile Rank in Class of Athletes, by Conference,
Gender, and Sport, 1995 Entering Cohort

	Ivy League Universities	UAA Universities	NESCAC Colleges	Coed Liberal Arts Colleges (Other)
Men				
Baseball	30	57	30	40
Basketball	26	54	33	37
Crew	43		43	
Cross country	40	56	49	57
Fencing	43			
Football	21	40	26	25
Golf	44		34	44
Ice hockey	26		30	
Lacrosse	29		34	38
Other sports	38	52	42	51
Sailing	53		40	
Soccer	35	46	41	44
Sprint football	44			
Squash	46		40	
Swimming	28	37	42	29
Tennis	46		53	50
Track	34	43	40	35
Wrestling	24		20	
Women				
Basketball	37	49	50	49
Crew	48		52	
Cross country	47	61	59	62
Fencing	51			
Field hockey	42		43	38
Gymnastics	34			
Ice hockey	38		35	
Lacrosse	43		43	42
Other sports	49	41	49	57
Sailing	53		57	
Soccer	50	45	51	51
Softball	38		46	47
Squash	46		49	
Swimming	41	60	53	56
Tennis	47	43	52	69
Track	38	52	53	54
Volleyball	46	50	46	56

Source: Expanded College and Beyond database.

APPENDIX TABLE 6.1

Underperformance of Athletes, by Gender, Recruit Status, and Type
of Sport, Controlling for High School Grades, Differences in Race,
Field of Study, SAT Scores, and Institutional SAT, 1995 Entering
Cohort, Ivy League Universities and NESCAC Colleges

	Without Controls for HS Rank	*With Controls for HS Rank*
Ivy League Men		
In top tenth of HS class		**7.8**
Recruited High Profile	**–19.0**	**–17.2**
Walk-on High Profile	**–7.2**	**–7.0**
Recruited Lower Profile	**–15.7**	**–14.3**
Walk-on Lower Profile	**–3.6**	**–3.6**
NESCAC Men		
In top tenth of HS class		**9.6**
Recruited High Profile	**–19.8**	**–19.0**
Walk-on High Profile	–4.8	**–5.0**
Recruited Lower Profile	**–11.1**	**–10.7**
Walk-on Lower Profile	**–3.8**	**–3.6**
Ivy League Women		
In top tenth of HS class		**5.0**
Recruited athletes	**–12.9**	**–12.5**
Walk-on athletes	**–5.2**	**–5.1**
NESCAC Women		
In top tenth of HS class		**10.9**
Recruited athletes	**–8.8**	**–7.9**
Walk-on athletes	**–5.3**	**–4.6**

Source: Expanded College and Beyond database.

Note: Numbers in **bold** are significant at the .05 level.

APPENDIX TABLE 6.2a
Underperformance of Male Athletes, by Conference, Recruit Status, and
Type of Sport, Controlling for Need-Based Financial Aid, Differences in Race,
Field of Study, SAT Scores, and Institutional SAT, 1995 Entering Cohort

	Without Controls for Need-Based Aid	*With Controls for Need-Based Aid*
Ivy League Men		
Received need-based aid		**−4.4**
Recruited High Profile	**−19.0**	**−18.0**
Walk-on High Profile	**−7.2**	**−7.7**
Recruited Lower Profile	**−15.7**	**−15.4**
Walk-on Lower Profile	**−3.6**	**−3.7**
NESCAC Men		
Received need-based aid		−0.6
Recruited High Profile	**−21.8**	**−21.7**
Walk-on High Profile	**−7.7**	**−7.6**
Recruited Lower Profile	**−12.1**	**−12.1**
Walk-on Lower Profile	**−3.9**	**−3.9**
UAA Men		
Received need-based aid		−0.1
High Profile athletes	**−7.2**	**−7.2**
Lower Profile athletes	−0.2	−0.2
Coed LAC (Other) Men		
Received need-based aid		**4.0**
High Profile athletes	**−10.6**	**−11.5**
Lower Profile athletes	**−7.0**	**−7.1**

Source: Expanded College and Beyond database.

Note: Numbers in **bold** are significant at the .05 level.

APPENDIX TABLE 6.2b
Underperformance of Female Athletes, by Conference and Recruit
Status, Controlling for Need-Based Financial Aid, Differences in Race,
Field of Study, SAT Scores, and Institutional SAT, 1995 Entering Cohort

	Without Controls for Need-Based Aid	*With Controls for Need-Based Aid*
Ivy League Women		
Received need-based aid		**–4.4**
Recruited athletes	**–12.9**	**–12.6**
Walk-on athletes	**–5.2**	**–5.5**
NESCAC Women		
Received need-based aid		1.8
Recruited athletes	**–11.3**	**–11.2**
Walk-on athletes	**–6.0**	**–5.8**
UAA Women		
Received need-based aid		2.4
Athletes	–2.4	–2.7
Coed LAC (Other) Women		
Received need-based aid		1.5
Athletes	–2.2	–2.1

Source: Expanded College and Beyond database.

Note: Numbers in **bold** are significant at the .05 level.

APPENDIX TABLE 6.3

Athlete-Aid Underperformance Interaction, by Gender and
Conference, Controlling for Differences in Race, Field of Study,
SAT Scores, and Institutional SAT, 1995 Entering Cohort

	Ivy League Universities	NESCAC Colleges	UAA Universities	Coed Liberal Arts Colleges (Other)
Men				
Main effects:				
Received need-based aid	**−6.1**	−2.7	−0.9	1.6
High Profile athlete			−13.6	−5.6
Recruited	**−18.9**	**−21.2**		
Walk-on	−4.8	**−12.2**		
Lower Profile athlete			−5.6	**−7.1**
Recruited	**−14.1**	**−12.4**		
Walk-on	**−4.4**	−3.1		
Interaction effects:				
High Profile athlete on aid			12.8	−8.1
Recruited	4.8	4.0		
Walk-on	−9.6	9.2		
Lower Profile athlete on aid			8.2	2.2
Recruited	1.8	5.1		
Walk-on	1.9	−2.4		
Women				
Main effects:				
Received need-based aid	**−7.4**	−1.1	0.5	−0.5
Athlete			−1.0	−1.1
Recruited	**−11.9**	**−8.4**		
Walk-on	**−5.5**	**−4.9**		
Interaction effects:				
Athlete on aid			−0.4	−0.1
Recruited	**5.3**	4.3		
Walk-on	2.7	1.2		

Source: Expanded College and Beyond database.

Note: Numbers in **bold** are significant at the .05 level.

APPENDIX TABLE 6.4

Athlete-SAT Underperformance Interaction, by Type of Sport,
Recruit Status, and Conference, Controlling for Differences in Race,
Field of Study, SAT Scores, and Institutional SAT, 1995 Entering Cohort

	Ivy League Universitites	*NESCAC Colleges*
High Profile Male Athletes		
Recruited		
Low SAT	**−19.2**	**−19.3**
Mid SAT	**−22.2**	**−25.8**
High SAT	−2.2	−8.4
Walk-on		
Low SAT	−10.6	**−8.2**
Mid SAT	−7.0	−7.2
High SAT	−3.5	−6.4
Lower Profile Male Athletes		
Recruited		
Low SAT	**−17.1**	**−9.4**
Mid SAT	**−17.0**	**−14.0**
High SAT	**−7.3**	**−9.8**
Walk-on		
Low SAT	−2.0	**−6.7**
Mid SAT	**−3.6**	**−4.5**
High SAT	**−4.0**	−3.3
Female Athletes		
Recruited		
Low SAT	**−16.0**	**−13.3**
Mid SAT	**−11.6**	**−11.9**
High SAT	−5.4	−5.2
Walk-on		
Low SAT	**−5.9**	**−6.9**
Mid SAT	**−4.9**	**−7.0**
High SAT	**−5.2**	−2.1

Source: Expanded College and Beyond database.

Note: Numbers in **bold** are significant at the .05 level.

APPENDIX TABLE 6.5

Underperformance of Walk-On Athletes, by Year, Gender, Type of Sport, and
Whether Playing, Controlling for Differences in Race, Field of Study, SAT
Scores, and Institutional SAT, 1995 Entering Cohort, Ivy League Universities

	Freshman	*Sophomore*	*Junior*	*Senior*
Lower Profile Male Athletes				
Played	**–3.2**	**–6.0**	**–5.3**	–3.2
Did not play	–2.6	–0.2	**–4.1**	**–5.1**
Female Athletes				
Played	**–6.1**	**–6.2**	–3.3	–2.3
Did Not Play	–3.6	**–5.2**	–1.9	–1.5

Source: Expanded College and Beyond database.

Note: Numbers in **bold** are significant at the .05 level.

APPENDIX TABLE 6.6

Underperformance of Athletes, by Level of Play, Recruit Status,
and Type of Sport, Controlling for Differences in Race, Field
of Study, SAT Scores, and Institutional SAT, 1995 Entering
Cohort, Ivy League Universities and NESCAC Colleges

	Without Controls for Varsity Only	*With Controls for Varsity Only*
Ivy League Men		
Varsity only		−0.7
Recruited High Profile	**−13.8**	**−13.3**
Walk-on High Profile	−4.0	−3.8
Recruited Lower Profile	**−12.6**	**−12.1**
Walk-on Lower Profile	**−3.9**	−3.6
NESCAC Men		
Varsity only		**−5.3**
Recruited High Profile	**−23.4**	**−19.0**
Walk-on High Profile	**−13.4**	**−10.6**
Recruited Lower Profile	**−13.6**	**−9.3**
Walk-on Lower Profile	**−5.4**	−2.0
Ivy League Women		
Varsity only		−0.4
Recruited athletes	**−12.1**	**−11.8**
Walk-on athletes	**−4.1**	**−3.9**
NESCAC Women		
Varsity only		1.8
Recruited athletes	**−14.8**	**−16.2**
Walk-on athletes	**−7.1**	**−8.1**

Source: Expanded College and Beyond database.

Note: Numbers in **bold** are significant at the .05 level.

APPENDIX TABLE 6.7

Underperformance of Male Athletes, by Conference, Field of Study, Recruit Status, and Type of Sport, Controlling for Differences in Race, Field of Study, SAT Scores, and Institutional SAT, 1995 Entering Cohort

	Social Science and Business Majors	Other Majors
Ivy League Men		
Recruited High Profile	**−20.5**	**−16.5**
Walk-on High Profile	**−10.0**	−3.4
Recruited Lower Profile	**−16.9**	**−14.3**
Walk-on Lower Profile	−1.5	**−5.0**
NESCAC Men		
Recruited High Profile	**−21.6**	**−18.3**
Walk-on High Profile	**−8.3**	−6.3
Recruited Lower Profile	**−11.1**	**−11.5**
Walk-on Lower Profile	−2.7	**−5.6**
UAA Men		
Recruited High Profile	−9.8	−5.3
Walk-on High Profile		
Recruited Lower Profile	3.2	3.3
Walk-on Lower Profile	−7.1	1.4
Coed LAC Men		
Recruited High Profile	**−8.0**	**−8.6**
Walk-on High Profile		
Recruited Lower Profile	**−6.0**	**−7.7**
Walk-on Lower Profile	−2.1	−4.9

Source: Expanded College and Beyond database.

Note: Numbers in **bold** are significant at the .05 level.

APPENDIX TABLE 6.8

Underperformance of Athletes, by Conference,
Gender, Recruit Status, and Team Type, Controlling for
Differences in Race, Field of Study, SAT Scores, and Institutional SAT,
1995 Entering Cohort, Ivy League Universities and NESCAC Colleges

	Ivy League Universities	NESCAC Colleges
Men		
Recruits on low-recruit teams	**−18.3**	**−10.1**
Recruits on high-recruit teams	**−14.9**	**−11.5**
Walk-ons on low-recruit teams	**−3.2**	−3.0
Walk-ons on high-recruit teams	**−4.2**	**−7.9**
Women		
Recruits on low-recruit teams	**−13.0**	**−10.7**
Recruits on high-recruit teams	**−12.8**	**−11.3**
Walk-ons on low-recruit teams	**−5.7**	**−5.5**
Walk-ons on high-recruit teams	**−4.6**	**−5.1**

Source: Expanded College and Beyond database.
Note: Numbers in **bold** are significant at the .05 level.

Average Athletic Expenditures, by Conference and Gender, Academic Year 2000–01

	Recruiting Expenses	Travel Expenses	Total Operating Expenses	Total Expenditures	Number of Participants	Number of Teams
All Women's Sports						
Ivy League universities				$2,462,403	479	17
UAA universities	$36,983	$246,332	$312,199	$853,255	193	9
NESCAC colleges	$1,700	$144,720	$209,070	$703,405	330	15
Coed liberal arts colleges (other)	$1,190	$100,457	$154,364	$522,429	209	11
All Men's Sports						
Ivy League universities				$3,971,480	615	17
UAA universities	$40,480	$273,329	$361,413	$1,014,368	267	10
NESCAC colleges	$5,873	$169,658	$260,707	$952,343	403	14
Coed liberal arts colleges (other)	$20,352	$102,414	$181,086	$680,200	242	11
Total Expenditures						
Ivy League universities	$615,831		$2,006,713	$8,325,254	1094	34
UAA universities	$93,049	$521,613	$693,752	$2,545,981	460	19
NESCAC colleges	$9,348	$334,820	$505,429	$1,962,248	732	29
Coed liberal arts colleges (other)	$90,123	$216,470	$468,344	$1,578,671	451	22

Source: Equity in Athletics Disclosure Act worksheets and tables.

Note: UAA universities values include only Carnegie Mellon University, Emory University, New York University, the University of Chicago, and Washington University, St. Louis. NESCAC colleges values do not include Trinity College.

APPENDIX TABLE 7.2a

Average Athletic Expenditures, by Conference and Sport, Men's Sports Only, Academic Year 2000–01

	Recruiting Expenses	Travel Expenses	Total Operating Expenses	Total Expenditures	Number of Participants
Football					
Ivy League universities			$248,519	$1,188,749	103
UAA universities	$17,396	$61,907	$70,307	$351,695	90
NESCAC colleges	$2,914	$21,238	$44,458	$220,802	80
Coed liberal arts colleges (other)	$1,190	$17,108	$40,804	$184,014	56
Basketball					
Ivy League universities			$109,562	$413,440	22
UAA universities	$11,994	$54,634	$241,892	$191,772	21
NESCAC colleges	$771	$19,597	$26,516	$91,986	17
Coed liberal arts colleges (other)	$2,859	$10,087	$21,173	$74,574	16
Sports Other Than Football and Basketball					
Ivy League universities			$829,922	$2,369,280	490
UAA universities	$18,049	$181,551	$229,341	$605,780	192
NESCAC colleges	$2,479	$130,947	$194,179	$661,634	313
Coed liberal arts colleges (other)	$9,358	$65,965	$108,481	$380,572	170

Soccer					
Ivy League universities			$45,883	$120,247	33
UAA universities	$4,563	$37,234	$48,929	$67,847	28
NESCAC colleges	$434	$9,791	$15,727		28
Coed liberal arts colleges (other)	$1,451	$8,414	$11,125	$51,156	25
Tennis					
Ivy League universities			$42,447	$61,587	15
UAA universities	$2,185	$14,421	$19,184	$36,755	14
NESCAC colleges	$110	$6,532	$8,550		13
Coed liberal arts colleges (other)	$725	$5,769	$8,766	$38,455	11
Swimming and Diving					
Ivy League universities			$50,833	$106,771	31
UAA universities	$2,359	$35,277	$41,126	$53,651	23
NESCAC colleges	$191	$11,567	$14,608		23
Coed liberal arts colleges (other)	$1,644	$13,798	$18,705	$65,445	17

Source: Equity in Athletics Disclosure Act worksheets and tables.

Note: UAA universities values include only Carnegie Mellon University, Emory University, New York University, the University of Chicago, and Washington University, St. Louis. NESCAC colleges values do not include Trinity College.

APPENDIX TABLE 7.2b

Average Athletic Expenditures, by Conference and Sport, Women's Sports Only, Academic Year 2000–01

	Recruiting Expenses	Travel Expenses	Total Operating Expenses	Total Expenditures	Number of Participants
Basketball					
Ivy League universities			$89,230	$322,758	16
UAA universities	$11,577	$54,037	$70,307	$181,495	16
NESCAC colleges	$277	$13,578	$19,675	$70,095	14
Coed liberal arts colleges (other)	$1,190	$9,370	$18,744	$67,494	13
Sports Other Than Basketball					
Ivy League universities	$25,406	$192,295	$729,480	$2,185,014	463
UAA universities	$1,424	$131,142	$241,892	$647,774	177
NESCAC colleges	$8,375	$80,653	$189,395	$633,310	316
Coed liberal arts colleges (other)			$123,637	$417,628	196

Soccer

Ivy League universities	$7,443		$49,084		33
UAA universities		$40,898	$52,109	$112,232	28
NESCAC colleges	$226	$12,046	$18,870	$64,892	26
Coed liberal arts colleges (other)	$1,067	$6,929	$12,936	$42,003	24

Tennis

Ivy League universities	$2,972		$37,390		15
UAA universities		$16,742	$21,167	$67,740	19
NESCAC colleges	$64	$6,638	$8,672	$34,837	11
Coed liberal arts colleges (other)	$656	$8,414	$11,125	$39,466	10

Swimming and Diving

Ivy League universities	$3,764		$50,530		30
UAA universities		$36,683	$43,184	$111,588	23
NESCAC colleges	$188	$10,533	$14,022	$48,956	30
Coed liberal arts colleges (other)	$1,849	$15,833	$20,924	$73,399	25

Source: Equity in Athletics Disclosure Act worksheets and tables.

Note: UAA universities values include only Carnegie Mellon University, Emory University, New York University, the University of Chicago, and Washington University, St. Louis. NESCAC colleges values do not include Trinity College.

APPENDIX TABLE 8.1
Sears Cup Rank of Study Schools, by Conference and Year

	1995–96	1996–97	1997–98	1998–99	1999–00	2000–01	2001–02
NESCAC							
Amherst College	6	7	9	4	12	14	7
Bates College	58	51	49	79	35	50	45
Bowdoin College	9	45	62	55	56	53	27
Colby College	119	65	62	133	69	118	58
Connecticut College	105		116	59	211	244	148
Hamilton College	111	125	116	71	24	41	89
Middlebury College	15	12	4	2	5	2	4
Trinity College	206	90	76	34	116	66	55
Tufts University	39	31	84	45	40	24	59
Wesleyan University	197	121	167	208		168	108
Williams College	1	1	4	1	1	1	1
UAA							
Brandeis University	79	53	40	34	142	170	63
Carnegie Mellon University	65	134	94	79	127	123	68
Case Western Reserve University	84	183	197	133	110	59	66
Emory University	7	4	14	22	14	4	5
New York University	101	42	66	59	103	95	53
University of Chicago	195	38	66	79	69	80	177
University of Rochester	24	40	101	114	183	247	133
Washington University	33	35	10	13	23	16	17

Coed Liberal Arts Colleges (Other)

Carleton College	28	83	149	114	149	104	77
Denison University	45	36	29	15	27	19	44
Kenyon College	22	20	12	22	30	46	50
Macalester College	169	112	84	31	57		177
Oberlin College			197	208	139	189	
Pomona College	53	33	101	114	72	93	79
Swarthmore College	104	93	128	155	132	99	220

Women's Colleges

Bryn Mawr College	197	177	149		153		223
Smith College	124		128	71	77	148	160
Wellesley College							

Ivy League (Division I)

Brown University	95	40	74	51	46	62	68
Columbia/Barnard	161	169	82	163	96	112	148
Cornell University	79	90	202	163	79	122	72
Dartmouth	65	54	43	68	96	65	79
Harvard University	54	35	43	60	60	43	49
Princeton University	23	60	25	31	33	24	21
University of Pennsylvania	114	132	107	107	87	89	54
Yale University	154	111	127	141	141	86	69

Source: "Sears Directors' Cup Final Standings," as reported at the National Association of Collegiate Directors of Athletics (NACDA) Web site (http://www.nacda.com).

Note: Empty blocks denote that the school was not ranked that year.

APPENDIX TABLE 8.2a

Study Schools Reaching Final Eight in Division I NCAA Championships,
by Sport and Year, Academic Years 1998–2001, 1986–89, 1976–79, 1966–69

	Men			Women		
	1998–99	*1999–2000*	*2000–01*	*1998–99*	*1999–2000*	*2000–01*
Baseball						
Basketball						
Cross country						Yale University
Field hockey				Princeton University		Princeton University
Football						
Golf						
Ice hockey						
Indoor track						
Lacrosse		Princeton University	Princeton University*			
Outdoor track and field						
Soccer			Brown University	Dartmouth College		
Softball						
Swimming and diving						
Tennis						
Volleyball						
Wrestling						

	1986–87	1987–88	1988–89	1986–87	1987–88	1988–89
Baseball						
Basketball						
Cross country	Dartmouth College	Dartmouth College		Yale University	Yale University	
Field hockey					University of Pennsylvania	University of Pennsylvania
Football						
Golf						
Ice hockey	Harvard University		Harvard University*			
Indoor track						
Lacrosse	Cornell University	Cornell University			Harvard University	Harvard University Princeton University
Outdoor track and field						
Soccer	Harvard University					
Softball						
Swimming and diving						
Tennis						
Volleyball						
Wrestling						

continued

APPENDIX TABLE 8.2a (Continued)

	Men			Women		
	1976–77	1977–78	1978–79	1976–77	1977–78	1978–79
Baseball						
Basketball			University of Pennsylvania			
Cross country						
Field hockey						
Football						
Golf						
Ice hockey			Dartmouth College			
Indoor track			Dartmouth College Harvard University			
Lacrosse	Cornell University*	Cornell University				
Outdoor track and field						
Soccer	Brown University		Columbia University			
Softball						
Swimming and diving						
Tennis			Princeton University			
Volleyball						
Wrestling						

	1966–67	1967–68	1968–69
Baseball		Harvard University	NYU
Basketball			
Cross country			University of Pennsylvania
Field hockey			
Football			
Golf			
Ice hockey	Cornell University*	Cornell University	Cornell University Harvard University
Indoor track		Harvard University	Harvard University
Lacrosse			
Outdoor track and field			
Soccer	Trinity College	Brown University	Harvard University University of Pennsylvania
Softball			
Swimming and diving	Yale University	Yale University	Yale University
Tennis			
Volleyball			
Wrestling			

Sources: National Collegiate Athletic Association (NCAA), *Official 2001 NCAA National Collegiate Fall Championships Records Book, Official 2001 NCAA National Collegiate Winter Championships Records Book, Official 2001 NCAA National Collegiate Spring Championships Records Book,* available at the NCAA's Web site (http://www.ncaa.org).

  * Division I Champion.

APPENDIX TABLE 8.2b

Study Schools Reaching the Final Eight in Division III NCAA Championships,
by Sport and Year, Academic Years 1998–2001, 1986–89, 1976–79

	Men			Women		
	1998–99	*1999–2000*	*2000–01*	*1998–99*	*1999–2000*	*2000–01*
Baseball	Brandeis University	Emory University				
Basketball	Connecticut College Trinity College		University of Chicago	New York University Washington University* Williams College	Washington University*	Washington University* New York University
Cross country	Brandeis University Williams College		Williams College	Carnegie Mellon University Middlebury College University of Chicago Williams College	Hamilton College Macalester College Middlebury College Williams College	Middlebury College* Williams College
Field hockey				Middlebury College* Trinity College	Amherst College	Williams College
Football						
Golf	Emory University					
Ice hockey	Amherst College Middlebury College*	Middlebury College	Middlebury College			
Indoor track	Amherst College			Williams College	Tufts University Williams College	Williams College
Lacrosse	Denison University Middlebury College	Middlebury College*	Denison University Middlebury College*	Amherst College Bowdoin College Middlebury College*	Hamilton College Middlebury College Williams College	Amherst College Hamilton College Middlebury College*

Outdoor track and field	Hamilton College Williams College	University of Chicago Williams College	Williams College			
Soccer	Tufts University	Macalester College Williams College	Hamilton College Williams College	Williams College	Williams College	Macalester College Williams College
Softball		Tufts University				
Swimming and diving	Case Western Reserve University Denison University* Emory University Kenyon College Williams College	Denison University Emory University Kenyon College* Williams College	Amherst College Denison University Kenyon College* Williams College	Carnegie Mellon University Denison University Emory University Kenyon College*	Denison University Emory University Kenyon College* Hamilton College	Denison University Emory University Kenyon College* Middlebury College
Tennis	Amherst College Emory University Pomona-Pitzer Colleges Williams College*	Amherst College Emory University Kenyon College Williams College	Amherst College* Williams College	Emory University Williams College*	Emory University Williams College	Emory University Trinity College Williams College*
Volleyball	Washington University Wellesley College	Wellesley College	Washington University Wellesley College			
Wrestling						

continued

APPENDIX TABLE 8.2b (*Continued*)

	Men			Women		
	1986–87	*1987–88*	*1988–89*	*1986–87*	*1987–88*	*1988–89*
Baseball						
Basketball		Washington University				
Cross country		Brandeis University University of Rochester	Brandeis University University of Rochester	University of Rochester	Carleton College University of Rochester	Carleton College
Field hockey						
Football						
Golf						
Ice hockey						
Indoor track		Carleton College	Bates College MIT	University of Rochester	Carleton College	Tufts University University of Rochester
Lacrosse		Denison University				
Outdoor track and field	Denison University Pomona-Pitzer Colleges	Carleton College	MIT		Smith College	
Soccer	Washington University	Emory University		University of Rochester*		University of Rochester
Softball						
Swimming and diving	Denison University Kenyon College* University of Rochester	Carleton College Denison University Kenyon College*	Denison University Kenyon College* Williams College	Denison University Kenyon College* Pomona-Pitzer Colleges	Denison University Emory University Kenyon College*	Denison University Emory University Kenyon College*
Tennis	Swarthmore College University of Rochester	Emory University Swarthmore College	Pomona-Pitzer Colleges Swarthmore College	Emory University Kenyon College	Emory University Kenyon College Pomona-Pitzer Colleges Smith College	Emory University Kenyon College Pomona-Pitzer Colleges
Volleyball				Washington University	Washington University	Washington University
Wrestling						

	1976–77	1977–78	1978–79	1976–77	1977–78	1978–79
Baseball	Brandeis University	Brandeis University				
Basketball		Brandeis University				
Cross country	Bates College Brandeis University		Brandeis University Carleton College			
Field hockey						
Football		Carnegie Mellon University	Carnegie Mellon University			
Golf			University of Rochester			
Ice hockey						
Indoor track						
Lacrosse						
Outdoor track and field		Brandeis University				
Soccer		Washington University	Brandeis University Denison University Washington University			
Softball						
Swimming and diving						
Tennis						
Volleyball						
Wrestling						

Sources: NCAA, Official 2001 NCAA National Collegiate Fall Championships Records Book, Official 2001 NCAA National Collegiate Winter Championships Records Book, Official 2001 NCAA National Collegiate Spring Championships Records Book, available at the NCAA's Web site (http://www.ncaa.org).

* Division III champion.

APPENDIX TABLE 9.1
Acceptance Rates, by Conference and School, 1990, 1993 and 2000 (percent)

	1990	1993	2000
Ivy League Universities			
Brown University	23	26	16
Columbia University	28	29	13
Cornell University	30	37	31
Dartmouth College	26	26	21
Harvard University	18	16	11
Princeton University			12
University of Pennsylvania	42	42	23
Yale University	20	23	16
NESCAC Colleges			
Amherst College	22	23	19
Bates College	42	45	29
Bowdoin College	27	30	28
Colby College	41	47	37
Connecticut College	45	51	32
Hamilton College	43	57	39
Middlebury College	40	34	25
Trinity College	50	59	30
Tufts University	46	47	26
Wesleyan University	40	43	27
Williams College	28	30	24
UAA Universities			
Brandeis University	67	66	48
Carnegie Mellon University	72	60	36
Case Western Reserve	86	81	71
Emory University	66	49	45
New York University	54	53	29
University of Chicago	46	47	44
University of Rochester	62	63	51
Washington University	59	68	30
Coed Liberal Arts Colleges (Other)			
Carleton College	47	59	44
Denison University	70	83	68
Kenyon College		70	65
Macalester College	56	51	53
Oberlin College	54	64	39
Pomona College	37	36	30
Swarthmore College	32	39	24
Women's Colleges			
Bryn Mawr College	60	57	59
Smith College	63	55	53
Wellesley College	49	43	43

Sources: College Board, *College Handbook* 1992, 1995, 2002.

APPENDIX TABLE 9.2

Acceptance Rates for Recruited Athletes, Minority Students,
and All Other Applicants, by Gender, SAT Scores,
and Conference, 1999 Applicant Pool (percent)

SAT Scores	Male Recruited Athletes	Male Minority Students	Male Students at Large	Female Recruited Athletes	Female Minority Students	Female Students at Large
Ivy League Universities						
Below 1000		0	1	4	1	0
1000–1099	7	3	1	26	11	0
1100–1199	42	23	2	53	26	3
1200–1299	48	27	4	60	36	5
1300–1399	66	47	8	78	65	10
1400–1499	74	59	18	80	63	22
1500–1600	82	53	36	80	54	40
NESCAC Colleges						
Below 1000	29	23	3	14	27	5
1000–1099	38	53	5	29	42	5
1100–1199	46	46	9	50	63	10
1200–1299	65	64	17	69	68	19
1300–1399	76	71	36	78	84	40
1400–1499	78	66	54	89	70	59
1500–1600	96	100	68	87	62	75
Coed Liberal Arts Colleges (Other)						
Below 1000	19	24	5	27	20	6
1000–1099	36	45	14	47	50	18
1100–1199	58	62	21	58	63	27
1200–1299	71	68	34	66	76	41
1300–1399	75	78	47	80	87	52
1400–1499	85	63	62	87	88	67
1500–1600	94	76	77	83	89	79
Women's Colleges						
Below 1000				11	8	2
1000–1099				47	41	10
1100–1199				79	67	26
1200–1299				70	67	45
1300–1399				83	74	64
1400–1499				92	93	78
1500–1600						84

Source: Expanded College and Beyond database.

APPENDIX TABLE 12.1

Conference Rules Governing Length and Activities of Traditional and Non-Traditional Sports Seasons

Conference	Maximum Total Season Length (All Sports)	Traditional Fall Season	Traditional Winter Season	Traditional Spring Season	Non-Traditional Season	Off-Season
Ivy League	26 weeks	17 weeks	20 weeks	18 weeks	12 practices 2 dates of competition Voluntary conditioning	**Impermissible activities:** "Any meeting, activity or instruction involving sports-related information and having an athletic purpose, and held for one or more student-athletes at the direction of, or supervised by, any member or members of an institution's coaching staff." **Permissible activities:** 1. Supervised, voluntary conditioning 2. Small group skills instruction 3. Review of game films (football only)
NESCAC	Same as traditional season	10 weeks	16 weeks	12 weeks	None	**Impermissible activities:** 1. Teaching of skills by athletics staff 2. Contests or scrimmages with outside teams **Permissible activities:** 1. Conditioning programs 2. Organizational meetings
UAA	21 weeks	14 weeks	Up to 21 weeks	Up to 21 weeks	Limited to 5 weeks 5 dates of competition No class time can be missed	**Impermissible activities:** Team competition or practice **Permissible activities:** Voluntary conditioning

Centennial Conference	21 weeks	13 weeks	Up to 21 weeks	Up to 21 weeks	Limited to 5 weeks 18 practices 3 dates of competition No class time can be missed	**Impermissible activities:** Team competition or practice **Permissible activities:** Voluntary conditioning
NCAC	21 weeks	11 weeks	Up to 21 weeks	Up to 21 weeks	Limited to 5 weeks 5 dates of competition No class time can be missed	**Impermissible activities:** Team competition or practice **Permissible activities:** Voluntary conditioning
NEWMAC	21 weeks	14 weeks	Up to 21 weeks	Up to 21 weeks	Limited to 5 weeks 5 dates of competition No class time can be missed	**Impermissible activities:** Team competition or practice **Permissible activities:** Voluntary conditioning
MIAC	21 weeks	13 weeks	Up to 21 weeks	14 weeks	7 practices No competition No class time can be missed	**Impermissible activities:** Team competition or practice **Permissible activities:** Voluntary conditioning
SCIAC	Same as traditional season	14 weeks	16 weeks	20 weeks	Voluntary skills instruction No team competition or practice	**Impermissible activities:** Team competition or practice **Permissible activities:** Voluntary conditioning

Sources: Council of Ivy Group Presidents (2001), NESCAC (2002), UAA (2002a), 2002–2003 *Centennial Conference Manual, NCAC 2002–03 Policies and Procedures Handbook, NEWMAC EBook 2002, MIAC Policy Book 2002–03, Constitution and Bylaws of the Southern California Intercollegiate Athletic Conference,* NCAA (2001a), and NCAA (2001b).

Note: The traditional season covers the time from the first practice through the conference championship, if there is one. The traditional season does not include the NCAA or other championships. Values are approximate averages for all sports in a given traditional season. The non-traditional season includes sanctioned practice and playing time outside of the traditional season. The maximum total season length is the maximum allowed length of the traditional and non-traditional seasons combined. Off-season is all time outside of the traditional and non-traditional seasons.

References

Amherst Faculty Committee on Admission and Financial Aid. 1999. *Admission to Amherst: A Report to the Faculty and Administration.* September.

Amherst Special Committee on the Place of Athletics. 2002. *The Place of Athletics at Amherst College: A Question of Balance.* May.

Anderson, Susan. 1997. "A Review of the History of the Academic Index." Report prepared for The Andrew W. Mellon Foundation. August 12.

———. 2002. "Memorandum to William G. Bowen Regarding Nontraditional Season Deliberations." January 16.

Arenson, Karen W. 2001. "Yale President Wants to End Early Decisions for Admissions." *New York Times,* December 13, p. D1.

Art & Science Group, LLC. 2001. "Intercollegiate Athletics Have Little Influence on College Choice—Intramural and Recreational Opportunities Matter More." *StudentPOLL,* 4(4): 1–12.

Astin, Alexander W., William S. Korn, and Eric L. Dey. 1990. *The American College Teacher: National Norms for the 1989–90 HERI Faculty Survey.* Los Angeles: Higher Education Research Institute, UCLA.

Austin, Ethan. 2002a. "Under a New Ruling, Athletes Must Now Wait until Season." *Tufts Daily,* October 31, online edition.

———. 2002b. "Captain's Practice Rule Ain't All It's Cracked up to Be." *Tufts Daily,* November 7, online edition.

Avery, Christopher, Andrew Fairbanks, and Richard Zeckhauser. 2003. *The Early Admissions Game: Joining the Elite.* Cambridge, Mass.: Harvard University Press.

Bates College. Office of Institutional Planning and Analysis. 2001. "Memorandum on *The Game of Life* at Bates and NESCAC Follow-up Study." December 10.

Baumgarten, David. 2002. "Tops in Ivies, but Weak Outside, Field Hockey Faces Old Dominion." *Daily Princetonian,* October 4, online edition.

Bell, Taylor. 2001. "A Junior to the NBA?: Nation's Top 100 Seniors." *Chicago Sun-Times,* August 19, p. 119.

Bennet, Douglas J., Nancy Hargrave Meislahn, and John Biddiscombe. 2002. "Return to the High Ground." Interview by William Holder. *Wesleyan,* Spring, pp. 22–23.

Berkow, Ira. 2002. "College Football: A Button for All Occasions, Including Brown vs. Harvard." *New York Times,* September 28, p. D1.

Bernstein, Mark F. 2001. *Football: The Ivy League Origins of an American Obsession.* Philadelphia: University of Pennsylvania Press.

Biddiscombe, John. 2002. "Comments and Perspectives on Division III Athletics." Paper commissioned by The Andrew W. Mellon Foundation for this study.

Bloom, Alfred H. 2001. "Letter to Alumni, Parents, and Friends [of Swarthmore College]," June 1. Available at http://www.swarthmore.edu/Home/News/Media/Sources/abloom2.html.

Bochner, Owen. 2002. "Taking Time Out of the Year." *Cornell Daily Sun,* September 6, online edition.

Bollinger, Lee C. 1999. Paper read at the Macalester College Forum on Higher Education, St. Paul, Minn., June 3. Cited in Shulman and Bowen, p. 85.

Bowen, William G., and Derek Bok. 1998. *The Shape of the River: Long-Term Consequences of Considering Race in College and University Admissions.* Princeton, N.J.: Princeton University Press.

Brand, Myles. 2001. "Academics First: Reforming Intercollegiate Athletics." Address delivered to the National Press Club, January 23, 2001. *Vital Speeches of the Day* 67(12) (April 1): 367–71.

Bray, Corey, comp. 2002. *1982–2001 NCAA Sports Sponsorship and Participation Report.* Indianapolis, Ind.: National Collegiate Athletic Association.

Brennan, Stephen J., ed. 2000. *Inside Recruiting: The Master Guide to Successful College Athletic Recruiting.* Vol. 3. Omaha, Neb.: Peak Performance Publishing.

Broussard, Chris. 1999. "College Football: One Team Had to Win: It's Swarthmore Routing Oberlin." *New York Times,* September 5, section 8, p. 9.

Brown, Gary T. 2002. "Management Councils Take Mountain-Sized Steps at Denver Session." *NCAA News,* April 15, online edition.

Burstein, Rachael. 2001. "Football Players at Swarthmore Talk about Past Year after Sport Is Cut." *Swarthmore Phoenix,* December 13, online edition.

Byers, Walter, and Charles H. Hammer. 1995. *Unsportsmanlike Conduct: Exploiting College Athletes.* Ann Arbor: University of Michigan Press.

Campbell, Amy. 2002. "Division III Intercollegiate Athletics." Paper commissioned by The Andrew W. Mellon Foundation for this study. April.

Cantor, Nancy E, and Deborah A. Prentice. 1996. "The Life of the Modern-Day Student-Athlete: Opportunities Won and Lost." Paper presented at the Princeton Conference on Higher Education, March 21–23, Princeton, N.J.

Carnegie Foundation for the Advancement of Teaching. 2002. *The Carnegie Classification of Institutions of Higher Education,* 2000 edition. Second revision. Electronic data file. Available at http://www.carnegiefoundation.org/Classification/CIHE2000/downloads.htm.

Centennial Conference. 2002. *2002–2003 Centennial Conference Manual.* N.p.: Centennial Conference, August 9.

Center for the Study of Athletics. 1988. *Report No. 1: Summary Results from the 1987–88 National Study of Intercollegiate Athletics.* Palo Alto, Calif.: American Institutes for Research.

Chace, William M. 2002. "Athletics and Academic Values Don't Have to Compete at a Research University." *Emory Edge,* February, p. 1.

Chronicle of Higher Education. 2002. *Chronicle of Higher Education: Facts & Figures: Gender Equity in College Sports.* Available at http://chronicle.com/stata/genderequity/.

Clemens, Teri. 2000. "Closing the Deal in Division III." In *Inside Recruiting: The Master Guide to Successful College Athletic Recruiting,* edited by Stephen J. Brennan. Omaha, Neb.: Peak Performance Publishing.

College Board. 1992. *College Handbook.* Princeton, N.J.: College Board.

———. 1995. *College Handbook.* Princeton, N.J.: College Board.

———. 2002a. *College Handbook.* Princeton, N.J.: College Board.

———. 2002b. *College Search.* Available at http://www.collegeboard.com. Accessed October 25.

Cook, Philip J., and Robert H. Frank. 1993. "The Growing Concentration of Top Students at Elite Schools." In *Studies of Supply and Demand in Higher Education,* edited by C. T. Clotfelter and M. Rothschild. Chicago: University of Chicago Press.

Council of Ivy Group Presidents. 2001. *The Ivy Manual 2001–2002.* Princeton, N.J.: Council of Ivy Group Presidents.

———. 2002. Statement. June 20.

Covell, Daniel Dexter. 1999. "To Keep a Proper Perspective on the Role of Athletics: An Examination of the Perceived Role of Intercollegiate Athletics in the New England Small College Athletic Conference." Ph.D. dissertation, University of Massachusetts at Amherst, Amherst, Mass.

Covell, Dan, and Carol A. Barr. 2001. "The Ties That Bind: Presidential Involvement with the Development of NCAA Division I Initial Eligibility Legislation." *Journal of Higher Education* 72(4): 414–52.

Dartmouth College. 2002. "Dartmouth Announces Elimination of Varsity Swimming and Diving Programs." Press release. November 25.

Dowling, William C. 2002. "The Liberty League: It's Time." *Daily Targum,* September 10, online edition.

Drake Group. 2002. Drake Group Web site. Available at http://www.thedrake group.org.

Eastern College Athletic Conference. 2002. Web site. Available at http://www. ecac.org.

Eisner, Jane R. 2001. "Title IX Levels Field in Aspects Good and Bad." *Arizona Republic,* January 29, p. B7.

ESPN. 2002. *Worst College Football Teams of All Times.* September 16. Available at http://espn.go.com/page2/s/list/colfootball/teams/worst.html.

Fainstein, Norman. 2002. "Statement on NESCAC Reforms." Sent to authors December 20.

Falla, Jack. 1981. *NCAA: The Voice of College Sports: A Diamond Anniversary History, 1906–1981.* 1st ed. Mission, Kan.: National Collegiate Athletic Association.

Fallows, James. 2001. "The Early-Decision Racket." *Atlantic Monthly,* September, pp. 37–52.

Fatsis, Stefan. 2002. "March Brings Usual Madness: Basketball over Academics." *Wall Street Journal,* March 22, online edition.

Feigelson, Suzanne. 1998. "A Recruit's Confession." *Amherst Student,* December 2, online edition.

Festle, Mary Jo. 1996. *Playing Nice: Politics and Apologies in Women's Sports.* New York: Columbia University Press.

Fielitz, Lynn R. 2000. "Using the Internet for Athletic Recruiting." *Journal of Physical Education, Recreation and Dance* 71(2): 13–15.

Fincher, Cameron. 1974. "Is the SAT Worth Its Salt? An Evaluation of the Use of the Scholastic Aptitude Test in the University System of Georgia over a Thirteen-Year Period." *Review of Educational Research* 44(3): 293–305.

Finley, Bill, with Brandon Lilly. 2002. "St. John's Cites Fairness in Cutting 5 Men's Teams." *New York Times,* December 14, p. D5.

Fish, Mike. 2002. "Lights Out for Knights? Rutgers Football Facing a Struggle—On and Off the Field." *CNN Sports Illustrated,* September 27. Available at CNNSI.com.

Fiske, Edward B. 2001. "Gaining Admission: Athletes Win Preference." *New York Times Education Life Supplement,* January 7, pp. 22–23, 40–41.

Fitting, Matthew. 2002. "Taking a Swing at a New Way of Slotting." *Swarthmore Phoenix,* October 3, online edition.

Fleisher, Arthur A., Brian L. Goff, and Robert D. Tollison. 1992. *The National Collegiate Athletic Association: A Study in Cartel Behavior.* Chicago: University of Chicago Press.

Flores, Christopher. 2002a. "Wrestling Coaches Sue Department of Education over Title IX." *Chronicle of Higher Education,* January 17, online edition.

———. 2002b. "U. of North Carolina at Chapel Hill Abandons Early-Decision Admissions." *Chronicle of Higher Education,* April 25, online edition.

Ford, Susan F., and Sandy Campos. 1977. *Summary of Validity Data from the Admissions Testing Program Validity Study Service.* Princeton, N.J.: College Board.

Frank, Robert H., and Philip J. Cook. 1995. *The Winner-Take-All Society: How More and More Americans Compete for Ever Fewer and Bigger Prizes, Encouraging Economic Waste, Income Inequality, and Impoverished Cultural Life.* New York: Free Press.

Friends of Smith Athletics. 2003. *About FOSA.* Available at http://www.smith. edu/athletics/fosa_aboutfosa.html. Accessed January 13.

George, Anjali. 2001. "The Trials and Tribulations of an Ex-College Athlete: What Happens When the Game Is Over?" *Barnard Bulletin,* February 21, pp. 12–13.

Gerdy, John R. 2001. "Facing up to the Conflict between Athletics and Academics." *Priorities* 16 (Summer): 1–15.

Giamatti, A. Bartlett. 1981. "Yale and Athletics." In *The University and the Public Interest.* New York: Atheneum. Adapted from a speech delivered to the Association of Yale Alumni, April 1980.

Glasser, Jeff. 2002. "King of the Hill." *U.S. News & World Report* (March 18): 56.

Goodman, Ellen. 2002. "No Letup in Myth-Making About Women and Sports." *Boston Globe,* June 20, p. A15.

Gross, Jane. 1982. "Reformers Try to Halt Academic Abuse." *New York Times,* March 24, p. B9. Cited in Covell and Barr, pp. 430–31.

———. 2002. "Different Lives, One Goal: Finding the Key to College." *New York Times,* May 5, p. 1.

Guttmann, Allen. 1991. *Women's Sports: A History.* New York: Columbia University Press.

Hanford, George H. 1974. *An Inquiry into the Need for and Feasibility of a National Study of Intercollegiate Athletics.* Washington, D.C.: American Council on Education.

Hartigan, Rachel Shea, and Justin Ewers. 2002. "Work Hard, Stay Sane—and Get In." *U.S. News & World Report,* September 21, online edition.

Hartill, Lane. 2001. "Some Schools Make a Tough Call: Drop Football." *Christian Science Monitor,* February 6, p. 14.

Hartocollis, Anemona. 2002. "Harvard Faculty Votes to Put the Excellence Back in the A." *New York Times,* May 22, p. A20.

Hawes, Kay. 2002. "Financial Aid Audit Takes One Step Back, Two Ahead." *NCAA News,* April 1, online edition.

———. 2003. "Division III Convention Actions Speak Louder Than Words in 'Future' Issue." *NCAA News,* January 20, p. 1.

Hensley, Larry D. 2000. "Current Status of Basic Instruction Programs in Physical Education at American Colleges and Universities." *Journal of Physical Education, Recreation and Dance* 71(9): 30–36.

Hoberman, John. 2001. "Mind Games." *Wall Street Journal,* February 16, p. W12.

Holder, William. 2002. "NESCAC Fights the Trend." *Wesleyan,* Spring, p. 18.

Hong, Anne. 2002. "M. Tennis Defeats Penn in Near-Brawl, W. Tennis Drops Match to Quakers." *Daily Princetonian,* April 2, online edition.

Hooks, David Taylor. 1998. "Complying with Title IX: An Examination of the Effects on Three NCAA Division III Colleges in Pennsylvania and the Difficulties the Law's Interpretation Has Created for Small Colleges Attempting to Achieve Gender Equity." Ed.D. dissertation, University of Pennsylvania.

Hoxby, Carolyn M. 1997. "The Changing Market Structure of U.S. Higher Education." Mimeo, Harvard University.

———. 2000. "The Effects of Geographic Integration and Increasing Competition in the Market for College Education." May 2000 revision of NBER Working Paper No. 6323.

Hutchins, Robert Maynard. 1936. *No Friendly Voice.* Chicago: University of Chicago Press.

———. 1938. "Gate Receipts and Glory." *Saturday Evening Post,* December 3, pp. 23, 73–77.

Jacobson, Jennifer. 2002. "Dashing from Classroom to Locker Room: Professionalization of Sports and the Demands on Professors Make the Dual Role Difficult." *Chronicle of Higher Education,* May 3, p. A39.

Jenkins, Sally. 2002. "Title IX Opponents a Bunch of Sad Sacks." *Washington Post,* June 24, p. D01.

Jensen, Mike. 2000. "Swarthmore Dropping Football Creates a Firestorm." *Philadelphia Inquirer,* December 10, online edition.

Johnson, Abigail. 2000. "Dartmouth Coaches Face Own Early Decisions." *The Dartmouth,* November 22, online edition.

Josefowitz, Nicholas F. 2002. "Ending Athletic Preference." *Harvard Crimson,* April 29, online edition.

Karch, Brendan. 2000. "Football Commitment Perceived as Incomplete." *Swarthmore Phoenix,* December 7, online edition.

Katz, Andy. 2001a. "Why Wait? Recruits Choosing Colleges Early." ESPN.com, July 18, updated July 22.

———. 2001b. "Unofficial Visits Are Becoming Way to Go." ESPN, August 17.

Kerr, Clark. 2001. *The Gold and the Blue: A Personal Memoir of the University of California, 1949–1967.* Vol. 1. Berkeley: University of California Press.

Killpatrick, Frances, and James Killpatrick. 1999. *The Winning Edge: The Student-Athlete's Guide to College Sports.* 6th ed. Alexandria, Va.: Octameron Associates.

Kimball, Emily. 2000. "For Athletes, Brown U.'s Recruiting Requirements Jump-Start College Admission Process." *Brown Daily Herald,* September 13, online edition.

King, Billie Jean. 2002. "For All the Good Things It Has Done, Title IX Is Still Plagued by Myths." *New York Times,* June 23, sports section, p. 7.

Kingsley, Karla. 2002. "Ivy League Reconsiders Role of Athletics in Admissions." *The Dartmouth,* May 2, online edition.

Kline, Kenneth A. 1997. "The Relationship between Academic Achievement and Athletic Participation of Female and Male Athletes at the NCAA Division III Level (Women, Men)." Ph.D. dissertation, University of Connecticut.

Knight Foundation Commission on Intercollegiate Athletics. 2001. *A Call to Action: Reconnecting College Sports and Higher Education.* Miami, Fla.: John S. and James L. Knight Foundation.

Lambert, Craig. 1997. "The Professionalization of Ivy League Sports." *Harvard Magazine* 100 (September–October): 36–49 ff.

Larson, Joseph S. 2002. Letter to the editor. *Chronicle of Higher Education,* May 10, p. B22.

Lee, Min, Sonia Scherr, and Nathan Ashby-Kuhlman. 2000. "Finding the Right Balance: Making Athletics and Academics Work Together." *Swarthmore Phoenix,* April 27, online edition.

Lester, Robin. 1999. *Stagg's University: The Rise, Decline, and Fall of Big-Time Football at Chicago.* Illini Books edition. Urbana: University of Illinois Press.

Letlow, Paul, and Barry Johnson. 2002. "I-A Schools Set to Adapt Sports for Rule Changes." *News-Star* (Monroe, La.), April 28, p. 1A.

Levison, Lee M. 1981. "Origins of the New England Small College Athletic Conference." Unpublished paper, Trinity College.

Lewis, Stephen R. 2002a. "Further Thoughts on Division IIIA." Memorandum to Bowen. January 25.

———. 2002b. Letter to "Colleagues Interested in the Place of Intercollegiate Athletics." March 4.

Licht, Jeremy. 2002."Players, Coaches Unhappy with Ivy Changes." *Yale Daily News,* September 5, online edition.

Lindholm, Jennifer A., Alexander W. Astin, Linda J. Sax, and William S. Korn. 2002. *The American College Teacher: National Norms for the 2001–2002 HERI Faculty Survey.* Los Angeles: Higher Education Research Institute, UCLA.

Lipsyte, Robert. 2002. "Backtalk: Lesson No. 1: Mixed Messages Part of Curriculum." *New York Times,* January 20, Section 8, p. 11.

Litvack, James. 2002. "Ivy League Reforms." Paper commissioned by The Andrew W. Mellon Foundation for this study.

Lord, Mary. 2002. "Athletics for All: Harvard Tops the Scoreboard with a Sporting Smorgasbord to Foster Sound Bodies and Minds." *U.S. News & World Report* March 18: 68–69.

Loury, Glenn C. 2000. Foreword to *The Shape of the River: Long-Term Consequences of Considering Race in College and University Admissions,* by William G. Bowen and Derek Bok. Paperback edition. Princeton, N.J.: Princeton University Press.

———. 2002. *The Anatomy of Racial Inequality.* Cambridge, Mass.: Harvard University Press.

Lovenheim, Mike. 1998. "If You Let Me Play. . . ." *Amherst Student,* December 2, online edition.

Malekoff, Robert. 1998. "The Non-traditional Season: Turning Point or Full Speed Ahead?" *Intercollegiate Athletic Forum*, December, pp. 1–2, 4.

———. 2002. "Division III Athletics: Issues and Challenges." Paper commissioned by The Andrew W. Mellon Foundation for this study.

Maloney, Michael T., and Robert E. McCormick. 1993. "An Examination of the Role That Intercollegiate Athletic Participation Plays in Academic Achievement: Athletes' Feats in the Classroom." *Journal of Human Resources* 28 (Summer): 555–70.

Marcus, David L. 2000. "Student Athletes R.I.P.? Swarthmore College Cans Its Football Program." *U.S. News & World Report* (December 18): 57.

———. 2001. "What Are Your Chances of Getting in through the Coach's Door?" *U.S. News & World Report* (September 17): 94.

Massey, Douglas S., Camille Z. Charles, Garvey F. Lundy, and Mary J. Fischer. 2003. *The Source of the River: The Social Origins of Freshmen at America's Selective Colleges and Universities*. Princeton, N.J.: Princeton University Press.

Massey, Douglas S., and Mary J. Fischer. 2002. "Stereotype Threat and Academic Performance: New Data from the National Longitudinal Survey of Freshmen." Mimeo, University of Pennsylvania. June.

McCallum, Jack. 1999. "Streak Buster: After 28 Straight Losses, Swarthmore Finally Won a Ball Game, but That Wasn't What Made the Day Special." *Sports Illustrated* (September 13): 54.

McGrath, Charles. 2002. "The Way We Live Now: 9-15-02: A Whole New Ballgame." *New York Times Magazine*, September 15, p. 21.

McKissic, Rodney J. 1998. *How to Play the Sports Recruiting Game and Get an Athletic Scholarship: The Handbook and Guide to Success for the African-American High School Student Athlete*. Phoenix, Ariz.: Amber Books.

McPherson, Michael. 2001a. "A Statement from the President on Football at Macalester College." Memorandum to the Macalester community. September 18.

———. 2001b. "The Future of Macalester Football: Statement by President Michael McPherson." November 27.

Menand, Louis. 2001. "Sporting Chances: The Cost of College Athletics." *New Yorker* (January 22): 84–88.

Middlebury Ad Hoc Committee on the Future of Athletics. 2002a. *Report of the Ad Hoc Committee on the Future of Athletics*. May 9.

———. 2002b. "Addendum to Report of the Ad Hoc Committee on the Future of Athletics: Elaboration of Recommendation 3." September 6.

Milem, Jeffrey F., Joseph B. Berger, and Eric L. Dey. 2000. "Faculty Time Allocation." *Journal of Higher Education* 71 (4): 454–75.

Minnesota Intercollegiate Athletic Conference (MIAC). 2000. *2000 Football Statistics*. Available at http://www.miac-online.org/Stats/Archivedstats/football stats2000.html. Accessed March 11, 2003.

———. 2001. *2001 Football Statistics*. Available at http://www.miac-online.org/ Stats/football2001/MAC.HTM. Accessed March 11, 2003.

———. 2002. *MIAC Policy Book 2002–03*. August. Available at http://www.miac-online.org/policy.html.

Morrison, Leotus. 2002. Presentation to Mary Baldwin College's Parents' Council, March 15.

Mrozek, Donald J. 1997. "The 'Amazon' and the American 'Lady.'" In *The New American Sport History: Recent Approaches and Perspectives,* edited by S. W. Pope, pp. 198–214. Urbana: University of Illinois Press.

National Association of Collegiate Directors of Athletics (NACDA). 2002. "Sears Directors' Cup Final Standings." Available at http://nacda.ocsn.com/searsdirectorscup/nacda-searsdirectorscup-previous-scoring.html. Updated June 18.

National Collegiate Athletic Association (NCAA). 1999–2001. *NCAA Convention Proceedings for 1999–2001.* Convention proceedings starting with 2001 are available at http://www.ncaa.org. Earlier years can be found in many libraries.

———. 2000. "A Brief Chronological History of the National Intercollegiate Championship Series." In *NCAA National Collegiate Championships Records,* pp. 9–12. Indianapolis, Ind: NCAA.

———. 2001a. *2001–02 NCAA Division I Manual.* Indianapolis, Ind.: NCAA.

———. 2001b. *2001–02 NCAA Division III Manual.* Indianapolis, Ind.: NCAA.

———. 2002a. *Division III Financial Aid Audit Proposal,* March, online edition.

———. 2002b. *2001 NCAA Membership Report.* April 1. Available at http://www.ncaa.org/library/membership/membership_report/2001.

———. 2002c. *Division III Facts and Figures.* Available at http://www1.ncaa.org/membership/governance/division III/factsheet_d3_2. Updated May 8.

———. 2002d. "National Collegiate Athletic Association Proposed Budget for Fiscal Year Ended August 31, 2003." July 30. Available at http://www.ncaa.org/financial/2002-03_budget.pdf.

———. 2002e. *Official NCAA Football Records 2002.* August. Indianapolis, Ind.: NCAA. Available at http://www.ncaa.org/library/records/football_records_book/2002/001-003a.pdf.

———. 2002f. *NCAA 2002 Graduation-Rates Report.* September 26. Available at http://www.ncaa.org/grad_rates.

———. 2002g. "Future of Division III." Available at http://www1.ncaa.org/membership/governance/division_III/d3_future. Accessed October 4.

———. 2002h. "NCAA Revenue Distribution: Total Distribution to Members." Available at http://www1.ncaa.org/finance/7-yr_conf_summaries/total_distribution. Accessed November 26.

———. 2003. Web site. Available at http://www.ncaa.org. Accessed March 12.

National Federation of State High School Associations. 2002. "National Federation of State High School Associations Participation Study 1971–2001." In *1982–2001 NCAA Sports Sponsorship and Participation Report,* compiled by Corey Bray. Indianapolis, Ind.: National Collegiate Athletic Association.

National Science Board. 2002. *Science and Engineering Indicators—2002.* Arlington, Va.: National Science Foundation.

National Women's Law Center. 2002. "The Battle for Gender Equity in Athletics: Title IX at Thirty." A report of the National Women's Law Center. June.

Naughton, Jim. 1998. "Judge Approves Settlement of Brown U.'s Title IX Case." *Chronicle of Higher Education,* July 3, p. A31.

New England Small College Athletic Conference (NESCAC). 2001. "NESCAC Presidents Decision on Post-season Participation: Teams Permitted to Accept NCAA At-large Bids for 2001–02." News release. September 28.

———. 2002. *NESCAC Manual 2002–2003: Agreement and Official Interpretations.* Revised. N.p.: NESCAC, September 25.

———. 2003. "Statement by the NESCAC Presidents in Declining to Participate in a *U.S. News & World Report* Survey of NCAA Division III Athletic Programs." News release. February 11. Available at http://www.nescac.com/Releases/ NESCAC_U.S. News%20Survey%20Statement.htm.

New England Women's and Men's Athletic Conference (NEWMAC). 2002. *NEW-MAC EBook 2002.* Version 8.0. August 28. Available at http://www.orangekite .com/portfolio/newmaconline/ebook_toc.html.

New York Times. 1998. "Brown to Settle Title IX Suit." June 24, p. C3.

———. 2002a. "College Hoops and Academics." March 29, p. A28.

———. 2002b. "A Sporting Chance for Girls." Editorial. June 2, section 4, p. 12.

———. 2002c. "College Sports Gets Network." June 7, Sports Desk, p. D2.

Noll, Roger. 1999. "The Business of College Sports and the High Cost of Winning." *Milken Institute Review* (third quarter): 24–37.

North Coast Athletic Conference (NCAC). 2002. *NCAC 2002–03 Policies and Procedures Handbook,* 19th edition. N.p.: NCAC, September.

"Not Worth the Candle." 2002. *The Phrase Finder 2000.* Available at http://phrases. shu.ac.uk/bulletin_board/6/messages/1018.html. Accessed December 2.

Oostdyk, Scott. 1982. "Where Have All the Fans Gone?" *Princeton Alumni Weekly,* December 15, p. 16.

Osmar, John. 2002. "College Football As It Used to Be." Letter to the editor. *New York Times,* January 6, Section 8, p. 7.

Ostman, Per. 2002. "The Death of Sport." *Cornell Daily Sun,* October 11, online edition.

Paige, Roderick. 2003. "Statement Regarding Final Report of Commission on Opportunity in Athletics." February 26. Available at http://www.ed.gov/Press Releases/02-2003/02262003a.html.

Pennington, Bill. 2002a. "Unusual Alliance Forming to Rein In College Sports." *New York Times,* January 17, online edition.

———. 2002b. "More Men's Teams Benched as Colleges Level the Field." *New York Times,* May 9, pp. A1, D4.

Peterson's. 2002. *Peterson's Four-Year Colleges 2003.* Princeton, N.J.: Peterson's.

Pfister, Gertrud. 2002. "Her Story in Sport: Towards the Emancipation of Women?" Paper presented at the 2002 World Conference on Women and Sport, May 16–19, Montréal.

Philadelphia Inquirer. 2002. Editorial. July 30, p. A10.

Potter, Amy. 2002. "Ivy Presidents Announce Recruitment Changes." *Daily Pennsylvanian,* August 29, online edition.

Princeton Trustee Committee on Student Life, Health and Athletics. 1994. *Report on Princeton Athletics.* Princeton, N.J.: Princeton University. November 30.

Pulley, John L. 2002a. "Oberlin College, Facing a $5-Million Deficit, Sees Years of Belt Tightening Ahead." *Chronicle of Higher Education,* April 16, online edition.

———. 2002b. "Well-Off and Wary: Even Small, Wealthy Private Colleges like Oberlin Are Feeling the Economic Pinch." *Chronicle of Higher Education,* June 21, online edition.

Ramist, L., C. Lewis, and L. McCamley-Jenkins. 1994. *Student Group Differences in Predicting College Grades: Sex Language, and Ethnic Groups.* College Board Report No. 93-1, ETS RR-94-27. New York: College Board.

Rasmussen, Richard A. 1997. "The Role of Intercollegiate Athletics in the Academy—A Case Study of the Formation of the University Athletic Association." Ed.D. dissertation, University of Rochester.

———. 2002. "Perspectives on Trends and Issues in Division III Athletics." Paper commissioned by the Andrew W. Mellon Foundation for this study. May.

Rasmussen, William M., and Rahul Rohatgi. 2002. "Ivy League Debates Recruiting Reduction." *Harvard Crimson,* May 15, online edition.

Ratnesar, Romesh. 1999. "A Quaker Beating: When Swarthmore Routed Oberlin in the Season Opener, It Won Much More than a Game." *Time* (September 20): 8.

Richards, Shaunette, and Elizabeth Aries. 1999. "The Division III Student-Athlete: Academic Performance, Campus Involvement, and Growth." *Journal of College Student Development* 40(3) (May–June): 211–18.

Robst, John, and Jack Keil. 2000."The Relationship between Athletic Participation and Academic Performance: Evidence from NCAA Division III." *Applied Economics* 32(5) (April): 547–58.

Rodrick, Stephen. 2001. "Big Man Temporarily on Campus." *New York Times Magazine,* November 25, pp. 56, 58–59.

Rosovsky, Henry, and Matthew Hartley. 2002. *Evaluation and the Academy: Are We Doing the Right Thing?* Cambridge, Mass.: American Academy of Arts and Sciences.

Sack, Allen L., and Ellen J. Staurowsky. 1998. *College Athletes for Hire: The Evolution and Legacy of the NCAA's Amateur Myth.* Westport, Conn.: Praeger.

Savage, Howard J. 1929. *American College Athletics.* New York: Carnegie Foundation for the Advancement of Teaching.

Sax, Linda J., Alexander W. Astin, Marisol Arrendondo, and William S. Korn. 1996. *The American College Teacher: National Norms for the 1995–96 HERI Faculty Survey.* Los Angeles: Higher Education Research Institute, UCLA.

Sax, Linda J., Alexander W. Astin, William S. Korn, and Shannon K. Gilmartin. 1999. *The American College Teacher: National Norms for the 1998–99 HERI Faculty Survey.* Los Angeles: Higher Education Research Institute, UCLA.

Schneider, Jodi. 2002. "The Fairness Factor." *U.S. News & World Report* (March 18): 63–65.

Short, Bryan C. 1980. Letter to the editor. *Yale Alumni Magazine and Journal* 44(1) (October): 42.

Shulman, James L., and William G. Bowen. 2001. *The Game of Life: College Sports and Educational Values.* Princeton, N.J.: Princeton University Press.

Shultz, George. 2003. Speech delivered at the Ivy Football Association Award Dinner, New York, January 22.

Slobogin, Kathy. 2002. "Toddler Athletes a Growing Trend." CNN.com, June 7. Available at http://www.cnn.com/2002/HEALTH/06/06/cov.super.toddlers/index.html.

Slovenski, Peter. 2002. "How You Play the Game." Unpublished essay sent to James Shulman and William G. Bowen, February 14.

Southern California Intercollegiate Athletic Conference (SCIAC). 1989. *Constitution and Bylaws of the Southern California Intercollegiate Athletic Conference.* September 27 (corrected to April 21, 1999). Available at http://www.galcit.caltech.edu/SCIAC/const.html.

Sperber, Murray. 1990. "The NCAA as Predator: The Rape of the Association for Intercollegiate Athletics for Women." In *College Sports, Inc.,* pp. 322–32. New York: Henry Holt.

———. 2001. "The Sports Authorities." *University Business,* April, online edition.

———. 2002. "The NCAA's Last Chance to Reform College Sports." *Chronicle of Higher Education,* April 19, p. B12.

St. John, Warren. 2002. "And the Band Misbehaved On," *New York Times,* September 29, section 9, p. 1.

Staurowsky, Ellen. 2002. Letter to the editor. *NCAA News,* May 13, p. 4.

Steele, Claude M. 1997. "A Threat in the Air: How Stereotypes Shape Intellectual Identity and Performance." *American Psychologist* (June): 613–29.

Suggs, Welch. 1999. "CBS to Pay $6-Billion for TV Rights to NCAA Basketball Championships." *Chronicle of Higher Education,* December 3, p. A54.

———. 2001a. "Can Anyone Do Anything about College Sports?" *Chronicle of Higher Education,* February 23, p. A50.

———. 2001b. "Male Basketball Players' Graduation Rates Fall Again." *Chronicle of Higher Education,* September 10, online edition.

———. 2001c. "Left Behind." *Chronicle of Higher Education,* November 30, pp. A35–A37.

———. 2002a. "Colleges in New England Cut Back on Admitting Athletes." *Chronicle of Higher Education,* January 11, p. A48.

———. 2002b. "Tipping the Athletic Scale: Williams Struggles with Athletics and Admissions." *Chronicle of Higher Education,* March 8, online edition.

———. 2002c. "Women's Law Group Warns 30 Colleges about Imbalances in Athletic Scholarships." *Chronicle of Higher Education,* June 19, online edition.

———. 2002d. "Title IX at 30." *Chronicle of Higher Education,* June 21, pp. A38–A42.

———. 2002e. "Education Department Announces Panel to Review and Strengthen Title IX." *Chronicle of Higher Education,* June 28, online edition.

———. 2002f. "A Split Decision? The NCAA's Division III Debates Whether to Divide into 2 Groups." *Chronicle of Higher Education,* September 20, online edition.

———. 2003a. "New NCAA President Calls for Gender Equity, Stronger Commitment to Reform." *Chronicle of Higher Education,* January 13, 2003, online edition.

———. 2003b. "Smoke Obscures Fire in Title IX Debate as Federal Panel Adjourns." *Chronicle of Higher Education,* February 7, online edition.

———. 2003c. "Cheers and Condemnation Greet Report on Gender Equity: Federal Panel Focuses on Protecting Men's Sports, to the Dismay of Women's Advocates." *Chronicle of Higher Education,* March 7, online edition.

Swarthmore College Athletics Review Committee. 2000. Press release, December 4. Available at http://www.swarthmore.edu/Home/News/Media/Releases/00/athletics.html.

———. 2001. *Report to the Board of Managers.* May 5. Available at http://www.swarthmore.edu/news/athletics/report.html.

———. 2002a. "Minutes of the Athletics Review Committee." April 26. Available at http://www.swarthmore.edu/news/athletics/Minutes-Apr%2026,%202002.pdf.

———. 2002b. *Athletics Review Committee Final Report.* July 26. Available at www.swarthmore.edu/news/athletics/final_report.html.

———. 2002c. Chart A, Swarthmore College Men's 1999–2000 Intercollegiate Athletic Teams. Available at http://www.swarthmore.edu/news/athletics/chart1.html. Accessed September 12.

———. 2002d. "FAQ—Answers to Frequently Asked Questions." Available at http://www.swarthmore.edu/news/athletics/faq.html. Accessed September 12.

Thelin, John R. 1996 [1994]. *Games Colleges Play: Scandal and Reform in Intercollegiate Athletics.* Baltimore: Johns Hopkins University Press.

———. 2000. "Good Sports? Historical Perspective on the Political Economy of Intercollegiate Athletics in the Era of Title IX, 1972–1997." *Journal of Higher Education* 71(4): 391–410.

Tidball, M. Elizabeth, et al. 1999. *Taking Women Seriously: Lessons and Legacies for Educating the Majority.* Phoenix, Ariz.: Oryx Press.

Tilghman, Shirley. 2002. "Why a Moratorium for Student-Athletes?" *Daily Princetonian,* December 4, online edition.

Tobin, James. 1980. "The Ivy League and Athletics: The President's Views Deserve Support." *Yale Alumni Magazine and Journal* 44(1) (October): 40–41.

Turner, Sarah E., and William G. Bowen. 1999. "Choice of Major: The Changing (Unchanging) Gender Gap." *Industrial and Labor Relations Review* 52(2) (January): 289–313.

Turner, Sarah E., Lauren A. Meserve, and William G. Bowen. 2001. "Winning and Giving: Football Results and Alumni Giving at Selective Private Colleges and Universities." *Social Science Quarterly* 82(4) (December): 812–26.

U.S. Department of Education. Office of Postsecondary Education. 2002. *IPEDS College Opportunities Online.* Available at http://ope.ed.gov/athletics/.

U.S. Department of Education. Secretary's Commission on Opportunity in Athletics. 2003. *"Open to All": Title IX at Thirty.* February. Washington, D.C.: Department of Education. Available at http://www.ed.gov/inits/commissionsboards/athletics.

U.S. General Accounting Office. 2001. *Intercollegiate Athletics: Four-Year Colleges' Experiences Adding and Discontinuing Teams: Report to Congressional Requesters* (GAO-01-297). Washington, D.C.: The Office.

University Athletic Association (UAA). 2002a. *Background Information, 2001–2002.* Available at http://www.uaa.rochester.edu/. Accessed January 2.

———. 2002b. *UAA: University Athletic Association: Where Theory Meets Practice.* Available at http://www.uaa.rochester.edu/. Accessed January 2.

University of Iowa. 2000. Gender Equity in Sports Project. Available at http://bailiwick.lib.uiowa.edu/ge. Last updated October 16, 2000.

van der Werf, Martin. 2002a. "Endowment Losses Force Dartmouth to Cut Its Budget." *Chronicle of Higher Education,* August 26, online edition.

———. 2002b. "Many Colleges Could Close or Merge Because of Financial Problems, Standard & Poor's Warns." *Chronicle of Higher Education,* November 27, online edition.

Vélez, Karin. 1997. "The New England Small College Athletic Conference, 1971–1997: A Retrospective." Unpublished report submitted to the NESCAC presidents on August 9.

Vladeck, Steve. 1998. "A College Divided: Athletics and Amherst." *Amherst Student,* December 2, online edition.

Walker, Teresa M. 2000. "Justices Consider Dispute over Prep Sports Recruiting." *Associated Press State and Local Wire,* October 8, Sports News.

Welch, Paula D. 1999. *Silver Era, Golden Moments: A Celebration of Ivy League Women's Athletics.* Lanham, Md.: Madison Books.

White, Gordon. 1980. "Colleges Find Advantages in Conferences." *New York Times,* February 24, p. S10.

Williams Ad Hoc Faculty Committee on Athletics. 2002. *Report on Varsity Athletics.* May.

Williams, Lena. 2000. "Women Play More, but Coach Less." *New York Times,* May 3, p. D8.

Wilson, Robin. 2002. "Report Says Undergraduate Education Has Improved in Recent Years." *Chronicle of Higher Education,* March 22, online edition.

Witkin, Gordon, and Jodi Schneider. 2002. "College Sports." *U.S. News & World Report,* March 18, pp. 48–50.

Wu, Ying. 1997. "The Demise of the AIAW and Women's Control of Intercollegiate Athletics for Women: The Sex-Separate Policy in the Reality of the NCAA, Cold War, and Title IX." Ph.D. dissertation, Pennsylvania State University, December 1997.

Wulff, Jennifer. 1998. "Playing the Game." *Dartmouth Alumni Magazine,* March, pp. 20–23.

Yale University, Admissions Policy Advisory Board. 1966a. "Second Report and Addendum: Problems in Admitting Artists." October 31.

———. 1966b. "Addendum to Second Report of October 31, 1966." December 6.

Young, Jeffrey R. 2002a. "Yale Drops Early Decision, but Defies Admissions-Counseling Association's Guidelines." *Chronicle of Higher Education,* November 7, online edition.

———. 2002b. "Stanford U. Revises Early-Admissions Policy, Adopts a Nonbinding Plan Similar to Yale's." *Chronicle of Higher Education,* November 8, online edition.

Index

Page numbers for entries occurring in figures are suffixed by an f; those for entries in notes, by an n, with the number of the note following; and those for entries in tables, by a t.